IN THE LAND OF
TIGERS AND SNAKES

THE SHENG YEN SERIES IN CHINESE BUDDHIST STUDIES

THE SHENG YEN SERIES IN CHINESE BUDDHIST STUDIES

Edited by Daniel B. Stevenson and Jimmy Yu

Funded jointly by the Sheng Yen Education Foundation and the Chung Hua Institute of Buddhist Studies in Taiwan, the Sheng Yen Series in Chinese Buddhist Studies is dedicated to the interdisciplinary study of Chinese language resources that bear on the history of Buddhism in premodern and modern China. Through the publication of pioneering scholarship on Chinese Buddhist thought, practice, social life, and institutional life in China—including interactions with indigenous traditions of religion in China, as well as Buddhist developments in South, East, and Inner/Central Asia—the series aspires to bring new and groundbreaking perspectives to one of the most historically enduring and influential traditions of Buddhism, past and present.

Michael J. Walsh, *Sacred Economies: Buddhist Business and Religiosity in Medieval China*

Koichi Shinohara, *Spells, Images, and Maṇḍalas: Tracing the Evolution of Esoteric Buddhist Rituals*

Beverley Foulks McGuire, *Living Karma: The Religious Practices of Ouyi Zhixu (1599–1655)*

Paul Copp, *The Body Incantatory: Spells and the Ritual Imagination in Medieval Chinese Buddhism*

N. Harry Rothschild, *Emperor Wu Zhao and Her Pantheon of Devis, Divinities, and Dynastic Mothers*

Erik J. Hammerstrom, *The Science of Chinese Buddhism: Early Twentieth-Century Engagements*

Jiang Wu and Lucille Chia, editors, *Spreading Buddha's Word in East Asia: The Formation and Transformation of the Chinese Buddhist Canon*

Jan Kiely and J. Brooks Jessup, editors, *Recovering Buddhism in Modern China*

Geoffrey C. Goble, *Chinese Esoteric Buddhism: Amoghavajra, the Ruling Elite, and the Emergence of a Tradition*

Dewei Zhang, *Thriving in Crisis: Buddhism and Political Disruption in China, 1522–1620*

Erik J. Hammerstrom, *The Huayan University Network: The Teaching and Practice of Avataṃsaka Buddhism in Twentieth-Century China*

Chün-fang Yü, *The Renewal of Buddhism in China: Zhuhong and the Late Ming Synthesis*, Fortieth Anniversary Edition

John Kieschnick, *Buddhist Historiography in China*

IN THE LAND OF TIGERS AND SNAKES

Living with Animals in Medieval Chinese Religions

HUAIYU CHEN

Columbia University Press

New York

Columbia University Press
Publishers Since 1893
New York   Chichester, West Sussex
cup.columbia.edu

Library of Congress Cataloging-in-Publication Data
Names: Chen, Huaiyu, 1974- author.
Title: In the land of tigers and snakes : living with animals in medieval Chinese
    religions / Huaiyu Chen.
Description: New York : Columbia University Press, 2023. | Series: The Sheng Yen series
    in Chinese Buddhist studies | Includes bibliographical references and index.
Identifiers: LCCN 2022022632 (print) | LCCN 2022022633 (ebook) | ISBN 9780231202602
    (hardback) | ISBN 9780231202619 (trade paperback) | ISBN 9780231554640 (ebook)
Subjects: LCSH: Animals—Religious aspects—Buddhism.
Classification: LCC BQ4570.A53 C44 2023 (print) | LCC BQ4570.A53 (ebook) |
    DDC 294.3/5693—dc23/eng/20220709
LC record available at https://lccn.loc.gov/2022022632
LC ebook record available at https://lccn.loc.gov/2022022633

Columbia University Press books are printed on permanent
and durable acid-free paper.

Printed in the United States of America
Cover design: Milenda Nan Ok Lee
Cover image: Courtesy of *Dunhuang shiku quanji, 2000*

Contents

Illustrations

Acknowledgments

Getting this book ready for publication has been a long journey. It began in 2005 when Takata Tokio invited me to give a talk on the classification of animals and plants in medieval Chinese Buddhism at Kyoto University. In 2009, when I published this talk as my very first article, the late Denis Sinor helped edit it. Since then, numerous colleagues and friends have helped me at various stages of preparing, writing, revising, and editing different sections of the manuscript. In particular, I would like to thank the following mentors, colleagues, and friends for their invaluable support: Barbara Ambros, Jinhua Chen, Nicola Di Cosmo, Mădălina Diaconu, Thomas DuBois, Vincent Durand-Dastès, Zhe Ji, Yan Jin, Xiaofei Kang, Keith Knapp, Li-ying Kuo, Victor H. Mair, Alfreda Murck, Tamar Novick, Reiko Ohnuma, Lisa Onaga, Willard J. Peterson, Xinjiang Rong, Dominic Sachsenmaier, Dagmar Schäfer, Wutian Sha, Meir Shahar, Shengkai, Madeline Spring, Roel Sterckx, Jacqueline I. Stone, Stephen F. Teiser, Edward Q. Wang, Zhanru, Guangda Zhang, Tao Zhang, and Xing Zhang. I am also very grateful to many colleagues at Arizona State University for their trust and support: Stephen R. Bokenkamp, Robert Joe Cutter, Anne Feldhaus, Joel Gereboff, Juliane Schober, Hoyt C. Tillman, and Stephen H. West. Many administrators of the School of Historical, Philosophical, and Religious Studies (SHPRS) and the School of International Languages and Letters (SILC), faculty heads, and school staff helped facilitate my research and sabbatical leaves.

Numerous programs and institutions have invited and hosted me to share my research with colleagues and a broader audience. I acknowledged them here with profound gratitude: Buddhist Studies Workshop at Princeton University, Institute for Advanced Study in Princeton, Clare Hall of Cambridge University, Department of East Asian Studies at Cambridge University, Department of East Asian Studies at University of Göttingen, Department of East Asian Studies at

State University of New York in Albany, Department of Asian Studies at the University of British Columbia, Department of East Asian Studies at Tel Aviv University, Department of Asian Studies at Hebrew University of Jerusalem, Department of Philosophy at Tsinghua University, Department of South Asian Studies at Peking University, School of History at People's University of China, Department of Philosophy at Sun Yat-sen University, Center for the Study of the Yellow River Civilization and Sustainable Development at Henan University, the Sheng Yen Education Foundation, Institut national des langues et civilisations orientales (INALCO), and Max Planck Institute for the History of Science in Berlin (MPIWG). At Arizona State University, the Center for the Study of Religion and Conflict (CSRC), the Center for Asian Research (CAR), and the Institute for Humanities Research (IHR) offered travel and seed grants to support my research. A junior scholar grant from the Chiang Ching-kuo Foundation (CCKF) in 2009 helped the early stage of this project. The last stage of the manuscript benefited from a research grant of the Gerda Henkel Foundation in 2021.

Tremendous gratitude to the editors of the Sheng Yen Series in Chinese Buddhist Studies at Columbia University Press, Chün-fang Yü, Daniel Stevenson, and Jimmy Yu, for their support. I am so grateful to Lowell Frye for his patient and compassionate help guiding me through every step of this publication project. Thanks to Leslie Kriesel, Mary Bagg, and Cynthia Col for their professional efforts in producing, copyediting, and indexing the book. Three reviewers offered very constructive, meticulous, and comprehensive reports. Thanks to them for their collegiality, professionalism, and support. All errors and shortcoming remain my sole responsibility.

Some sections of the chapters previously appeared in the following publications: "A Buddhist Classification of Plants and Animals in Early Tang China," *Journal of Asian History* 43, no. 1 (June 2009): 31–51; "Transforming Beasts and Engaging with Local Communities: Tiger Violence in Medieval Chinese Buddhism," *Pakistan Journal of Historical Studies* 3, no. 1 (2018): 31–60, © Indiana University Press; "The Road to Redemption: Killing Snakes in Medieval Chinese Buddhism," *Religions* 10, no. 4 (2019): 247 (Creative Commons CC BY 4.0 license); "The Other as the Transformed Alliance: Living with the Tiger in Medieval Chinese Daoism," *Polylog: Zeitschrift für interkulturelles Philosophieren* 45 (2021): 4–22. I thank these journals for the permission to reproduce and adapt these already published materials.

Lastly, I thank my wife, Fei, and my kids, Sarina and Linden, for their companionship, and the animals who enrich our family life in the past, present, and future.

IN THE LAND OF
TIGERS AND SNAKES

Introduction

In 2016 an account of a strange homicide case appeared in the *Washington Post*. The previous year, a forty-five-year-old Michigan man named Martin Duram had been fatally shot five times in his Michigan home. His wife Glenna, found lying nearby with a gunshot wound to her head, had survived. The only witness to the murder was Bud, the couple's African gray parrot, who later began to mimic male and female voices having an argument, in which the man's last words were "Don't [expletive] shoot." Although Bud's "testimony" could not be presented in court, investigators who heard the parrot's account of Martin's final moments began to view Glenna as a suspect. In fact, she had attempted but failed to commit suicide after shooting her husband. And based on apologetic notes she wrote to her children, she was charged with and convicted of first-degree murder.[1]

This account reminds me of a similar case in medieval China, although there the parrot was treated as a legal witness. The story, as it appeared in *Anecdotes from the Kaiyuan and Tianbao Periods* (*Kaiyuan Tianbao yishi*), a collection of oral histories relating to the High Tang period gathered by Wang Renyu (880–956), tells of Yang Chongyi 楊崇義, a rich resident in Chang'an who inherited a large fortune from his forebears.[2] His wealth surpassed even that of many princes and dukes in the capital city. Mrs. Liu 劉氏, Yang's beautiful wife, was having an extramarital relationship with a neighbor, Li Yan 李弇, and the lovers hatched a plan to murder Yang. So, one day when Yang returned drunk to his room, Liu and Li killed him and buried him in an abandoned well. None of the attendants in Yang's house witnessed the homicide, but a parrot had been standing in the living room while it occurred.

After the murder, Liu dispatched household attendants to search for her husband; she then reported him as missing to the government, saying she feared bandits may have killed him. Officials began to search for suspects. They arrested some of the attendants and interrogated them without turning up any clues. When they went to Yang's residence for further investigation, the parrot in the living room suddenly began to squawk, and one official asked the parrot what happened. Though we are not told the exact words it uttered, the parrot identified the murderers as Liu and Li. Both were arrested and later sentenced to death.

Emperor Xuanzong 玄宗 (Li Longji, 685-762, r. 713-756) was astonished by the intelligence of this parrot. He issued an edict to bestow an honorific title, "The Green-Clothes Messenger," upon the parrot. The prime minister, Zhang Yue 張說 (663-730), even composed a biography for it, which was widely circulated in the capital. Many stories in medieval China credited the parrot with spiritual qualities such as righteousness, compassion, loyalty, and filial piety—attributes that enabled it to assist in the judgment of legal cases and to serve other sentient beings. In general, the parrot was portrayed as an articulate and intelligent bird in both Buddhist and non-Buddhist writings. This story is a stunning manifestation of the relations between animals and humans, men and women, as well as state power and the local community in medieval China; it is thus integral to this book's central theme for exploring how the changing power relations between humans and animals shaped the ecological, social, political, and cultural order in medieval Chinese society.

In the Land of Tigers and Snakes grew from my interest in examining how Buddhism adapted and adopted ideas about animals in medieval China. Since some animals in early Buddhist narratives did not exist in China's natural environment, the ways in which Chinese writers interpreted and modified the religious and cultural implications of these exotic animals during the spread of Buddhism deserve further study. For instance, lions, tigers, and leopards, considered as apex predators, have played significant roles as decorative and symbolic animals in the lives of political and religious figures in Africa, Asia, and Europe.[3] In many cultures across these regions, lions and tigers have earned reputations as noble animals for displaying dignity, ferocity, power, and might—features that happen to coincide with qualities expected of rulers in human society. While wielding political and military power over their regimes, kings, emperors, and dictators often enhanced their political and cultural rhetoric by invoking the symbolic power of beasts.

The lion is one of the most important animals in early Buddhist literature. But it was often usurped in Chinese textual sources by the tiger, a dominant East Asian feline species, because the medieval Chinese audience was more familiar with tigers, the ruler of the natural environmental order in traditional Chinese understanding and perception. In examining how Buddhist depictions of the natural world and native Chinese taxonomies mutually enriched each other, I offer a special perspective for understanding how Buddhism as a religious culture took root in Chinese society. With this book I also aim to interest other scholars in looking at the natural world and Chinese religions with a view to inspiring further research across multiple disciplines.

In the Land of Tigers and Snakes explores how Buddhism and Chinese culture together shaped the discourses, thoughts, knowledge, rituals, and practices about understanding, contacting, handling, taming, and combating animals as well as dealing with human-animal encounters in general during the medieval period. In Buddhist cosmology, the animal kingdom was viewed as one of the six realms inhabited by sentient beings, the others being deva (gods), asura (demigods), humans, hungry ghosts, and hells. Since Buddhist cosmology and the Buddhist concept of the natural world were new exotic ideas at the time of their introduction to Chinese religious life, I am interested in how they were transformed as they were rendered into the Chinese Buddhist literature and how the definitions and concepts of animals changed over time. Although Buddhists tended to classify animals according to three etic categories—animals belonging to the natural world; animals created by Chinese Buddhist literature, such as animal spirits; and animals transformed by their Chinese context—the images, roles, and functions of animals in Chinese Buddhism should not be separated from the political, social, cultural, and religious milieu of medieval China.

To some extent, this study expands the focus of an earlier book I wrote in Chinese about animals in medieval China, especially regarding various symbolic meanings of animals as cultural capital for constructing political and religious order.[4] Several friends and colleagues who read that book kindly asked if I plan to pen a work in English for a readership beyond the sinological realm and thus facilitate a wider range of conversation and discussion. *In the Land of Tigers and Snakes* answers that call. Indeed, I hope this book will interest not only scholars of Chinese Buddhism but also those who research animals (whether in the context of Buddhism or other religions) and those who study China or Asia, or religion and environment, in general. To that end I have consulted various sources from multiple disciplinary perspectives including literary criticism, religious studies, ritual studies, art history, the history of science, and environmental studies.

SPREAD OF BUDDHISM AND INFLUENCE OF ANIMALS

Theoretically and methodologically, in the past two decades, scholarly interests in the relationships between religions and nature, the environment, and animals have grown apace. Researchers have often attempted to understand the interconnected web of culture, society, and nature that has shaped religious traditions. Human beings develop their cultures, and construct their societies, through interactions with nature. Although Buddhism originated in South Asia around the sixth century BCE, it became a dominant cultural and religious tradition in medieval East Asia, traveling both by land and sea routes across Central Asia and Southeast Asia to reach East Asia. The vast continent of Asia has marvelous landscapes of forests, deserts, rivers, mountains, and meadows. These landscapes, and their ecological systems, have had a crucial impact on Buddhist cosmology, doctrines, and knowledge. Among these landscapes the Sundarban forests, the Himalayan mountain ranges, and the Taklamakan deserts are renowned for their ecological diversity.[5] Animals in these areas have played indispensable roles in the historical and cultural experiences of Buddhists.

The introduction and adaption of Buddhism is one of the most important changes in medieval Chinese cultural, economic, political, religious, and social life. In the past, scholars focused on textual sources for understanding the history of early Buddhism and interpreted doctrines from reading these textual sources. Recently, contemporary scholarship in religious studies has drawn attention to how the materialist turn, animal turn, and affect turn[6] have had a powerful impact on Buddhist studies.[7] The early members of the Buddhist community lived in a world with sounds and materials, such as the sounds of verbalized teachings, and those of animals. The psychological experiences of these early Buddhists were generated not only from the concrete content of the oral teaching, or texts, but also from the physiological marks and sounds of the Buddha. Many scholars are motivated to think about how nontextual materialist elements were crucial to early religious practitioners.

Religious culture shares similarities with political culture; the symbolic use of animals, especially beasts, is very common to both. In the medieval period, for example, the rulers *and* the ruled tended to understand the human social structure and order as mirrored in the structure and order of nature. Order in the animal kingdom is not very different from order in human society: both involve the dynamic between predator and prey. Contemporary scholars have attempted to use animals for analyzing numerous social and cultural phenomena. But with the rise of animal-oriented studies as a new field, the literature began to emphasize multiple definitions of nonhuman animals, depending on different human experiences and perceptions. For instance, Alan Bleakley has suggested that there are three categories of animals in human culture, based on the experience of human beings: biological, psychological, and perceptional.[8] Animals sometimes appeared in the daily life of Buddhists, but they might also appear as imagined, or in psychological or artistic contexts. For instance, the *nāga* and dragon in Asian culture are sentient beings created in literature and art by human imaginations and perceptions. The mystic *nāga* in early Buddhism was transformed into the Chinese dragon with the introduction of Buddhism into China. My Chinese-language study showed that the translators of an early Mahāyāna Buddhist text, the Lalitavistara Sūtra, replaced the two *nāga* brothers, who bathed the newly born Siddhartha, with the Chinese concept of nine dragons, perhaps as a symbol of royal legacy and power for glorifying the mighty Buddha.[9]

The spread of Buddhism to China beginning in the common era brought Buddhist ideas, rituals, institutions, and practices to the land, introducing as well the Buddhist knowledge of animals and plants. Echoing John Kieschnick's book *The Impact of Buddhism on Chinese Material Culture*, we might wonder how and if Buddhism affected Chinese animal culture in the medieval era. For instance, while studying Buddhist cosmology, scholars have focused on the impact that several new, crucial concepts such as karma, reincarnation, and rebirth had on Chinese culture. Yet they have paid less attention to how the idea of the animal realm challenged the Chinese concept of animals than they have to how the deva, asura, hungry ghost, and hell realms seemed exotic to the Chinese audience. Indeed, Stephen F. Teiser has masterfully contributed three great monographs on the Buddhist introduction and acceptance of hungry ghost and hell realms in medieval China.[10] The animal realm would likely have caused much confusion because the Chinese had already developed a very rich animal culture before Buddhism arrived—and some preeminent animals in the Buddhist tradition that hailed from South Asia could not be found in China. In the case of the animal realm in medieval Chinese Buddhism, it would be interesting to examine the gap between

Buddhist ethical principles and practical activities, the gap between doctrinal and discursive rhetoric in canonical texts, and the actual responses toward imminent threats from animals in the daily lives of local communities.

In this book I have chosen to focus on how the power relations between animals and humans shaped the cultural, political, religious, and social order in medieval China from the sixth to the twelfth century. During this time the interaction between Buddhism and indigenous Chinese traditions most closely concerned the natural world in general and animals in particular. In applying historical, religious studies, literary analysis, and anthropological approaches, I explore how animals were defined in Chinese religious traditions and how they were written into the Chinese religious literature across the porous boundaries between Buddhism, Confucianism, and Daoism. Although animals have been studied in religious traditions such as Buddhism, Christianity, Judaism, and Islam from various disciplinary perspectives, including religious studies, literature, anthropology, archaeology, and history—there is no single monograph devoted to studying the sophisticated human-animal relationships in medieval Chinese religions.

A number of monographs and articles have been devoted to the study of animals in Chinese history, literature, and religions in general, for which I hope my study will enrich this scholarly tradition. Edward H. Schafer laid a foundation for studying some important animals in medieval Chinese literature and culture.[11] Other scholars have written about animals in Chinese literature and art: for example, Madeline Spring on animal allegories in Tang literature,[12] Hou-mei Sung on some animals in Chinse art,[13] Rania Huntington on the fox in Chinese narrative literature,[14] and Wilt Idema on insects and the mouse versus the cat in Chinese literature.[15] In the field of Chinese history, several monographs have demonstrated the significance of animals. Roel Sterckx published a book on animals and religion in ancient China and also an edited volume with other scholars on ancient knowledge and management of animals.[16] Keith Knapp published a series of articles dealing with birds and noble animals in early medieval Confucianism and religions.[17] Xiaofei Kang wrote a book on the fox in later imperial and modern China.[18] Vincent Goossaert published a book on beef and ox culture in traditional China.[19]

Scholars who have discussed animals in Chinese Buddhism or Buddhism in general have tended to focus on animals from the perspective of nonviolent Buddhist thought and practice.[20] The Buddhist deployment of animals is far more varied and interesting than their roles in rebirth and vegetarianism, and it cannot be adequately studied without comparative and connective studies with other cultural and religious traditions in China, especially in the medieval period.[21] In the medieval period, multiple forces including intellectual, political, and literary thoughts and writings, powers, and artistic representations helped shape the images and roles of animals in medieval Chinese religions and culture. For example, I previously analyzed how medieval Chinese Buddhist monks introduced the concept of five phases (*wuxing* 五行) when they discussed zodiac animals in Buddhist literature; eventually the monks transformed these twelve zodiac animals from the reincarnations of calendrical bodhisattvas into the reincarnations of demons who kept insulting meditating monks.[22] I call this the Chinese Buddhist version of the legend of fallen angels.

STRUCTURE AND THEMES OF THIS STUDY

I intend *In the Land of Tigers and Snakes* to help echo some concerns from scholars working on the interplay between religion, environment, ecology. Most studies addressing this connection have focused on animals in the Judeo-Christian tradition. The question goes back to the ultimate ontological debate on the status of humankind in the history of the universe in natural science and the divine order in theology. From Lynn White Jr. to Aaron Gross, and then to Bron Taylor, questions concerning the extent to which religions are responsible for the ecological, environmental, and species crisis in traditional and modern society have generated numerous insightful and proactive discussions, not just for the sake of scholarship but also with a view to understanding and informing possible and plausible routes out of this crisis.[23] Scholars of Chinese environment studies have also presented their contributions to the crisis in traditional China.[24] in the spirit of these discussions, I attempt with this book to provide some fresh observations and trace some contemporary concerns back to the medieval period.

In particular, I analyze how animals played roles in the human-human, animal-human, and religion-religion relations in medieval China by focusing on four interacting power agents including the state, animals, local community, and religious community. I articulate how the powers of these four agents were constructed, challenged, undermined, and enhanced in order to deal with the tensions among different stakeholders of medieval Chinese cultural, ecological, political, religious, and social order.

First of all, different cultural, political, and social groups in medieval Chinese society talked about, discussed, portrayed, and categorized animals differently for their own specific interests. Recently I have realized more fully the extent to which animals appear as spirits, demons, and companions in Chinese religious writings from the perspective of human-animal conflicts and violence. In ana-lyzing the images of animals that are foregrounded in these writings, I attempt to reveal how various social groups, such as the medieval state, eminent monks, literati, and lay people applied their zoological and ethnographical knowledge about animals, nature, and the environment, their beliefs and practices in Bud-dhism and Daoism, and their established Confucian values, to define animals, classify animals, develop symbolic meanings for animals, transform animals, and wrestle with animals in their own sociocultural relations. The central issue is to understand how animals have played roles in shaping humans' historical, cultural, religious, and life experiences, and how these experiences have been manifested in literary imagination and visual representation. In short, it is worth thinking about how medieval people redefined animals and themselves, based on their literary, cultural, and life experiences with animals.

The second aspect I focus on concerns animal-human relations. From the per-spective of environmental history, in medieval China, with the increasing human population, Buddhist monks, Daoist priests, local villagers, and government administrators all faced threats from tigers and snakes. Indeed, these were the two biggest physical and psychological threats according to religious and nonre-ligious sources (appearing in the medieval Chinese discourse as so-called tiger ter-ror and snake disaster). Local communities struggled with these threats. Bud-dhist and Daoist clergy attempted to help local communities overcome tiger violence and snake disaster. Taming tigers and killing snakes became crucial cul-tural capital for both religious traditions to show their power, both in reality and rhetoric. Intellectually, for instance, killing snakes had a long history in Dao-ism. Daoist priests developed many techniques and rituals for taming and kill-ing snakes. And Chinese Buddhism seemed not to refute the possibility of learn-ing from Daoism. Auspicious violence in the Mahāyāna tradition offered the option and doctrinal foundation. Also, with the development of Tantric Bud-dhism in medieval China, killing snakes was no longer a taboo. Religiously, the competition between Buddhists and Daoists became fierce in medieval China.

Third, animals played an explicit role in religion-to-religion relations in medi-eval China. Besides local authorities ordered to kill tigers to protect villagers and their livestock, Buddhism, Confucianism, and Daoism developed their respective strategies and rhetoric for responding to this challenge. Based on the correlative theory in the Confucian political discourse, local governments addressed the tiger issue by developing a rhetoric of virtuous governance for driving violent tigers away. Daoist priests used their talismans and magic for avoiding conflicts with violent tigers. Medieval Chinese Buddhism offered an alternative. Buddhist hagiographical narratives constructed images of eminent monks, renowned for their ability to tame and convert violent tigers with their wisdom and compassion. These Buddhist narratives served as the rhetorical tool for making holy images of Buddhist saints, not dissimilar to medieval Christian hagiographies. In the meantime, they ventured into the boundary between the human and natural world by taming and converting tigers. Similarly, medieval Chinese narratives also depict the unstable boundaries between the humans and the animal world, which is explicitly manifested by the "were-tiger" issue. Traditional Chinese yin-yang theory and five-phase theory lay philosophical foundations for narratives on the were-tigers (or tiger transformation from humans), with the tiger regarded as the beast of "gold" among the five elements, which could be transformed in accordance with certain historical context. The Buddhist theory of retribution and reincarnation enriched the narratives on the were-tigers in medieval China.[25]

The six chapters in this book deal variously with how medieval Chinese religious traditions categorized, transformed, tamed, conquered, contested, and sanctified some of the most visible and significant animals—including tigers, pheasants, locusts, snakes, and parrots—that have profoundly meaningful lives in medieval Chinese sociocultural, literary, and religious life. Out the millions of animal species that lived in medieval China—too vast a number to be covered here—these animals became central figures in my book because of their prominent positions in manifesting three power relations among animals, humans, and religions. The written texts from medieval authors and compilers offer more detailed information about how those other animals were depicted, used, and interacted, symbolically, literarily, and religiously. Also, the animals I discuss are more representative of the ecological environment of mountains and waters in medieval Chinese culture and the classical Chinese categorization of animals in four groups (birds, beasts, worms, and fish), as well as domesticated/wild and indigenous/exotic animals, as the educated class depicted them. In each chapter I diachronically examine the historical origins and evolving developments of thoughts, rituals, and practices concerning animals in the medieval Chinese context; and I synchronically analyze the interactions and negotiations between animals and humans, between Buddhism and other Chinese traditions, and between the state and local communities.

In the first chapter I present the classification of animals in a medieval Chinese context. By analyzing a seventh-century Buddhist document that mainly offered guidelines for handling materials that were donated to the medieval Chinese monastic community, I explore how a medieval Chinese Buddhist monk combined doctrinal foundations in the early Buddhist monastic code, historical traditions, and his own personal daily experiences for developing three categories of animals relevant to maintaining Buddhist monastic order. I suggest that medieval Chinese categorization of animals appears to reflect a local and regional biodiversity that was different from that of early Buddhism. In particular, many tropical plants and animals were evidently recorded and discussed with some frequency in early Buddhism. But various animals that appeared in medieval Buddhist accounts were only active in northern China, which demonstrates how Chinese writers adapted their work to the daily experiences of a northern audience.

Chapter 2 focuses on the cultural and symbolic meanings of some important unruly animals for the agricultural society in medieval China, such as tigers, locusts, and pheasants. Tigers appeared as the symbols of powerful local families who had political, economic, and cultural authority and resisted the power of the court or central government. In reading epigraphic accounts of the pacification of tigers in a Confucian context, I analyze how tigers were used in political ideology. Tigers appeared as dissenting political "others" that were tamed and governed by the imperial sovereign. In Confucian political discourse, harmonizing tigers in the governed region symbolized the power of virtuous governance over local subjects. According to this doctrine, the tiger refers to a strong local power that might not be submissive to the authority of the central government and might be aggressive or even violent toward local residents. An official who was dispatched by the central government needed to pacify this local power and build a loyal relationship with the crown, thus stabilizing the imperial political order. Locusts refer to a powerful destructive force that endangered the productivity of the local agricultural order. The conquest of locust disasters was part of the local governance objectives that served to construct a stable economic order. Pheasants symbolized uncivilized marginal social groups, and they became the targets of the cultural transformation by imperial governments. Both Confucianism and Buddhism developed discourses on domesticating wild pheasants as ideological transformations to manifest their individual power over animals.

I turn in chapter 3 to the perhaps surprising topic of interactions between monks and tigers. I offer insight on stories about tiger taming in medieval Chinese Buddhism through my readings of various hagiographies selected from the biographies of eminent monks. Based on analysis of the stories about taming violent tigers in order to assist local villages, I suggest that the monks who tamed tigers lived an eremitic life, mostly in the forest, where they were likely to often encounter tigers and other beasts. The special place tigers held in Chinese culture, where they were regarded as the king of beasts and the most dangerous of all animals, suggested rhetorical constructions for the hagiographic association between tiger taming and monastic practice. Thus, the tiger replaces the lion as a central figure in Chinese Buddhist literature. Monks expanded their monastic order by transforming tigers and the natural order represented by these tigers. Since violent tigers were a major threat to the safety of humans and livestock in local villages, taming them became one of the major methods for the Buddhist monastic order to help local villages. It also reveals an alternative way for handling problems tigers with Buddhist compassion and wisdom, which is different from the local government under Confucian virtue and ideology. The taming of wild tigers in Buddhist narratives also raises an issue of boundaries between the realm of nature and the realm of Buddhism or Buddhist civilization. By taming tigers, monks were seen to expand the Buddhist realm and therefore to civilize the wildness from a Buddhist perspective.

Chapter 4 shifts to my discussion of Daoist engagement with tigers. As the apex predators in the ecological system in medieval China, tigers posed a challenge not only to local communities but also the Daoist hermits who lived in rural areas and mountains. Daoists developed new discourses and strategies for dealing with the so-called tiger violence problem. Their new discourses and strategies were shaped and reshaped by the Daoist textual and doctrinal traditions, the daily experience of living with the natural environment and animals, the interactions with local community, and the competition with Buddhists. Given that Daoism in medieval China was diverse and sophisticated, I limit my discussion on the medieval Daoist hagiographical sources to examine how they mirrored some issues in the medieval Buddhist hagiographies from a perspective of comparative monasticism. In these Daoist hagiographies, it appears that Daoist priests regarded tigers as companions, threats, and weapons in their daily and religious lives. Some medieval Daoists transformed tigers to companions during their solitary practices as hermits in mountains. Some Daoists confronted tigers as violent threats to local communities. By taming violent tigers, Daoists helped maintain social-ecological order and eased the tension between humans and wild animals in order to serve local communities. Taming and pacifying tigers became cultural and religious capital for the Daoists, helping to expand the Daoist realm. Some Daoists also transformed tigers into weapons against Buddhists for protecting Daoist property and assets. Daoist approaches to tiger violence in medieval China illustrate that on the one hand Daoists preserved doctrinal and ethical traditions rooted in their cosmology, and on the other hand they developed new strategies for responding to new challenges from the natural environment and religious competition.

In chapter 5, I analyze the changing images of snakes and serpents from early Buddhism to Chinese Buddhism and their roles in shaping the relationship between Buddhism and Chinese traditional values and religions, especially Confucianism and Daoism. The snake is one of the most important animals in Indo-European religious cultures, bearing several symbolic meanings. It was the evil animal that tempted Adam and Eve to eat a corrupting apple. In Buddhism, the image of the snake is also negative. It appears as one of three animals symbolizing anger in Buddhism responsible for the arising of suffering. In medieval Chinese sources, on the one hand, many stories depicted the snake-form reincarnation of humans as a severe punishment for bad karma. For instance, Emperor Wu of the Liang dynasty, Xiao Yan, was married to a woman named Xi Hui. For damaging Xiao Yan's Buddhist scriptures, she was punished to become a snake. Stories like this also reflected gender issues and stereotypes. Alternately, other stories attempted to demonstrate the power of Buddhist wisdom for defeating poisonous snakes as succubus by eminent monks in the medieval period. In Daoist hagiographies, however, snakes or serpents appeared as allies of Daoist priests for attacking the monks who took over Daoist property or threatened Daoist local communities.

Chapter 6 addresses the intelligence of animals in terms of how medieval Chinese Buddhists developed a theory concerning the enlightenment of animals, and I focus on analyzing the enlightenment story of the parrot in medieval Chinese Buddhist narratives. First, I discuss images of parrots in early Buddhist Jātaka stories and those in medieval Chinese Buddhist narratives. The differences show that medieval Chinese narratives addressed the abilities of parrots (their verbalization of human language, wisdom, and intelligence) as properties of this enlightened bird. Medieval Chinese Buddhist narratives equated parrots with sages from ancient Chinese civilizations who both combined animal bodies and human abilities of language, wisdom, and intelligence; this strategy aimed to demonstrate to the Chinese audience familiar with Chinese legends of cultural heroes that both parrots and sages shared similar properties of sentient beings.

In the epilogue I move from retrospective thinking to a prospective view by briefly summarizing key issues of this book and addressing their impact on contemporary issues. I pay particular attention to the historical implications of power relations between humans and animals and their interactions with the state and local communities in Chinese religions.

CHAPTER 1

Buddhists Categorizing Animals

Medieval Chinese Classification Systems

People in ancient and medieval periods used classification systems to establish an order by which they could not only make sense of nature and society, but also locate their positions within that order. Geoffrey E. R. Lloyd, a historian of ancient science and medicine, evaluates the strengths and weaknesses of three types of animal and plant classification: biological, cross-cultural universalist, and cultural relativist. Based on reading the texts of Aristotle as well as the *Huainanzi*, a compendium of Western Han philosophy and statecraft, Lloyd compares the classifications of animals and plants in ancient Greece and China; the two cultures, he says, share some significant similarities: "both make heavy use of animals to express differences between humans, and in both cultures the classifications are hierarchical or otherwise heavily value-laden." But he also emphasizes "a broad contrast between a Greek insistence on stable essence and a Chinese focus on processes, transformations, interdependence."[1] By studying how people in ancient and medieval periods classified animals we can understand how they observed and categorized the natural objects and other species they interacted with in their social and spiritual lives.

Before the rise of modern science, the classification of animals often focused on their social function or potential usefulness to society, and on how their symbolic meanings figured in moral teachings. Classifiers observed animals and primitively categorized them according to their folk genus/species—although some would try to make sense of their physical forms and rank the various organisms. But as David Clough remarks, "The first appearance of other animals in human narratives that we are aware of is in Aesop's fables, where they were classified morally, rather than physically, in order to teach moral truths, launching a tradition that continued in the moral and spiritual descriptions of animals that

continued in the Book of Physiologus and the bestiaries."[2] While anthropologists
and historians draw attention to how premodern people understood the natural
order and its relationship to their value system,[3] in this chapter I propose that
classifying animals in ancient times reflects certain dynamics at work in the developing relations between humans and animals. A Buddhist classification of animals, for example, reveals the Buddhist community's sense of power over animals.
By focusing on the writings of Daoxuan (596–667), a Buddhist master in medieval China, I examine how traditional Chinese zoological knowledge, Buddhist
literary and doctrinal tradition, and the individual master's personal experience
shaped this power.

As I detail later this chapter, various scholars have already contributed to our
knowledge of traditional animal classification in China. Be we can learn much
from how Buddhists approached classifying plants and animals, and from the
encounters and interactions between Buddhist and Chinese cultures in terms of
their different approaches. In medieval China, Buddhist authors left some fragmentary accounts of classification methods in their commentaries, biographies,
and ritual manuals. Some biographical sources in the Buddhist canon show how
the Buddhist community lived, wrote, and came to terms with animals and plants
in daily life. Daoxuan, one of the most prolific Buddhist scholars in Chinese history, is thus a rich source for this chapter's case study.

DAOXUAN'S VIEWS ON ANIMAL CLASSIFICATION

Drawing upon several sections in Daoxuan's *Ritual of Measuring and Handling Light
and Heavy Property* (*Liangchu qingzhong yi*), I examine how he classified the natural
world in early Tang China. He first talks about fields, gardens, and plants.[4] Then
he lists animals in three categories based on their standing in monastic communities: (1) domesticated animals (camels, horses, donkeys, sheep and goats, and
cows, which were used for economic purposes); (2) wild animals (such as apes,
monkeys, deer, and rabbit, which were not used for economic purposes); and
(3) animals prohibited by monastic code (Vinaya).[5] Indeed, Daoxuan's lists are
important resources for understanding plants and animals as the fundamental
physical basis of the Chinese Buddhist monasticism.[6] Although he intended his
original text to deal with property bequeathed to the monastic community by
deceased members, his classification of all monastic property is primarily based on

thirteen categories specified in the Four-Part Vinaya (Dharmaguptaka Vinaya, *Sifen lü*), which was part of his disciplinary training. But he also consults other sources, especially the Ten-Stanza Vinaya (*Shisong lü*, or commonly called Sarvāstivāda Vinaya). Since the sources of Vinaya were not sufficient to deal with all categories of monastic property in the Chinese context, Daoxuan introduced his own understanding of Buddhist doctrines to justify his ways of handling such property.[7] Although animals constituted the fundamental physical basis of the monastic community, the Buddhist community had to learn about how animals and plants might affect individuals as they strive toward enlightenment—particularly monks, who must do so in accordance with the regulations in the Buddhist monastic codes.

Daoxuan touches on the relationship between animals and humans in numerous cases in his writings. Given that Buddhists consider animals to be sentient beings, let me clarify that use of the word "animals" in this study refers only to nonhuman animals living in nature and society: Skt. *tiryañc*; Pali. *tiracchāna*; Ch. *chusheng, bangsheng,* or *hengsheng.*[8] He applies generic terms to creatures and nature, however, without considering the practicality of those terms in China. For instance, he uses *sisheng* (four forms of births) to refer to all creatures in the world, yet does not explain how to understand this term.[9] Nonetheless, *Ritual of Measuring and Handling Light and Heavy Property* remains one of the most significant documents in offering a set of practical regulations in the context of Chinese Buddhist monasticism.[10] It shows how Daoxuan adjusts the monastic regulations of dealing with animals and plants to the context of Chinese Buddhism in general,[11] and specifically to Tang Buddhists.

Although Daoxuan turns to canonical Buddhist sources, especially Vinaya texts, when writing about plant and animal classification, he does not limit himself within the tradition of the Four-Part Vinaya, part of the training he inherited from his masters. He consciously and unconsciously draws on his cultural and life experiences as well as the prevailing environment, to develop hybrid and ambivalent interpretations on the classification of plants and animals; his writings are confined to North China based on where he lived and traveled during his lifetime.

Daoxuan's list allows us to explore various doctrinal, historical, and geographical implications. Plants and animals provided the physical foundations for the daily lives of the medieval Chinese Buddhist monastic community. Further, they also provided the companionship and counterpart to Chinese Buddhists for cultivating their faith and practice, their views of the world, nature, and history. By means of looking at and examining plants and animals, making sense of them, and categorizing as well as classifying them, Chinese Buddhists also redefined their identity as Buddhists, and as Chinese Buddhists. Dealing with plants and animals is part of social relationships at large in Buddhist monasticism.

In sum, with this chapter I show how historical, geographical, religious, and cultural elements should be brought together to understand Chinese Buddhist writings on animals.

INFLUENCES ON AND OF BUDDHIST ZOOLOGY

Classifying animals is an important component of the relationship between human beings and animals as well as between human beings and nature more broadly. Only recently has contemporary scholarship become aware of the subject of classifying animals in traditional China.[12] Since the medieval Chinese monastic community was not isolated from the natural world, it was not to be designed as a separate space inhabited only by human beings. Animals always took part in the daily activities of Buddhist monastic members. Many social historians have viewed this participation as merely economic. But I believe it should be examined in a larger context and scrutinized according to multiple considerations, among them being religious, ethic, economic, and even biological. In terms of Buddhist ethics, dealing with animals remains a very significant subject.[13] Before discussing Chinese Buddhist classification of animals, however, I introduce the classification of animals in medieval Christianity and then trace the idea of animal classification back to early Buddhism.

Although the study of animal classifications in medieval Chinese Buddhism and even Chinese religions in general is still an underdeveloped field, contemporary scholars have produced a large number of works on animals in medieval Christianity.[14] Joyce E. Salisbury, for example, focuses on the status, roles, and classification of animals in the Middle Ages.[15] The themes of her scholarship include animals as property, food, role models for human beings, and human beings as animals. Salisbury notes that the concept of animals as human property might have originated with the domestication of dogs to assist human beings in hunting. Later, cattle and pigs became domesticated, and goats and sheep were introduced into Europe from the Mediterranean region. The domestication of horses followed. These animals mainly served as sources of food and labor. She also points out that when early Christian theologians realized animals could become property, they also viewed animals as destroyers of property. Given God's control of wild beasts and human beings' ability to tame and domesticate animals, she therefore concludes that wild beasts and domesticated animals became the prevailing concepts of animals in Christian discourse. But there are some exceptions, Salisbury indicates, such as cats. Cats were not domesticated animals, but they shared spaces with human beings and sometimes served the activities of human beings in hunting down mice. Based on her understanding, there are at least three types of animals: wild beasts, domesticated animals, and those that are neither. As I show in this chapter, this system is very close to the medieval Chinese classification of animals in the Buddhist context.

Furthermore, Salisbury suggests that under the overwhelming influence of Christianity, in the Middle Ages it was well accepted that animals were inferior to human beings. In the eleventh century, the Christian church instituted a law claiming the superior status of human beings over animals in every respect. In the Middle Ages, animals were considered the property of humans in three respects: first, humans ate animal meat and made clothing from animal skins and fur; second, humans trained animals to perform labor that aided in agriculture and production; and third, humans used animals as symbols of the economic status and identity of their owners.

Salisbury's study also touches upon how views of animals in Christian thought changed over time. Christian narratives of the Edenic era depicted (unclothed) humans as vegetarians who had no need for animal meat, skin, or fur. In medieval Christian culture, however, different animals were portrayed in different ways. For instance, European Christians demonized the goat, transforming it from a sacrificial to an evil animal, whereas sheep always appeared in sacrificial roles.[16] In medieval life, cattle, sheep, goats, pigs, horses, cats, and dogs were important animals in urban life,[17] and they also played a role in shaping medieval social and religious customs.

Looking back at early Buddhism, animals were viewed as intellectually inferior. Although Buddhism does not apply a clear hierarchical structure to the world of animals, according to monastic code the killing a small animal should be punished in the same way as killing a large animal.[18] In the theory of reincarnation, animals were viewed as human beings and could be reborn based on their deeds (karmas), but the path of animals was inferior to the path of human beings.

Lambert Schmithausen points out that in early Buddhism, animals seemed to be in misery and lived a more painful life than humans, because animals were enslaved, controlled, and tortured by human beings.[19] Rebirth in the animal realm was inferior to rebirth in the human realm. This concept might be paralleled to the social caste system in ancient India. People from higher castes could enslave or torture those from lower castes. Since animals were viewed as inferior to humans, this also reflected the anthropocentric worldview in ancient India. Transmigration theory tells that humans could be reborn as animals and animals could be reborn as humans, a concept rooted in the Vedic religion.[20]

Chinese Buddhists were aware of the animal path and its relationship to the classification of animals. Daoshi 道世—a contemporary of Daoxuan who resided with him at Ximing Monastery—provided a preliminary classification of animals, based on how many feet they had, in his encyclopedia *Pearl Forest of the Dharma Grove* (*Fayuan zhulin*). He identified animals without feet and those with two feet, four feet, and multiple feet. Animals without feet included the needlemouth worm (Skt. *nyaṭkūṭa*), as well as any worm who used its belly to move. Animals with two feet included many birds. Animals with four feet included dogs, foxes, horses, elephants, and so forth. And animals with more than four feet included insects such as the centipede.[21] Daoshi further noted in Lokasthāna Sūtra (Da lou-tan jing) that there were three kinds of animals: fish, birds, and beasts (6,400 species of fish, 4,500 species of birds, and 2,400 species of beasts). He also cited Saddharmasmṛtyupasthāna Sūtra (*Zhengfa nianchu jing* 正法念處經) and said that there were four billion animals in general. This fish-bird-beast classification system seems to be close to the Chinese classification of animals that was based on the categories listed in the *Erya* 爾雅, a lexicon dating to approximately 250 BCE, which included four categories: birds, beasts, worms, and fish. Although Daoxuan was very familiar with Daoshi's works, he did not mention his classification system at all.

From an ethical perspective, Paul Waldau discusses animal rights in the Buddhist tradition.[22] The first precept of no killing, he states, provides a basis to promote universal compassion toward animals as an ethical absolute. By tracing some scriptures in the Pāli canon, Waldau suggests that *tiracchāna* (animals) are different from humans because they do not have mental dimensions. He thus concludes, "The Buddhist tradition confirms the ancient nature of a concern for living beings, a concern which has been dominated in the other major religious and philosophical traditions by a tendency to ethical anthropocentrism."[23]

Therefore it is not surprising when Daoxuan, a medieval Chinese Buddhist master, talks about animals in the context of their economic and religious applicability.

Categorizing humans and animals together as sentient beings has a long history in Indo-Iranian religious traditions. The term "sentient beings" refers to organisms with certain intelligence and emotions. These emotions include fear of death and the experience of suffering. In Zoroastrianism, animals are grouped in two categories: good animals and evil animals. Mahnaz Moazami examined the crucial implications of *xrafstars* (evil animals) in Zoroastrian rituals based on Avestan and Pahlavi literature.[24] He points out that this bifurcation of animals was decided by the Zoroastrian dualistic worldview. The good animals were pure and therefore could be used to make sacrifices to gods. The evil animals were creatures of evil spirits designated for evil purposes. They lived in a dark world, attacking good animals, destroying water, soil, and plants, causing pollution and impurity. According to Moazami, *xrafstars* named either as *xrafstra-* in Avestan or *xrafstar* in Pahlavi both refer to reptiles and amphibians, such as frogs, scorpions, lizards, and snakes. Bigger beasts such as felines and wolves were also creatures of evil spirits, but they were called *dadān*, literarily "wild animals" or "beasts." Zoroastrian texts also provided information concerning techniques and rituals for killing these evil animals. According to Zoroastrian ethics, anyone killing these evil animals would accumulate merits for helping to purify the world. The texts also stipulate that hell was located in the north, where it was cold, narrow, stinking, and full of wild animals, such as wolves, reptiles, and even cats.

The categorization of animals also has its role in Manichaeism. As early as the 1920s, George Sarton (1884–1956) noted that Manichaeism attempted to classify everything with pentads.[25] Hans-Peter Schmidt explains: "The Manichaean pentad comprises men, quadrupeds, flying, aquatic, and creeping creatures. It occurs in Parthian, Sogdian, and Turkish texts, and it is also mentioned by Augustinus (in inverted order)."[26] As Schmidt notes, in this system, all creatures were classified into five groups: two-legged human beings, four-legged living beings, flying living beings, living beings in the water, and living beings creeping on the ground on their belly. In Latin, respectively, they are *animalia/bipedia*, *quadrupedia*, *volantia*, *natantia*, and *serpentia*. In this list, human beings were classified with animals, though humans were listed as the first category, as per the approach of Daoxuan in medieval Chinese Buddhism.

Daoxuan also stipulated regulations for dealing with animals. Some points from his text should be noted here. First, he lists slaves, servants, and animals together. Although it is not surprising to list animals and humans together, since animals are also sentient beings in Buddhist cosmology, it seems that in the case of Daoxuan's list, economic status is the principal basis of classification. Daoxuan appears to view both animals and slaves as contributors to monastic income, thus making the same kind of offerings as devout donors.[27] Plants were also viewed as in terms of income for the monastic community, but they were "produced" from the lands and fields owned by the monastic community, rather than offered by donors. Listing human labor, plants, and animals in this way is common in Buddhist texts. In the Sutra of the Great Renunciation (Abhiniṣkramaṇa Sūtra, *Fo benxing ji jing* 佛本行集經) translated by Jñānagupta (523-619, Shena jueduo 闍那崛多) in the Sui dynasty, it is stated that there was a Brahman whose surname was Mahākātyāyana. His range of expansive wealth spanned jewels, slaves, six categories of animals, grains, wheat, beans, houses, gardens, and other sources.[28] In this list, slaves, animals, and plants were grouped together. Even a popular Mahāyāna text for bodhisattva precepts, the Brahmajāla Sūtra (*Fanwang jing* 梵網經, The Scripture of the Brahma Net) grouped slaves and six categories of animals together. It seems that Daoxuan inherited this conventional listing tradition from Buddhist texts.

As we saw earlier in the chapter, Daoxuan places the animals that could be owned by the monastic community into three categories—domesticated animals, wild animals, and animals rejected in the monastic code—based on the relationship between animals and human society.[29] In particular, Daoxuan classifies animals according to their potential use in monastic economy. We know that all five domestic animals on Daoxuan's list were the same as the animals classed as domestic in ancient India: camels, horses, donkeys, sheep and goats, and cows. In fact, as shown by Jacques Gernet's study on monastic economy, which he based on the Dunhuang manuscripts, the medieval Chinese Buddhist community did own and trade cows, at least in northwestern areas.[30] Daoxuan's third category reveals how this system of classification depended on regulations in the Buddhist community that were shaped by monastic ethics.

We can tell from this list that this system of classification must have been justified by the traditional Buddhist view of animals to fit within the contemporary context of Daoxuan's era. Brian K. Smith suggests that in ancient India animals were similarly classified as either domesticated (*grāmya*, "of the village") or wild (*āramya*, "of the jungle").[31] According to the Baudhāyana-Śrauta Sūtra (24: 5), each of these groups included seven types of animal: "The seven village animals are the cow, horse, goat, sheep, man, ass, and camel as the seventh; some say that mule [is the seventh]. The seven jungle animals are [wild] cloven-hoofed animals, animals having feet like dogs, birds, crawling animals, elephants, monkeys, and river animals as the seventh."[32]

Francis Zimmermann offers a more detailed discussion on the classification of animals in ancient India by paying more attention to Vedic cosmology.[33] He conducted a close reading of *The Sushruta Samhita* (*Miaowen benji* 妙聞本集) and attributed it to Sushruta (Miaowen). This is a medical text from the Ayurvedic literature tradition, and its classification of animals was strongly connected with the classification of meat in the Vedic tradition. Although this text distinguished wild from domesticated animals, it did introduce other classification systems based on other criteria. For example, taking the geographical and biological environment into account, it classified animals in two groups: those from dry land and those from wet land. It also classified animals into other subgroups, such as those living near water and those living in swamps; those known to be meat-eaters; and those considered whole-hoofed. Zimmermann noticed that human beings were sometimes categorized as meat-eaters, and animals appeared as either the food of human beings or the enemies of human beings.

Like other old traditions, ancient Indian tradition did not differentiate true animals from those that were imagined, and beasts were often mixed in categories with demons. Animals also served as the vehicles of gods and goddesses. Using the sources in the Purāṇa, Zimmermann also concluded that the groups classified as domesticated (*grāmya*) and wild (*āraṇya*) each included seven animals. Cattle, goats, humans, sheep, horses, mules, and donkeys made up the former, while the latter included animals that were hunted, artiodactyl beasts, elephants, monkeys, birds, amphibians, and reptiles. Interestingly, we see that human beings were listed as domesticated animals. But in the Vedic tradition, domesticated animals actually refer to animals that could be sacrificed to the gods. In Vedic literature, humans, horses, cattle, sheep, and goats were used as sacrificial offerings. In the Indian epic *Mahābhārata*, wild animals refer to seven species of four-footed creatures: lions, tigers, cattle, buffalo, elephants, bears, and monkeys.

Zimmermann also reveals another system of animal classification in the ancient Indian Sanskrit lexicon Amarakośa. This text explains an interesting cosmology.

Aryans lived in the heartland and so-called barbarian inhabitants lived in the wilderness. Human beings were categorized by four social castes with four different ranks, and they corresponded to four categories of animals. For instance, the Kṣatriya caste corresponded to elephants and horses that were trained to serve in the court. The Vaiśya caste corresponded to cattle and other animals used in agricultural activities. Dogs and pigs were animals for the Śūdra caste. This classification reflects the typical design of social classes by the Brahman priests.

Whereas Smith and Zimmermann mostly rely on textual sources from ancient India, Roswith Conard examines archaeological evidence and traces the following domesticated animals in the ancient Indus civilization: cattle, sheep, goats, pigs, horses, camels, dogs, and fowl. She also lists animals such as the bull, buffalo, elephant, cat, dove, and peacock as possibly domesticated. The dove, peacock, tiger, and rhinoceros played an important role in the religious life of ancient India.[34] In the Harappa area, on an ancient seal, a figure appeared sitting on a throne with his legs crossed, surrounded by an elephant, tiger, rhino, and cattle.[35]

In Brahmanic and Buddhist mythology, various animals always appeared as symbols of gods and goddesses. Each god or goddess had his or her partners, descendants, sacred sites, epithets, Avatara, images, weapons, colors, numbers, flowers, garments, jewels, decorations, mantras, attendants, and vahanas. The god Brahma's vahana was a goose. Vishnu was sitting on a snake. Shiva used cattle as his vehicle. Kartikeya's vahana was a peacock.[36] It seems that these animals also helped define the identity of different gods and goddesses.

The scholarship of Hermann Oldenberg has laid a foundation for modern studies on the animals in the religious rituals of India; especially noteworthy is the first chapter of his monumental work *The Religion of the Veda*, where he devoted seven sections to discussing the subject.[37] For him, the relationship between gods, demons, and animals was key because in the Vedic religion those animals with a brutal nature were messengers or representatives of deities and demons. In ancient Indian religious culture, gods could transform themselves into numerous forms of other species, including animals. The highest god could become a fish, a turtle, a dwarf, or a man-lion; when appearing as Rama, a monkey became his companion; when appearing as Krishna, cows surrounded him. This can be seen in Srimad Bhagavata, Book I, Discourse III: 5.[38] Many deities and demons, especially those who were hostile and brought on plague, were portrayed as animals. *Ahi budhnya* and *aja ekapād* were two typically evil ones. *Ahi budhnya* looked like the deity of earth, yet *aja ekapād* was regarded as the pillar of heaven and earth to support the whole world. Many animals appeared as the servants, slaves, and vehicles of deities and demons. Just like humans domesticated and tamed animals, deities and demons also domesticated, tamed, and dispatched their animals, especially hawks, horses, and goats. Only a small number of animals such as cows could be regarded as useful animals to humans. Many animals, such as serpents, white ants, turtles, and horses, were the objects of worship cults.

Oldenberg also explored animal representations in the Vedic rituals. Bulls, horses, and goats were sacrificed to Indra and Agni. Particular animals appeared as the totems of tribes, as some family names such as Matsya (fish) and Aja (goat) suggest. The ancestor of the Kaśyapa clan in the Brahman caste was said to be the turtle, and the deity of the turtle was viewed by this clan as Prajāpati, creator of the universe. Some other surnames from animals include Gotama, Śunaka, Kauśika, and Māṇḍūkeya.

Precedent for Daoxuan's classification of animals can be found in the many Buddhist canonical texts that provide lists of animals. The *Discourse on the Ten Stages* (*Daśabhūmika-vibhāṣā, Shizhu piposha lun* 十住毗婆沙論) had a long list of beasts, including pigs, dogs, foxes, cats, mice, monkeys, tigers, wolves, lions, rhinoceroses, leopards, bears, elephants, horses, cattle, snakes, serpents, scorpions, raptors, hawks, doves, fish, turtles, and many more.[39] Some Vinaya texts listed animals in relation to the monastic community. For instance, the Mahāsāṃghika Vinaya (*Mohe sengqi lü* 摩訶僧祇律) mentioned that animals not permitted to be received in the monastic community included elephants, horses, cattle, buffalos, donkeys, sheep, river deer, deer, pigs, peacocks, parrots, and hens.[40] In the Ten-Stanza Vinaya, the list included cattle, horses, camels, donkeys, mules, pigs, sheep, dogs, monkeys, river deer, deer, geese, peacocks, and so forth.[41] The Mūlasarvāstivāda Vinaya Bhikṣuvibhaṅga (*Genben shuo yiqieyou bu pinaiye* 根本說一切有部毗奈耶) classified animals into two groups: those with two feet, and those with four feet. Two-footed animals included humans and birds. Four-footed animals included elephants, horses, camels, donkeys, cattle, sheep, river deer, deer, pigs, and rabbits.[42] The list in the Samantapāsādikā (*Shanjian lü piposha* 善見律毗婆沙) included river deer, deer, monkeys, peacocks, pheasants, and so forth.[43] It is notable that elephants, horses, cattle, sheep, donkeys, monkeys, river deer, deer, peacocks, and pheasants appeared relatively frequently in canonical texts, which might indicate that these animals were often seen in ancient India.

Most of the animals mentioned in the monastic codes could live peacefully among humans, but some, such as lions, tigers, and wolves, brought trouble. In

Four-Part Vinaya and Ten-Stanza Vinaya texts, the evil animals included lions, tigers, leopards, wolves, bears, and brown bears, all considered typical beasts in the Buddhist context. Evil animals referred to those capable of attacking others, and those under the threat of such attacks. In Daoshi's Buddhist encyclopedia *Pearl Forest of the Dharma Grove*, he attributed being reborn as an animal to bad karma. Medieval Chinese Daoism seems to have borrowed the idea of the animal path and a human's rebirth as an animal from Buddhism. But as the Daoist text indicated, the animals that human beings were reborn as included birds, beasts, worms, and fish, which reflected traditional Chinese categorization of animals.[44] Basically, medieval Daoist classification of animals hybridized the Buddhist idea of transmigration and rebirth and the Chinese idea of four categories of animals.[45]

In Daoxuan's classification, we saw that domesticated animals included camels,[46] horses, donkeys, bulls, sheep, and so forth.[47] All of these animals could legally belong to the permanent dwelling sangha (*changzhu sengqie* 常住僧伽). Their affiliated saddles, saddle blankets, ropes, railings, folds, mangers, and stables could belong to the monastic community as well. But whips and sticks could not; in fact, the monastic community destroyed whips and sticks because they were used to torture domestic animals. Although the enslavement of animals seems to conflict with Buddhist attitudes toward animals, Schmithausen summarized a common view in early Buddhism: "Existence as an animal is a very unhappy one, much more painful than human existence. One of the reasons is that animals are enslaved by man: used as vehicles, beaten and exploited."[48] Daoxuan rejects the use of whips and sticks for bringing pain to animals, yet he does not reject the idea of animals transporting members of the monastic community. Using animals in this way would require training, prodding, and disciplining them with whips and sticks. This practice, then, seems to be contradictory to the compassionate ideal of the Buddhist monastic community, as many Buddhists claimed.[49]

In the same text, Daoxuan also used another term for domesticated animals, *liuchu* 六畜 (six animals). "Six animals" appeared in many early Chinese texts, such as *Zuozhuan* 左傳 (Zuo's commentary on the Spring and Autumn) and *Zhouli* 周禮 (Rituals of the Zhou dynasty). According to an early Chinese lexicon *Erya* 爾雅, the so-called six animals were horses, cattle, sheep, pigs, dogs, and roosters; these were the most familiar domesticated animals in ancient Chinese social and economic life. I believe that Buddhist texts borrowed this term from indigenous Chinese texts for referring to domesticated animals in general.

Yet Buddhist texts never explicitly offered a list of six animals. The Ekottarika Āgama (*Zengyi Ahan jing* 增壹阿含經) mentioned six animals briefly, but only listed the following five animals: pigs, roosters, dogs, cattle, and sheep.[50] This list aligns perfectly with the five animals (*wuchu* 五畜) specified in the *Basic Questions* (*Suwen* 素問) of the *Yellow Emperor's Inner Classics* (*Huangdi neijing* 黃帝內經). Another early Chinese translation of the Buddhist text Avadānaśatakaṃ (*Zhuanji baiyuan jing* 撰集百緣經) used the term "six animals" but listed only four: elephants, horses, cattle, and sheep,[51] and elephants were not even considered domestic. In the Dharmapada, *Udānavarga (*Chuyao jing* 出曜經), the term "six animals" appeared but there were seven animals listed: camel, mule, donkey, elephant, horse, pig, and dog.[52] So it seems that sometimes the term "six animals" in Chinese translations of Buddhist texts just indicates animals in general. Daoxuan uses the term in this way, too.

Daoxuan classifies the domesticated animals of his era that were not used for economic purposes as wild animals: apes (*yuan*), monkeys, river deer (*milu*), deer, bears, ringed pheasants, rabbits, mountain cocks, and wild geese. Apes, bears, and geese were also listed as wild animals in ancient India.[53] These wild animals and their necessary cages and confinements were not to be accepted by the monastic community even if donated. River deer and deer sometimes served as food for local people. In Chinese Buddhist texts, all these animals, river deer, deer, bears, and brown bears were regarded as evil, which means that they could damage the daily monastic practice and corrupt the monastic morality. According to Daoxuan, if the monastic community received these animals, it was bound to release them, because they were considered obstacles on the Buddhist path.[54] At this point, Daoxuan does not claim the value of compassion; rather, he emphasizes that the austere life in the monastery would prevent its members from keeping animals whose needs surpassed what the community could provide.

When some domesticated animals died, the monastic community would provide funerary services for them. The Dunhuang manuscripts include prayers for use during such rituals dating from the ninth to tenth centuries. One manuscript (P. 2940) of purification and lament (*Zhaiwan wen* 齋琬文) specified the deceased animals for which the funerals could be performed: the horse, ox, camel, donkey, sheep, dog, and pig.[55] These animals were certainly crucial to the economic life of local people in medieval Dunhuang. The ritual was part of the feast for honoring the Buddha for his blessings to these animals; the feast also included the ritual of releasing and redeeming animals. Even though the monks would not keep some domesticated animals in their monastic community, it seems likely that they could perform the redeeming and releasing ritual on behalf of the local people.

Another manuscript (S. 5637) from Dunhuang offers an example of the prayer model in the medieval period. This text provides details of the rituals for numerous deceased sentient beings, both humans and animals. Three separate sections were designed, for a deceased horse, ox, and dog. According to this prayer text, after the horse died its owner hosted a feast, prayed for blessings, sacrificed burnt offerings, and made a wish to the deceased horse. The prayer also praised the horse for its mighty appearance and its loyalty—saying, for instance, that the nature of this horse was ultimately the best, its color looked like peach flower, and its eyes were as bright as a hanging mirror. To indicate compassion, the owner provided an array of vegetarian food and burnt incense during the funeral service. The host wished for his deceased horse not to be reborn in three bad realms and to avoid eight difficulties, and to even surpass six realms of life and death. In other words, the host wished his horse to reach enlightenment.[56] Directly after the section dedicated to the deceased horse, the text focused on the rituals for a deceased ox; it stated that the owner domesticated and fostered the beast and used it as an alternative source of labor. The ox died from an illness, so a feast was held for blessings. The figure and color of this ox were extraordinary, and its power and energy were unparalleled. The host wished for the deceased ox to receive the human form and to cultivate his merits and virtues for being reborn in the realm of heavens (*devas*). This wish for the ox is different from the one for the horse and did not include the blessings for being reborn beyond six realms. In the third section, the dog was praised for its loyalty to its owner and for its awareness of the owner's benevolence. It also praised the dog for protecting the gate and courtyard day and night, for recognition of acquaintances and strangers, and for patrolling the field and garden.

Hens, ducks, and geese are commonly known as domestic birds (*jiaqin* 家禽) in the Chinese tradition. In Daoxuan's list, however, they were labeled as wild animals, which is a Buddhist tradition. But the concept of domestic birds does appear in Buddhist biographies. For example, in the biography of Faxiang 法相 in Huijiao's *Biographies of Eminent Monks* (*Gaoseng zhuan* 高僧傳), it is stated that Faxiang could recite Buddhist scriptures containing more than one hundred million characters. Birds (*qin* 禽) and beasts (*shou* 獸) often attended him and stayed by his side, having been tamed just like domestic birds.[57] Occasionally, these domestic animals also accompanied other monks. For example, Falang 法朗 was said to have cultivated his Buddhist practice to elicit a response from the spirits of other sentient beings. His dormitory room was full of geese, ducks, roosters, and dogs. These animals could spiritually respond to Falang. When he went to sleep, all birds and beasts in the room observed silence. When he walked around, these animals started making noise.[58]

This kind of experience with animals is rare in Buddhist history. Certainly Daoxuan would not support trying to cultivate such behavior in the monastery. Moreover, he does not make a distinction between birds and beasts; instead, he only distinguishes wild animals from domestic animals. And for him, the wild animals refer to those animals not allowed to be received and kept in the monastic community. Even hens, ducks, and geese were listed as wild animals because in Daoxuan's eyes they did not serve the economic and daily needs of the monastic community. Therefore, in this sense, Daoxuan did not borrow the traditional Chinese concept of domestic birds in his discussion on Buddhist classification of animals.

Some common animals in ancient India, such as the jackal (Skt. *sigāla*, Ch. *yegan* 野干),[59] lion, rhinoceros, elephant, parrot, and peacock, were neither active in China nor particularly visible to Chinese Buddhists in the medieval period; this explains why they did not appear on Daoxuan's list. Some Chinese Buddhist pilgrims encountered these animals in South Asia. For example, in his travel account, Huichao 慧超 described that there was a stupa near the place where the Buddha achieved nirvana in Kuśinagara and many pilgrims who traveled to this place were hurt by rhinoceroses and tigers. Xuanzang witnessed a lot of wild elephants in central India. Wild foxes often appeared in early Buddhist texts and Tang dynasty novels,[60] which might indicate that these foxes were active in India and the Western Regions.

The lion, though a common animal in India, Sri Lanka, and Central Asia, as well as West Asia, was exotic for the Chinese. Persian and Indian kingdoms were said to have offered lions as gifts to the Chinese court.[61] But less privileged people, including common monks, might not have had opportunities to see them. Therefore, it is not surprising that the lion is absent from Daoxuan's list even though he surely had textual knowledge about them. And it might be a mistake to assume that knew nothing about their presence in China, since a lion was offered to the Tang court, and Daoxuan lived in Chang'an for a long time. When the lion reached Chang'an in the early Tang period, many famous literati composed poems praising this exotic animal, of which Daoxuan was most likely aware.

But the animal's lack of significance in the Chinese monastic community caused Daoxuan to keep it off his list.

The tiger was another important animal absent from Daoxuan's list. In both India and China, the tiger was a common beast living in the wilderness. At least two species, the Siberian tiger and South China tiger, were active in the north and the south respectively. In medieval Chinese Buddhism, many biographers of monks told stories of their subjects' encounters with tigers in mountains and temples from the north to the south. For example, as the biographer of Senglang 僧朗 indicated, in the Mount Tai (Taishan) area, tiger violence was a big problem for local people. The biographer of Zhikuan 志寬 also stated that tigers threatened local villagers in the Sichuan area and explained how Zhikuan helped ease this violence by setting up a vegetable feast, walking the path, and bestowing eight precepts. Facong 法聰 helped resolve the violence of tigers by bestowing them three-refuge precepts in Mount Sangai (Sangaishan 傘蓋山), Xiangyang Prefecture. All of these biographers attempt to praise the moral virtue of monks whose dharma power could remove the violence of tigers; in sum, although many might have exaggerated the dharma power of eminent monks in terms of helping to pacify violent tigers, they did deliver a message that tigers were active and had contacts with monks in mountains in a number of areas, such as Shandong, Sichuan, Hubei, and Fujian.

It is worth noting that Daoxuan does not include the elephant in any of the three animal categories he lists. The elephant was a significant animal in ancient Indian economic and religious life, and in non-Buddhist sources mentions of elephants in southern China were not uncommon. There could be many reasons why Daoxuan omitted them from his list. First, the elephant (like the tiger) does not seem to be important to the medieval Chinese monastic community, at least, not as important as in India. Second, elephants tended to live in southern China, which was an unfamiliar area for Daoxuan. In other words, Daoxuan was not particularly aware of this animal since it had nothing to do with his daily life experiences.

The rhinoceros was also absent from Daoxuan's list. This animal usually appeared together with the elephant in medieval Chinese sources, both in Buddhist biographies and non-Buddhist historical sources. Buddhist lexicons such as *A Collection of Names and Their Explanations in Buddhist Translations* (*Fanyi mingyi ji* 翻譯名義集)[62] and *Pronunciation and Meaning of All Scriptures* (*Yiqiejing yinyi* 一切經 音義)[63] list entries containing the rhinoceros. Some biographers of well-known

Buddhist figures occasionally mentioned products derived from rhinoceros horn. For instance, the biographer of Huisi 慧思 stated that a military governor Wu Mingche 吳明徹 in the Chen dynasty (the fourth and last of the Southern Dynasties during the Southern and Northern Dynasties period), presented a pillow made by rhinoceros horn to Huisi who preached dharma in the Southern Marchmount (Hengshan, Mount Heng in Hunan) because he admired Huisi so much.[64] Famous Tiantai master Zhiyi 智顗 was also said to own a rhinoceros horn.

In early Buddhism, the rhinoceros was a very important animal in terms of symbolizing the *dhūta* practice/cultivation of a Buddhist, which means that a Buddhist practiced asceticism alone, walking in the forest and wilderness. The Rhinoceros Sutra, which was discovered in the Gandhādī manuscripts, testifies to the importance of this Buddhist teaching in Central Asia.[65] In Rāṣṭrapālaparipṛcchā Sūtra, one sentence reads: "He lives alone like a rhinoceros; he is ever fearless like a lion."[66] This praised the virtue of a Mahāyāna bodhisattva. Some other texts such as Moon Lamp Samadhi Sutra (Samādhirāja-candrapradipa Sūtra, Yuedeng sanmei jing 月燈三昧經) and Mahāyāna Jeweled Cloud Sutra (*Dasheng baoyun jing* 大乘寶雲經) used the same metaphor. Basically, the rhinoceros was viewed as a crucial metaphor when describing solitary practices in Buddhist literature.

The absence of the rhinoceros can be explained in similar terms as the absence of elephant on Daoxuan's list. This rhinoceros was mostly active in southern China, an area unfamiliar to Daoxuan, though he did know that such an animal existed. Elephant tusks and rhinoceros horns were two of the most precious gifts offered in the south to the central court in medieval China. But the animals themselves rarely had a significant impact on monastic life, and thus were of little interest to Daoxuan.

Some animals on Daoxuan's list tended to live in northern China. As Xu Tingyun showed, the river deer was common in central and northwest China, especially in Shaanxi, Shanxi, Ningxia, Henan, and Anhui.[67] In contrast, the sources Xu examined do not mention the situation in southern China. Apes and monkeys mainly lived in southern China in the Tang period, however, and in tracing these two animals in Tang poems, Xu suggests that they might be active in Guizhou, Sichuan, Hunan, Hubei, Jiangxi, Zhejiang, and Anhui, or the area around the two banks of the Yangtze River. Occasionally, Tang people also encountered monkeys in Shaanxi and Henan. According to Xu, tigers and elephants were also active in many areas. In Guangdong and Anhui, people saw heads of elephants, while tigers were seen in both urban and rural areas in northern

China. Bears were active in the Guangling area (modern day Jiangsu). In north-western China, cattle became the favorite hunting animal of Emperor Xuan-zong. Therefore, it seems that most of the animals mentioned by Daoxuan resided in the farmed lands of northern China.

When Daoxuan discussed hens, ducks, and pigs he emphasized that they could carry pollution, though he did not specify what type. By indicating that pure Buddhist monastics and monks should not keep these birds, he was perhaps just following the monastic code he read.[68] All cages and pens used to confine these wild animals, he said, should be burned. Daoxuan also pointed out that the monastic community should destroy bows and arrows, as well as other weaponry used to hunt animals. Interestingly, animals such as hens and pigs are classified as domesticated in non-Buddhist society. Thus, this category seems to be a Chinese Buddhist invention.

The third category in Daoxuan's list included other animals prohibited by the monastic code, such as cats, dogs, eagles, and mice, which suggests that this category mainly referred to pets. One story handed down regarding dogs as pets comes from the Four-Part Vinaya, which stated that during the Buddha's stay in Kashmir, the Buddhists there kept dogs. These dogs barked when they saw Buddhist monks, and when the monks reported this to the Buddha, he told them to not keep dogs.[69] Looking at medieval Europe, the concept of "pets" had been developed by that time. Christian theology had a profound impact on lay people's knowledge and understanding of animals. Pets, for medieval Europeans, included at least cats, dogs, and monkeys. Some archaeological evidence even suggests that apes and parrots had been introduced into England from other places.[70]

The term used to describe the third group of animals, those being against monastic codes or prohibited according to monastic codes, is *elüyi* 惡律儀 (literarily "evil behaviors against code and ritual"). This categorization can be found in the Ten-Stanza Vinaya but not in the Four-Part Vinaya. In Buddhist canonical sources, there are two discourses on evil behaviors against codes and rituals which concern animals. One counts twelve behaviors, and the other sixteen behaviors. The twelve evil behaviors found in Sutra on Repaying the Buddha's Compassion for his Great Skillful Means (*Da fangbian Fo bao'en jing* 大方便佛報恩經) include killing animals (for eating their meat or selling them to make a profit), rearing chickens for meat, rearing pigs for meat, hunting or trapping birds, fishing, hunting beasts to eat or sell, stealing, taking the lives of those prisoners who were sentenced to death, being prison officers, casting incantations on dragons and snakes, killing dogs, and waiting to hunt beasts.[71] This discourse of twelve evil behaviors also appeared in the Sarvāstivādavinaya-vibhāṣā (*Sapoduo pini piposha* 薩婆多毘尼毘婆沙), Bodhisattvabhūmi (*Pusa dichi jing* 菩薩地持經), and at least two manuscripts from Dunhuang, the *Commentary on the Code and Precept Selections* (*Lüjieben shu* 律戒本疏) and the *Record on the Meaning of Bodhisattvabhūmi* (*Dichi yiji* 地持義記). In Dharmakṣma's translation of the Mahāparinirvāṇa Sūtra, however, the list was expanded to sixteen evil behaviors, with the following four additions: rearing lambs and killing them, rearing cattle and killing them, rearing cattle and selling them, and double-tongued speech.[72] Many other Buddhist translators and writers also adopted this discourse. See Zhiyi 智顗, Huiyuan 慧遠 (523–592, from the Pure Shadow Temple, Jingyingsi 靜影寺), and Zhanran 湛然 for example. Huiyuan in particular offered a lengthy explanation about these sixteen behaviors in his *Essay on the Meaning of Mahāyāna* (*Dasheng yi zhang* 大乘義章).[73] For these Buddhist writers, raising any domesticated birds and beasts was prohibited, as were fishing and hunting. Yet the animals in the list included sheep, cattle, and pigs, appeared in Daoxuan's list of animals as domesticated. His list of animals against the monastic code mostly included pets. This shows a clear difference between Daoxuan's ideas and those of several contemporaries.

In Daoxuan's interpretation, the monastic community should not be involved in killing and trading animals because the bad deeds accumulated from such acts would bring terrible retribution to the monks. Buddhism has a long tradition that prohibits injuring animals and other living beings. As Schmithausen remarks, "In the so-called ascetic religions of Ancient India (Jainism and Buddhism), killing or injuring living beings is regarded as both unwholesome and fundamentally immoral; for, on the one hand, killing or injuring them is bad karma entailing evil consequences for the perpetrator after his death, and on the other all living, sentient beings are afraid of death and recoil from pain just like oneself."[74] Schmithausen points out that in ancient India, not only humans and animals but also plants and seeds were regarded as sentient beings. This no-killing tradition was inherited by Chinese Buddhists. In the early Tang period, Daoxuan states that selling animals was even eviler than simply killing them. For the monastic community, when dealing with animals the principle of compassion was to be strictly obeyed. According to Daoxuan, the monastic community should erect its sacred house of compassion (*cibei shengzhai*).[75]

Unlike Confucianism, in medieval Chinese Buddhism animals were not to be used for sacrifice, not even to the Three Jewels: the Buddha, dharma (doctrine, or teaching), and sangha (monastic community).[76] Thus, the animals donated by lay people were not to be *dedicated* to the Buddha or the sangha but instead intended for the daily use of the monastic community.[77] Current scholarship on animals from the Confucian perspective suggests that in ancient China, Confucians may have viewed animals in light of their values of benevolence and reciprocity.[78] Historically, Buddhism protected animals from being sacrificed in ancient India. This compassion toward animals served as a powerful tool against old Brahmanical ritual in which animals were sacrificed.[79]

It seems that in Chinese Buddhist monasticism, Vinaya masters were instrumental in classifying animals. Daoxuan, who classified everything a monastic community might have owned, based his classification of animals mainly on the monastic code (Vinaya) of the Indian Buddhist tradition. But there are many Chinese translations available for a variety of monastic code traditions. Therefore, Chinese Vinaya masters had to justify their classifications to fit with changing situations. In pre-Buddhist Chinese society, rulers or sage-kings had authority in classifying animals.[80] It is still debatable to what extent Chinese taxonomy of animals was borrowed from the Indian tradition, and the issue deserves thorough exploration.[81] In ancient Indo-Iranian civilization, religious priests were responsible for classifying everything (including living beings); the classification of animals in Indo-Iranian culture has been discussed mainly in sacred scriptures, such as the Ṛgveda and the Bundahiśn. Most systems developed in these sacred texts were based on their religious values, and reflected their religious features, or even served their religious needs. For example, in the Zoroastrian system animals were classified as good or evil based on whether they were created by the bright god (Ahura Mazdā / Ohrmazd) or the dark god (Angra Mainyu / Ahriman).[82]

CONCLUSION

First, Daoxuan's knowledge of animals is significant for combining Buddhist tradition with Chinese indigenous tradition. He not only justifies his knowledge of animals based on his reading of the monastic code, doctrinally and literarily, but also considers contemporary Chinese knowledge about animals, from both the Chinese traditional zoological knowledge and his own personal experience. His broad knowledge of Buddhist texts offered him a unique position in discussing animals in the Chinese monastic community and helped him jump from early

Buddhist tradition to Chinese tradition. Although he was ordained and trained in the Four-Part Vinaya tradition, he was also familiar with other Vinaya texts that had been translated into Chinese. He lived in Chang'an, so he was familiar with Xuanzang's journey to the Western Regions. But as the analysis in this chapter shows, his textual knowledge and practical experience with animals in a certain historical context by no means could offer a generalizable image.

Second, in classifying animals, Daoxuan views them as inferior to human beings, even though he lists animals and monastic laborers together. His guiding principle is whether the animals benefit the individual monastic members in their enlightenment. In other words, the animals by any means must serve the monastic needs. He does not view animals as equivalent to human beings in terms of their karma. From his viewpoint, classifying animals matters because the monastic community has to decide whether they can keep these animals within the monastic community. Thus, the compassion Daoxuan supports in his text has nothing to do with liberation in modern discourse; rather, it has to do with the purification of monastic individuals, the cultivation of these individuals. Daoxuan does not speak against the use of animals as labor, which reflects a typical anthropocentric worldview in medieval monasticism. This worldview seems to transcend cultures and also appeared in medieval Christianity.

Third, most of the animals listed by Daoxuan were found or cultivated in northern China, reflecting his observations of the monastic community in that part of the country.[83] Ironically, his ideal model of Chinese Buddhist monasticism is the Buddhist monasticism in southern China.[84] Through an examination of Daoxuan's ideas about dealing with animals, we can also conclude that the ownership of animals was restricted to the Buddhist community, and prohibited to individuals. This suggests that so-called asceticism in Chinese Buddhist monasticism was practiced strictly in the sense of individuals, rather than a communal behavior.

Finally, as I emphasize in this chapter, many Buddhist concepts in daily life, including the classification of animals, were transformed from early Buddhist culture to Chinese culture. Although current scholarship has largely neglected these common concepts, this chapter offers an example of how we should pay attention to these changing concepts while understanding Buddhism in its wider context of Asian history.

CHAPTER 2

Confucians Civilizing Unruly Beasts

Tigers and Pheasants

In chapter 1 we saw that Daoxuan objected to the ownership and use of wild animals in Chinese monastic communities. In day-to-day life, however, there was no way for either Buddhists or non-Buddhists to avoid interacting with the animal realm. And wild animals especially played vital roles in the political, socioeconomic, cultural, and religious life of medieval China. Encounters between humans and wild animals were often seen in terms of confrontation and power struggles that could be likened to the way powerful entities such as the state, or local and religious communities, took advantage of human apprehensions and interests to mobilize both political and cultural capital.

The tension and negotiation centered on wild animals between Buddhism and Confucianism in medieval China caught my attention when I came across a very interesting detail in my research. Specifically, this was a Buddhist stupa inscription beside the tomb of Sun Liao (458–524 CE), dedicated to him by his sons on September 8, 524.[1] According to the inscription, Sun Liao was a native of Dingzhou (modern Dingzhou, Hebei Province) but his ancestors were from Taiyuan. He turned to study Buddhist doctrines during childhood. When he was eighteen, he started to practice vegetarianism and also abstained from consuming alcohol. Later, he demonstrated further devotion by cutting off two of his fingers and burning them as an offering to the Buddha. Although he often engaged in prolonged periods of meditation, he accepted an appointment between 512 and 515 as the magistrate of Lancang County (modern Li County, Gansu Province). His virtuous governance was praised for following models of previous local administrations, especially that of Lu Gong 鲁恭 (32–112 CE).[2] Continuing its eulogy of Su Liao, the inscription states that his political virtue swept across about one hundred *li* and mentions how the autumn locusts had flown away. Here, the so-called sweeping of about one hundred *li* refers to the size of the geographical area a county magistrate would oversee in ancient China, and the mention of massive flying locusts refers to one of the most disastrous threats in medieval Chinese agriculture.

It may seem odd to find a historical reference praising Lu Gong's virtue as the magistrate of Zhongmou County in the first century on the stupa that Sun Liao's sons commissioned some four hundred years later to fulfill their filial piety. But the inscription explicitly reveals the peaceful coexistence of Buddhist and Confucian values: Sun Liao, a devoted Buddhist and a local administrator, modeled his virtuous governance on the Confucian political ideal that shaped Lu Gong's successful career as a county magistrate. But aside from sharing similar political values, both magistrates would have needed to confront the swarming locust problem.

Wild animals had significant impacts on local villages in traditional Chinese agricultural society. Numerous sources that documented animals of all kinds in ancient times reveal that along with locusts, tigers and pheasants were two of the most common unruly animals found in the wilderness, seriously challenging local government officials in medieval Chinese political and social order, practically and symbolically. Tigers were the most ferocious animal, endangering local villagers and their livestock, which means danger to the local economic and ecological order. Politically and economically, maintaining the order of local agricultural production was one of the most important duties for local governance in imperial China. In the meantime, in ancient and medieval China, shooting pheasants was a popular and fashionable sport among literati and officials. Culturally, tigers and pheasants were also granted special symbolic meanings by elite Confucian scholars and writers who attached themselves to the Han-centric worldview in their era. More interestingly, in medieval Chinese mentality, the pheasant appeared to symbolize the marginal and so-called barbaric groups[3] who were waiting to comply with the teaching and transforming order of the imperial government in its frequent attempts to extend its cultural influence to the local regions, frontiers, and borderlands.

In this chapter, as I examine how the tiger and pheasant figured as symbolic wild animals in medieval Chinese political culture, I consider the intellectual foundation for the roles these wild animals played in the face-to-face confrontation between Confucianism and Buddhism in the medieval period. My discussion reveals that there were two transformations in the metaphorical and practical approaches to tigers and pheasants from the Confucian perspective. Generally, in the medieval political culture, tigers were regarded in terms of the disaster that might harm local villagers and their livestock, so local government adopted a legalist approach for trapping and killing tigers to maintain the socioeconomic order. At the same time, pheasants were wild animals that the noble class hunted and trapped for sport. Both practices of trapping and killing displayed inhumane attitudes and supremacy concerning wild animals. But based on their benevolent and righteous values that often emphasize the power of teaching and transforming society, ancient and medieval Confucian elites developed new approaches to counter the inhumane approaches to tigers and pheasants, which meant keeping tigers and pheasants alive and reaching a peace between humans and these wild animals. These new approaches also produced symbolic cultural implications as tigers and pheasants were granted new symbolic meanings for special social groups in the political life of medieval Chinese society.

THE QUESTION OF UNRULY ANIMALS IN MEDIEVAL POLITICAL CULTURE

In the past decade, the study of medieval tombstone epigraphy has flourished. Numerous collections of medieval tombstone inscriptions offer rich sources for our understanding of medieval political, socioeconomic, cultural, and religious life. Many of these inscriptions made typical historical allusions to political rhetoric that includes mention of wild animals such as the pheasant, locust, and tiger. I begin with several interesting sentences from some tombstone inscriptions of deceased officials in the medieval period.

First, the tombstone inscription for Yang Jian 楊緘 (608–665) reads: "His governance mixed both hardness and softness, suppressing abundance with simplicity. The roaming zither was in control, which was the same as the pure rules of Zijian. The baby pheasant came to be domesticated, which followed Zhongkang's marvelous transformation."[4] Zijian refers to Mi Zijian 宓子賤, the administrator of Shanfu (modern Shan County, Shandong Province). According to the *Spring and Autumn Annals of Master Lü* (*Lüshi chunqiu* 呂氏春秋), Mi Zijian was one of Confucius's disciples and was appointed the administrator of Shanfu. "The roaming zither" refers to stories that Mi Zijian always played the traditional zither and did not leave his office for field work, yet his region was well governed and political order was harmonious, as mention of the domesticated baby pheasant in this inscription infers. As the Confucian narrative of political governance developed, Mi Zijian's manner became its ideal model for administrators. Cui Baozhen's (?-685) 崔抱真 tombstone inscription reads: "[His political accomplishments] transformed fish and domesticated pheasant; . . . once [he] governed the suburb of the capital city, the governance was harmonious, and the family was well supplied. His virtues and rites spread to the capital, and his mighty compassion were settled in his governing region. The flying locust quietly stopped, and the domesticated pheasant was pacified."[5] Cui's tombstone inscription also used domestication of the pheasant to praise his virtuous governance. The tombstone inscription of Lu Pude (611-680) also said that Lu's governance was harmonious, so the pheasant was domesticated; and his compatible transformation moved locusts out of his governing region.[6] These inscriptions eulogized the political accomplishment of the deceased local administrators by introducing the domestication of the pheasant as a metaphor. Notably, this metaphor only applied to the virtuous governance of county magistrates. In the first inscription, Yang Jian held the positions of magistrate of Jiangyang 江陽 County, Yangzhou 揚州, and Xinfeng 新豐 County, Yongzhou 雍州. The second inscription eulogized Cui Baozhen for his appointment as the magistrate of Wuzhi 武陟 County, Huaizhou 懷州. Lu Pude was appointed as the magistrate of Yanling County 鄢陵 and later as the magistrate of Xiuwu 修武 County.

There are some cases concerning the tiger in medieval epigraphy. The tombstone inscription of Tan Bin 檀賓 (464-524) reads: "[He] then moved to be the grand protector of Wei Prefecture (Wei jun). After he had inaugurated his job, since the western bank of the Yellow River [that he governed] neighbored with the borderland 'barbarians,' local people embraced different will. If [Tan Bin's governance] cannot make tigers float and locusts fly away, how could he rectify the 'barbaric' stupidity?"[7] Tan Bin was the grand protector of Wei Prefecture 魏郡 so he had to deal with nomadic tribes in the frontier region. This passage indicates that the central government of the Northern Wei dynasty, even though the regime itself had originated with a nomadic tribe, regarded other frontier tribes as "barbarians" equivalent to wild and unruly tigers and locusts considered them to be targets in need of pacifying and transforming. A similar rhetoric can be found in the tombstone inscription of Yuan Ti 元悌 (506-528), who served as the grand protector of Henan 河南尹. It said that when he governed the capital region his governance not only kept tigers away but also made locusts fly away.[8] These two cases just used generic terms for referring to the tiger and locust. Yet on the tombstone of Yu Zuan (458–527) 于纂, the inscription claimed that in 512 when he was appointed the grand protector of Xiurong 秀容 Prefecture, he was reputable for his blessings and benevolence in ruling his people. His style of dealing with situations was fair and straightforward, refuting bribery and corruption. Therefore, it said that he was like Song Jun, who made tigers move away, and also like Lu Gong, who made locusts fly away.[9] This similar rhetoric continued, appearing in various tombstone inscriptions of the Northern Qi dynasty. In the tombstone inscription of Helian Yue (488–531) 赫連悅, his political achievement as the grand protector of Henei 河內太守 was also praised: "The flying locusts gathered in the distance [away from his governed region], so there was no disaster. The cruel tiger was embarrassed [for guilt in killing innocent people], waiting to be killed."[10] Although the tiger was often associated with the grand protector, in the Northern Qi dynasty, the tigers and locusts metaphor appeared in the tombstone inscriptions of county magistrates. The inscription eulogizing Liu Shuangren 劉雙仁 (480–570) states said that while serving as the magistrate of Gaoyi County, Yinzhou, he made cruel tigers flee and the disastrous locusts stay away from his region.[11] Later, similar rhetoric appeared in the period of Wu Zetian's reign (690–705), when Dong Xiling 董希令 was the magistrate of Liangxiang County 良鄉縣 in Youfu 幽府 (present-day Beijing), the locusts and tigers fled away.[12]

Allusions to pacifying tigers and locusts, as well as to domesticating pheasants, appeared in many historical and literary works of the medieval period. In the Tang dynasty (618–907), literary works also used these allusions in the context of political discourse. Dugu Ji 獨孤及 wrote in one poem that he "loved the emperor and cultivated his governance like cultivating himself; [he attracted] single men and widows come to follow him, and the baby pheasant came to be domesticated 愛君修政若修身，鰥寡來歸乳雉馴."[13] In Liu Zongyuan's 柳宗元 writings it is clear that he rejected the idea that supernatural powers brought disasters. But he did engage in dialogue with his subordinates when asked whether deities or humans were responsible for natural disasters, specifically whether humans should be credited when locusts did not trouble people, and the tiger took her babies and fled.[14]

Various genres of medieval writing portray the tiger and locust as animals that submitted to the power of virtuous governance by grand protectors, whereas the pheasant and locust reached peace under local county magistrates. In terms of rhetorical strategy, the authors of medieval tombstone inscriptions used certain vocabulary and references to political ethics to appeal to historical memory and engage in the moral persuasion of educated audiences and readers. Those readers who were trained to serve in the government must have been familiar with these historical allusions associated with wild animals. And they knew that different wild animals in these historical allusions from various marvelous stories referred to officials with different ranks, which were medieval political conventions.

Before I discuss the historical allusions to wild animals that were incorporated into scholarly training for those pursuing careers in government, let us look at the historical context for how these wild animals mattered in medieval Chinese daily life. As is well known, in ancient East Asia, the tiger was the mightiest wild animal that could be seen and encountered by common people. In medieval Chinese sources, the trouble brought by tigers was often called "tiger violence" (*hubao* 虎暴) or "tiger disaster" (*huzai* 虎災), as when tigers invaded local villages from their forest dwellings and brutally took the lives of humans and domestic animals.

The tiger "problem" seemed to be widely acknowledged in southern China in particular. For example, when Xiao Xiang 蕭象 (498–536) was appointed as the prefect of Xiangzhou 湘州 Prefecture (modern Changsha, Hunan Province), that area was troubled by tiger violence; according to the official history the problem later disappeared due to his virtuous governance.[15] Yu Qianlou 庾黔婁 (c. 470–510), a magistrate of Bian County 編縣 (modern Jingmen, Hubei Province) who later became one of twenty-four filial exemplars, also experienced tiger violence, but his virtuous governance seemed to prevent tigers from further entering his county.[16] Sun Qian's 孫謙 biography reveals an interesting interaction with tigers in Lingling 零陵 (modern Lingling, Hunan Province), where he was appointed as prefect in 507. Even though by then he was very old, Sun Qian still exercised his power and fulfilled his duty. He diligently urged and encouraged local people to participate in agricultural activities. Local officials and commoners were grateful for his governance. Before he took up the post, this prefecture had many violent tigers. Once he arrived, these tigers disappeared. At night when he left, the tigers came out to threaten the local people again.[17]

A similar phenomenon was recorded in the Tang dynasty when Li Shen 李紳 (772–846) was appointed the prefect of the Chu 滁 and Shou 壽 areas. Within his governed territory, many tigers were active in the Mount Huo 霍山 region, where they threatened tea pickers. The local government sent archers to shoot these tigers but failed. When Li Shen arrived, all the tigers just disappeared. At the beginning of the Kaicheng period (836–840), Li Shen became the prefect of the Henan area and he pushed hard against powerful local families and forced them to leave, bringing the loyalty of the local community back to the central government. Later he became military commissioner of the Xuanwu region. It is said that although his territory was hit by drought, his virtuous governance prevented locusts from entering.[18]

In medieval Chinese political culture, local officials were committed to pacifying "tiger violence," and they implemented many laws and regulations to deal this violence, to protect both humans and livestock. In the Han and Jin dynasties, laws were enacted that rewarded hunters who trapped and captured tigers. In the Han dynasty, the reward for one tiger was three thousand coins (*sanqian qian* 三千錢); in the Jin dynasty, the reward was changed to three bolts of silk (*sanpi juan* 三匹絹).[19] In the Tang dynasty, Xuanzong once ordered Li Quanque 李全確, a talented magistrate of Lianshui 漣水 County (modern Lianshui, Jiangsu), to teach the method of capturing violent tigers in the Huainan 淮南 area because of an outbreak of "tiger disaster." Li Quanque used to be the magistrate of Qiupu County (Chizhou, Anhui). In both counties where he served as magistrate, he earned a reputation for dealing with violent tigers and bringing tranquility back to his people.[20] During the Han and Tang periods, eliminating tiger violence was an important task for local administrations; the tiger problem became less serious in the Song dynasty, and the ransom was accordingly decreased.

Policies toward tigers in the medieval period also indicated that "tiger disaster" spread across the country as a result of increased agricultural, social, and cultural activities. Trapping, capturing, and killing tigers reflects a legalist approach to the so-called tiger violence, which demonstrates that the government viewed the tiger as a threat from a wild "other." But transforming the tiger and moving it away by means of virtuous governance, instead of trapping and killing the tiger, not only shows benevolence toward the animal but also offers an alternative approach to Confucian political ideology, the basis of discursive political rhetoric in the medieval Chinese context.

The pheasant was also a familiar creature to medieval Chinese people, often appearing along with the tiger in both textual and inscriptional sources. Broadly speaking, the pheasant was viewed as one of the most hunted birds in the world. In traditional China, it was one of the most popular birds in historical and literary writings, appearing in numerous Confucian classics and official histories. Although the wild baby pheasant symbolized the marginal and "barbaric" (non-Han) groups in the Han historical writings as I noted earlier, in Confucian classics, the feather patterns in the domesticated pheasant symbolized civilized culture.[21] This discourse continued to the Tang dynasty. In the *Old History of Tang*, interestingly enough, a passage mentioned the domesticated pheasant as the symbolic animal of the civilized world under the governance of the sage kings: "The sun, moon, and stars shed their shining lights on the ground earth. The mountains distribute their clouds and rains, which symbolizes that the sage kings took care of the governed people with their kindness. The dragon is always changing without rules, which symbolizes that the sage kings preach their teachings in accord with various situations. The flowered insect, the pheasant, with five colorful stripes, symbolizes the sagely kings' civilized bodies."[22] The discourse of the pheasant having many colorful stripes already appeared in the *Classic of Documents* (*Shangshu* 尚書). It seems that the pheasant appearing in ancient sources referred to the domesticated pheasants with magnificent striped patterns on their bodies.

In contrast to the tiger, the pheasant posed no threat to the people living in medieval Chinese society. But the pheasant was otherized and victimized by privileged medieval Chinese aristocrats who abused them for sport. Hunting pheasants has a very long history. As early as 514 BCE in the Lu kingdom 魯國, an official Jia Xin 賈辛 was married to a beautiful woman. But she did not talk or laugh for three years. He started to hunt pheasants to please her, and the first time he shot a pheasant she started to laugh.[23] As Zhou Yiliang 周一良 noted, in the Han and Wei periods, the art of shooting pheasants was well established among the aristocratic class.[24] Usually, the aristocratic sportsmen would first set up a shooting field with a screen. They put a domesticated pheasant behind the screen to attract wild pheasants. Once the wild birds entered the field, the shooters would start hunting them down. Hu Sanxing 胡三省 noted in his commentary on the *Comprehensive Mirror for Aid in Government* (*Zizhi tongjian* 資治通鑒) that, "Since the Cao Wei period, human lords mostly liked going out for shooting pheasant by themselves 自曹魏以來，人主率好出自射雉。"[25]

Indeed, many rulers liked shooting pheasants. In the Wei kingdom, Cao Cao 曹操 once hunted sixty-three pheasants in Nanpi 南皮 (modern Nanpi, Hebei) in a single day. In the Wu kingdom, Sun Quan 孫權 often shot pheasants, which irritated his subject Pan Jun 潘濬. Pan admonished Sun Quan that as a ruler Sun should realize the instability of the political order under heaven and waste no time in shooting pheasants. Pan even destroyed Sun's shooting screen. After that, Sun Quan abandoned his pastime. The sixth son of Sun Quan, Sun Xiu 孫休, was a big fan of shooting pheasants. Even though he originally spent a lot of time reading, when the hunting season arrived, he often spent the entire day shooting pheasants. His addiction to shooting pheasants was always criticized as his weakness by the later generation.[26] This popular sport among the aristocratic class continued in the East Jin and Southern dynasties.

Medieval Chinese official histories also record numerous stories about hunting wild pheasants. Xiao Baojuan 蕭寶卷 (commonly known as Donghunhou 東昏, 483-501), was another ruler whose favorite hobby was shooting pheasants.[27] He set up 296 ranges for this purpose. The screens were decorated with curtains and barriers lined with green and red silk. His crossbow was engraved with gold and silver, and his arrows were decorated with the shells of hawksbill sea turtles. The Song emperor Xiaowu 宋孝武帝 (Liu Jun 劉駿, 430-464) was said to often go pheasant hunting. One time when he finished offering his sacrifice in the ancestral tombs and went to shoot pheasants for fun, Cai Xingzong 蔡興宗, an official holding the imperial seal, admonished him that it was wrong to do this right after having offered sacrifices to the ancestors. The Song emperor Mingdi 宋明帝 (Liu Yu 劉彧, 439-472) always hunted pheasants with his subjects. He even ordered that his subject Liu Xiuyou 劉休祐 should be killed as a punishment for failing to hunt down a pheasant. The Southern Qi emperor Wudi (Xiao Yi 蕭頤, 440-493) also engaged in this pastime, but he was always admonished by Xiao Ziliang.

Like the rulers and court officials, some local officials in the Qi dynasty often entertained themselves by shooting pheasants. For instance, Xiao Min 蕭敏, the prefect of Xin'an 新安, was a fan, and this predilection kept him away from the office. Many case litigants had to meet him in the hunting field. Later he died from an injury to the waist inflicted by an open crossbow. Huan Xibo 桓僖伯 was very skilled in shooting pheasants, so he was favored by Emperor Wudi. An official named Zhang Xintai 張欣泰 bought a house facing a mountain and shot pheasants as entertainment during leisure time. All these examples show the popularity of this activity among government officials who also left numerous poems about pheasant hunting, such as Pan Anren's 潘安仁 "The Rhapsody on Shooting Pheasant (Shezhi fu 射雉賦)"[28] and Han Yu's poem "The Pheasant with an Arrow (Zhi dai jian 雉帶箭)."[29]

In both political and literary culture, the medieval nobility seemed to be familiar with wild pheasants. Shooting wild pheasants, similar to trapping and killing tigers, was regarded as a legal and justifiable action for the noble class. But Confucian political ideology also offered an alternative approach to wild pheasants:

domesticating them and allowing wild pheasants befriend children. This approach emanated from the Confucian political ideal of virtuous governance. Domesticating wild pheasants manifested the Confucian ethical values of benevolence and righteousness.

ANIMAL ALLUSIONS AND THE CORRELATIVE THOUGHT

The origins of these allusions can be traced back to some stories in the Han dynasty. The most comprehensive story about pacifying locusts and pheasants was from Lu Gong. According to the *Record of the Han Dynasty from the Eastern Pavilion* (*Dongguan Han ji*) 東觀漢記 and the *History of the Later Han Dynasty* (*Hou Han shu* 後漢書), when Lu Gong was the magistrate of Zhongmou County 中牟令, neighboring grand protectors all suffered from locust disasters that destroyed their agricultural crops. But these locusts did not enter Zhongmou County, which drew the attention of Yuan An 袁安, the grand protector of Henan 河南尹. So Yuan An sent inspector named Fei Qin 肥親 to seek the truth. Lu Gong accompanied Fei Qin walking on the paths in the field. They sat under a mulberry tree. A pheasant passed by, and a child walked along with it. Fei Qin asked why the pheasant was not hunted. The child answered that the pheasant was just a baby. Fei Qin was surprised, so he told Lu Gong that he discovered three marvels while inspecting Lu's approach to political governance: "Now the locusts do not trouble your borders, which is the first marvel. Your transformation has reached wild birds and beasts, which is the second marvel. And even a child has a mind of benevolence, which is the third marvel 今蟲不犯境，此一異也。化及鳥獸，此二異也。豎子有仁心，三異也。"[30] As a county magistrate, Lu Gong successfully fulfilled his political duty of protecting agricultural crops and transforming the local wilderness, the behaviors of unruly locusts and the baby pheasant indicate. A similar story concerns Wang Fu 王阜, who was a magistrate of Chongquan in the late Han dynasty. According to the *Record of the Han Dynasty from the Eastern Pavilion*, Wang Fu's direct and unequivocal governance earned the respect of the entire county. Both officials and commoners turned to the transformation under his guidance. The auspicious *Luan* bird gathered in the public academy. While Wang was ordering the academy head clerk Sha Die to play official music, these birds started dancing in accord with the music.[31] Although this story does not clearly mention the pheasant, it shows that the local governance of a county magistrate could have an impact on the behavior of an auspicious bird.

The story about tigers reacting to virtuous governance and fleeing without troubling the local region can also be traced back to the late Han dynasty in tales concerning at least two figures. One was Liu Kun 劉昆,[32] the grand protector of Hongnong Prefecture 弘農, and another was Song Jun 宋均, the grand protector of Jiujiang Prefecture 九江. Although they were both reputable grand protectors who prevented the so-called tiger violence, Song Jun's name often appeared in medieval epigraphic writings, yet Liu Kun's name did not. So here I focus on the legend about Song Jun. According to his biography in the official history, before Song was inaugurated in his position in Jiujiang, numerous tigers dwelled there and always troubled the local community. Once Song Jun arrived and heard the situation, he spoke to his counties:

> Tigers and leopards stay in the mountains. Tortoises and turtles live in the water. They relied on individual places. And wild beasts in the Yangtze and Huai Rivers are [the] same as wild birds and hounds in the northern lands. Now the reason why these beasts troubled local people is because of the cruelty of local officials. The efforts for hunting them are not the principal solution of benevolent practice. The solution is to prevent corruption and lust, and to consider cultivating loyalty and kindness, removing confines and pitfalls, and eliminating and cutting taxes and controls.[33]

Since Song took up his position in Jiujiang, these violent tigers left eastward over the Yangtze River, no longer troubling people in this area. In the first year of the Zhongyuan period (56 CE), locusts brought disasters to some neighboring prefectures, but never entered the Jiujiang area. In the biography of Song, Fan Ye praised his political accomplishment as a grand protector whose benevolent governance successfully transformed wild animals, especially tigers, and prevented them from troubling the local community.

Although the local government officials shifted their focus from shooting pheasants to domesticating them and from killing tigers to moving them away, their nonviolent approaches to wild animals do not convey their morality vis-a-vis protecting the environment. Their approaches only concerned political virtues. The narrative about officials who were compelled to make wild tigers float away is particularly interesting. I argue that the Chinese character for *fu* 浮 (float-ing) depicts the performative act of the tiger, which demonstrates two sets of displays and witnesses. On the one hand, tigers are witnesses for displaying the efficacy of the power of correlative thinking in Confucian ideology. If the correla-tive thinking does not work, the tiger would not move away. On the other hand, local villagers become witnesses who can verify the outcome of the virtuous gov-ernance of local officials by seeing tigers floating away. If the tiger swims under the water, nobody can really see it. So "floating" in the river is very important, because this act can be visually verified by the observer.

Although the allusion to Song Jun often appeared in medieval epigraphy, it seems that the visual manifestation of this allusion was uncommon. As Hou-mei Sung has suggested in her study *Decoded Messages*, the tiger became fully estab-lished as an independent subject of painting in the tenth century, and some com-mon tiger themes were developed in the Song paintings, including the tiger's crossing the river.[34] In the Jin (Jurchen) dynasty (1115-1234), Li Yu was said to pos-sess three tiger paintings, *A Tiger Watching His Cubs*, *Tigress and Cubs*, and *Three Tigers Cross the River*. But she has found that no Song examples of the theme on the tiger's crossing the river have survived. Only one Ming example survives in the Palace Museum, Beijing, which came from Zhu Duan (1501-1521). She notes that the tiger's crossing the river referred to the legend of Liu Kun 劉昆, the Han dynasty governor of Hongnong. Zhu Duan's painting delivered the message that perfectly suited the political climate of the mid-Ming court, because at that time the literati officials struggled against increasing corruption by pursuing Confu-cian ideology, and thus encouraged the wise administration of a regional official to practice benevolent rule.

A close look at the context of political thought in ancient China might reveal that these stories about wild animals in the careers of local officials were instru-mental in advocating the correlative relationship between Confucian benevolent governance and the transformation of wild beasts and birds that could be traced in the Han dynasty. It echoes what Deborah Cao has noted:

> Importantly, animals are not segregated and excluded from the moral cosmos and they are given consideration in traditional Chinese philosophical ideas or practical philosophy, such as Confucianism and Daoism/Taoism, as part of the moral and ethical pursuit of the betterment of life and society. It can be argued that in traditional Chinese thought, animals, together with humans,

form part of the moral universe of the exemplary humans; such exemplary humans should be models of benevolence and compassion. Furthermore, compassion and benevolence extend beyond humans to other life forms in nature.[35]

The so-called virtuous governance was based on the Confucian model of cosmological and political harmony. Cosmologically, a ruler must act in accordance with the norms created by heaven. The ruler is supposed to maintain the communion and harmony between him and heaven through his ritual and political performance. On the one hand, he offered sacrifices on behalf of his regime for demonstrating his piety toward heaven. On the other hand, he must exercise his power by possessing virtue and benevolence toward his subjects so he could create a political harmony within his regime. If his acts satisfied both heaven and the ruled, good omens would appear as evidence of heaven's silent approval, which also signified the legitimacy of his regime.[36] In this correlative thinking of Confucian ideology, bad governance could result in locusts destroying crops on the ground. In the Tao Gong chapter of the *Records of Rites* (*Liji* 禮記檀弓篇), it is stated that Confucius once lamented that harsh governance was more harmful than the actions of cruel tigers to local people, which illustrates the long history of the cruel tiger appearing as a symbol of harsh local governance, such as excessive taxation.[37] Contemporary scholarship has focused more on the connection between heaven and governance, in particular, the resonance between heaven and humans 天人感應, so-called correlative Confucianism by scholars.[38] As Charles Holcombe writes:

It was not just that the self-cultivated literatus was assumed to understand better the workings of heaven, earth, and man: he was even supposed to have a physical influence over them. During the Han dynasty, Confucian theorists, such as Tung Chung-shu (Dong Zhongshu), had devised the elaborate system of correspondences, linking the behavior of individuals to that of the broader cosmos. It was theorized that, because heaven and earth are interconnected through a universal web formed of the substance known as Ch'i 氣 and because of the resonance that exists between all mutually related categories, the rectification of a ruler's heart at the center would exert a kind of gravitational pull outward upon the entire world and bring even the seasons into their proper sequence. Although much of the "Han Confucian" worldview was discredited after the fall of the Han, this theory of an intricate network of correlations between the human and natural orders remained popular.[39]

In this Confucian correlative ideology, if a local official failed to fulfill his obligations, his governed subjects suffered punishment from heaven.

In terms of the correlative relationships between human activities and animal behaviors, Roel Sterckx has explicitly demonstrated that in ancient China, there were two major themes concerning animal transformations, which indicates that both music and Confucian moral teaching could transform the behaviors of wild animals.[40] As he notes: "Through the moral influence of music unruly and unknown people or strange lands could be brought under the instructive command of a central ruler. Just as local climates were thought to influence the shape and character of a region's human and animal inhabitants, the local musical 'airs' or 'winds,' viewed as components of the indigenous natural environment, were the cosmic embodiment of the morals and customs of a particular people or community.... Underlying these characterizations of music as a means of moral transformation is the notion that music foremost constitutes a principle linked with the creation of order ranging from the emancipation of humankind from a state of primordial bestiality to the establishment of sociopolitical and ritual order."[41] Thomas Allsen also writes: "In China, the appearance of tigers (*hu*), understood as bandits as well as great cats, was typically equated with bad government, which benevolent rule could overcome. Music, it was thought by some, could be used to exercise control over the natural world, creating there and in the human sphere the proper harmony and hierarchy."[42] In contrast to other value systems such as Buddhism and Daoism in transforming animals, Confucian transformation of beasts and birds is virtuous and, with the exception of music, it occurs without ritual performance such as reciting prayers, offering sacrifices, and doing sympathetic magic.

Animals have natural spirits, which are the same as the heavenly spirits in the Confucian correlative system. In the writings dominated by Confucian values, the phrase "communicating with the heavenly spirits 通于神明" was often used.[43] The local people viewed their officials as spirit-mediums who could communicate with higher spirits in a hierarchical cosmological order. Empowered with their virtues and morality, these officials could communicate with all kinds of spirits, including both heavenly spirits and natural spirits. The local officials believed that benevolence was a powerful means for showing their kindness and for communicating with wild animals. The tension between the human world and animal world could be negotiated.

In a broad context of world history, in terms of the supernatural controlling power over animals, Allsen states that in many religious traditions—including Mesopotamian, Western Christian, Eastern Christian, Islamic, and Indian religions, and local religion on the Malay Peninsula—beasts, especially birds, lions, wolves, stags, snakes, alligators, and tigers could be trained by goddesses and holy saints to be companions and servants. He also discusses the model kings of antiquity credited with the ability to communicate with animals. This suggests that the king's physical ascendancy over animals and his moral and spiritual domination of wild beasts were extensively publicized. The king also had the power to mediate and negotiate the relationship between nature and culture; for the king nature was a threat, and royal restraint was necessary. Nature was especially menacing because "wild animals threaten human interests in a variety of ways: as household pests, competitors for forage with domesticated animals, competitors for prey with human hunters, and, most important for us, as crop raiders and predators on livestock and people."[44] In the context of Chinese history, the emperor in the central court was also very concerned about animals and their symbolized powers in local areas. It was important to understand the communication between local officials and wild animals and the communication between local officials and people. In the eyes of local people, transforming wild animals means that the virtue of local officials lies in their ability in "communicate with the heavenly spirits." In this sense, animals might be viewed as being governed by heaven, or that heaven controlled the spirits of animals. It might also indicate that officials could transform the spirits of animals directly, which signifies the communication between the local officials and wild animals.

In the stories of domesticated pheasants and fleeing tigers and locusts that date to the later Han dynasty, local areas were viewed as regions full of wild creatures waiting to be fostered and cultivated with rites, and as such become civilized by Confucian values. But their original wildness was also viewed as an undermining force to the political order in the local area. Tigers were violent and could potentially disregard local authority dispatched by the central government. Tigers also threatened the local economy because they could harm livestock and people. Locusts could ruin crops and agricultural products.[45] The people of this region were similar to the uncivilized imperial citizens and could not be viewed the same as cultured people who understood Confucian etiquette and rites. These people were far away from the political center, such as the capital city of the empire, and might not comply with orders from the court. Local officials dispatched from the central government were obligated to pacify these threats and nurture the wild animals from the local wild areas. Local officials and their governed subjects were in a similar relationship to that which exists between parents (or father) and children (or sons). The father was the elite, literate, civilized person who stayed in the center of the power within a family.

Local officials knew the political and cultural as well as ritual conventions. They were obligated to maintain local political order. The local people had the potential to betray and even threaten the centralized order and authority from the court, without considering Confucian etiquette and rites. In remarking on mourning rites in imperial China, Miranda Brown writes: "Unlike their Warring States and Western Han predecessors, Eastern Han ritualists did not treat mourning for one's father as a strictly personal affair, or a personal obligation that interfered with official duty. Instead, they considered sons' mourning for fathers analogous to the mourning that subjects performed for lords."[46] Norman Kutcher also points out: "In Confucian discourse, the parallel conception of society by its nature ran counter to hierarchical and authoritarian models of societal organization. In the parallel society, the emperor's power over a minister came not from coercion, but from encouraging his ministers to be filial to their own parents. In the same way, a local official obtained the obedience of the common people by encouraging their devotion of their parents—which he taught them by his devotion to his own parents."[47] The local officials faced the pressures from tigers and locusts as well as pheasants, as these creatures symbolized strong local power and uncivilized people. On the one hand, they were obligated to mobilize local resources for serving the needs of the central government; on the other hand, they were also told to transmit the rites and values of the central court to the local area, and to civilize and cultivate the local area.

Within the epigraphic texts discussed here, the local officials could not rely on military or other armed forces to suppress their subjects in the local area. Instead, relying on Confucian governance, the officials had to extend their virtuous benevolence to their governed local people. If these local people were transformed under Confucian sympathetic governance, they would willingly support the central court by offering tributes as taxes, such as grains and silks. The local government was actually also supported by the local people, which constructed a parent-child relationship between local officials and ruled people. In the mind of local officials, as the "parenting" officials,[48] they had to take care of their child-like people—and the latter then were willing and able to support their officials. This relationship could also be viewed as a political version of filial piety practice or a collective practice of filial piety. In protecting local people from cruel governance and wild animals, the needs of local officials would be fulfilled. In this sense, if the local people did not support their parentlike officials, they were viewed as "barbarians" who did not know Confucian rites of filial piety.[49] The healthiest relationship between local officials and people should be thus: local officials practice benevolence toward their governed people and the latter return with filial piety-like practice, which can be called righteousness in Confucian terms.

THE POLITICAL RHETORIC OF LOCAL GOVERNANCE

As I noted earlier, the writers of medieval epigraphy and other historical and literary texts were obligated to follow particular political and ritual conventions in their thinking and writing. Writers had to know what allusions could be used for certain ranks of deceased officials. They also had to follow certain cultural values and habitus. In particular, the writers must choose the right allusions to eulogize the deceased officials without violating political, ritual, and cultural conventions. Some historical changes also shaped and modified these conventions. Different allusions about tigers, locusts, and pheasants applied to different officials who served as grand protectors, prefects, and county magistrates. From the Han to Tang periods, these posts experienced changes as well. Thus, it is not surprising to see shifting patterns of different animal allusions in medieval writings. Moreover, perceptions about the governance of local people shifted from the early medieval period—when the grand protector was viewed as having a major role in ruling them—in terms of who was responsible for transforming these people and suppressing strong local power.

A close reading of many epigraphical sources shows that there are two historical changes behind the patterns of animal allusions. First, from the Han to Tang periods, the political and civil systems of regional administration shifted from the *jun* 郡 (prefecture) and *xian* 縣 (county) system to the *zhou* 州 and *xian* system. This administrative change resulted in new titles for regional leaders and new ways of ruling local regions. Originally in the Han dynasty, *zhou* 州 was a temporary regional unit under an inspector (*cishi* 刺史) who represented the emperor and examined and evaluated the performance of local officials. There were thirteen *zhou* units in the Han dynasty when it was institutionalized by the Han emperor Wu 漢武帝 in 106 BCE. During the Southern and Northern Dynasties (220–589 CE), the inspectors gradually extended their powers to the local civil administration. In the Sui dynasty (581–618), the central government ordered the abandonment of the system of *jun* units, and the political functions of all *jun* were transferred to the *zhou* units. Thus the head of a *jun*, the grand protector, also gradually faded away in civil administration and was replaced by the *cishi*, the inspector. Since the grand protector disappeared in local administration, the historical allusions about fleeing tigers were then used to refer to inspectors instead of grand protectors in medieval writings about local officials.

As for the second historical change behind the shift in animal allusions, the county was the local civil administrative unit under the *jun*, which meant a lower control level, and for the central power, meant direct contact with the local region. The literati and officials were aware of how big a region a local administrator could rule and govern. As some medieval texts have shown, the grand protector governed a region within one thousand *li* 千里, yet a county magistrate ruled a region within one hundred *li* 百里. For example, Wang Ze's 王則 tombstone inscription composed in 652 said that as the magistrate of Bochang County in Qing Prefecture, he preached his teaching for one hundred *li* in the region and his transformation moved locusts away and made beasts cross the river.[50] The tombstone inscription of Han Cheng clearly shows the difference between one thousand *li* and one hundred *li* as the geographical coverages for a grand protector and a county magistrate. It said that Han Cheng's grandfather Han De was a grand protector of Guangping Prefecture in the Northern Qi dynasty, so he expanded five rites and proclaimed six rules thoroughly in one thousand *li*. Yet Han Cheng's father Han Jie was a magistrate of Guoxian, County Nanyang, in the Sui dynasty, so his virtue was expanded to only one hundred *li*.[51] It seems that during the Southern and Northern Dynasties, in the minds of the elite literati, the grand protector was the official who could be directly accessed by the local people. But in the minds of the Tang literati, the county magistrate could directly govern the local people. Based on his analysis of Buddhist sculptural inscriptions from the Northern Dynasties, Hou Xudong has pointed out that the local people in the Northern Dynasties might have a threefold view on prevailing social stratification: the state (emperor), the heads of prefectures and counties, and the local people themselves including family members. When the local people commissioned sculptures and carved inscriptions, they prayed for the state, especially the emperor, the heads of local governments, and their family members.[52] Hou has also noted that the political discourse in the Northern Wei dynasty observed a classification based on four political groups within the empire: the emperor (*wang* 王), dukes and marquises who were major officials in the central government (*gongqing* 公卿), local government officials who ruled local people (*zaimin* 宰民), and the local people (*qianshou* 黔首). From the perspective of the court and the officials, the local people were both the subject of being civilized and the economic and human resources for the state's finance and military forces.[53]

The relationship between the central court and the local region was a crucial issue for all dynasties of the Chinese Empire through the ages. Even today it remains a significant political issue for the Chinese government. In medieval China, the major political governance duty for local officials was to promote five rites (*wuli* 五禮) and six rules (*liutiao* 六條), which originally appeared in the Han dynasty. As Anne Cheng notes: "In the ritual treatises of the early Han, the rites are presented as essential in the harmonization of the sociopolitical community and the prevention of disorder, while the laws play only a secondary role by intervening most of the time a posteriori to sanction an already committed crime."[54]

Governing the local area has been a crucial political subject for the Chinese government for a long time. There were many discussions on the means by which the central government could better rule the local regions. Numerous thinkers in ancient China developed political theories. Masubuchi Tatsuo has suggested that legalism developed in the Warring States period, centered on virtue (*de* 德) and method (*shu* 術). Virtue in this theory indicated that a talented ruler could grant benefits to a virtuous official who helped the ruler. The method 術 referred to the punishment in which the order of a ruler could be carried out without resistance. Masubuchi has also discussed how the Han administration advanced a system that helped the emperor maintain control over officials in both central and local governments. In the central government, censors (*yushi* 禦史) were granted privileges to impeach other officials to maintain disciplinary surveillance over officialdom. Regional inspectors (*cishi*) were sent to supervise local officials.[55] But Masubuchi does not touch upon the meanings and functions of the five rites and six rules in Han imperial ideology.

In the meantime, the five rites played a crucial role in the political ideology of Han China. The wild pheasant symbolized the local people who did not know the Confucian value system promoted by the central government, and who needed to be domesticated by the government officials who were trained in the civilized culture, especially its morality. This Confucian value system was particularly reflected by the five rites. The heads of local governments also transformed local traditions and customs 移風易俗 and persuaded local people to accept the Confucian rite system.[56] According to a modern understanding, the Confucian moral nobility had three characteristics: filial devotion (*xiao*), humanness (*ren*), and ritual decorum (*li*).[57] The central government required local administrators to extend these moral values to their ruled community.

These concepts and variant practices continued in the medieval period. I suggest that the five rites aimed to transform baby pheasants (or the uncivilized local people they symbolized), and the six rules targeted violent tigers (or the powerful local officials or petty officials they symbolized). In particular, the six rules targeted officials and petty officials from the local area who suppressed local people and resisted the authority of the central court. Officials should not abuse their powers, as this could generate resistance to law and order imposed by the central government. Cruel beasts such as wild tigers were apt symbols for these oppressive local officials.

In the Tang dynasty, local petty officials were often viewed by the central government as a morally corrupt group that required monitoring and regulation by the heads of local governments. These petty officials were seen as an evil force between the local officials appointed by the central government and the local people. They treated local people cruelly and pursued their own political and economic interests. They also resisted the control of local officials who represented the power of the state.[58] Therefore, these petty officials were not trained in morality under the guidance of the Confucian value system as the central government promoted. Their activities had to be regulated, and punished as necessary, by the heads of local governments. In the medieval period, the responsibility of civilizing the local area rested on the shoulders of the grand protectors. For example, again in the Tang dynasty, the grandfather of Xing Xianji 邢仙姬 as a grand protector of Cangzhou in the Northern Qi dynasty implemented six rules to guide Confucian customs and expanded five rites to admonish local people.[59] A tombstone inscription concerning Huangfu Hui 皇甫惠 dated in 697 delivered similar messages about the duty of a county magistrate who served near the borderland between central China and nomadic tribes.[60] When Huangfu Hui was appointed as the magistrate for Hehe 合河 County of Lan Prefecture 嵐州 (modern Xing County, Shanxi), he was praised for domesticating wild pheasants and for creating harmonious social order that could be attributed to his generosity and strictness as a local administrator. This rhetorical tone indicates that a local official must transform the marginal local subjects and civilize them from the perspective of Confucian political virtue, which means to admonish local people to accept the Confucian rites and teachings advocated by the central government. The local officials considered "teaching" and "jurisdiction" as the political tools to serve this civilizing purpose. Interestingly, the two distinctive characters *hu* 胡 and *han* 漢 were used to indicate two different worlds, uncivilized and civilized.

The local officials were persuaded by their superiors and their education or training to bring civilized order to the land they governed. This civilized order was defined by the central government under Confucian principles, in particular the Confucian rites and imperial law. This persuasion was transferred within the circle of officials, generation by generation, through their education, training, and writing practices. The so-called *li* 禮, though generally referring to five rites in Confucian political thought, sometimes explicitly indicated the traditional patriarchal order. A tombstone inscription for Yao Bianyi 姚辯義 (died in 718), the magistrate of Linji County 臨濟縣 (modern Jiyang, Shandong), briefly outlined the political career of his father, Yao Demin 姚德敏. As the magistrate of Xiao County 蕭縣 (modern Xiao County, Anhui), Yao Demin was praised for "initially domesticating pheasant in the wilderness and embodying the political essentials of Lu Gong."[61] His son Yao Bianyi was appointed magistrate of Wucheng Xian 武城縣 (modern Wucheng County, Shandong) and his virtue was eulogized by the men of his county. During his tenure, he refused bribes and exercised honesty, and thus powerful local noble families had to retract their power. Eventually, he became the magistrate of Linji County. Yao Bianyi guided local people to practice Confucian rites and brought men and women back on their distinctive tracks.

This distinction between men and women was important for preserving the local economy, social norms, and political order. In the eyes of the central government, this transforming process by local officials aimed to civilize local regions. In fact, many scholars note the transforming power of Confucian ideology. For example, Thomas Metzger suggests a transformative moral ideal in Chinese high culture.[62] As P. Steven Sangren notes: "The Chinese Empire, which the Chinese called 'All Under Heaven' (Tianxia 天下), was conceived as a pervasive order, in contrast to the chaotic world of barbarians outside its domain."[63] Ogata Isamu has analyzed the conflict between the family and the state in ancient China and the dilemma of the literati officials in resolving this conflict. He does not agree that there was a parallel structure between the filial piety of family and the loyalty of state polity; he suggests that filial piety was limited to within the family. Thus a debate ensues regarding the superiority of filial piety or loyalty as the obligation of an official. Ogata's discussion mostly focuses on the Qin and Han dynasties as he discusses the concepts of the private and public in ancient China. Nevertheless, he argues that no clear boundary existed between private and public concepts in the ancient Chinese world. He notes many conflicts between family rites and state rites and offered some examples in which the rites between the ruler and ministers were viewed as superior to the rites within the family.[64] In his understanding, there was a political discourse on leaving family and returning to family. For him, a man leaves family and becomes an official, then retires from the government and returns to the family: leaving family and becoming an official means entering from the private family realm into the public political realm.[65] In the context of the political discourse of the Tang dynasty, Howard J. Wechsler has briefly discussed the idea of *Tianxia wei jia*, which he translates as "the world constitutes a family."[66]

Thus the representations of power in Confucianism can be understood and interpreted in many ways. In a religious interpretation, Confucianism is not a separated world. As C. K. Yang notes: "Even taking into consideration the relative difference in the belief in magic and miracles, the Confucians did not constitute a group separate from the general current of religious life of traditional Chinese society. They shared with the rest of the population a basic system of religious belief in Heaven, fate, and other supernatural concepts." He also states: "Accepted by the rulers and the people alike, Heaven represented not merely a powerful but also a morally meaningful body of forces, operating on ethical principles which were fully binding on man as an integral part of the universe."[67]

Local officials perceived the governed people as savage beasts, as the Han Chinese perceived nomadic tribes as savage beasts—for beasts did not fully master Confucian values of benevolence, righteousness, filial piety, and loyalty. From the perspective of Confucian social and political ideology, these values were important in running a family and an empire successfully. Without filial piety, a family was at risk of destruction, which meant the family tradition would not be carried on. Without loyalty, the authority of an empire would be undermined, and the empire might disintegrate into parts. Benevolence was the rightful attitude of the father toward his child, and also of a political power of the empire toward the governed, in exchange for the governed people's loyalty. Teaching these values to the so-called savage was a way of extending moral transformation. This transformation made the "savage people" from local areas or afar become civilized or domesticated like savage animals. One of the most important duties of the local officials was to change old cultural habitus, or remove the atmosphere and transform traditions and customs 移風易俗—which included removing or suspending unauthorized local worship 淫祠 or unregulated offerings 淫祀,[68] such as worshipping animals or the god of natural objects, especially the god of water or river 河神.[69] The code of rites did not allow the making of offerings to these deities until the authorization process was completed. As we will see in later chapters, other institutionalized religions including Buddhism and Daoism also attempted to replace these local shrines and sacrificial rites.

Carving stone with inscriptions was a crucial part of the burial rite, which was regulated in the five rites in medieval China. According to Du You's *Comprehensive Statutes* (*Tongdian* 通典), the Tang code of rites has five sections called the five rites.[70] One of these is the rite of ill omen, *xiongli* 兇禮. This set of rites—including funeral, mourning, and burial rites—was designed to memorialize deceased people.[71] *The Six Codes of the Great Tang* (*Tang liudian* 唐六典) compiled under the supervision of Li Linfu 李林甫 (683–753) also contained regulations for establishing the memorial stelae and shrines that testified to the virtuous governance of local officials (*dezhengbei* 德政碑).[72] If these officials were credited for their achievements, the local government would report to the Department of State Affairs (Shangshusheng 尚書省) with attention to the Bureau of Rites to apply for a permit. The Department of State Affairs would approve it and report it to the emperor. Then the local government could establish a memorial stele.

The memorial stele inscription for eulogizing the virtue of a local official also used historical allusions to pacifying animals. It followed exactly the same conventions as the tomb stele, but mostly mentioned baby pheasants and locusts, without tigers. Here is an example of one such inscription for virtuous governance. Li Ren 李仁 was a Tang official; it was copied and circulated in local gazetteers. He was the magistrate of Gaoyuan 高苑 County, Zizhou 淄州 (modern Zichuan, Shandong). The inscription praising his virtuous governance in the Confucian sense contained references to baby pheasants and children as well as to locusts and the inspector.[73] Clearly, the allusions came from the story of Lu Gong whose virtuous governance set a model for local administrators. The stele inscription also claimed that virtuous governance encourages agricultural production as the means to benefit local people economically and ritually, supplying those that are poor and supporting those that are struggling. Overall, a local administrator should transform the local community by advocating Confucian customs.

The surviving family and friends of the memorialized official would erect a stone stele so that the reputation of the deceased would not perish. In her study of memorial stelae inscriptions from the Han dynasty, Miranda Brown argues: "Although some inscriptions portrayed their subjects as loyal dynastic ministers, many others de-emphasized the connection between the deceased and the Han dynastic house, instead focusing on the subject's relationship with the population." As she suggested, "More than gifts from the court presented at death, extreme expressions of popular grief bore testimony to the deceased's virtue."[74] Brown attributes the reason for building a link between Han stelae and many Southern Song shrines to their strong thematic resemblances. They both emphasized the contribution officials made to the local area by improving local economic welfare and virtuous teaching—in other words, both the stele and the shrine commemorated benevolent administration. The tombstone inscriptions from the medieval period offered evidence to bridge the Han stelae and Song shrines in emphasizing the contribution of officials to improving the practice of social welfare and rites. Fleeing tigers and domesticated pheasants also illustrate how local officials used Confucian virtues to transform the local population, pacifying local bullies, and civilizing local people. These officials were not required to manifest their loyalty to the dynastic house.

Given the political institutions and religious practices in medieval China, I believe that writing a tombstone inscription was also a ritual practice. As such, the writer knew how to compose the tombstone inscription, using logic and a set of terms as historical allusions. Gilbert Lewis emphasizes that the procedure of ritual performing was more important than its meaning for ritual performers.[75] James L. Watson also suggests that the performers might know how to carry out the rites but could not "provide ready explanations (in words) for what was being expressed, communicated, or symbolized."[76] I would argue, similarly, that the composers of medieval tomb inscriptions knew what explanations should be expressed, communicated, or symbolized in the historical allusions they used in their writings. A composer equipped with Confucian education and training would understand that specific historical allusions and certain terms must be used in accordance with the ranks of the deceased officials, following a set of rigid political and cultural conventions.

CONCLUSION

Some wild beasts that played important roles in political life, especially tigers, were viewed as unruly, unrestrained, undisciplined, and disruptive sentient beings. Wild beasts did not follow human rules and principles; instead, they have their jungle rules. Ferocious tigers may disobey the command of humans. They may rebel against human interests and harm humans and livestock in local communities. They are perfect equivalents to local powers. These local powers refer to non-Han nomadic groups in northern China and other peripheral groups including landlords and local officials who were not legally or politically ruled by the central state. These local powers politically, economically, and culturally countered the influence of the central state. That the central state could mobilize its political and military power to hunt down and kill these local powers is often regarded as a legalist approach to handling local regions.

But by accepting Confucian political ideology and attempting to display its superiority in terms of education, culture, and civilization, the central state was said to be taming the rebellious local powers by its virtuous governance. So, it extended its principles and rules to discipline and civilize these savage powers in local areas. In this sense, the central state positioned itself like a religious community. The Chinese regime could be viewed as an institutionalized, textualized, and ritualized community. Institutionally, the central state imposed its prefecture and county administration system and deployed inspectors for checking and balancing the local administrators. For instance, earlier in the chapter we read about Fei Qin, an inspector who checked up on the magistrate of Zhongmou, a representative of the central state acting as an arbitrator between the local powers and the ruled subjects.

Officials were educated in classical texts and were expected to spread the classics and promote classical education in areas they ruled. Ritually, they were expected to extend the Confucian rites for civilizing local communities. If we combine all these elements, there is not much difference between the political regime under Confucian ideology and Buddhist and Daoist communities that also attempted to impose their institutions, rules, principles, rituals, and texts. All these ideologies aimed to expand their civilized realms and mobilize local residents, which again indicates that these institutionalized teachings are concerned with educating and transforming (*jiaohua*) local people and extending their power over animals. In other words, all three teachings endeavor to impose their order over the order of nature.

In particular, we have seen from the discussions above that in the historical allusions contained in tomb inscriptions there was a shift in the use of pacified animals—from tigers and locusts to pheasants and locusts from the Southern and Northern Dynasties to the Tang period. This shift, as I argue, reflects the shift of local control from the grand protector to the county magistrate from the early medieval to medieval periods, which indicated the expansion of the power of central government in local areas.[77]

In this chapter I also suggest that these historical allusions of pacified animals reflected the education and training of the composers of tomb inscriptions, who not only followed the literary conventions but also political and cultural conventions of writing them. Confucian values were clearly illustrated in their compositions. In particular, the local administrators were persuaded to extend the five rites and six rules to local areas. These rites and rules indicated that the government's political control came from both Confucians and legalists. The local administrators negotiated with local people through both morality and regulations. In terms of the historical allusions discussed here, the writing of the tomb stele does not differ much from the writing of the memorial stele. I suggest, however, that the tomb stele and memorial stele represent two sets of evaluation systems and two sets of expectations from different audiences in the central government and the local area. The memorial stele inscription was an institutionalized writing and had to be authorized by the Bureau of Rites in the central government. The tombstone inscription could be more private, representing the expectation of the owner and his surviving family.

Interestingly, the Confucian values of benevolence and compassion met their Buddhist counterpart in the early medieval period. With the introduction of Buddhism, some members from noble families refused to participate in hunting. For example, when the Wu emperor of the Southern Qi dynasty asked Wang Ji to shoot pheasants, Wang Ji pretended he was ill to avoid breaking with his Buddhist faith.[78] As I noted in chapter 1, killing animals was not allowed in medieval Chinese Buddhist monastic rules. Instead, medieval Chinese Buddhist community developed various discourses and rituals for transforming and taming wild animals. Buddhist narratives indicated that some eminent monks could tame tigers and pheasants. In the next chapter I focus on discussing how eminent monks handled tigers.

But here I would like to highlight that medieval Buddhist hagiographies indicated that some eminent monks "domesticated" wild pheasants by preaching Buddhist doctrines and conveying Buddhist precepts. For example, in the period from 550 to 559, a monk named Seng'an 僧安 gathered about twenty disciples so that he could lecture them on the Mahāparinirvāṇa Sūtra. Just as he began explaining the title of this text, a wild female pheasant came to his seat and listened to his dharma talk. During the lunch break, she too walked out for food and drink and came back to the lecture again. Although most disciples were surprised, Seng'an told them that this pheasant must be reborn in the human realm so she could understand the dharma talk. Several years later, a woman met Seng'an and asked to become a nun. She was regarded as the reincarnation of this female pheasant.[79] Similarly in 640, when an eminent monk named Daohong 道洪 presented a dharma lecture on the Mahāparinirvāṇa Sūtra, a wild white pheasant came to listen, looking like a domesticated pet.[80] These two stories both mentioned a dharma talk on the same sutra, which might indicate that nonhuman animals were reborn as humans so they could understand the talk. Nevertheless, the wild pheasants in both stories were portrayed as domesticated animals who converted to Buddhism. In other words, Buddhism transformed their animality.

Another story claimed that a wild pheasant could even receive Buddhist precepts. In 597, when a monk named Lingcan 靈燦 went to Huaizhou 懷州 (modern Qingyang, Henan Province) to supervise the construction of a stupa for housing the relics, it is said that a wild male pheasant came down to the site without fear because of the virtue possessed by this eminent monk. Lingcan then bestowed three precepts on this pheasant, seemingly now domesticated after listening to the dharma preach. It turned out that this was an auspicious bird.[81] To a great extent, these stories echo the theme in Confucian political ideology that wild pheasants could be domesticated, an act conveyed here in face-to-face rhetoric between Buddhism and Confucianism.

In the medieval period, transforming birds including pheasants, and beasts such as tigers, was a common idea among all three teachings in medieval China. The Daoist approaches to tigers are the focus in chapter 4. Looking ahead, I offer a brief note on Daoist approaches to pheasants. An essay by Ming Sengshao 明僧紹 (d. fifth century) on Daoism and Confucianism suggested that the divine virtue of Daoist teaching reached various animals, including the resonant response of large animals, such as Kirin 麒麟 and Phoenix, as well as the transformation of the little ones such as birds and pheasants.[82] In the Jin dynasty, Zong Bing also cited the allusion of fleeing tigers to support his claim that the strong honesty of local administrators could bring up the resonant miracle, and he said that "Lu Yang and Geng Gong modeled Song Jun, the Jiujiang administrator from a long time ago, so they could turn the Sun back, make the spring fly, and also make locusts and tigers avoid the virtues, which are all resonated by the series of honesty. The resonance of the Divine Way was also the resonance of the Buddha."[83] In the early Daoist religious tradition, a similar idea of pacifying wild beasts was clearly shown in the *Heavenly-Written Scripture of True Text by Five Elders from the Primal Origin* (*Yuanshi wulao chishu yupian zhenwen tianshu jing* 元始五老赤書玉篇真文天書經), which was compiled in the Daoist canon as the first Numinous Treasure scripture, and also appeared in the Dunhuang manuscript (S. 5733). It said that there are twenty-four resonant responses on the ground as the celebration of divine truth being revealed by the Five Elders of the Primal Origin. Among these twenty-four resonant responses, the sixteenth stated that lions and wild beasts would stay with people in harmless companionship.[84] In the *Master Redpine's Almanac of Petitions* (*Chisongzi zhangli* 赤松子章曆), one of the chapters offered a ritual to eliminate disasters caused by tigers. According to this chapter, Daoist priests would request the North Dark Lord and his 120 attendants to lead local deities and gods of mountains, heaven and earth, and earth together to eliminate the danger of tigers and wolves.[85] Tigers, wolves, and other wild beasts might hurt local residents and domestic animals, so Daoist priests offered the service to drive them away. The Confucian literati inscribed their ideology of using benevolent governance to receive the resonant miracle of making tigers flee on the tombstones of their officials.

CHAPTER 3

Buddhists Taming Felines

The Companionship of the Tiger

C hinese animal culture may have benefited tremendously from the ancient textual, ritual, and doctrinal traditions of Buddhism, the ecological reality of the physical landscape in medieval China certainly helped to shape it. Although various animals played significant roles in ancient China, in the context of medieval Buddhism some animals were more preeminent than others. For instance, the lion was one of the most visible animals in Asian Buddhist culture. But in medieval China, tigers frequently appeared in hagiographical sources.[1] In this chapter I focus on how Buddhist monks engaged with local communities by dealing with the challenges and power dynamics presented to them by the tiger.

In traditional Chinese culture, the tiger is known by such names as the Lord of a Hundred Beasts or the King of the Forests. Two major species of tiger were commonly found around various mountains across the Chinese Empire in the medieval era: the Northeast China tiger (often called the Siberian tiger or Amur tiger) and the South China tiger.[2] They often interacted with Buddhist monks who commonly lived an ascetic life in the mountains and forests through practicing *dhūta* cultivation.[3] From time to time, Buddhist monks fled to the mountains from urban areas under the threat of warfare or political persecution. While staying in the mountains and forests, these Buddhists often encountered beasts such as tigers that they would not usually meet in urban areas. For example, in 573 CE, a monk named Fazang (546–629) left his monastery for the mountains. Then, in 574, the Northern Zhou dynasty prohibited both men and women from becoming monastic members. Since Fazang was hiding in the mountains, he was able to retain his monkhood. During his stay in the mountains, he made the valley his dwelling place and took on birds and beasts as his disciples and companions.[4]

With the growth and expansion of human settlements in medieval China, the conflict with tigers increased.[5] Chinese sources recount numerous legends of tiger attacks on travelers and livestock in local villages, events generally known as "tiger violence" (*hubao*) (figure 3.1).[6] As a significant threat to the social order at the village level, tiger violence became a key concern for the central court in the Chinese Empire. The central court often passed laws and instructed local government officials to control and eliminate tiger violence. Local government officials issued orders rewarding local hunters who killed tigers and thus prevented further disasters. The Buddhist monastic society in medieval China responded to the needs of local villages demanding a solution to the issue of tiger violence by developing a new narrative for how eminent monks could serve and engage with local communities by pacifying violent tigers. This new narrative can be found

3.1 A tiger pursuing a person, depicted in the mural of South Wall, Mogao Cave 159, Dunhuang. c. 8th century.

© *Dunhuang shiku quanji*, 2000.

in numerous legends in medieval Chinese hagiography, which seems to serve as a rhetorical tool for constructing holy images of the Buddhist saints, not unlike what occurred in medieval Christian hagiographies.

In the many related legends about monks who transformed wild animals into their disciples and companions, tigers appeared, perhaps surprisingly, more often than many other animals in medieval Chinese Buddhist sources.[7] By investigating and analyzing these legends I intend to show not only why tigers became one of the most important animals they portrayed, but also how monks lived with and wrote about tigers.[8] In this chapter I draw on and interpret the historical and cultural context of medieval China behind these legends.

Medieval Chinese Buddhist hagiographies documented various animals playing different roles in the lives of monks. Sometimes creatures were said to surround the tombs of deceased monks, and to pay tribute and mourn the death of these monks. Other legends recounted how some animals converted to Buddhism and could understand the preaching of eminent monks. Taming tigers was one of the most popular themes in some legends. These legends should be examined from multiple perspectives.[9] Historically, the scenes of animals as mourners cannot be authenticated as facts; therefore, such images and stories should be understood as Buddhist folk tales. But legends about how animals lived with monks may be real, as many Tarzan-like stories have been observed across the globe in the past and present.

As Alan Bleakley suggests, animals should be understood according to three dimensions of human experience. First, humans encounter animals in nature, which reflects the biological experience. Second, human beings imagine animals in their psychological experiences based on their culture. Third, human beings create animals as symbols by means of their writing, which constitutes the conceptual experience of animals.[10] While discussing animals in medieval Chinese Buddhist writing, especially tigers, it is important to analyze the role of animals through the application of these three experiential dimensions for Chinese monks. Some monks did encounter real tigers in their daily lives as they practiced their faith in solitude in mountains and forests.[11] Sometimes, tigers appeared as imagined subjects through cultural and psychological experiences whenever the monks felt that tigers were surrounding the tombs of their Buddhist masters. When Buddhist monks practiced meditation and entered a deeper state of consciousness, they could also encounter imagined tigers. Certain special tigers might well have been the creation of medieval Chinese Buddhist writers who used descriptions and narratives to portray tigers, not based on nature but with the purpose of manifesting Buddhist power.

Although lions also played a crucial role in early Buddhist life, they were not native to ancient China; instead, tigers were commonly regarded as the king of the animal realm. In Confucian political and social discourse, tigers appeared as the animal symbol of the strong and cruel ruling class—especially the powerful local clans and administrators who took possession of both property and lives of the masses, just as tigers did to local villagers. Sometimes, law enforcement officials directly dispatched from the central government were given the nickname "tiger," symbolizing their service as if they were the literal claws and teeth of the emperor grasping those officials who endorsed corruption and brought injustice.

As we saw in chapter 2, the state mobilized two approaches to the threat of the tiger. One approach was the legalist practice, by which the state requested local government administrators to hunt, trap, and kill tigers to prevent them from posing a risk to human lives and local livestock. The other concerns political ideology, by which the state developed the Confucian rhetoric of virtuous governance for moving tigers away. According to this rhetoric, if a local administrator, especially a prefect, executed his benevolent and virtuous governance in the local area, the strong local clans would not be able to easily take away the property and lives of local people. Virtuous governance was also believed to generate auspicious events, such as when tigers no longer crossed the river to disturb the benevolently governed area. In this sense, the political ideal of Confucian discourse was to control the problem of cruel local clans able to harm local people as much as violent tigers did. Interestingly, medieval Chinese Buddhism developed an alternative discourse for taming tigers and protecting the property and lives of local people.

THE CULTURAL USE OF THE LION IN EARLY BUDDHIST TRADITION

Some animals, especially so-called apex predators such as lions and tigers, became more preeminent than others in the history of Asian Buddhism because of their position in the food chain. In this chapter I examine how the Buddhists in South and East Asia came to terms with apex predators in their religious lives, and how the dynamic environment shaped their changing understanding and symbolic use of these apex predators. Early Buddhist discourse on the lion was by no means univocal: it evolved in a process of constant change. Multiple elements shaped this process. Early Buddhism benefited from much South Asian intellectual thought, and it developed its sophisticated narratives and interpretations by adapting new elements to serve the ideological and cultural needs of its followers. As we see in this chapter, aside from the narratives about the Buddha as a lion in his previous lives, the physiological features of the lion have been used to describe the Buddha's physical movements in preaching his teachings. The sound of the lion's roar, and the color of the lion's skin, inspired the followers of the Buddha in creating their rhetoric for the growing Buddhist community.

Biologically, both lions and tigers belong to the genus *Panthera* of the Pantherinae subfamily, within the Felidae family. The lion's modern biological name is *Panthera leo*, and the tiger's is *Panthera tigris*. In the genus *Panthera*, there are two other animals: *P. onca* (the American jaguar); and *P. pardus* (the leopard). The Latin word *Panthera* might come from the Sanskrit word for tiger, *pundarikam*.[12] These animals from the genus *Panthera* are often viewed as apex predators in different geographical regions.[13] But across the continents of Asia and Africa, lions have occupied the most dominant position for a long time. There are two species of lions active in Asia and Africa, which are often called Asiatic lions (*P. leo persica*) and African lions (with many different Latin names). In Asia, most wild lions live in the Gil reservation region of India and, in Africa, wild lions mostly live in sub-Saharan regions. Currently, there are no longer any wild lions living in West Asia and North Africa. Historically, there were nine species of tigers in Asia,[14] but only a few of them have survived to the present day. Tigers are indigenous to Asia, and they are never found in other continents. In Central Asia, Caspian tigers have been extinct for many years. Bali tigers and Javan tigers have been extinct since the mid-twentieth century. To date, four tigers including Siberian tigers,[15] South China tigers,[16] Sumatran tigers, and Bengal tigers are still present in Asia, though most of them do not live in the wild.[17]

The lion seems to be the most important animal in the political and religious life of ancient South Asia, and it has been an instrumental symbolic animal since the Vedic era. In the Ṛgveda, the lion is used to symbolize the power and vigor of some important deities, such as Indra, Parjánya, and Agni. The lion is also regarded as the king of all animals, and the protector of Śiva.[18] In early Buddhist literature, the lion is often associated with the Buddha to symbolize his might, nobility, authority, power, and wisdom. In the following discussion, we first see how the Buddha was depicted as a religious leader whose power was decorated with the symbolism of the lion in early Buddhist literature. We then explore how the Buddhist discourse on the lion underwent a transition from early Buddhist literature to early Mahāyāna Buddhist literature.

The historical Buddha preached his teachings orally, and there is no immediate textual source available to document them. Buddhism remained a minority teaching in South Asia but as it spread, long after the historical Buddha's death, the early Buddhist community gradually developed its textual tradition. Many texts portrayed the Buddha as a unique spiritual leader, and the historical Buddha became a glorified cultural hero. Before he became the Buddha, Gautama Siddhārtha heralded from the Kṣatriya caste, and he lived in a small republic. His clan seems to have been powerful, but father was not a king. Nevertheless, he was portrayed as a prince in early Buddhist literature; his followers reconstructed his entire clan as a genealogical succession of kingship, creating a mighty and noble royal background for Gautama Siddhārtha. For this purpose, numerous narratives in early Buddhist literature have attempted to associate the Buddha with the lion, a symbolic animal of royalty in general, but also a crucial symbolic animal of royal power in South Asian political history.[19] For instance, the Buddha was called "Śākyasiṃha," the lion of the Śākya.[20] A new genre of early Buddhist narrative called "Śākyasiṃhajātaka" appeared for depicting the heroic behaviors of the Buddha in his previous lives.[21]

As a result of the Buddha's glorification in early Buddhist literature, many titles associated with the lion have been given to the ancestors of the Buddha and the Buddha himself to highlight their mighty and noble virtues and qualities. For example, in the early Buddhist text Aggañña Sutta (*Qishi jing*), it is stated that the great-grandfather of Gautama had two sons, and they were called Siṃhahanu[22] and Siṃhapāda. Siṃhahanu had four sons, and the oldest son Gautama's father.[23] It appears that both Siṃhahanu and Siṃhapāda are titles, rather than names, and they both incorporate the word for a lion. Some similar titles have appeared in the kingship of ancient India, such as Siṃhakesarin, Siṃhakośa, Siṃhagupta, Siṃhajaṭi, Siṃhadanshtra, Siṃhadeva, Siṃhanāda, Siṃhabala, Siṃhabāhu, Siṃhabhūbhṛit, Siṃhamahīpati, Siṃharāja, Siṃhasāhi, and Siṃhaksha.[24] Even some Chinese sources from the sixth and seventh centuries mentioned titles of kings in ancient South Asia incorporating the word for a lion, such as Siṃhapārśva, a king in West India appearing in an account by Chinese pilgrims. The Chinese historian Zhou Yiliang pointed out that, in medieval South India, the title Rājasiṃha 獅子王 was very popular. Around 699, while on his way to Ceylon to worship the Buddha's tooth relic, the acclaimed Tantric Buddhist master Vajrabodhi met a king called Narasiṃha Potavarman in South India.[25]

Early Mahāyāna Buddhist literature reveals that many titles incorporating the word for lion (*siṃha*) were associated with or given to the Buddha, thus equating his ruler status in human society with that of the lion in the animal realm. In the Mahāratnakūṭa Sūtra (*Da baoji jing*), Gautama was praised as being as fearless as Rājasiṃha. In other texts, there are numerous titles for the Tathāgata Buddha that incorporate *siṃha*, such as Siṃhaghoṣa, Siṃhadhvaja, Siṃdhadhvaja, and Siṃhagaṃdha. These titles, along with the titles the Buddha's ancestors received, appeared only after Gautama achieved enlightenment.

The lion was not always depicted as the ruler of the animal realm in early Buddhist literature, even though its power was well acknowledged. In the Mahīśāsaka Vinaya, a Jātaka story shows that the lion was once ruled by the wild fox and became part of the animal army attacking human society.[26] According to this story, a wild fox listened as a hermit named Māṇava recited texts in a mountain cave. Being ambitious and cunning, the fox realized that if he could understand these texts, he might be able to become the king of all animals. So, he mobilized all the wild foxes to tame all the elephants, and then mobilized the elephants to tame all the tigers. Eventually, he drove these tigers to tame all the lions, and so he became the king of all beasts. After he had conquered the animal kingdom, he gave up the idea of marrying a beast, and set his eyes on a human lady instead. He then brought his animal army to surround the kingdom of Kāsī and requested to marry the princess of this kingdom. But it turns out that a wise court official used a cunning strategy to help the king defeat the animals; he suggested that the king should ask the lion within the wild fox's animal army to roar before the two sides engaged in war. Once the lion roared, the heart of the wild fox was shaken so much that it broke apart. Then, all the beasts fled. In this story, the king of Kāsī was the previous life of the Buddha, the wise official was the previous life of the Buddha's disciple Śāriputra, and the wild fox was the Buddha's opponent Devadatta.

Many Jātaka stories in which the lion was considered to be the Buddha in a previous life praised him for his virtue and wisdom, especially his sacrifice for the benefit of all sentient beings,[27] as in this story from the *Scripture of the Wise and Foolish* (*Xianyu jing*).[28] Once upon a time, there was a lion with golden skin who followed the Pratyekabuddha to cultivate himself and become a vegetarian, no longer harming other sentient beings. A hunter, who had shaved his head and wore ascetic robes, saw this golden-skinned lion and sought to hunt it down, so he could offer the lion skin to the king. The lion found out about this danger and was nearly ready to attack this hunter. But the lion ceased the attack, thinking that because this hunter was wearing ascetic robes, he might achieve enlightenment in future. The lion was then killed by the hunter, and the hunter offered the lion skin to the king. The king read some Buddhist texts and realized that a beast with golden skin must be the manifestation of a bodhisattva. He therefore asked the hunter if there were any auspicious signs before the lion died. After he had received the answer, he ordered that the lion skin be honored by placing it on a seven-jeweled vehicle. He also used a golden coffin to preserve the lion skin, and he housed it in a stupa. In this story, the Buddha sacrificed himself in his previous life for the cultivation of the hunter. It seems that the discourse of the Buddha's sacrificing his lion life is very popular in the Jātaka tradition, and it has been depicted in many wall paintings in caves where early Buddhist art is found.[29]

Aside from the time when the Buddha appears as a lion in his previous lives in the Jātaka tradition, the cultivation and virtues of the Buddha are always associated with the lion. As the Ekottarika Āgama (*Zengyi ahan jing*) teaches, the highest status of the Buddha's meditation is called the Siṃhavijṛmbhita, which reflects the rapid vigor of the lion. The Buddha taught that there are four periods of meditation. Once a practitioner completed all four periods of meditation, he or she would enter the highest status.[30] The Buddha himself experienced all these four periods and reached the highest status, so he eventually reached the enlightenment and cut off all delusions.[31]

The Buddhist text Mahāparinirvāṇa Sūtra offers a detailed, paralleled analogue between the Buddha's spiritual body and the lion's physical body. The Buddha is fully enlightened, so his wisdom is as sharp as a lion's claws and teeth, his wish-fulfilling mindset is likened to a lion's feet, his paramitas (perfections) are like a lion's body, and his compassion is as soft as a lion's tail. The Buddha is powerful and mighty, and he stays in a clear and pure house, as a lion stays in his clear and pure cave. He would roar for sentient beings, like a lion, to destroy the demonic army and make those who have fears feel peaceful and safe.[32] This scripture also illustrates that both the Buddha and the lion share eleven marvelous things: (1) the Buddha can perceive and reveal those who did not reach enlightenment but only pretended to do so; (2) the Buddha may roar like a lion to test his powerful ability to be enlightened; (3) the Buddha can make his cultivation place clear and pure, without being disturbed by Mara; (4) the Buddha can help his followers understand what he cultivated, and where he preached his Dharma; (5) the Buddha can teach his followers the fearless mind; (6) the Buddha can enlighten those who fall asleep; (7) the Buddha can convey happiness to sentient beings by manifesting his presence (8) the Buddha can enlighten sentient beings who are in chaos and delusion; (9) the Buddha often motivates sentient beings to seek constant cultivation, without giving up their right efforts; (10) the Buddha can tame heretic practitioners and convert them; (11) the Buddha can also preach his teachings to his friends, relatives, and attendants. It is well known in the Buddhist community that the preaching behavior of the Buddha is called *sīhanāda* (the roaring of the lion) in Buddhist texts, because it can destroy demons and heretics, similar to what the lion did in the forest. John Strong suggests that this roaring rhetoric also indicates the Buddha's ability to resolve any doctrinal doubts held by his followers.[33] Thus it appears that the roaring rhetoric not only targets the threat from outside the Buddhist community, but also demonstrates the Buddha's authority of wisdom within the Buddhist community.

In early Mahāyāna Buddhist sources, the roaring of the lion was granted as an ability of the Buddha when he was born. The sound of the lion's roaring certainly comes from the daily experience of early Buddhists who were witnesses to this sound in South Asian forests. The sound of the Buddha's preaching, which is paralleled with that of the lion's roaring, is not only a literary metaphor, but also a historical memory of the day-to-day experiences of those who observed lions and their activities. This metaphor was popular later in Chinese Mahāyāna Buddhist sources, though the Chinese Buddhists rarely saw lions in their daily lives.

The early Buddhist community also associated the Buddha's preaching of his teachings with his seat, decorated with lions. In early Mahāyāna Buddhist texts, the dharma-preaching practice is simply called "ascending the lion seat" or "ascending the golden lion seat," referring to the position and gesture of the Buddha when preaching his teachings. Ascending the lion seat is a Buddhist ritual for preaching, but from the perspective of material culture, the lion seat should be noted as a metaphor of the authority and power of the Buddha. This is similar to the South and Central Asian political rulers' method of symbolizing their political authority and power. For instance, King Aśoka (?–232 BCE) used lions to decorate his monumental pillars. Many sources have indicated that in South Asia and Central Asia, some kings used golden lion seats as their thrones. A Chinese source stated that in the Kucha 龜茲 Kingdom, the king once honored Kumārajīva with a golden-lion chair, decorated with a silk cover, from the Eastern Roman Empire. In the Hephthalite 嚈噠 Empire, the emperor sat on a golden chair, decorated with the sculptures of six white elephants and four lions.[34]

Generally, in early Buddhist traditions, especially in early Mahāyāna Buddhism, the lion is the most important animal associated with the Buddha for symbolizing his authority and power. The lion's physiological features and vocalizations inspired early Buddhists to create narratives to establish the metaphor between the spiritual leader of the human realm and the ruler of the animal realm: the Buddha, and the lion, respectively.

THE SHIFT FROM LION TO TIGER IN MEDIEVAL CHINESE BUDDHISM

The lion is not indigenous to China but, as early as in the Warring States period (478–221 BCE), the lion had already appeared in Chinese art. The Chinese word *shizi* 獅子 (lion) is a transliteration of an ancient Iranian word. Many scholars have discussed an early Tocharian B manuscript, discovered in Kucha, which uses the word *secake/śiśäk* for lion.[35] But a real lion did not enter China until the first century CE. According to Chinese sources, in the first century many countries from the Western Regions, such as the Arsacid Empire 安息 and the Rouzhi 月支 Kingdom,[36] offered lions as tributes to the court of the Han Empire. Later, in the Northern Wei and Tang dynasties, many rulers from Sogdiana and Persia gave lions as tributes to the Chinese court. Nevertheless, real lions appear to have been observed by only a limited, privileged group of people, mostly the Chinese ruling classes, especially those in the capital city. For the Chinese, the tiger is the head of the animal realm. Historically speaking, the tiger is one of the most preeminent animals in South Asia and East Asia.[37] But in South Asia, unlike East Asia, it never earned the same high position as the lion.[38]

In ancient Chinese political and religious culture, the tiger occupies a unique position: it symbolizes controlling power and force. The icon of the tiger is used to symbolize the power and status of royalty in the rites of birthday celebrations, weddings, funerals, and burial ceremonies. As the symbol of royal power and authority, the icon of the tiger is designed for public display, and it appears on court ceremonial robes and royal vehicles. In one of the oldest lexicons of China,

Explaining Simple Graphs and Analyzing Compound Characters (*Shuowen jiezi*), the tiger is said to be the lord of all mountain beasts.[39] In the medieval period, the tiger was commonly viewed as the most powerful beast, and many stories discuss the tiger as the ruler of the forest.[40] Many rulers of nomadic ethnic groups incorporated "tiger" in their titles,[41] possibly for similar reasons that "lion" was used in the titles of South Asian royalty.

One of the most interesting cases concerning the tiger's symbolism of royal authority and power is the "tiger warrior" (*huben* 虎賁) system. The tiger warrior was first established in the Zhou dynasty (1045-256 BCE), when King Wu instituted the tiger warriors as his close military guards. The members of this army were stringently selected, and they were regarded as the finest fighters able to defend the king. Their main duties were to protect the royal palace, and they were present as honor guards during royal funeral rites. These two functions continued in later dynasties, throughout the history of the tiger warrior institution, until the medieval period. The robes of these tiger warriors were decorated with the patterns of tiger skin.

Due to its ferocity, the tiger was used as the symbol for tyrannical governance in ancient China. In the *Book of Rites* (*Liji*), it is stated that Confucius once sighed, saying that "tyranny is more dreadful than a dangerous tiger."[42] Thus, the tiger became the symbol for tyranny or bad governance. In the Han dynasty, the central court began to impose the Confucian ideology as its political foundation for so-called virtuous governance, and it started to extend its power to many local areas, and to spread its recognized rites for civilizing its subjects. The central court then developed a new political rhetoric, in which the tiger appeared as the symbol of powerful local families who might compromise the authority of the central court, while pheasants symbolized the uncivilized local villagers, who did not fulfill the institutionalized five rites in their daily lives.

When Buddhism came to China, the Buddhist community quickly realized the central position of the tiger in Chinese cosmology. Although the Buddhist community has its own traditional cosmology, when faced with a Chinese audience, it had to negotiate with the Chinese understanding of the tiger in the political and religious culture. In terms of textual and visual sources, there are many cases where tigers replaced lions, and became the eminent animal in the Buddhist community with the spread of Buddhism to Central and East Asia. In particular, the tiger earned the higher position in East Asia, which it would never earn in South Asia. In replacing the lion with the tiger, one of the most interesting cases concerns a story in the ancient South Asian collection, the *Book of Five Sections* (*Pañcatantra*). The third story in the fifth section talks about four Brahmins. Three Brahmins are erudite, while the fourth is not knowledgeable, but very rational. They found a pile of bones from a dead lion in the forest. One Brahmin suggested combining these bones to wake up the dead lion. Once all the bones were combined by the three erudite Brahmins, the fourth Brahmin warned that a wakened lion would bring disaster to these Brahmins. He therefore climbed up a tree. When the lion resurrected, it devoured three Brahmins.[43] Boris I. Marshak has identified a similar story on the murals in Panjikent. But on these murals, the story is depicted as three Brahmins and one dead tiger. The tiger was resurrected, and it ate the third Brahmin who had woken up the tiger.[44] The reason for this modification is unclear. The replacement of a lion with a tiger might stem from Chinese influences, since the Sogdian culture in Central Asia received numerous influences from Chinese Buddhism, especially given that many Sogdian Buddhist texts were translated from the Chinese versions.[45] Also, the *Book of Five Sections* itself had an impact on Chinese literature.[46]

Another example concerns how a Chinese Buddhist master Zhiyi 智顗 (538–597) used the tiger to replace the lion while commenting on the Chinese translation of the early Mahāyāna Buddhist text Mahāvaipulya-mahāsamghāta Sūtra (*Da fangdeng daji jing*). The first Chinese translation was carried out by Dharmakṣema between 414 and 426. A section in chapter 23 discusses how twelve zodiac animals manifested themselves to teach and transform those animal-form sentient beings in the samsara, the cycle of life, death, and rebirth. These twelve animals take turns, coming from the four cardinal directions, centered on Mount Sumeru, the center of six realms for sentient beings. In each direction, there are three animals. Among these animals, in the north, there are the lion, the rabbit, and the *nāga*.[47] This might reflect the early understanding of geographical information in ancient South Asia. But when Zhiyi commented on this section, he shifted the north to the east and replaced the lion with a tiger.[48] This is a Chinese-led transformation, because Zhiyi was attempting to attract a Chinese audience. He also implemented other indigenous Chinese ideas, including yin-yang 陰陽 theory, Five-Phase theory (*wuxing* 五行), and Twelve-Terrestrial-Branch (*dizhi* 地支) theory, to reinterpret the twelve zodiac animals in this early Mahāyāna Buddhist text.

How the tiger earned a crucial position in Chinese Buddhist culture can be shown by its appearance in honorary titles: One the one hand, in medieval Chinese Buddhism an earlier Buddhist tradition of incorporating the lion in the honorary titles of the Buddha (such as Tathāgata Buddha) continued, while on the other hand the medieval Chinese Buddhist community developed a new tradition of using the tiger in the honorable titles of eminent monks. For example, those eminent monks who were regarded as skillful masters in Vinaya learning were called "the tigers of Vinaya" (*lühu* 律虎), and those eminent monks who mastered scriptural doctrines were called "the tigers of exegetic learning" (*yihu* 義虎). Fayuan 法願 (524–587), a Vinaya master who was active in the Northern Qi dynasty, focused his Buddhist learning on Vinaya studies. For his cutting arguments against other Vinaya commentators, he earned the title of "the tiger of Vinaya." In the early Sui dynasty, he became the abbot of the Great Xingguo Monastery 大興國寺.[49] In the Tang dynasty, Yuanlin 元林, who resided at the Lingquan Monastery 靈泉寺, was also called the tiger of Vinaya.[50] Even as an Indian diaspora monk staying in China, Zhizang 智藏 (741–819) received the same title.[51] Although Zhizang used to be a Buddhist monk residing in western India, he did not receive a title incorporating the word for a lion. This indicates that the Chinese Buddhist community attempted to honor him in the new tradition of the tiger of Vinaya. Other monks, such as Chengchu 澄楚 (889–959) and Zanning 贊寧 (919–1001), were also called the tigers of Vinaya. In the medieval period, many monks, including Huirong 慧榮 (early seventh century), Daoguang 道光 (682–760), Wu'en 悟恩 (?–986), Xizui 希最 (?–1090), and Depu 德普 (1025–1091), were referred to as tigers of exegetic learning.

The tiger of Vinaya, as a new tradition, appeared in the Vinaya learning community. The prime concern of medieval Vinaya masters, such as Daoxuan, was the survival of the Buddhist community, and how this survival was to be sustained by the strict observance of the precepts and profound learning of Vinaya texts. Daoxuan was particularly concerned about the degeneration of morality within the Buddhist monastic order. He accused many monks of lacking the right attitude toward these precepts and Vinaya learning. He once attributed the political persecution against Buddhism in the Northern Dynasties to the disorder within the monastic community. For him, a Vinaya master should serve to police discipline within the monastic order. The tiger, as an important symbol of power and authority, fit well in the Buddhist mentality during the medieval period. For the Chinese audience, as the king of all animals in East Asia, the tiger symbolized the protector of law and order of nature.

It should be noted that both the experiences of Chinese monks in their daily lives, and the literary and writing tradition by which these monks were trained and educated, contributed to the appearance of these titles incorporating the word for a tiger. The Buddhist historiography that created those titles was influenced by traditional Chinese narratives of political figures. The title of tiger, used in Chinese political culture, appeared in the later Han dynasty 後漢. The first noted official who was called the tiger was Dong Xuan 董宣, the prefect of Luoyang 洛陽令. He was a restless, tough persecutor, and he once killed a servant of Princess Huyang 湖陽公主 for his crime. He thus earned a reputation as a fearless tiger who could confront any government corruption, even if high-profile figures were involved. Many tough government officials that maintained the political and legal order in the Southern and Northern Dynasties, including Zang Jue 臧厥 (495-542), Xiao Huikai 蕭惠開, and Li Chong 李崇, have been called tigers, according to their biographies in the official histories. Among these officials, the case of Xiao Huikai is unique, because he was a good friend of a Buddhist monk, Senghou 僧侯. Apparently, in the medieval period, Chinese texts drew parallels between these "eminent" officials and "eminent" monks, given that titles incorporated the word for a tiger.

In medieval Chinese Buddhist historiography, interestingly, a great number of the biographies compiled about monks portrayed them as eminent.[52] One feature that defines them as eminent is their ability to tame tigers.[53] Tigers are the most dangerous and ferocious animals in medieval East Asian nature. Since these monks had the ability to tame these tigers and convert them to Buddhism, medieval Chinese Buddhism developed a new tradition for conquering the animal kingdom. Buddhist monks became the teachers and spiritual guides of the most powerful animal in East Asia. This rhetoric helps medieval Chinese Buddhism expand its dharma realm into the realm of animals.

Thus, it is clear that the Buddhist images of apex predators experienced a transition with the spread of Buddhism from South Asia to East Asia, particularly China. The lion seems to be the most important animal in Buddhist tradition before Buddhism entered China. But after Buddhism's arrival in China, its view of animals had to compete with the Chinese view of animals. The Buddhist literary and historical use of lions would have seemed foreign to the Chinese audience, who were more familiar with tigers. Although the old tradition of the lion being used as a symbol of the Buddha's authority and power continued in medieval Chinese Buddhism, the Chinese Buddhist community, based on their literary tradition and daily life experiences, gradually developed new ideas and concepts, as well as the cultural practice of leveraging the tiger as the new symbol of Buddhist power and authority, especially for eminent monks. First, some eminent monks who had mastered Vinaya and exegetic learning were granted honorable titles, incorporating the word for a tiger, for their prowess in argumentation, while some Vinaya masters earned a title incorporating the word for a tiger for their contribution to maintaining moral discipline within the monastic order. Second, some eminent monks are portrayed as the conquers of nature, who could tame tigers and convert them to Buddhism; therefore, they helped local villages remove the most dangerous threat from the natural world, which was a new way for the Chinese Buddhists to engage with local society.

THE CHANGING ATTITUDES OF BUDDHISM TOWARD TIGERS

In early southern Asian Buddhist literature and early Chinese translations of Buddhist literature, the tiger was portrayed as an evil animal. First, in Jātakamālā stories, the tigress was described as a cruel animal who ate Prince Mahāsattva and consumed his blood and flesh to feed her cubs.[54] The Jātakamālā story was well known to ancient Chinese Buddhists, appearing in many entries of a Chinese Buddhist encyclopedia titled *Differentiated Manifestations of the Sutras and Vinayas* (*Jinglü yixiang*) compiled by Baochang 寶唱 (c. 495–528) in the early sixth century. It was also depicted in many different ways in medieval Chinese Buddhist art, such as mural paintings in Dunhuang (figure 3.2). This story has many different versions that share a common theme, casting the tigress as the attacker who fulfilled the vow Prince Mahāsattva made as a bodhisattva to sacrifice himself and save other sentient beings such as tiger cubs. Second, in early Buddhist literature, tigers often appeared as violent animals who might endanger human lives in the wilderness. Third, in early Buddhist literature, tigers were considered to be the reincarnation of people who had committed very bad deeds. But in early examples of Buddhist Vinaya literature such as the Mahāsāṃghika Vinaya (translated into Chinese in 416), the killing of tigers was prohibited. Notably, although early Buddhist monks were disturbed by tigers, they attempted to find a capable person to tame them, because killing a tiger would result in the offense of *pāyattika* (falling into the hell realm) in this monastic code.[55]

In some medieval Chinese translations of Buddhist texts such as *Treatise Spoken by the Buddha on the Abhidharma for Living in This World* (*Foshuo lishi apitan lun*), tigers were listed with lions, leopards, bears, and other beasts as attackers who would take the lives of other sentient beings. This was understandable to

3.2 Prince Bodhisattva sacrifices himself to a tigress. Mogao Cave 428, east wall.
© *Dunhuang shiku quanji*, 2000, 54, no. 39.

Chinese readers because in medieval China, once travelers entered the wilderness, especially the ancient forests across the country, an encounter with wild beasts such as tigers, wolves, and wild dogs was imminent. As for the conflict between the animal world and the human world, there was not much difference between South Asian and Chinese literature since at that time, at least in China, there was a vast wilderness for animals to live in peace and have little interaction with humans. In Buddhist cosmology, the tiger was from the animal realm, one of the six realms, and travelling across realms was possible. For instance, if human committed bad deeds, their karma could be affected adversely, and eventually they could be downgraded and reborn as a tiger in the next life. According to another highly popular medieval Chinese Buddhist encyclopedia, *Pearl Forest in the Dharma Grove (Fayuan zhulin)*, sentient beings would fall into three evil realms if they had done something terribly wrong. Even if they had a body from the heavenly (*deva*) realm, once their life came to an end, they could be reborn in the realm of animals, as a lion, tiger, wolf, elephant, horse, or cow, and be hunted for life. The sentient beings who consumed large amounts of meat were also likely to be reborn as animals.

Interestingly, some legends in the *Pearl Forest in the Dharma Grove* suggest that human beings may be reborn as tigers as a consequence of a strong ego and a stubborn attitude. A Buddhist text discovered in the Dunhuang manuscripts, Scripture Spoken by the Buddha on the Causes and Effects of Good and Evil Actions (*Foshuo shan'e yinguo jing*), echoes this view and claims that those men who hated their wives would be reborn as tigers.[56] It suggests that medieval Chinese readers accepted the idea that tigers and stubborn people shared one feature: a strong ego. Thus the latter could be reborn as the former because of this shared bad trait. At the time, people had a number of opportunities to observe tigers in the wild; witnessing the fury of tigers may gave made an impact on their daily lives, and those experiences were preserved as cultural memory in recorded in Buddhist writings of the period. The story of the tiger eating the bodhisattva and thereby helping him achieve the ultimate goal of compassion was well known to medieval Chinese Buddhists. Many legends in Chinese Buddhist hagiographies portray monks following the paths of Prince Mahāsattva and imitating his behavior by renouncing their bodies and succumbing to tigers, an act clearly manifest in the early Buddhist heritage of Jātakamālā stories in medieval Chinese Buddhism. For instance, an early eleventh-century monk Xingming 行明 was a native to Changzhou 長洲 (modern Suzhou), in the Wu prefecture. He once told his fellow monks that he would not like to be cremated on a wooden pyre as many others had been, or share the fate of Qu Yuan 屈原 (who ended his life as fish food in a lake), but that he had made a vow to learn from Prince Mahāsattva and had overcome numerous *kalpas* to eventually achieve the "holy fruit." He often mentioned his will to fellow monks, yet nobody took him seriously. One day, this young monk surrendered himself to a group of tiger cubs who immediately feasted on his body. What was left of his corpse was cremated, and the ashes were retrieved.[57] In this case, because Xingming sacrificed his life to tiger cubs like the Buddha had in a previous life, it appears that the medieval Buddhist community acknowledged him as an enlightened monk; his ashes remaining after his cremation were venerated as a relic.

But medieval Chinese hagiographies also note that some monks survived attacks from beasts in the mountains. A monk called Xichen, a native from Bingzhou 并州 (modern Taiyuan, Shanxi), once offered himself to wolves and tigers in a mountain valley. Some beasts approached him yet shied away after smelling him.[58] There is no way to authenticate the account but it may be that the monk looked and smelled like a beast, hence other beasts did not eat him because he was one of them. In the medieval Chinese Buddhist literature that concerns miracles, some legends depict the transformation of human beings into tigers. For instance, in a collection titled *Records of Equality and Harmony* (*Qixie ji* 齊諧記), it is said that in Taimo 太末, a county of Dongyang 東陽 Prefecture (modern Longyou, Zhejiang), in the year 408, a person named Wu Daozong 吳道宗 lost his father as a child and lived with his mother. One day when he left the house, neighbors heard a strange noise coming from within. They went inside to investigate and found a black-striped tiger, but Wu's mother was not there. The neighbors were worried that the striped tiger had harmed his mother, so they recruited more people to try and save her. When they entered Wu's home again, they found the mother sitting calmly, and she spoke with them as though nothing unusual had happened. The mother had once told her son that people would be transformed into tigers if they had been guilty of wrongdoing in a previous life. Later, Wu's mother disappeared again, and reports came in from Taimo County, where a black-striped tigress had been spotted. Local residents had gathered and attacked this tigress, wounding her severely. The tigress then returned to Daozong's home where she eventually died on the mother's bed without changing back into her human form. Wu Daozong realized that the tigress was his mother and buried her honorably.[59]

There are similar legends about people transforming into tigers from other areas that carry the same message. These legends confirm that a human who committed a crime would suffer immediate consequences in this life by turning into a tiger or tigress, rather than being reborn as a tiger or tigress in the next life.[60]

HANDLING "TIGER VIOLENCE" IN MEDIEVAL CHINESE BUDDHISM

Many legends record that medieval monks could survive encounters with beasts such as lions and tigers. In Chinese Buddhist literature, monks from other lands were the first to demonstrate this power of being able to tame tigers. As early as the fifth century, tales of how monks survived encounters with tigers became increasingly common. One of the earliest cases was that of Buddhayaśas (Fotuo

Yeshe 佛陀耶舍, c. fourth to fifth centuries), a monk from Kashmir. He turned to monastic life at the age of thirteen and often travelled with his master. One day Buddhayaśas and his master encountered a tiger in the wilderness, and when the master tried to find shelter, Buddhayaśas assured him that the tiger would not attack them, since he looked like he had just had a meal and was satiated. The tiger did in fact leave them and walk away.[61] In this story, Buddhayaśas did not tame the tiger, but he understood the nature of the beast and could make a judgment about its behavior. Yet another story tells of a dedicated monk from Kashmir named Gunavarman (Qiuna Bamo 求那跋摩, 367-431), an outstanding student who after his ordination recited millions of words from Buddhist texts. Gunavarman once traveled to Java, where he was given a house by the king who referred to him as the master. In Java, tigers were rampant in the mountains and often attacked local villagers. Gunavarman understood the problem and told the king that he would like to move into the mountains. Upon his arrival, the tigers apparently calmed down and stopped harming villagers.[62] It appears that Gunavarman helped the local people to pacify the tigers. A third monk from Kashmir was Dharmayaśas (Tanmo Yeshe 曇摩耶舍, c. fifth century) who was believed to have mastered scripture and vinayas even as a young boy. When he grew up, he often traveled alone in the mountains, but tigers never attacked him.

Chinese narratives have portrayed these three monks from Kashmir as eminent for their ability to pacify tigers without being harmed, yet there is no way to establish if they carried this extraordinary ability from their training in Kashmir or if they developed it after they arrived in China. At least one thing is clear: around the late fourth and early fifth centuries, the extraordinary abilities of some foreign monks to keep tigers pacified was recorded in medieval Chinese literature. Some Chinese monks of the time have also been credited with having had this ability, for example, a monk called Fawu 法晤 (411-489) who practiced solitary ascetic cultivation. He often recited the Mahāprajñāpāramitā Sūtra, the Prajñāpāramitā Sūtra, and the Lotus Sutra (*Fahua jing*). While traveling around mountains and marshes, he was not afraid of tigers and wild buffalo.[63] Faxu 法緒 (c. fifth century), another monk from Gaochang (modern Turfan, Xinjiang), observed his precepts strictly and practiced vegetarianism as well as meditation. He later entered the Sichuan region, where he found a mountain valley for his *dhūta* practice/cultivation, where tigers and wild buffalo did not harm him. He often recited the Lotus Sutra, the Vimalakīrti Nirdeśa Sūtra (*Weimojie jing*), and the Golden Light Sutra (*Jin' guangming jing*).[64] Tanchao 曇超 (419-492), a monk from

Qinghe 清河 (modern Qinghe, Hebei), traveled to the Shixing 始興 area (modern Shaoguan, Guangdong), and found shelter under the trees on the land he owned. It is recorded that beasts such as tigers never disturbed him. Huimi 慧彌 (439–518), a monk from Hongnong 弘農 (modern Sanmenxia 三門峽, Henan), devoted himself to solitude. He entered the Zhongnan Mountains, and it is said that tigers never attacked him.[65] In the sixth century, a monk from Kuaiji 會稽, Dazhi 大志, also practiced solitary, ascetic cultivation and offered himself to tigers but they turned away. While he lived in the mountains he survived on wild vegetables.[66]

It is noteworthy that many of these legends from medieval Chinese Buddhist hagiographies follow a distinct narrative pattern. Some of them reflect on the daily activities of medieval Chinese monks. Others are more generic and rhetorical and not based on actual fact. Those focusing on daily activities comprise biographies of monks who either lived alone in the forests or mountains by cultivating their ascetic practice and were thereby more likely to have encountered tigers. Those not based on the actual lives of monks often mention tigers and wild buffalo. The reason these animals appear in monastic biographies is more complex. First, tigers were regarded as a major threat to local communities, and local residents and monks had to deal with this constant threat. Second, the tiger was considered the king of the animal kingdom in East Asia. For medieval Buddhists, if a monk could deal with a ferocious tiger, he thereby demonstrated his ability to handle any other beast. Third, medieval people perceived tigers and wild buffalo as mighty and arrogant, so legends using these characteristics metaphorically could attract readers beyond the Buddhist community and potentially convert them.

Regional differences can be seen in the narratives of Buddhist hagiographies. Many legends associated with tigers and wild buffalo tell of the experiences of monks who traveled or lived in southern China,[67] while legends told by monks in northern China often enlist tigers, wild dogs, and leopards. For instance, in the seventh century, a monk called Puji 普濟 from Yongzhou 雍州 (modern Xi'an, Shaanxi) often wandered in the wilderness but was always successful in avoiding wild dogs and tigers (figure 3.3).[68] He was a devoted monk who studied the Avataṃsaka Sūtra (Huayan jing), and recited this text once every two days. His biography indicates that his dedicated study of sutra text was responsible for his extraordinary ability to survive while living among wild dogs and tigers.[69] Another monk, Pu'an 普安 (c. sixth century) from Jingyang 涇陽 (modern Jingyang, Shaanxi), cultivated ascetic practice and pretended to die in the wilderness, and

3.3 A Buddhist monk surrounded by a herd of beasts, including a tiger, a dog, a snake, and more. Mogao Cave 74, Dunhuang. c. 8th century.

© *Dunhuang shiku quanji*, 2000.

although he tried to offer his body to wild dogs and tigers, they would only smell him and turn away.[70] These two legends emanate from the area commonly known as the Guanzhong 關中 (the area within the pass, Tongguan 潼關) in the medieval period.

Even though we should be cautious when considering the authenticity of these monastic legends, they reflect some part of the reality of the time, such as monks living and traveling in the wild for long periods of time, how they may have appeared and smelled like animals, and so on. One legend in medieval Chinese Buddhism concerns a monk from Silla, Wuxiang 無相 (679–756), who lived for a long time in the mountains and often slept on the ground. His robes became tattered, and his hair grew very long. A hunter once caught sight of him and, considering him an exotic animal, was about to shoot him when he stopped because he realized Wuxiang was a human being.[71] This story suggests that Wuxiang looked like a beast in the eyes of another man, although no mention is made as to whether he smelled like a man or a beast.

Gunavarman was probably the first monk in early medieval Chinese Buddhist narratives believed to possess the ability to tame tigers. According to his biography, while traveling during the day or at night, wherever he encountered a tiger he would pacify it by touching its head with a Buddhist scepter.[72] Gunavarman was a monk from Kashmir, and his story is not found in Central Asian sources. This may be because Chinese writers attempted to trace the genealogy of this tradition to Central Asia for Chinese readers. They had some reason to believe this too. First, tigers were not sighted in Central Asia with such frequency and, second, they were not dangerous, man-eating tigers. So, legends of monks taming tigers would not go down well in Central Asia where the lion remained a more feared beast. Besides, medieval Chinese Buddhists struggled to legitimize Buddhism as a tradition indigenous to China, divorcing it from its South Asian and Central Asian roots. After Gunavarman, many Chinese monks were portrayed as masters able to tame and pacify tigers by lecturing on the dharma, bestowing the precepts of the Three Refuges, reciting scripture, and even imitating Prince Mahāsattva by giving up their lives and sacrificing their bodies.

Around the fifth century, a monk called Tancheng 曇稱 was believed to have developed a reputation for compassion. At the end of the Liu Song period, in the Pengcheng 彭城 area (modern Xuzhou, Jiangsu), tigers were active on Jia Mountain 駕山 and constituted a serious threat to local villagers. Tancheng decided to sacrifice his body to prevent tiger attacks. He told local villagers that if he was eaten by tigers, the tragedy would come to an end. The villagers tried to stop him but he sat alone on the grass and chanted: "I use my body to placate your hunger and thirst and mitigate your willingness to cause harm, and in the future, you shall only eat high dharma food." At midnight, tigers came out to eat Tancheng, leaving only his head. Local villagers built a memorial mound to house his head and there were no tiger attacks in this area after his sacrifice.[73]

Over time, legends grew about how the mere presence of eminent monks could drive away the tiger. Other methods of pacifying tigers included setting up vegetable feasts (*zhaihui* 齋會), following the ritual of a circumambulating procession (*xingdao* 行道),[74] and bestowing precepts (*shoujie* 授戒). Zhikuan 志寬 (565–643) was a monk who traveled to Sichuan where hundreds of tigers attacked villages and harmed livestock and humans. One tiger was apparently the leader of this group. Zhang Xun 張遜, the military governor of Suizhou 遂州, heard that Zhikuan was a compassionate monk whose devotion was well known, so he dispatched a messenger to invite Zhikuan to resolve the crisis. Zhikuan taught local people how to set up vegetable feasts, to walk the path, and to observe the eight restrictions. It is recorded that by the evening, tiger violence had ceased.[75] Many other legends convey the benevolent influence of eminent monks. In medieval

Chinese Buddhist rhetoric, their virtues produced supernatural power that prevented tigers from disturbing the local area. Daochan 道禪 (457–527), a monk from Jiaozhi 交趾 (modern Vietnam), had a reputation for observing monastic precepts. He moved to reside and practice in a temple in Xianzhou Mountain 仙洲 (modern Wuyishan 武夷山, Fujian) where tiger violence was a huge problem for the local community, but upon his arrival it dissipated.[76]

In medieval Chinese Buddhist texts, while the tiger was regarded as an animal, its reputation had grown beyond that. The tiger could appear with mountain spirits and demons in interaction with men from the monastic order, even sometimes as the mountain spirit itself, a concept from traditional Chinese cosmology and not from the Buddhist tradition. Medieval Chinese monks had to deal with both mountain spirits and beasts such as tigers in their daily lives. According to his biography, an eminent monk named Hongming 弘明 (402–486) was a native of Shanyin 山陰, Kuaiji 會稽 (modern Shaoxing, Zhejiang) who went into the monastery at a young age. He practiced reciting the Lotus Sutra in the Cloud-Gate Temple (Yunmensi 雲門寺) in Shanyin and also practiced meditation and confession rituals. Each morning, as he sat down to meditate, he found his water jug full. Curious to find out who was doing him this service, he realized that the water was offered by heavenly beings (*devas*) who were moved by his sincere devotion. Once, a tiger entered his chamber while he was meditating and crouched beside his bed. It is written that the tiger did not leave but observed Hongming for a long time. Later, Hongming moved to the Shilao Temple (Shilaosi 石姥寺) in Yongxing 永興 (modern Xiaoshan 蕭山, Zhejiang) for further meditation, but he was disturbed by a mountain spirit. Hongming captured this mountain spirit and immobilized it with his rope belt, whereupon the spirit confessed and requested to be freed. So Hongming released it, and it never appeared again.[77] This story seems to show that monks could deal with at least two sorts of sentient beings, beasts from the Buddhist tradition and mountain spirits from the Chinese tradition.[78]

There are other examples of this dual ability. In the Sui dynasty, Zhenhui 真慧 (535–607) was another monk able to get along with the tiger and the mountain spirit. He practiced in the cave of a tiger during the summer and, as a result, the tiger evacuated the cave. When fall arrived, he left the cave and the tiger returned. When he was meditating, the mountain spirit helped him keep the time and alerted him whenever he was behind schedule. This story illustrates that both a tiger and mountain spirit could interact with a monk during meditative practice.[79] Some other examples show that mountain spirits and tigers accepted Buddhist teaching and converted. One case was that of Yu Falan 于法蘭 (c. fourth century). While living in a mountain cave, a tiger came to his stone chamber and turned into a domesticated animal. His biography also states that some mountain spirits came to accept his teaching because his virtue could move these spirits and other sentient beings. Zhidun 支遁 (314–366) wrote a eulogy praising his virtue and achievements.[80] Daoxing 道行 (751–820), a monk who was ordained in the Southern Marchmount 南嶽, went to Fengyang 灃陽 (modern Fengxian 灃縣, Changde, Hunan) to build a wooden chamber to serve as his residence. Tigers and leopards from the mountain crouched on his bed and chairs. His biography indicates that local mountain deities and spirits helped him with the construction of the chamber. In the mid-Tang dynasty, a monk named Weikuan 惟寬 was also skillful in taming a tiger in the Kuaiji area in 791 and bestowed the Eight Precepts to a mountain spirit in 792.[81]

In Korea, mountain spirits were often depicted in literature as wearing yellow robes and walking with a tiger. The tiger was regarded as the lord of the mountain and also the spirit of the mountain; therefore, it was worshiped by local villagers. The Chinese concept of mountain spirits protecting the monastic community and the state while helping monks in caves had an impact on medieval Korean culture.[82] In medieval China, the mountain spirit was sometimes portrayed in yellow robes and turned out to be a tiger, the king of the forest. A monk called Sengda 僧達 (c. sixth century) grew up in Daibei (modern Datong, Shanxi). He thoroughly studied Vinaya teachings and travelled from Luoyang to Jiankang 健康 (modern Nanjing, Jiangsu) where he received respect and patronage from the Liang emperor Wudi 梁武帝. He settled in the famous Tongtai Temple 同泰寺. With the fall of the Liang regime, he returned to northern China and entered the city of Ye 鄴城. The Northern Qi emperor Wenxuan 文宣帝 constructed the Honggu Temple 洪谷寺 in Mount Linlü 林廬山 for him. One day, as Sengda climbed a mountain, a ferocious tiger blocked his path. He explained to the tiger that he had come to the temple to benefit all sentient beings and the tiger yielded the way to him. Later, the tiger transformed into a mountain spirit wearing a yellow robe to visit him and requested to be called by the spirit's true name and to receive blessings. Then Sengda asked his disciple to recite the *Golden Light Sutra*. But one day the tiger was caught in the act of eating a dog and Sengda realized that his disciple had been lazy and failed to recite the Buddhist scripture to bless the tiger. He interrogated his disciple who confessed that he had recited the Vimalakīrti Nirdeśa Sūtra rather than the Golden Light Sutra. He asked his disciple to worship the Buddha and to burn incense and explained to the tiger that reciting the Vimalakīrti Nirdeśa Sūtra was enough to bring blessings. The tiger then released the dog into the temple.[83] This story clearly shows that in medieval Chinese Buddhist hagiography, tigers could understand different Buddhist scriptures and knew which sutra brought blessings. The tiger could transform into a mountain spirit to communicate with eminent monks and perhaps even had the intelligence to converse with revered monks.

Taming beasts, especially tigers, gradually came to be regarded as one of the most important credentials of an eminent monk. As Shen Yue 沈約 (441-513) noted in his "Preface to Inner Scriptures" (Neidian xu 內典序), eminent monks often changed their bodily appearance and marks to tame wild buffalo and tigers.[84] Non-Buddhist medieval Chinese literature rarely discusses how to tame a tiger. It may have been possible for a villager or a hunter not to be afraid of a tiger, yet actively taming or taking a tiger as a disciple seems to be the preserve of eminent monks, according to medieval Chinese Buddhist hagiographical narratives. For these monks, taming tigers was not a technique similar to the skills of a modern-day lion tamer, because the monks relied on Buddhist wisdom and practiced high virtue. There were three kinds of practices in this respect: precepts, concentration, and wisdom. It appears that monks could interact with violent tigers in multiple ways such as driving them away, taming them, and transforming them into companions.

Major techniques used by monks to tame tigers included employing the power of the dharma scepter (or mace), reciting Buddhist scripture, and bestowing them with precepts. In medieval Chinese Buddhist discourse, when a monk's meditation and cultivation reached a high level, he could use his consciousness to transform the surrounding environment into a forest of virtue and merit, which became a consecrated ritual space keeping beasts and demons away. If beasts and birds entered this space, monks could use their power to tame them and transform them into disciples. The dharma scepter was a powerful tool for taming tigers in medieval Chinese Buddhist writings. Benru 本如, who was a master in lecturing on the Lotus Sutra, the Nirvana Sutra, the Golden Light Sutra, and the Amitāyurdhyāna Sūtra, saw a tiger sleeping in the southwestern corner of his temple. He used his scepter to touch the head of the tiger and told it that the temple was not the right place for sleeping.[85] The tiger woke up and left immediately. Later, a pavilion was constructed in the place where the tiger was sleeping, which later became known as the famous Tiger-Creek Pavilion 虎溪亭 of the White Lotus Temple 白蓮寺.[86] This story suggests that the power of Benru's mace followed from his long-term lecturing on many important scriptures.

Another monk, Faxiang 法響 (553–630), left his parents at the age of sixteen and became the disciple of Master Zhiyi 智顗. He recited the Lotus Sutra and constructed a dharma-lotus hall beside the Qixia Temple 棲霞寺. Without telling the others, he also practiced the concentration (*samādhi*) confession ritual and achieved enlightenment. The area where he lived was threatened by frequent tiger attacks, and one day local villagers set up a vegetable feast to pray for release from the terror of the tiger. Suddenly, a tiger appeared at the assembly and caught one person in its jaws. Faxiang called out to the tiger that the feast had been set up for it and requested the tiger to leave that person alone. The tiger then released the captive. Later, a group of tigers came to join in the feast and participants were afraid and started to run away. Faxiang presented himself and used his mace to touch the heads of these tigers and lecture them on the dharma. After the feast, the village never experienced tiger attacks again and, indeed, all the tigers moved away from this village.[87]

Besides using the dharma mace to tame tigers, medieval monks also used their hands to caress their head and back, or to bestow precepts to tigers. Benjing 本凈 (c. eighth century) helped tame a group of tigers in the mountain by caressing the head of the leader, who left without blocking the path of the woodcutters.[88] According to these narratives, bestowing the precept of the Three Refuges to tigers could also tame them. Facong 法聰 (468–559) resided on Sangai Mountain 傘蓋山 in Xiangyang 襄陽 where he had constructed a small house in which to pursue cultivating his mind. In his house, two tigers often stayed with him. The Liang Prince of Jin'an 晉安王 Xiao Fangzhi 蕭方智 (543–558) came to visit him and was afraid of the tigers but Facong told the tigers not to harm his friend. Xiao asked Facong for help in stopping tiger attacks in his area. Facong responded by immediately going into meditation, upon which seventeen large tigers entered his house. Facong bestowed the precepts of Three Refuges on these tigers and commanded them not to harm local villagers. It is said that the tigers accepted his demand and left the area.[89]

According to medieval Chinese Buddhist hagiographies, tigers not only converted to Buddhism but also studied it by listening to sutra recitation. Sengsheng 僧生 (c. fourth to fifth centuries) was a monk from the Sichuan area who became the head of the Sanxian Temple 三賢寺 in Chengdu 成都. He had a reputation for reciting the Lotus Sutra and his meditation was exemplary. It was stated that once, when he went to the mountain to recite the Lotus Sutra, he attracted tigers to listen.[90] Although taming tigers by reciting sutras was a Chinese convention, the tradition of reciting sutras to beasts can be traced back to early medieval Chinese Buddhist narratives. According to the *Biographies of Eminent Monks*, Faxian 法顯 (337–422), the famous Chinese pilgrim who traveled to South Asia, once encountered lions and recited sutras to avoid being harmed by them. When he journeyed to Rāja-gṛha 王舍城, he was told by monks in a nearby temple that, along the way, he may encounter black lions. Faxian insisted on continuing his journey and arrived at a mountain. He burned incense and was praying at midnight when three black lions came to attack him. As Faxian carried on reciting the sutras and also kept taking the Buddha's name, the lions were enticed to lie down at his feet. Faxian touched their heads and said, "If you want to harm me, please allow me to finish the recitation." Soon after he finished the recitation, the lions left.[91] This story is not supported by other sources, such as Faxian's memoir. It might be an addition of the biography compiler. There is no evidence to verify whether Faxian recited the sutras in Sanskrit or in a local dialect of Central Asia, or even in the Chinese language, but whatever language he used, the biography indicated that three black lions understood his recitation.

The legends in the previous discussion also indicate that many popular Mahāyāna texts were an important part in this narrative of monks taming tigers in China. The Lotus Sutra was one of the most important such texts. Other texts include the Avataṃsaka Sūtra, the Diamond Sutra, the Golden Light Sutra, and the Vimalakīrti Nirdeśa Sūtra. The Diamond Sutra became more popular in the late Tang dynasty. Daoyin 道蔭 (c. ninth century) was a monk devoted to reciting the Diamond Sutra. In the early ninth century, he encountered a tiger who jumped out in front of him during a walk. He was scared and began reciting the Diamond Sutra for protection. The tiger withdrew and crawled back into the grasses without making any aggressive move.[92] Many biographies of monks in medieval China record incidents where eminent monks verbally communicated with tigers; that is how they could live together. An Indian monk, Zhu Fodiao, 竺佛調 (c. fourth and fifth centuries) resided in the Changshan Temple 常山寺 for several years. On a lone trip to the mountains, he was stalled by a snowstorm and entered a cave where a tiger resided. When the tiger came back in the night, Fodiao talked to it and explained why he was there: the tiger was not angry and left him alone.[93] Fashi 法施 (c. seventh century) was a monk who lived in the Dhūta

Temple near Jiangling 江陵 (modern Jingzhou 荆州, Hubei). A tiger served as an attendant in his room. When a guest came to visit Fashi, he spoke to the tiger and asked him to close his eyes to avoid scaring the guest. He referred to the tiger as "the Buddhist gentleman" (fozi 佛子). Once the tiger understood the directive, he lowered his head and closed his eyes. Fashi treated this tiger as a family pet.[94]

Three other biographies mention how eminent monks could communicate with tigers. Fachong 法沖 (c. early seventh century) was a native of Chengji 成紀, Longxi (modern Tianshui 天水, Gansu). He was in the mountains when he found a cave under a huge cliff, but it belonged to a tiger. So he spoke to the tiger, asking permission for a place to sleep, and the tiger understood and allowed him to stay.[95] Daocheng 道澄 (c. 803) was at a summer retreat on Yunyang Mountain 雲陽山 (modern Chaling 茶陵, Hunan) when a tiger accidentally ran into his room. He talked to the tiger, who shook his tail and left.[96] The third story is about Huiwen 慧聞 (c. seventh century) who used his mace to touch a tiger and a leopard and talked to them while traveling. Interestingly, all these legends illustrate that the communication was one way, with the monks speaking to the tigers. It is quite possible that several eminent monks dwelled in the mountains for long periods, and after becoming familiar with the habits of beasts were thus able to communicate with them. In Chinese Buddhist literature, the first translator, An Shigao, was said to be able to master the sounds of birds and beasts, in addition to his other miraculous abilities, his knowledge in medicine and astrology, and other skills.[97]

In medieval Chinese Buddhist legends, monks seem to have kept tigers as companions and pets. One particular monk named Huiyong 慧永 (332–414) had a tiger as his companion in his meditation chamber at the top of a peak on Mount Lu. His patron was Tao Fan 陶范, the prefect of Xunyang 潯陽 (modern Jiujiang, Jiangxi), who offered a house and converted it into a temple on Mount Lu for Huiyong. If a guest came to find shelter in Huiyong's meditation chamber, Huiyong usually moved a tiger out and gave the room to the guest. Fajin 法進, a monk who lived in the Jade Maiden Temple 玉女寺 in Mianzhu 綿竹 County (modern Mianzhu, Deyang, Sichuan) near Yizhou 益州, meditated in the bamboo forest behind his temple. Four tigers often accompanied him.

One story describes a tiger that served as the travel guide for nuns. A nun named Minggan 明感 from Gaoping 高平 (modern Gaoping, Jincheng, Shanxi) attempted to find a place to practice ascetic cultivation within the mountains but lost her way. She then encountered a tiger who was only a few feet away from her. At first, she was frightened until she noticed how the tiger walked ahead of her and guided her for several days until she finally reached Qingzhou 青州 (modern Qingzhou, Shandong). As she entered the village, the tiger disappeared.[98] There are other stories about how tigers guarded and observed the practice of nuns. Jingcheng 靜稱 was a nun who lived alone in a mountainous area. A tiger always stayed beside her and observed her while she meditated. There was a nunnery in the area where those who had taken their vows but violated the precepts went to confess. The tiger became restless when the nun did not confess soon enough, but it showed his joy when she did so quickly.[99]

According to legend, Huizhong 惠忠 (683-769), the sixth patriarch of the Oxhead School of Chan Buddhism, was also protected by tigers. In a village with a grain barn for storing the monastery's food supplies, bandits came to steal the food one night. A tiger that served Huizhong jumped out of the bush and roared, frightening the bandits away and waking up the guard. The local magistrate Zhang Xun 張遜 came to visit Huizhong and asked him if he could meet some of his disciples. Huizhong replied that he had between three to five disciples and then tapped his bed three times. Three tigers jumped out from around him to prove that Huizhong actually considered these tigers to be his disciples.[100]

A Chan master named Shanjue 善覺, who resided in the Hualin Temple 華林寺 in Tanzhou 潭州 (modern Changsha 長沙, Hunan) was said to have two tigers as his servants. The Surveillance Commissioner of Hunan (Hunan guancha shi 湖南觀察使) Pei Xiu 裴休 (791-864) came to visit him. When Pei asked the master if he had any servants, Shanjue answered yes and called out their names, "Big Emptiness" 大空 and "Little Emptiness" 小空. Two tigers jumped out to meet them, taking Pei by surprise. Shanjue eventually asked the tigers to leave, and they roared and left. In the Song dynasty, the Chan master Fazhong 法忠 (1084-1149) was believed to have the power to summon dragons to bring rain, and to ride tigers in his daily life. According to his biography, Fazhong was from Siming (now the eastern region of Zhejiang) and began to study the Tiantai tradition after he received his full ordination at the age of nineteen. He then traveled to visit eminent Chan masters for further learning and practiced asceticism in Lu Mountain, where he lived with snakes and tigers. During the Xuanhe period (1119-1125), the Xiangtan area experienced extreme drought. Local residents prayed for rain to no avail until Fazhong decided to help and summoned a dragon that brought rain. He lived in the South Marchmount (Nanyue) for a while and often rode a tiger to go from place to place. Whenever local Confucians and Buddhists saw him, they paid homage.[101] This narrative highlights Fazhong's extraordinary ability in summoning a dragon and riding a tiger,[102] which of course aims to boost his image as an eminent Chan master. As we see in the next section, a similar narrative also appeared in the biographies of eminent figures in Daoism.

A COMPARISON WITH MEDIEVAL EUROPEAN HAGIOGRAPHIES

In discussing the possibility of comparing ancient East and West, Walter Scheidel points out that "transcultural comparison, by contrast, tends to focus on a potentially universal repertoire of possible forms of features and processes (power, production, socialization, cultural symbolism, etc.)."[103] He suggests that any comparison should have a clear agenda about what goal should be accomplished and what questions should be answered.

The focus thus far in this chapter has been on the taming of tigers in medieval Chinese Buddhist hagiographies and portraying the image of Buddhist monks as eminent monks. Tigers are cruel and violent beasts, and they were said to hurt livestock and take human lives. Eminent monks appeared as cultural heroes who could purportedly tame these beasts in nature and extend their religious power to the wilderness by using their wisdom and compassion. The narratives about this taming practice serve to highlight the power of these revered monks for their spiritual wisdom and compassion. These narratives became the monastic rhetorical tools for contemporary Buddhist readers who would read and accept the Buddhist values of eminent monks. A comparative question, then, would be whether medieval Christian accounts have the same strategy and rhetoric for creating narratives about the taming of beasts by Christian saints or if these Christian hagiographies used similar narratives of taming beasts for portraying their saints to persuade their actual and potential followers to admire and venerate them.

In Christian narratives, unlike tigers in medieval Chinese religions, other beasts often appeared. The discussion of taming beasts in medieval Christian hagiographies began with St. Francis of Assisi's (1182–1226) story, which of course is much later than the historical period of focus in this chapter. His taming a wolf with compassion in Gubbio became a well-known legend in the Franciscan tradition. In his era, a wolf lived in the suburb of Gubbio and threatened local residents. When he saw this beast, he displayed his Catholic cross, and in the name of Jesus he commanded the wolf to stop attacking humans. He also explained Christian theology to this wolf and denounced its sin for committing murder. This wolf obeyed St. Francis and promised not to disturb the local community. Then St. Francis brought it to the village where it behaved like a lamb.[104] The principle and structure of this story is exactly the same as what we have learned about the eminent monks who tamed violent tigers and brought peace to the local community.

In medieval European literature, the forest was commonly regarded as barbaric and chaotic. It seems as if southwest China was conceived similarly, a place full of disease and plague with deep forests in which travelers often became lost. For medieval European Christians, Christian saints could conquer the forest—the barbaric, dangerous, and chaotic place. A lot of anthologies told such stories and they certainly reflect the propaganda from the medieval Christian church regarding the power and impact of Christian morality. This conquering power of Christian saints was widely believed by Christians. They believed that these saints could travel to many remote places and survive in the dangerous and dark wilderness without being harmed. Both the ideology developed in the Christian church and the common perception among Christians together created the intimate connections between beasts and Christian saints.

Some common features are highlighted in a comparison of medieval Chinese monks with medieval European Christian saints. In general, the encounters between eminent monks and tigers should be read as personal experiences, and many cases of taming the tiger could be read in terms of the individual behaviors of each monk. When these stories were written into the biographies of eminent monks, they illustrated the collective experience of the monastic community and the collective memory recorded in Buddhist history. Such accounts resonate closely with the encounters of Christian saints with beasts in medieval Europe. In medieval European Christian hagiographies, there were numerous stories about the encounters between saints and beasts.[105] The intimate connection between Christian saints and beasts can be traced back to the story of St. Anthony in the third century. In the Christian tradition, he is regarded as one of the founders of early Christian monasticism.

When St. Anthony learned of a hermit called Paul who had practiced asceticism within a cave for about sixty years, he was intent on finding him in the desert. He received assistance from a wolf during his journey, and eventually this wolf helped him locate the cave where Paul was practicing. St. Anthony and Paul quickly became good friends. Even a crow brought food for them. Later, Paul passed away, and two lions came to dig a grave for him. They did not return to the nearby forest until Paul was buried.[106] This story in Christian lore sought to tell readers that Paul was a highly cultivated and accomplished Christian saint whose virtue attracted animals to serve him both during his life and after his death.

As contemporary scholarship has demonstrated, according to *Vita Antonii*, a fourth-century biography of St. Anthony written by Athanasius (293–373), the desert was portrayed as a landscape full of various beasts, demons, and supernatural beings. These beings became threats to the self-identity of humans, especially Christian ascetics. In ancient times, it was commonly believed that if humans entered the desert, they had to deal with all these nonhuman beings. So early Christian writers created an image of St. Anthony as a human figure who could calmly face these challenges from nonhumans and play a vital role in Christian history. As an ascetic, he could endure poverty, hardship, and overcome all difficulties for manifesting the will of God. These characteristics secured his survival in the desert.[107]

From a theological perspective, Clarence J. Glacken suggests that the intimate connection between animals and humans reflected a special ideal in medieval Christianity. To achieve this ideal, after humans were corrupted by the temptation in the Garden of Eden, they purified their sins and recovered from corruption by gaining a supernatural ability to rule nature and to command beasts.[108] In medieval Christian concepts, those ascetic saints who practiced in solitude were endowed with innocence and holiness so they could face beasts with their tranquil and harmonic attitudes. These traits of innocence, holiness, tranquility, and harmony originated from the situation in which Adam and Eve were living with the natural world without any conflict. Thus, medieval Christian literature took these qualities for saints to develop a harmonic relationship with the natural world, including beasts who lived in nature.[109]

The early period of human history in Christian tradition looks similar to what we know about Daoism in ancient China, since in Daoism it was said that there was a harmony between humans and nature as well as animals, an ideal condition in the history of mankind. Later this condition was disrupted by those people who did not follow Dao, the Way.

Laura Hobgood-Oster suggests that there were four types of relationships between saints and animals in medieval Christian hagiographies: animals as exemplars of piety, animals as sources of revelation, animals as saintly martyrs, and animals as primary intimate others.[110] The first type refers to animals who attended Mass in church, were baptized, received the Holy Eucharist, listened to church preaching, and participated in worship. From the earlier discussion of eminent Buddhist monks and tigers in medieval China, it is clear that there are some similarities here. These monks also brought tigers to attend Buddhist rituals; they ordained tigers and invited tigers to share their vegetarian feasts. In some cases, eminent monks had tigers sit as the audience to listen to their lectures or recitations on the Lotus Sutra, Diamond Sutra, or the Golden Light Sutra.

The second type refers to those animals who served as messengers of the divine to human beings, the bearers or carriers of the incarnation of the sacred, and the bearers of Christ. Hobgood-Oster specifically used a story about how a stag delivered the divine message to a Roman soldier named Placidus. In medieval Chinese Buddhist hagiographies, animals, especially tigers, were not portrayed as messengers of the Buddha; yet in the Buddhist tradition, animals often appeared as reincarnated beings who taught Buddhist morality to followers. Numerous stories in the Jātaka contain such narratives. Medieval Chinese Buddhist encyclopedias absorbed these narratives and made them widely available to medieval Chinese monks and lay Buddhists. For example, many stories appeared in *Differentiated Manifestations of the Sutras and Vinayas* and *Pearl Forest of Dharma Grove*.

The third type refers to animals as martyrs and servants. As Hobgood-Oster notes, "Following the example set by Jesus, martyrs claimed a second and ultimate baptism in blood. Their stories were told throughout Christianity to strengthen the commitments of believers facing repression. But some of these martyrs are not just symbolically but literally sacrificial lambs."[111] She offers the horse, pig, lamb, and several other animals as examples, concluding that "the symbol of animals as sacrificial victims and even as savior is central to Christianity."[112] She particularly highlights lambs as common sacrificial victims and lions as servants in death and funeral rituals.

It should be noted that in medieval Chinese Buddhism, animals were not used for sacrifices. Yet some eminent monks sacrificed themselves to tigers, also following what the Buddha did in his previous life as Prince Mahāsattva, as the tigress story in the Jātakamālā told. In medieval Chinese Buddhist hagiographies and the biographies in Chinese official histories, it was stated that after the death of eminent monks and filial officials, some animals would come and surround their tombs and mourn. This also happened with many Christian saints. After St. Regulus passed away, a group of deer gathered around his tomb in mourning. When St. Fingar died, a deer came and prayed before his corpse.

The fourth type of relationship refers to animals that appeared as primary others to medieval Christian saints. Many hermits and desert dwellers such as St. Jerome (c. 340-420), St. Giles, and St. Blaise in early Christian monasticism lived with animals as companions. The story of St. Jerome having a lion was widely known to Christians, and the story was often depicted in Christian art. Besides lions, an ass also appeared as his pet. St. Jerome saved a wounded lion while he was studying in a Christian monastery and transformed this lion into his servant.[113] St. Euphemia's life was connected with a lion and a bear. The lion played an important role in the lives of John the Silent, Simeon, and Gerasimus of Jordan.[114] In short, none of these stories are unique in medieval European Christianity, and many of similar descriptions could be found in medieval Chinese Buddhist narratives.

As we have seen in this chapter, many eminent Buddhist monks had tigers as their companions in the wilderness. As in Buddhism, beasts in Christian hagiographies occasionally played the role of heroes who save humans from trouble. In the story of St. Malchus, for instance—a Christian hermit captured and enslaved by the Ishmaelites—he and a fellow Christian escaped and were saved by a lioness. This story is similar to medieval Chinese Buddhist hagiographies in which eminent monks could save a tiger, and the tiger could, in turn, save eminent monks from bandits.[115]

CONCLUSION

Taming tigers and stopping tiger violence became crucial methods used by medieval Buddhists to produce religious and cultural capital and to compete for followers with Confucianism and Daoism. For medieval Chinese Buddhist monks, teaching and transforming tigers occurred with the purpose of civilizing them. For these monks, the boundaries between humans and animals were the same as those between Buddhism and non-Buddhism, and to those between the space of enlightenment and the space of nature.

In this chapter we see that the narratives of tiger taming by eminent monks appeared as unique characteristics in medieval Chinese Buddhist hagiographies.

This type of narrative did not originate in southern Asia where tigers were neither culturally nor religiously significant animals. This narrative was not from
Central Asia, where tigers were extinct. In ancient China, the idea of communicating with the spirit of animals had a long history and certainly an impact on
the development of Buddhist thought regarding the taming of tigers. In this sense,
the medieval Chinese Buddhist narratives on taming tigers were a hybrid tradition mixing traditional Chinese thought on communicating with animals and
Buddhist thought regarding compassion toward beasts as sentient beings.

Interestingly, Buddhist taming violent beasts in medieval China might remind
us of the Buddha's story of taming the maddened elephant Nāḷāgiri in early Buddhist Jātaka narratives. As Reiko Ohnuma notes, "The Buddha's effortless and
instantaneous taming of the maddened elephant Nāḷāgiri dramatically demonstrates his absolute mastery over the forces of nature, animality, and passion, as
well as his superior masculinity in comparison to the many male disciples who
surround him."[116] Ohnuma thus analyzes the taming of the maddened elephant
as a grand public spectacle. Indeed, on the one hand, medieval Chinese Buddhist
narratives on taming tigers seem to echo this Buddhist sentiment of mastering
nature and animality with their power of compassion. On the other hand, in most
cases, medieval Chinese Buddhist monks' taming of tigers were depicted in the
private scenes without public display. The taming scene by no means could be
regarded as the grand public spectacle and usually could not be witnessed by
numerous audiences. Furthermore, though only some talented and highly accomplished monks could access the power of taming, this power does open to the
nuns. As I mention earlier in the chapter, nuns occasionally also demonstrated
their Buddhist power of taming tigers, which means in medieval Chinese Buddhist monasticism the power of taming was not limited to the masculine group.

The advent of tiger taming in medieval Chinese Buddhism was a crucial development in helping Chinese Buddhism create roots in Chinese society, as it
offered an alternative for eminent monks to serve and save local communities.
These monks traveled from their monastic spaces to mountains and forests, and
they often met beasts in nature. They viewed the mountains and forests as ritual
places for their cultivation and performance. Taming, teaching, and transforming
beasts was the manner of their religious life in the wilderness, since beasts were
also sentient beings in the cycle of life, death, and rebirth.

In the meantime, medieval Chinese Buddhist narratives seemed to be highly
selective and exemplary. They highlighted the ability of monks to tame violent

and cruel tigers—the mightiest beasts in the natural environment of East Asia. On one hand, the monks lived in solitude in the mountains and forests. It was highly likely that they would encounter beasts, especially tigers. After all, in medieval China, tigers were common across the country. If monks expanded their activities into nature, they would certainly invade the territory traditionally ruled by tigers. In other words, this extension of monks into the wilderness defined an intersection between human beings and the animal kingdom.

On the other hand, in ancient China, tigers were regarded as the king of the animal realm and the ruler of all beasts. For people in medieval China, taming tigers was the biggest challenge one could face in nature. Taming a tiger or being spared by a tiger demonstrated extraordinary ability and success. Taming violent tigers also indicated a supreme control over nature. From a Buddhist perspective, because violent and cruel tigers would harm livestock and humans, they would appear as destructively powerful and uncivilized sentient beings. Taming them and converting them to Buddhism would bring these savage beasts into Buddhist civilization, which was not only the responsibility of monks but also a requirement of monks for moving toward final enlightenment.

In general, it appears that the encounter of monks with tigers produced three levels of relationships. First, medieval Chinese monks may not have been afraid of tigers, or they simply did not run away from tigers, since they knew that the power of their wisdom and virtue would prevent tigers from harming them. When tigers met these monks, the tigers just walked away without further interaction. Second, when medieval Chinese monks encountered tigers, they made friends with tigers and had tigers as their companions, indicating mutual trust and respect. They could live together harmoniously in the mountains and forests rather than compete for space and resources. Third, medieval Chinese monks converted tigers into Buddhists, and even into disciples, and transformed the space where tigers lived into the realm of Buddhist teaching.

In this chapter I interpret the taming of tigers in medieval Chinese Buddhist hagiographies as a narrative, a Buddhist rhetoric, a ritual, and a cultural trait that served as Buddhist teaching and transformation. First, the narrative of taming tigers serves to differentiate between prominent and common monks. It creates a new hierarchical order within the monastic community by creating exemplary figures and role models. Second, the narrative of taming tigers makes Buddhism different from other religious, cultural, and political Chinese traditions. In particular, it creates a boundary between Buddhism and Confucianism. In Buddhism, eminent monks did not hunt down or simply move tigers away by their virtue but tamed and converted tigers. Buddhism attempted to use its compassion and wisdom to transform tigers into Buddhists. Third, the narrative of taming tigers made Chinese Buddhism different from early Buddhism, or southern Asian Buddhism, due to its innovation of taming tigers as a new tradition. Eminent monks in medieval Chinese Buddhism could conquer and tame the rulers of the animal kingdom in East Asia, the tigers. Finally, the narrative of taming tigers in medieval Chinese Buddhism also made the human world different from the natural world. Eminent monks in the human world could tame and transform the beasts from the natural world. Buddhism could civilize the tigers and also other beasts and extend its power, compassion, and wisdom into the natural world, the mountains, forests, and jungles, or in the wilderness in general. By taming tigers, Buddhist monks in fact extended Buddhist culture or Buddhist civilization into the wilderness, for which the counterpart could be also found in medieval European Christianity.

By performing the ritual of taming tigers, medieval Chinese monks transformed the beasts they tamed into Buddhists and transformed themselves into eminent monks. In medieval Chinese Buddhist hagiographical narratives, only distinguished monks who had reached a certain level of virtue and wisdom could perform the ritual of taming tigers. Their eminence was verified by the efficacy of the ritual they performed. In other words, the prominence of the medieval Chinese Buddhist monks and the usefulness of performing rituals of taming tigers were mutually linked with each other.

From a broader historical context in Eurasian continent, in light of the animal-human relationship, there are similarities and differences between European Christianity and Chinese religions. In the traditions of both sides, religious saints were portrayed as power brokers superior to beasts. Both Christianity and Buddhism as well as Daoism developed a series of discourses and rituals for converting and taming animals in order to extend their powers into the from human realm to the natural world. Religious monasticism served as a dynamic organism marching from human society to nature. The discussion on Daoism and beasts in next chapter will further enhance this argument.

CHAPTER 4

Daoists Transforming Ferocious Tigers

Practical Techniques and Rhetorical Strategies

The challenges from ferocious tigers in medieval China were not unique to Confucian literati officials and Buddhist monks. With the rise of Daoist monasticism in medieval China, Daoist priests often encountered real tigers in the natural wilderness; they developed various strategies and techniques for handling tigers in their social and religious lives and for engaging with both the animal realm and local communities. But Daoist philosophies developed in ancient China already included fruitful discourses on the tiger. In fact, Daoist art and literature often depicted the tiger and the dragon as two of the most important symbolic animals. Therefore, there would always be a gap between traditional Daoist philosophical values and Daoist monastic practices in medieval China, which makes examining Daoist approaches to wild tigers in nature particularly interesting.

As wild animals, tigers played various roles in medieval Chinese Daoist apologetic and narrative literature; they could serve as companions to Daoist hermits in the mountains, as threats to Daoist practitioners, and as weapons used by Daoists against their rivals, such as Buddhists. In the medieval period, the expansion of human activities intensified conflicts between humans and animals in China, often disturbing the balance between the social and ecological order. With the constant growth of the Daoist ecclesiastical order, Daoist priests also expanded the scope of their interactions with the natural environment and local society. Daoism developed a more systematic textual tradition that included more details about the daily lives of Daoist priests, and Daoist hagiographies were composed and compiled to create images of eminent priests as role models in Daoist life. Daoists also left numerous fantastical stories to account for the practical techniques and rhetorical strategies they used to deal with beasts, including tigers.

Thus Daoist attitudes and approaches to the tiger reflect not only how medieval Daoists understood the cosmological, ecological, and social order, but also how they shaped their concepts of socioreligious life and the ecological system of their world.

In this chapter I analyze the attitudes and methods in the Daoist approach to handling tiger violence, and examine the ethics reflected in those approaches. I base my analysis on four elements: daily experiences and cognition vis-a-vis encounters with beasts and the natural environment; cosmological and doctrinal foundations; challenges by and competition from religious peers; and challenges from social and historical reality. Medieval Daoist hagiographical literature can tell us how these elements shaped and reshaped Daoist attitudes and methods for dealing with tiger violence, by providing numerous narratives about Daoist priests and devoted practitioners' interactions with the natural environment, local communities, and other religious and cultural traditions, which differ in their approach to nature compared to early Daoist philosophical texts, such as the *Daode jing* and the *Book of Zhuangzi*.[1] Within these four elements, I focus on the following three issues: First, how Daoists understood and dealt with the tiger was governed by doctrines and disciplines, cosmologically and ethically, which can be found in the Daoist textual tradition. Second, Daoists often changed their attitudes about animals by learning from and reacting to conflicts and competition with other traditions, especially Buddhism and Confucianism.[2] Third, Daoist cognition of animals was shaped and reshaped by daily experiences in both the natural environment and socioeconomic life. Many Daoists lived in the mountains and forests, and they were thus regularly faced with the challenge of beasts, including tigers; furthermore, some Daoists used domesticated animals in their social and economic lives, such as for agriculture and transportation, so conflicts between these domesticated animals and wild beasts also posed an issue.

THE SIGNIFICANCE AND POSITION OF THE TIGER IN DAOIST COSMOLOGY

The tiger has been a central subject in the study of medieval Daoist history. First, from an ecological viewpoint, the tiger was not only an apex predator in its own natural environment but was commonly perceived among the medieval Chinese populace as being ferocious and mighty. A subtle balance between the human and animal realms kept humans safe from attacks by wild animals, since these wild animals did not feel that their realm was invaded. When Daoist priests entered the wild forest and encountered tigers, they broke the natural boundaries between the human and animal realms. Those boundaries may have been flexible for the animals willing to retreat a bit as long as they had sufficient space to conduct a normal life. If their space became too constricted, though, confrontation with humans became inevitable. The stories we read about encounters between Daoist priests and tigers in the wilderness may sound spectacular, but we cannot simply dismiss them as fabricated legends. Instead, they reflect some historical and environmental realities of the real challenges that nature posed for Daoists who lived and traveled to the wilderness.

Second, from a historical and cultural perspective, one of the direst social problems in medieval China was the imminent threat to human and livestock from ferocious tigers. As noted in previous chapters, local communities were constantly endangered by "tiger violence" (*hubao* 虎暴). As we saw in chapter 3, medieval Chinese Buddhist hagiographical literature attempted to demonstrate the eminence of monks who were capable of taming and transforming tigers.[3] As a follow-up to these discussions, we can ask additional questions concerning how Daoists handled tiger violence: What rituals did they perform? How was their way of dealing with tiger violence different from that of the Buddhists in the medieval period? What was the doctrinal foundation behind the differences? Did they learn the attitude and method of facing the challenge of tiger violence from the Buddhists, or did they attempt to provide an alternative to local communities? Did they develop a new discourse against tiger violence to compete with their Buddhist rivals?

Third, in the eyes of medieval Chinese Daoists, the metaphor of the tiger occupies a unique position that can be traced back to the tradition known as miraculous birth of the Celestial Masters (Tianshidao). The Daoist hagiographical text includes a story about Zhang Daoling 張道陵, the founder of this Daoist tradition. When he was making his Divine Elixir of the Nine Heavens on a mountain in South China, a dragon and a tiger appeared. The green dragon and the white tiger—symbols of mercury and lead, respectively, the two ingredients for making elixirs—served as the main metaphors in the Daoist tradition for internal and external alchemy.[4] In commemorating this legend, Daoists named this mountain the Dragon and Tiger Mountain; it is located in modern Jiangxi Province.[5] So as a symbolic beast who witnessed the power of the founding master of Daoist tradition, the tiger plays a crucial role in the early history of Daoist doctrine and cosmology. The connection between alchemy and the symbolism of tiger and dragon has a long history in Daoist literature, but here I want to emphasize its association with the founder of the tradition in Daoist narratives.

Fourth, one of the important Daoist deities in medieval China, the Queen Mother of the West (Xiwangmu 西王母), has a strong symbolic connection with the tiger that can be traced back to ancient China.[6] Suzanne E. Cahill states that people as early as the Shang dynasty already linked their maternal deity with "the tiger, a symbol of the west since neolithic times, an agent of death and transportation to the spirit world."[7] In a scene on a pottery tomb relief, dated to the later Han dynasty and found in the vicinity of Chengdu, Sichuan, the Queen Mother of the West is depicted as a goddess with her entourage (figure 4.1) under a canopy, with a dragon to the left and a tiger to the right. The tiger and dragon signify

4.1 A pottery tomb relief from the later Han dynasty found in the vicinity of Chengdu, Sichuan Provincial Museum.

west and east, yin and yang, and death and life, respectively.[8] Martha L. Carter notes that as depicted in the *Classics of Mountains and Seas* Xiwangmu began her career as a forbidding combination of female and tiger, living alone: "The two symbolic animals depicted emerging from either side of her seat," she writes, "are a tiger and a dragon. . . . In Han China, the tiger and dragon are directional animals, affirming in a sense her power as a goddess of cosmic sway, but also they may be seen as theriomorphic incarnations of the goddess herself."[9]

Fifth (and last), despite the White Tiger's appearance as one of the four cardinal animals symbolizing the west, it was popularly regarded as a bloodthirsty demon. As the symbolic animal for the spirit of the Great White Star, it signified the destructive force of autumn. An encounter with the White Tiger Star was believed to presage death. Thus, it was believed that people born in the year of the tiger might bring harm to weddings, pregnancies, and newborn children. The Daoist text *Great Peace Scripture* (*Taipingjing*) regards the White Tiger as the stage of death in the cycle of life.[10]

Daoist attitudes toward the natural environment and animals are mixed and equivocal throughout Chinese history. Daoism is not a fixed and ahistorical tradition. Early Daoist philosophical works including the *Daode jing* and the *Book of Zhuangzi* laid some foundation for our understanding of nature and the ecological world in ancient China. E. N. Anderson and Lisa Raphals note that early Daoists sharply separated people from animals or humanity from nature. Daoists used animals for food, sacrifice, and service, but they maintained that animals should be used in ways based on their own natures. Anderson and Raphals also suggest that "early Daoism implies a morality of respect for the inner nature of things, and for the place of all things in the vast, ever-changing cosmic flow."[11] These attitudes gradually changed with the full establishment of Daoist ecclesiastical order in the medieval period.

Daily experiences would inform Daoist hermits in the mountains that the tiger had different eating habits from those of humans. Humans would not usually attack an animal as prey in the wilderness and eat its meat raw. When Daoist priests had to enter the wilderness, they needed to invent new discourses and rituals for overcoming potential difficulties. Would Daoist priests hold wilderness or nature in awe or respect? Not necessarily. They would feel awe and respect toward the Most High Lord of the Dao (Taishang laojun 太上老君) and the other Perfected Ones or "perfects" (*zhenren* 真人), their highest authorities of doctrines and their role model for practices. Medieval Daoist priests viewed the collapse of the natural ecology as the result of a disorder of the Dao, which means that living beings did not follow the leadership of the Dao and lost their faith in the Dao. The collapse of the ecosystem, then, does not reflect the wrongdoing of humans.

The balance of ecosystems, biodiversity, and environmental impacts are modern concepts that cannot be found in medieval Daoist cosmology. Modern emic and etic terminologies were created by modern scientific disciplines. As Paul R. Goldin reminds us, "we must avoid at all costs the myth that the ancients were somehow more in tune with nature, or that the deterioration of the environment is an exclusively modern phenomenon arising from the peculiar deficiencies of the modern outlook."[12] Although he does not believe that "the pre-industrial humans had a more profound comprehension of ecology or a more laudable attitude toward nature," he suggests that the Zhuangzian ideal of living in harmony with the external world could still inspire those people who might have accepted the typical Judeo-Christian way of viewing nature as a place for humanity to dominate.

The Zhuangzian ideal was based on early Daoist thought, yet I argue here that in medieval Daoism, the natural environment was dominated by the Daoist priests who could tame tigers and ride dragons. Medieval Daoist anthropocentric thinking still regarded the priests as the center of concern. The priests, not the natural environment, practiced and embodied the Way 道. The Way could only be found through the Daoist priests. Daoist priests could enlighten beasts such as tigers and leopards with what the Way was.

In medieval Daoist cosmology, the Most High Lord of the Dao is the highest sovereign responsible for creating and maintaining the cosmic order. In the power structure of this hierarchical order, divine figures such as the Most High Lord of the Dao are higher than human beings including Daoist priests, and the Daoist priests are higher than animals. The priests are working toward the status of transcendents. Among priests, the Heavenly Masters as community leaders enjoyed more respectful positions than common priests. Since the priests could command gods to drive tigers away, it seems that they are more powerful than tigers. Thus the tigers, even though they are regarded as apex predators in the natural realm, are inferior to human priests. John Snarey suggests that religious morality "can be a powerful force promoting the adaptation of a society to its environment."[13] For him, the continuing survival of a society depends upon the adherence to some moral codes that are commanded by a Supreme Deity who transcends society. It seems that in medieval Chinese Daoism, to ensure the survival of a Daoist order, the Most High Lord Lao appeared as a Supreme Deity and authorized the ethical power of Daoist practitioners to justify their attitudes toward the mountains and beasts. As Tuan Yi-fu also suggests: "An adaptive attitude toward nature has ancient roots in China. It is embodied in folklore, in the philosophical-ethical precepts of Taoism, and later, Buddhism, and it draws support from practical experience."[14] He notes some of the causes of deforestation, such as burning trees to deprive dangerous animals of their hiding places.

Daoism was a religious tradition created by humans, made within human society, and developed for humans. So, it is not surprising that its doctrines, rituals, and knowledge about nature, the environment, and animals are all centered on humans and serving the physiological, psychological, spiritual, and material needs of humans.

DAOIST TAMING OF THE WILD TIGER IN THE NATURAL WILDERNESS

Contemporary scholarship has paid attention to mountains in medieval Chinese religious life. With the construction of temples and religious sites, many mountainous regions were transformed.[15] While religious practitioners were living in the mountains, encounters with wild animals including tigers became inevitable. But the study of the roles of wild animals is still underdeveloped. Dealing with wild beasts such as tigers and snakes, as well as with the wilderness in which they lived, became an imminent task for those Daoist hermits who entered the mountains.[16] In *The Master Who Embraces Simplicity* (*Baopuzi* 抱樸子), Ge Hong 葛洪 (283–343) instructed that many Daoists went to live in the mountains either to practice the Dao and make medicines or to escape from constant wars and take shelter. People who did not know the correct techniques for entering the mountains might die of sickness or be attacked by tigers, wolves, and poisonous insects.[17] Those who did not have sufficient knowledge about the techniques for entering the mountains might encounter related difficulties, such as suffering from poisonous stings, being devoured by tigers and wolves, being killed by mountain specters, and dying from exposure to the cold or starvation in the valleys.[18] According to Ge Hong, one technique for entering the mountains was to know the calendar of taboos. In the longer months and shorter months, there were certain days on which both Daoist practitioners and common people entering the mountains would encounter tigers, wolves, and poisonous worms.[19] The image of the wilderness depicted by Ge Hong shares some similarities with that of the Judeo-Christian tradition in which, as Tuan Yi-fu points out, "wilderness is primordial chaos, a howling trackless waste, a dark world inhabited by monsters and evil spirits," and "wilderness is primeval chaos and potency, a threat and a lure."[20] Numerous early medieval Daoist texts specified various spirits and demons appearing as animals or other forms. Snakes, for example, were a constant threat, and the ritual killing of them was one of the most visible practices in early Daoism.

Early Daoist medical texts offered advice on the ritual healing of wounds caused by beasts as well as on controlling the tiger. A collection of medical recipes titled *Handy Therapies for Emergencies* (*Zhouhou beiji fang* 肘後備急方), attributed to Ge Hong, provided a recipe for healing the wounds from tiger and bear claws. It recommended smoking the wounds by burning a piece of green clothing 青布 to force poisons out of the body. The "soup" made from boiling lobed kudzu-vine root 葛根 was good for washing wounds, as was drinking the juice from boiling the smashed dried root for seven days and five nights. This medical text also included details about Daoist techniques to prevent a tiger from inhabiting the area by mobilizing the mountain deity to carry out a spell.[21] According to this text, the Daoist priest performing this ritual commanded the mountain deity to enter his lung. Then the White-Thearch deity of the lung—note each organ of the body was governed by its own deity, according to Daoist belief—would take away two eyes of the tiger and insert them in the lower part of the body of the priest. The priest then exhaled the air from his lung and moved to the mountain. In the mountain, the priest held thirty-five breaths, walked three steps while making gestures of touching the second knuckle joint of the fourth fingers of both hands, and prayed. If this ritual was carefully performed, the priest would not encounter any tiger in the mountainous area. Even if the priest accidently encountered a tiger, he could still summon the Lord of the Northern Dipper (Beidou jun 北斗君) to drive the tiger away. Ge Hong also taught that burning the horns of ox and goat could prevent tigers from approaching. Moreover, wearing a bag with smashed rabiagar 雄黃 and amethyst 紫石 would prevent tiger attacks.[22]

Daoist narratives portrayed Daoist priests as masters who could command deities, demons, and animals. These priests practiced the method of "pacing the void" and received talismans from the Most High via the Celestial Masters so they could command demons, deities, and animals. Therefore, tigers and wolves would not harm them while they walked in the wilderness. An early medieval Daoist text *The Declaration of the Perfected* (*Zhengao* 真誥) said that Daoist master Ge Xuan 葛玄 (164–244) could ride a tiger and command demons while traveling.[23] This ability was inherited and came from the Daoist tradition. Meanwhile, according to *Traditions of Divine Transcendents* (*Shenxian zhuan* 神仙傳), the Prince of Huainan, Liu An 劉安 (179–122 BCE), respected the Way and always welcomed Daoists with humble words and honorable rites. He once made the Eight Sires descend to his place in the wilderness, and they declared to Liu An that one of them held the ability to tame tigers and leopards, to summon dragons and krakens, and to dispatch spirits and ghosts.[24] Medieval Daoist texts claim that Ge Xuan bestowed numerous teachings and Daoist texts on his disciple Zheng Siyuan 鄭思遠,[25] including *Methods and Writs of Orthodox Unity* (*Zhengyi fawen* 正一法文) and others.[26] Zheng apparently continued Ge Xuan's legacy of taming the tiger. According to the eleventh-century Daoist encyclopedia *Cloudy Bookcase with Seven Labels* (*Yunji qiqian* 雲笈七籤), Zheng's benevolence was extended to birds and beasts. While living in the mountain Zheng adopted two baby tigers who lost their mother. And later the father of these baby tigers joined them to serve Zheng who was riding the male tiger and commanding baby tigers to bear books and medicines for him.[27] Daoist writers of later generations attributed Zheng's ability to command tigers to serve him to his high morality and virtue, which echoes the Confucian way of using morality and virtue to transform the behaviors of animals.[28]

Medieval Daoist priests developed talismans for controlling tigers. Zheng Siyuan's legacy came down to his disciple Ge Hong. In the "Inner Chapter" of Ge Hong's work titled *Master Who Embraces Simplicity*, he wrote that if he were equipped with a particular talisman from the Lord Lao, he would be protected in the forest. He could use red ink and write the talisman on white silk in the day of Jiayin 甲寅 (the day of tiger) and set it up on the table, worshiping toward the Big Dipper, offering meat soup, calling his own name, and receiving the talisman for attaching to his collar. This talisman could shield him from all mountain and water demons, tigers and wolves, as well as poisonous snakes.[29] Gradually, taming tigers was portrayed as an accomplished skill of many eminent Daoist masters in medieval Daoist sources. The tradition of Orthodox Unity said that Zhang Sheng's 張盛 oldest son Zhang Zhaocheng 張昭成 could let his spirit travel out of his body for several hundred *li* while he was sitting in his chamber, and he could also tame tigers and leopards.[30] According to the *Biographies of the Learners of the Way* (*Daoxue zhuan* 道學傳) compiled by Ma Shu 馬樞 (?–581) in the sixth century, a Daoist practitioner named Xiao Lianzhen 蕭廉貞 ate plant stalks and leaves as well as flowers and recited the *Scripture of Yellow Court* (*Huangting jing* 黃庭經). A tiger came to his bed and became his companion, so he treated the tiger as his dog.[31]

How could the tiger be tamed? And what does such taming mean for the Daoists? *The Book of Liezi* tells a story about how tigers could be reared. This work was likely compiled in the fourth century, but it was attributed to Lie Yukou 列禦寇, a scholar who was active in the fifth century BCE. The second section of the book, on the Yellow Emperor 黃帝, states that the groom of King Xuan of Zhou had a slave named Liang Yang 梁鴦 who was skillful in rearing beasts and birds. Liang had even tamed some savage animals, including tigers, wolves, eagles, and ospreys. So, the king ordered Mao Qiuyuan 毛丘園 to become Liang's apprentice, and Liang explained his taming skills to Mao: "Although tigers are a different species from man, when they fawn on the man who rears them it is because he lets them get their way; and likewise when they kill him, it is because he thwarts them. That being so, how would I dare to make them angry by thwarting them? But I do not please them by giving them their way either. For when joy passes its climax we are bound to revert to anger, and when anger passes its climax, we always revert to joy because in both cases we are off-balance. Now since in my heart I neither give them their way nor thwart them, the birds and animals regard me as one of themselves."[32] Liang Yang emphasized observing the natures of beasts and birds in order to seek a balance between thwarting them and giving them their way, to become one of them by earning their trust. This story was readily accessible to members of the Daoist community: In 741, the Tang emperor Xuanzong issued an imperial order to establish a nationwide Daoist school system. The students in these public schools had to study the *Book of Liezi* and Daoist classics, such as the *Daode Jing*, the *Book of Zhuangzi*, and the *Book of Wenzi*.[33]

In this context, to tame means to transform savage beasts into human beings' companions, servants, disciples, or guardians, or to adapt animals for use in the social and economic lives of humans. Many other stories in the medieval period convey how tigers could serve as companions to religious practitioners who cultivated themselves as hermits deep in the mountains. Thus tigers appeared as servants carrying books and as guardians protecting their lords. Essentially, taming is a cultural tool invented by humans: the tamed or domesticated animals must serve the social, cultural, spiritual, and economic needs of humans. Taming is a display of human dominance, either through ethical or ritual power. Two foundations seem to support the Daoist taming of the violent tiger. One comes from early Daoist philosophical writings that teach how to cohabit with wild animals in nature. The other comes from the discipline texts of early Daoism that outline the ethical rules of not killing animals.[34]

Notable interactions occurred between the Daoist discourse of taming the tiger and medieval Chinese political philosophy during the Datong period (535–551) of the Western Wei dynasty. For example, Chen Baochi 陳寶熾 studied the Daoist teachings for taming with Master Wang and Lu Jingzhen 陸景真, who witnessed him taming a white tiger while he practiced morning worship. As the story goes, a horde of tigers even knocked over a tree to alert him when a group of bandits or violent beasts approached him. The Western Wei emperor Wendi invited him to his court to solicit his advice on methods for governing subjects. Baochi created an analogy between tigers and ruled subjects: If human beings treated tigers well, he said, then tigers would not be a threat to humans. If the ruler tortured subjects, then subjects would resent him.[35] In this story, Baochi seems to distinguish between violent tigers and tamed tigers. Violent tiger were regarded the same as the bandits who could endanger humans, whereas tamed tigers could serve as guardians of humans.

A similar story appeared in the biography of Guo Wen 郭文, a native of Luoyang. He lived in a stone cave with a tamed tiger that served as his companion brought him essentials such as books, salt, and rice. The Emperor of the Jin dynasty invited him to a meeting and asked about his method of taming the tiger. Guo Wen advised just act naturally because if human beings were not willing to harm the tiger, then the tiger would not harm humans. This principle was the same as when governing subjects.[36] It is similar to Confucian thought on political ethics that emphasize the mutual relationship between the ruler and his subjects. The ruler treats his subjects with righteousness and benevolence, and the subjects, in return, treat the ruler with loyalty and respect. If the ruler treated his subjects well, then the subjects would respect the ruler. If the ruler tortured subjects, they would resent him. This metaphor comparing the tiger to the ruling subject illustrates a subtle adoption of Confucian ideology in medieval Daoist narratives about nature and beasts.

Medieval Chinese Daoism developed a set of rituals for constructing the Daoist cosmological order, within and beyond Daoist communities, working with both residents and animals. Daoist hermits residing in wild mountains were required to deal with beasts on a daily basis. According to Ge Hong, three talismans were designed for protecting humans and domesticated animals from beasts. The first, for anyone visiting or residing in a mountain, is "The Lord Lao's Talisman for Entering a Mountain" (*Laojun rushan fu* 老君入山符). Ge Hong then mentioned two talismans taught by a transcendent, Chen Anshi 陳安世. One is "The Talisman for Entering a Mountain and Removing the Tiger and Wolf" (*Rushan pi hulang fu* 入山辟虎狼符). This required writing the two-piece talisman in red ink on silk and hanging up four copies in the dwelling place.[37] For this method, Ge Hong uses the character *pi* 辟 for tigers and wolves, which literally means "removing and getting rid of." Medieval Chinese Buddhist hagiographies often stated that eminent monks would not yield to or avoid (*bubi* 不避) beasts when encountering them. Although sometimes the character *pi* might appear as the alternative character for *bi* 避, use of the former in Daoist texts may indicate the Daoist priests' intention to claim Daoist superiority over Buddhism. Chen Anshi also taught how to a make a second talisman carved on a two-inch block of jujube wood for worship, and how to wear it to prevent harm from hundreds of demons, snakes, tigers, and wolves.[38] All three talismans could be hung up around the chambers of domesticated animals such as cattle, sheep, and pigs for protection against tigers and wolves. As an alternative to the talisman, Ge Hong taught the method of controlling the tiger, which he claimed must be orally transmitted because writing could not fully communicate its sophistication. For example, one way is to conceive one's body as a vermillion bird and command the body, lengthened to three *zhang* 丈, to stand on the head of the tiger. At this moment, by suspending its pneuma (*qi* 炁), the tiger would just leave.[39]

In the fifth and sixth centuries, a ritual manual that was purportedly compiled by the noted Daoist priest Tao Hongjing 陶弘景 (456–536) taught methods for making five different talismans. This text was titled *Rituals Transmitted and Bestowed by Lord Tao* (*Tao gong chuanshou yi* 陶公傳授儀), and it survives in the Dunhuang manuscript (S. 3750, P. 2559, and BD. 11252 and S. 6301). The second section of the ritual is called the "Talisman Seal of Prohibiting Mountains 禁山符印," which teaches how to deal with beasts in the mountains. This section is translated as follows:

> [The Daoist priest] kneels down and prays: I, have my willingness in the mountains and forests, avoiding to reside among people. My body is not yet pure and void. My *qi* is still turbid with dust. My five organs are not stabilized. And I am afraid of evil birds. Today I am honored to receive the "Talisman Seal of

Prohibiting Mountains from the Duke of Western Marchmount" (Xiyuegong jinshan fuyin 西嶽公禁山符印), the "Petition of the Medium Yellow Tiger from the Most High" (Taishang zhonghuanghu zhang 太上中黃虎章), the "Talisman of Three-Five of Tiger King and Spirit Li from Zhang Tianhua" (Zhang Tianhua huwang lijing sanwu zhi fu 張天華虎王李精三五之符), which can suppress the mountain spirit from the top and control hundreds of birds from the bottom. I invoke the divine lord of Western Marchmount 西嶽神君, who is responsible for overseeing all deities. I also invoke the aged man of flying in the heaven who is responsible for eliminating tiger's gallbladder and breaking the *qi* of tiger's spirit. The medium yellow of the Ultimate Unity is responsible for swallowing *qi* and sending an edict to the tiger, running and smoking the ferocious eyes of the tiger. I also invoke jade lad of the Mysterious High, who is responsible for locking tiger's five organs and driving tiger to flee for seeking another dwelling. I invoke the ancient king of fierce beasts who can shake tiger and control birds and who can command them.[40]

This passage offers very detailed guidelines for how to control different parts of the tiger's body, such as its gallbladder, eyes, and five organs. It instructs a Daoist priest to invoke and command different deities to control different parts of the tiger. He will have to receive divine talismans and seals from his master to control tigers. The passage indicates that a Daoist priest equipped with talismans and seals could survive an attack by a ferocious tiger without getting hurt, but it does not say that the Daoist priest could bestow Daoist precepts on a tiger so a tiger could become a Daoist, as was noted in Buddhist writings I discussed in chapter 3.

It should be noted that the ability to handle a violent tiger was not limited to male priests. Even a Daoist priestess could seize the wild tiger. In Shangyu 上虞 County (modern Shaoxing, Zhejiang), the magistrate Liu Gang and his wife, Lady Fan, were both skilled Daoists. As *Zhongua Daozang* reports: "Liu Gang was out traveling when he encountered a tiger. [At first] it did not dare rise, but then it attempted to seize and devour him. Lady Fan seized the tiger and pressed its face to the ground so that it [could] not look at her. She bound it with twine and led it back to their home."[41] Later the tiger was tied up on their bed. This story reveals that in southeast China the Daoists could encounter the tiger while traveling, and that skilled Daoists, both male and female, could use their power to pacify the wild tiger.

DAOIST APPROACHES TO TIGER VIOLENCE AGAINST THE LOCAL COMMUNITY

In medieval China, both religious and nonreligious sources portrayed tiger violence as an imminent threat to the local communities and villages. Confucianism, as the state ideology, advocated virtuous governance as a way to provide
safety for local communities and protect them from tiger violence. Confucian
political philosophy taught that the local administrators could drive the violent
tiger away with their Confucian virtue. In their respective literatures, Buddhist
and Daoist clergies tried to facilitate social interaction and expand their religious
interests by demonstrating how they could help local communities stop tiger
violence. Buddhist monks claimed that they could tame the tiger and convert it
to Buddhism by bestowing Buddhist precepts and ordaining the tiger. Daoist
priests took a similar approach to dealing with the tiger violence issue by performing specific rituals. Local literati and government officials often disguised
and prohibited blood sacrifices to the local cults by local people. In the political
rhetoric of the state power in medieval China, such cults were either regarded as
being excessive or devoted to popular divinities, thus providing an escape from
the state-managed code of rites. Daoist priests, for example, competed and sometimes collaborated with local magicians and sorcerers concerning magic arts and
exorcisms.[42] They also exercised religious power by means of rhetorical strategies
such as calling attention to eminent Daoist priests.

In medieval China, then, to answer the call from local villagers, Daoist priests
joined the effort to deal with the tiger violence issue as a community crisis. This
echoes Terry F. Kleeman's observation: "The dominant tradition in Daoism is one
of service to the community of which the Daoist priest is an integral part, whether
this be a village in the mundane world or among the celestial cohorts in one of the
many Daoist heavens."[43] As the Daoist community transformed its method of handling tiger violence into religious rhetoric that manifested the power of Daoism,
Daoist priests continued seek and provide an alternative approach to the problem
of tiger violence. One option was to increase their religious capital by resolving
tiger violence and stop taking rewards from local government. Their social engagement would enhance the acceptance of the Daoist ideology in local areas where
Daoist priests might be regarded as the Honored Master of Taming Tigers.

Explicit references to the "tiger disaster" appear in early medieval Daoist literature and illustrate how Daoists at that time accepted the discourse of "tiger violence" endorsed by the Confucian state ideology. An important Daoist manual of petitions, *Master Redpine's Almanac of Petitions* (*Chisongzi zhangli* 赤松子章曆, c. fourth through sixth centuries), preserved a text titled "Petition for Stopping and Eliminating the Tiger Disaster" (Shouchu huzai zhang 收除虎災章). According to this text, villagers not only dealt with attacks by tigers and wolves but also, on one occasion, these beasts ate humans and harmed six domesticated animals. When villagers sought help from a Daoist priest, he would summon many deities and their attendants—such as the Lord of the Northern Darkness (Beixuanjun 北玄君) and his soldiers, as well as the Lord of Protecting Capital and Pacifying the North (Beiping hudu jun 北平護都君) and his soldiers—and ask them to work with the lords and deities of local mountains, rivers, soil, and grain to eliminate the harm from tigers and wolves.[44] By commanding some heavenly deities to work with local deities on the disaster issue, the priests could avoid direct engagement in the elimination of violent tigers. Daoist ritual may have empowered them to summon deities from the heavenly realm, but it did not help them gain the ability to handle savage beasts themselves. This is a very different approach from the Buddhist practice of stopping violent tigers.

In early medieval Daoist literature, the tiger was portrayed as an intruder that troubled the local community. For example, Ge Hong explained how tigers harmed livestock, such as cattle, in his era. A Daoist text titled *Secret Words of Embracing Simplicity* (*Baopu miyan* 抱樸密言), perhaps from the Eastern Jin dynasty, appearing as the appendix to the *Marvelous Essence Scripture of Eight Thearchs of the Cavern of Spirit* (*Dongshen badi miaojing jing*), illustrated a particular method Ge Hong used to stop tiger violence:[45] In 326, when Ge Hong owned a herd of some twenty cattle, his county suffered from tiger attacks but had no effective prevention methods or defense. Tigers came to harm his cattle and killed six or seven of them. So, he undertook a ten-day fast, invoking the lord of the high mountain and requesting him to eliminate the problem of violent tigers. At night during his ritual practice, he saw a figure wearing a single yellow garment and an official cap with a vermilion bird. This mighty figure was about the size of a human and his fingers were about one *chi* long. It turned out that he was the local high mountain lord who could stop the tiger violence. When tigers came to take the cattle again, this lord shot at them and killed one of the tigers in the bamboo forest. Afterward, no further tiger violence occurred in this area.[46]

Being a Daoist master, Ge Hong was able to invoke the lord of the mountains by performing a fasting ritual and command the lord to kill the tigers and restore order in the mountain region and local community. Ge Hong did not deal with the tiger violence in person by taming or killing the tigers; instead, he commanded local deities to do the job. Also, Ge Hong taught a technique of preventing tigers from harming domesticated animals. He taught that using the blood of a dark-colored goat and a red hen to make a cinnabar-colored pigment, and smearing it on the foreheads of cattle, sheep, and other domesticated animals, would shield them from plague and illness, as well as from the harm of tigers and leopards.[47]

Although cattle and tigers were animals, they were not equal in the eyes of Ge Hong. They had different identities in his world, and they played different roles in his social and economic life. The cattle were Ge Hong's private property, serving his social and economic needs. Tigers were savage beasts that could damage his social property. As a Daoist, Ge Hong valued his domesticated cattle more than he did barbaric tigers. The protection of a Daoist for his cattle could even cost a tiger its life. Ge Hong's understanding and practice of social justice seem to be based on his social and economic interests, rather than the ecological order of the animal realm in the natural environment.

Not every Daoist could master the skills of stopping tiger violence. Only the Daoist priests and laypeople who were portrayed as transcendents could prevent tigers from harming humans, as Ge Hong's Daoist hagiographical collection *Traditions of Divine Transcendents* (*Shenxian zhuan*) revealed. Ge Yue 葛越, whose Daoist name was Yellow Hut Master (Huangluzi 黃蘆子), could put prohibitive spells on tigers, wolves, all manner of noxious vermin, and flying creatures to prevent them from moving. Under his prohibitive spells, even the water of the river would reverse its course for one or two *li*.[48] Mao Ying 茅盈, a native of Xianyang 咸陽, practiced Daoism in Mount Heng 恆山 for twenty years. Later he moved to Mount Gouqu 句曲山 (modern Maoshan 茅山, Jiangsu) in southern China, and due to the power of his virtue, there were no disasters, such as floods, drought, plagues, disease, or locusts, and in the local mountain there was no threat from thorn grass, poisonous trees, tigers, or wolves.[49]

Methods for stopping tiger violence to help the local community appeared in both Buddhist and Daoist sources in medieval China, which suggests that there was a face-to-face competition and negotiation between the two religions in wrestling with cultural and religious power. After all, the winner of the competition would demonstrate religious superiority. Many stories depicted eminent Buddhist monks and Daoist priests either driving away violent tigers or eliminating the tiger violence. Two stories share a similarity in terms of the titles given to accomplished masters in both Buddhism and Daoism.

First, in the Tang dynasty, a Daoist master Pei Haozhong 裴浩中 resided in the Huadao Abbey 化道觀 in Yuntai 雲臺, Langzhou 閬州 (modern Langzhong 閬中, Sichuan). Apparently, he was more than a hundred years old, and he often used pollen branches to cultivate the pneuma (*qi*). While holding his breath and closing his eyes for this cultivation, a tamed yet ferocious tiger often served beside him. The tiger would also walk with him up to the cliff. Since the local area suffered from tiger violence, villagers made images of Pei to shield themselves from the attacks of tigers. He received the esteemed title Honored Master of Taming Tigers (Fuhu zunshi 伏虎尊師). In addition to his talent for taming tigers, he could also command dragons to make rain.[50] The taming of a tiger by a Daoist master (known as a "perfected") can be commonly found in some paintings in late imperial China.

Second, a story about the Song-dynasty Chan masters Zhifeng 志逢 (909-985) and Fazhong 法忠 (1084-1149), which can be found in medieval Chinese Buddhist narratives, tells of their ability to tame tigers and command dragons. These accomplishments earned them both the title of "Chan Master of Taming the Tiger" (Fuhu Chanshi 伏虎禪師).[51] The later appearance of this Buddhist title suggests that it might be a Buddhist variant phrase borrowed from Daoism.

As an alternate method of taming the tiger, some medieval Daoist narratives tell of Daoist priests who used force to attack the tiger and drive it away. According to the *Record of Marvels* (*Luyi ji* 錄異記) compiled by Du Guangting 杜光庭 (850-933) in the Tang dynasty, a Daoist named Jing Zhiguo 景知果 in the Sichuan area tamed tigers and leopards so that they became like domesticated dogs. Sometimes crows and vultures would sit on Jing's shoulders and limbs. A giant snake came out and then fled under his command. The tigers in his yard fought on moonlit nights, and when they got out of hand, Jing became cross and broke up the fight using a stick, so they scattered. Other beasts also befriended him.[52] This story appears to use taming beasts, even if it required a modicum of force, as a demonstration of the power of Jing Zhiguo, since his biography said he obtained the Way.

Although in the early medieval period, Daoist precepts often prohibited Daoists from taking the lives of animals, narratives dating to the late Tang dynasty show that Daoists did kill tigers to stop their attacks. Stopping tiger violence was a crucial theme in the *Record of the Numinous Efficacy of Daoist Teachings* (*Daojiao lingyan ji* 道教靈驗記) compiled by Du Guangting.[53] Although in most cases Daoists summoned local deities to handle savage tigers, one exception from Sichuan shows that killing tigers themselves was justified in medieval Daoism. This case appeared in a story told by He Yifan 何彝範, who served Gao Pian 高駢 (821–887), a highly acclaimed general in the late Tang. When Gao was the military governor in Chengdu (r. 875–879), a sly fox spirit often disturbed the brothel his soldiers patronized by throwing tiles and stones and displaying the transformations of exotic forms. Gao tried some talismans and prayers, but nothing worked. He Yifan then told him an old story about how Ge Hong had resolved the problem of tiger violence. When Ge Hong found the tigers that had harmed cows in his residential region, he followed the method taught in the *Inner Writ of the Sovereign of Earth* (*Dihuang nei wen* 地皇內文) to summon a deity for help. The next day, two dead tigers were found in the forest nearby. So, He Yifan recommended that Gao try the *Inner Writ* method. Then He helped Gao kill the old sly fox.[54]

All these example show that Daoism endorsed the killing of tigers by priests. By contrast, according to medieval Buddhist monastic rules and the *Biographies of Eminent Monks*, killing an animal was not regarded as an option for Buddhist monks who faced a violent beast. As we saw in Daoxuan's interpretation of classifying and handling animals, there were three ways of dealing with them: keeping them as monastic property on the monastic premise if they were domesticated, releasing them if they were wild, and raising them up for release if they were too young to currently be released to the natural environment.[55] While discussing the Daoist regulation text titled *One Hundred and Eighty Precepts*, Kristofer Schipper states that "Daoism developed institutions and regulations with the purpose of protecting the environment and to ensure that its natural balance would not be destroyed."[56] But as he also notes, in Daoism, killing living beings was allowed if the killing was not for consumption, for eating, for suicide, or for murder.

Medieval Daoism not only justified killing tigers, but it also justified mobilizing tigers to kill Buddhist monks, thereby portraying the tiger as a weapon for protecting Daoist property from non-Daoist political and religious powers. The appearance of the brave tiger warrior was leveraged as symbolic of the efficacy of Daoism against Buddhism. Du Guangting's collection *Record of the Numinous Efficacy of Daoist Teachings* told how in Guangzhou 廣州 there was a Daoist named Calamus Abbey 菖蒲觀, which was said to be the place where An Qi 安期 made

medicine a long time ago. In the Tang dynasty, it became a popular tourist desti-
nation known for its medical store, elixir well, and ancient pine trees. In this place,
an old Daoist abbey was once occupied by a group of Buddhist monks who built
a Chan temple. Horrible things often happened there. An elder told these monks
they could not take it over, and he warned them that tigers and leopards would
harm them if they did not move out. At first the monks did not believe the elder.
But about a month later, tiger attacked the monks and caused more than ten casu-
alties. The rest of the Buddhist group fled without speaking of the problem. So,
this place again became a Daoist abbey.[57] In addition to this story, Du's collection
included others about how efficacies were used against Buddhism. A similar story
appeared in Sichuan. On Mount Qingcheng 青城山, a group of Buddhist monks
took over the ancient Daoist Changdao Abbey 常道觀, forcing the Daoists out.
The monks then founded a temple called Feifu Monastery 飛赴寺, but the residents were often disturbed by spirit beings. Sometimes flying stones damaged the
buildings or the plaque was thrown off the cliff. Even the giant bell in the monastery was thrown into the mountain valley. Later, in 731, a Daoist named Wang
Xianqing 王仙卿 requested permission from the emperor to restore the Daoist
abbey on its original site and move the Buddhist monastery away.[58] Another story
also mentioned the conflict between Daoists and monks from the Feifu
Monastery.[59]

Sometimes tigers helped protect Daoist property. In the Southern Marchmount, the Transcendent Platform of Lady Wei, perched upon a giant rock in
front of the central peak, became a place for transcendents to stop and rest. One
night, a group of Buddhist monks arrived, carrying torches and sticks. They tried
to push the platform over but could not move it, and in frustration they left. Then
a tiger killed nine of the monks; only the monk who had not participated in push-
ing the platform survived. When the local villagers heard about this, they all felt
surprised and delighted.[60] In the same section, another story also told how a tiger
helped protect the Daoist land by drawing a boundary line in the dirt between
Buddhist and Daoist property.[61] In these stories, medieval Daoist priests acknowledged the physiological strength of the tiger and its mighty symbolic power as a
force that could prevent Buddhist monks from taking away Daoist property and
perhaps even kill the monks. So, Daoist priests mobilized the tiger and transformed it into a Daoist guardian animal. The tiger guardian figured prominently in the Daoist narratives that established a new social order to maintain
the ascendancy of Daoism, which can be regarded as a new development of Daoist

apologetics. In this order, the Daoist priests appeared to have greater power for taming and even killing the tiger, and the tiger was stronger than the Buddhist monks.

In the medieval period, the competitions of images, rituals, and practices became more intensive.[62] In analyzing medieval manuscripts and statues, Christine Mollier sheds new light on the intense contest for hegemony in the domains of scripture and ritual between Daoism and Buddhism.[63] I argue as well that Daoism and Buddhism engaged in the contest for hegemony in ruling wild nature by taming the ferocious tiger, the so-called king of all beasts in East Asia. Whichever tradition could tame and kill the king of all beasts would become more plausible, and therefore would have more cultural capital among the medieval audience.

THE DAOIST "WAY" OF ANIMALS

Medieval Chinese Daoist monasticism developed a strong anthropocentric tradition. More broadly, debates in contemporary scholarship examine how anthropocentrism developed in and affected religious traditions. In a renowned 1967 article published in *Science*, Lynn White Jr. held the anthropocentrism of Christianity and other religious traditions accountable for establishing the dualistic relationship of humans and nature, and the subsequent human exploitation of our planet's ecosystems.[64] In fact, there is a long tradition of Abrahamic religious anthropocentrism. Some scholars turn to the ancient sources of Asian traditions for environment-friendly ideas, and many agree that the religious traditions of South, East, and Southeast Asia promote responsible behavior toward the natural environment. These traditions tend to show a sense of the numinous in nature and the perception of sacred mountains, forests, groves, and rivers.[65] They appear to support the idea that the boundary between humans and nature is blurry. Some traditions believe in animism and the interdependence of all creatures. Nevertheless, in responding to the work of Lynn White Jr. nearly a half century later, some scholars remind us that, "it is inaccurate if not also blindly romantic to read retroactively Asian traditions as being in essence environmentally wise and concerned."[66]

Medieval Daoist narratives put forth the belief that the inferior moral agency and intelligence of animals prevented them from thoroughly understanding the

Way (Dao) through self-cultivation unless they had the guidance and instructions of Daoists. This view deemed some wild animals species different (in the sense of being "other") not only from humans but also from other domesticated animal species. Tigers, for instance, being wild animals—unlike some domesticated animals such as pigs, horses, and sheep—were neither sources of labor for supporting human economic life nor pets for daily companionship. The tiger, symbolizing the highest power of animals, served as cultural capital for the Daoist priests to maintain their image as superior moral cultivators wielding religious power and dominance. Medieval Daoist narratives developed religious rhetoric to explain that eminent Daoist priests could mobilize the power granted by the Lord of the Dao to command deities and demons to fight with the beasts.

Although tiger attacks on local villagers and livestock in medieval China might have been caused by human expansion and invasion into the realm of the tiger, Daoists, following prevailing norms in medieval Chinese society at the governmental and community levels, defined the attacks as tiger violence. By accepting this definition, some Daoist priests justified engaging in competition with local government and Buddhist community efforts to pacify this violence. On the one hand, Daoist participation could indeed help the local community by resolving the tiger problem. On the other hand, Daoist priests harvested cultural capital by exemplifying religious power. Even though the Daoist priests might not directly take the life of a tiger themselves, and instead mobilized demons and deities as proxy executors, the tiger was killed. From Daoist cosmological and ethical perspectives, killing is an act of violence that has to be justified; killing tigers seems to be based on the Daoist acceptance of defining tiger violence in terms of attacks. The methods medieval Daoist priests used to take the life of a violent tiger established their religious reputations, which were important in their competition with Buddhism.

Furthermore, killing tigers in medieval China might also have satisfied demands for tiger bones used in medical treatment. Ge Hong's *Handy Therapies for Emergencies* noted many recipes with ingredients consisting of various body parts from the tiger. Another text titled *Arcane Essentials from the Imperial Library* (*Waitai miyao* 外臺秘要) compiled by Wang Tao in 752 offered more details on the medical use of tiger body parts.[67] For instance, tiger head bones healed some illnesses such as malaria 瘧疾 (juan 5). Tiger claws treated heart and stomach pains caused by ghosts (juan 13). Skin from tiger heads treated speechlessness or lying because of extreme fear (juan 15). Tiger eyeballs treated lameness and illnesses caused by wind pathogens (juan 15).[68] Alcohol mixed with tiger bones treated other problems brought by deviant wind (juan 15) and liver problems (juan 16). Tiger bones also treated constipation and fatigue in the four limbs as well as renal disease (juan 16). Tiger body parts also treated other medical issues including gangrene (tiger excrement, juan 24), carbuncle of the back (tiger teeth, juan 24), hemorrhoids (tiger head bones, juan 24), archoptosis (tiger head bones, juan 26), and rabies (tiger teeth, juan 40). Tiger bones were often used to strengthen newborns and babies. For example, tiger head bones, boiled with some other plant ingredients, were used for bathing newborns (juan 35). In addition, babies who had sleep problems and cried unless given milk could be treated with a recipe containing a tiger eyeball (*hujing fang* 虎睛方). The tiger eyeball, along with rhino horn and herbal ingredients, can be mixed together and formed into small patties to feed sick babies. The recipe for healing eczema of the ear canal (juan 29) uses a balm made from tiger head bones (*hutougu* 虎頭骨) with duckweed (*fuping* 浮萍) and pig fat (*zhuzhi* 豬脂). In his preface to the *Arcane Essentials from the Imperial Library*, Wang Tao offers a list of several medical scholars from previous periods who compiled medical recipes, including Sengshen 釋僧深 (fifth-to-sixth century) and Sun Simiao 孫思邈 (581–682).

The medical, scientific, and cultural uses of tiger parts have long traditions in China, with at least three subspecies of tiger (the Amur tiger, the South China tiger, and the Bengal tiger) living across China throughout history. Before the mid-twentieth century, there were approximately half a million wild tigers in China. In 2017, according to data from the World Wildlife Fund, about five hundred wild Amur tigers lived in Russia's Far East and near the border between Russia and China. In Asia as a whole, agricultural, military, commercial, medical, and scientific activities have led to drastic reductions in the number of tigers.

On October 29, 2018, the State Council of China issued a new regulation that bans the sale, purchase, use, import, and export of all rhinoceros- and tiger-derived products in China; but it allows rhinos, tigers, and their related products to be used in scientific research with approval by the appropriate authorities. It also allows rhino horns and tiger bones to be obtained from farmed rhinos and tigers, excluding those raised in zoos.[69] This new regulation shocked the Humane Society International (HSI) based in Washington, DC. Iris Ho from HSI stated that China's reversal of its twenty-five-year ban on domestic trade in tiger bone and rhino horn would "set up what is essentially a laundering scheme for illegal tiger bone and rhino horn to enter the marketplace and further perpetuate the demand for these animal parts. This is a devastating blow to our ongoing work to save species from cruel exploitation and extinction, and we implore the Chinese government to reconsider."[70] Animal rights activists across the world urged China to reconsider this regulation. Therefore, on November 13, 2018, the Chinese government announced that it was postponing implementation of the policy change that would allow rhino horn and tiger bones from farmed animals to be used in traditional medicine, as well as for scientific and cultural purposes.[71]

CONCLUSION

Medieval Daoist narratives make a distinction between the violent tiger and its tamed counterpart based on the needs of the Daoist priests and community; this distinction serves the Daoists' rhetorical strategy of responding to the competition from medieval Buddhist monks, and to the challenge from local villagers. Tamed tigers could serve the social, cultural, economic, and spiritual needs of Daoist priests and local villagers. In medieval Daoist narratives, the tiger could be portrayed as the guardian, the companion, and the disciple of the Daoist hermits in the mountains and forests. The violent tiger was portrayed as a dangerous enemy, and in such cases killing the tiger as the enemy was justified, though traditional Daoist philosophical principles and early Daoist precepts did not endorse killing. Killing the violent tiger seems to illustrate that in medieval Daoist narratives there was still a clear boundary between wild and untamed nature and the civilized world of the Dao. The latter is part of human society and is governed by the principles of the Dao. Killing a violent tiger is a disturbance of the ecological order of wild nature, but it benefits the local village or the civilized world. So, in this sense, medieval Daoist narratives still value human society more than nature. Therefore, this distinction between the violent tiger and the tamed tiger is still a manifestation of anthropocentrism.

An important aspect of the relationship between the Daoist masters and the tiger in the wilderness is the boundary between the sacred and the profane in terms of human-animal relations. As Emile Durkheim states, "Sacred things are those which the interdictions protect and isolate; profane things, those to which these interdictions are applied and which must remain at a distance from the first. Religious beliefs are representations that express the nature of sacred things and the relations which they sustain, either with each other or with profane things. Finally, rites are rules of conduct which prescribe how a man should comfort himself in the presence of these sacred objects."[72] Mircea Eliade put it in the following terms: "Whereas profane space at the periphery is chaotic, wild, threatening, and dark, sacred space at the center is orderly and secure, yet it can inspire awe."[73] Both Durkheim and Eliade aim to use the sacred and the profane as universal concepts to analyze all religious phenomena. Jack Goody notes, however, that they do not apply in the case of a Western African religion, "neither do the Lo Dagaa appear to have any concepts at all equivalent to the vaguer and not unrelated dichotomy between the sacred and the profane."[74] It is interesting to see to what extent this pair of concepts could apply to medieval Chinese religions.

There was a distinction between the Daoist cosmic order and the order of nature. The Daoist cosmic order refers to the order in the Daoist realm governed by the Dao and administered by Daoist priests or celestial masters. The order of nature was governed by the tiger, the apex predator that sits on the top of the ecological hierarchy in medieval China. In a retrospective and reflexive discussion of humanistic thinking in the Judeo-Christian tradition as well as in the Enlightenment tradition, Aaron Gross points out that there is always the ascendancy of humans over animals in the Western tradition.[75] But the medieval Chinese religious world has a different set of concepts for drawing the boundary between humans and animals. In the medieval Daoist cosmic order, the Dao (Way) is the highest principle and law, but the executive power of interpretation lies in the celestial masters. The celestial masters created the Daoist sacred space by performing consecration rituals to exorcize demons and animal spirits. The natural wilderness is not consecrated by these masters, so it is not a sacred space for the Daoists. When the Daoist celestial masters entered the wilderness, they were equipped with consecrated items including amulets, talismans, spells, incantations, and other ritual objects. Although the Daoist masters did not actively perform rituals in the natural wilderness for transforming it into a sacred space, by using these consecrated ritual materials, they created multilayered shields to prevent the tiger and other wild beasts from harming them. This is very similar to the case in medieval Chinese Buddhism, but not Confucianism. In Confucian ideology, local officials could transform and move tigers away by their virtuous governance. Innate virtues granted officials the power to change the behaviors of wild beasts. In Daoism, the priests were empowered by external ritual tools such as talismans and verbal spells.

In medieval Chinese Buddhism, there was also a distinction between Buddhist cosmic order and the order of nature. The Buddhist cosmic order was governed by the Buddhist dharma, but the Buddhist community created a dharma realm by performing consecration rituals. The Buddhist dharma realm is defined by boundaries called Sīma. The Buddhist Sīma is created by a ritual of "making boundaries" as the Buddhist Vinaya texts explained, and the Buddhist Sīma is often dismissed following a reverse procedure. The creation of the dharma realm is often called "consecration" in Western-language scholarship. But the English word "consecration" might not be accurate for the Buddhist ritual of making boundaries, given the Buddhist context. The Buddhist dharma realm is different from the *bodhimaṇḍala*, which is literally translated into Chinese as *daochang*, and then in Japanese as *dōjō*. In the medieval Chinese Daoist context, the "consecration" might apply to the Daoist altar, the "ritual space (*daochang*)," which the Daoist priests made sacred. It can be used to exorcise evil spirits to heal illness and for other worldly benefits.

Similar to Confucianism and Buddhism, as I have discussed in chapters 2 and 3, Daoism also regarded untamed nature and beasts as "the other," and its texts in medieval China demonstrate strong teaching and transforming (*jiaohua* 教化) thought related to taming nature and beasts. Teaching and transforming means to convert wild animals to Daoism so that they are submissive to the Daoists who could command gods, deities, spirits, and animals through ritual techniques. Teaching and transforming the tiger, the chief of all beasts in the natural world, was a symbolic conquest of the natural world of wild animals, which indicates that medieval Daoism expanded its cosmological and spiritual order to cover all animals. When the Daoist priests entered the mountains and confronted untamed beasts, they chose to either prohibit them or tame them by teaching and transforming them to obey the Dao. If a violent tiger was not submissive, under extreme circumstances, killing it could be an option for the Daoists. In other words, to expand the Daoist realm and manifest the Daoist magical power, Daoist priests could take any necessary actions, even at the cost of the life of a tiger. Hence, teaching and transforming untamed beasts seems to be a shared strategy for all three organized teachings in medieval China, which also created a competition among them.

CHAPTER 5

Buddhists Killing Reptiles

Snakes in Religious Competition

We see from the discussion in chapter 4 that medieval Chinese Buddhist and Daoist hagiographical literature portrayed tigers and snakes as two of the most frequent beastly threats from the wilderness. Some medieval Buddhist hagiographies often included snakes and tigers together as two eminent threats.[1] Snakes, like other nonhuman animals, can exist in multiple layers of human experience. In ancient and medieval China, they could inhabit cultural, historical-physical, and psychological-cognitive domains. When encountering snakes as we read about and visualizing them in literature, legends, stories, paintings, and sculptures, we experience them as culturally constructed from the thinking and religious discourse of individual traditions: indigenous Chinese culture, Buddhism, and other traditions culturally constructed images of snakes in their own ways. Historical and physical experience refers to actual contact between humans and snakes, whether individually or in groups in the wilderness. Psychological and cognitive experience, meanwhile, refers to the imagined snakes that are both perceived and conceived from the previous two kinds of encounters. In the premodern period, these three different layers of experience often intermingled and mutually influenced each other. While discussing how medieval Chinese Buddhists handled the threat of snakes, it is worth noting that they had to deal with them on all three layers. The cultural experience of Buddhist monks comes from literary works, which include both indigenous Chinese writings and early Buddhist literature.

In the early twelfth century, there was a serpent's cave at the back of the Pure Dwelling Cliff 淨居巖 in the Southern Peak mountain ranges. A monk named Zongyu 宗譽 constructed a chamber as a temporary residence in this place. Because he was constantly being disturbed by a woman, he left for a temple on the mountainside. Later, in 1141, a monk named Shantong 善同 came to the Pure Dwelling Cliff and expanded the residence to several rooms. A twenty-eight-year-old traveling monk, Miaoyin 妙印, stopped by this area but died several days after a woman seduced him. Another monk who practiced alone in the same area also became sick. In the middle of the fourth month, a rainstorm with thunder and lightning suddenly passed through this area. Shantong saw a giant coiling snake in his chamber at midnight. Working with his monastic colleagues, Shantong managed to kill this snake in a vast cave, which stopped the rainstorm. Soon after, monks found out that this snake, which had rectangular black stripes, had killed eight monks and their attendants.[2] This story is instructive for many reasons. It reflects four types of conflict that deserve detailed scrutiny and discussion: conflict between humans and animals, between canonical rules and local justifications, between male monks and a feminized snake, and between organized religion and local cultic practice. In this chapter, I contextualize the discourse around, and the practice of, killing snakes, by exploring how Chinese Buddhists understood and handled these four conflicts.

In terms of the conflict between humans and animals, the story above reveals the confrontation between a group of monks who lived in the deep mountains and the snake that claimed the mountain as its realm. On the one hand, in Buddhist literature, snakes often appear as a threat. Monastic and lay Buddhists across Asia had to deal with snakes as they walked, lived, and practiced in the wilderness.[3] The story shows the monks facing threats of snakes, and of the rainstorm brought on by the snake, while they practiced alone or living as a group deep in the mountains.[4] Thus, living in the wilderness is dangerous because one might invade the realm of the snake. On the other hand, the conflict between humans and animals—including snakes—in the wilderness was already noted in pre-Buddhist literature in ancient China. A particularly common theme occurs in which people are vastly outnumbered by beasts in the ancient wilderness. As Han Fei 韓非 (279–233 BCE) noted: "In the earliest times, when the people were few and birds and beasts were numerous, the people could not overcome the birds, beasts, insects, and snakes. Then there appeared a sage who created the building up of wood to make nests to hide the masses from harm (then the people called him the One Having Nests)."[5] Thus, the struggle for living space would break out between human beings and animals. The monks could lose their lives to a venomous snake.

Attending to the conflict between canonical rules and local justifications, this story reveals the gap between the Buddhist Vinaya rule against killing and the local practice of execution. By the end of the story the serpent has killed eight monks and their attendants, so the serpent was killed as retribution for the bad karma it brought. Yet the monks' killing of a snake seems to violate the most important Buddhist precept that prohibits taking the life of any sentient being. As many scholars have noted, in Buddhist traditions monks should never kill sentient beings, whether human or animal.[6] The story I recount above is an exception in medieval Chinese Buddhism. It raises several questions, such as how a local Chinese Buddhist community justified the act of killing and what doctrinal and ritual resources could be mobilized by that community to make such a justification.

On the conflict between male Buddhist monks and a feminized snake, this story seems to liken the snake to a lustful woman who would sicken a man and eventually kill him. Although it does not explicitly state that the woman who killed Miaoyin was the giant snake transformed, the allegory here is of a weak male monk being corrupted and eventually destroyed both physically and spiritually by a snake-like woman. Both in Buddhist literature and in the pre-Buddhist tradition in ancient China, the woman and the snake were linked in an association that should be documented and analyzed. Similarly, the motif of monks facing a female sexual aggressor in the form of a coiling snake is also seen in Japanese Buddhist didactic tales.[7]

In regard to the conflict between organized religion and local cultic practice, this story tells that the snake was capable of bringing up thunder, lightning, and a rainstorm; these were common powers granted to the snake as a deity in ancient cultic beliefs. A conflict is revealed here between the Buddhist community and the local cult. Storms brought danger and threatened the monastic chamber and its residents, and the snake seems to be portrayed as the lord or deity in control of these natural forces.[8] But Buddhist monks, who represented human beings in this story, could keep these forces under control by killing the snake. Through this killing, the group of monks eventually brought forth a bright shining day, banishing the darkness. Finally, this group of monks used whatever was available to attack and kill the bothersome snake. The monks' use of weapons and force to defeat it seems to be well justified due to the fact that the snake had killed eight monks and their attendants. Afterward, the monks enjoyed a peaceful environment for their daily lives and practices.

In the following discussion, I hypothesize that several factors have played a role in shaping the attitudes and practices of handling these conflicts centered on the snake. The first factor is the tradition of killing snakes, which has a long history in ancient China. The second factor is the link drawn between women and snakes in ancient China, which was based on the discourse of the feminized snake in the traditional yin-yang theory. The third factor is the acceptance by the medieval Chinese Buddhist community of the Mahāyāna tantric tradition, which introduced rituals for killing sentient beings and justifications for doing so. The fourth factor is the competition between Buddhism with local cultic traditions and Daoism in medieval China. In medieval Chinese religious discourse, tigers and snakes appeared as the most dangerous threats against both the Buddhist and Daoist communities. Taming tigers and killing snakes became significant in terms of cultural capital—a way for both religious traditions to display their power. Chinese Buddhist and Daoist communities learned from each other in dealing with threats from dangerous animals at the local level. In other words, they could mobilize whatever resources were at hand when developing their strategies to deal with the challenges they faced.[9]

CONFRONTATIONS BETWEEN HUMANS AND SNAKES

Scientific studies indicate that venomous snakes have existed for about 60 million years. Colubroid snakes in Asia evolved a highly potent venom delivery system. Colubroid snakes include some deadly venomous snakes such as *Viperidae* (vipers and pit vipers), *Elapidae* (cobras, mambas, and coral snakes), and *Colubridae* (racers, gopher snakes, and kingsnakes).[10] Some scientists suggest that evolutionary exposure to snakes contributed significantly to the evolution of neural structures in mammals for detecting and avoiding them, and these structures associated snakes with fear.[11] Although people in ancient China did not possess modern knowledge of snakes, fear of snakes seems to have been universal across the empire.

The record on the confrontation between humans and snakes can be traced back to the sixth century BCE when snakes—along with tigers—were regarded as threats both to human lives and to the political and social order. In the sixth century BCE, Duke Jing of Qi (Qi Jinggong 齊景公, ?-490; r. 547-490) went out hunting and asked Yan Ying 晏嬰 (578-500) if it was inauspicious to see tigers on the mountains and snakes in the marshes.[12] But Yan Ying responded to him that only poor governance could bring up three inauspicious things for the state: having a wise man in one's midst without discovering him; knowing of his presence without employing him; and employing him without trusting him.[13] Although it seems that the tiger and snake served as metaphors in this story, it nonetheless clearly shows that the tiger and snake were considered dangerous threats to humans in the wilderness. In the Han dynasty, Wang Chong (27–100 CE) noted that there were numerous snakes and vipers in the south because of its humid environment.[14] But confrontations between humans and snakes spanned from the Yellow River region to the Yangtze River region.

In the ancient and medieval periods, the southern regions of China were described as teeming with threats from snakes. Humid weather in summer and lands exposed to water provided a hospitable habitat for numerous vipers and snakes carrying infectious diseases and plagues.[15] *Erya* 爾雅, an early Chinese lexicon that might be dated to the third century BCE, lists four major types of snake, including flying snakes (*tengshe* 螣蛇) and a mythical snakelike animal. But according to *The Classified Compendium of Literary Writing* (*Yiwen leiju* 藝文類聚), a collection of literary works compiled in 624, ancient and early medieval writers wrote about five major types of snake. This classification can be regarded as the literary tradition about snakes for early medieval China.[16] These five types of snake are the extremely venomous long snake (*changshe* 長蛇) that could bite anything, a mythical flying snake (*tengshe*), the giant, python-like Ba snake (*bashe* 巴蛇), a mythical giant snake (*jushe* 巨蛇) that could swallow an elephant,[17] and the two-headed "bramble-head snake" (*zhishou she* 枳首蛇).[18] The second type of snake is not a reptile species that can be found in nature, but the third type might be a sort of python.

In the Tang period, some local regions were famous for being home to different species of snake. The assumption was that some of them were venomous and should be despised and even killed, while others were not venomous and might simply be avoided. But some snakes were valued for economic, medical, and aesthetic reasons, so local governments authorized local catchers to obtain them as tributes to higher offices. For example, in the Tang dynasty, Qichun County (modern Qichun 蘄春, Hubei Province) offered numerous indigenous products as a local tribute to the court, including white clothing, deer-hair brush-pens, tea, white-flower snakes, and dried meat of black snakes.[19]

The Tang court had expectations for local areas within the empire to submit snakes as local tributes. The court then used the snakes or some of their body parts for making medicine. According to the *Comprehensive Statutes* (*Tongdian* 通典) compiled by Du You 杜佑 (735–812) in 801, many prefectures—including Xinping (modern Xianyang, Shaanxi), Qichun, Chaoyang (modern Chaozhou, Guangdong), Nanhai (modern Guangzhou, Guangdong), Gaoliang (modern Enping,

Guangdong), and Haifeng (modern Haifeng, Guangdong)–offered dried snake meat and snake gallbladders to the court.[20] Because of the high demand for these tributes, local governments mobilized some local residents to risk their lives to catch snakes. A vivid description of the life of snake catchers can be found in Liu Zongyuan's 柳宗元 (773–819) acclaimed essay "Catching Snakes." Liu states that there is an extraordinary kind of deadly snake having a black body with white rings in the wilds of Huguang (Hubei and Hunan). The flesh of this snake can nevertheless soothe excitement, heal leprous sores, exfoliate rough skin, and expel evil spirits. Therefore, the imperial court ordered each family to pay two snakes as the tribute every year.[21]

In medieval Chinese literature, snakes and tigers often appeared together as major threats toward local villages.[22] Medieval Chinese sources often mentioned "tiger violence" (*hubao* or tiger disaster) and "snake disasters" (*shezai* 蛇災) as set phrases. Dealing with violent tigers and disastrous snakes became leading concerns for local communities. For example, in Gan Bao's *The Account of Searching for the Spirits* (*Soushenji* 搜神記), a giant snake in a crevasse of the Yung range of the Dongyuan area killed several local officials. Local residents offered the snake oxen and sheep as sacrifices but with no luck. The local government also requisitioned children born to slaves of ordinary families and the daughters of criminals as offerings for the snake. Over several years, nine girls lost their lives to the snake. In Jiangle 將樂 County, Li Dan had six daughters. The youngest one, Li Ji 李寄, volunteered to deal with the snake. She brought a sword and a dog to the mouth of the cave where the snake was dwelling and eventually killed the snake.[23] Given all this conflict between human and snake at the local level, could medieval Buddhists provide the local community with alternative approaches to the snake problem? Social and historical realities brought many challenges to Buddhist monks who traveled in the wilderness. Local communities also called on monks for help in dealing with the serpent challenge.

CONFLICTS BETWEEN EARLY BUDDHIST PRINCIPLES AND LOCAL APPROACHES

Confronted with the threat of snakes in the wilderness, individual Buddhists and Buddhist communities responded with a mixture of different attitudes and practical approaches. Many elements may have shaped the attitudes of medieval

Chinese Buddhists toward snakes and the ways in which they handled snakes in
their social and religious lives. Collectively, medieval Chinese Buddhists lived in
a disciplined community that was ruled by Buddhist doctrines and moral codes.
The textual and literary tradition inherited and developed from early Buddhism
certainly had an impact on the attitudes of some Chinese Buddhists, which means
that some of the nonviolent doctrines and principles for handling snakes that were
taught in early Buddhist literature could still be found in Chinese Buddhism. I
first offer a general survey of the nonviolent handling of snakes in the early Buddhist textual tradition and then discuss how this nonviolent legacy continued in
Chinese Buddhism.

Snakes often represented the threat of real nonhuman animals in social and
religious life in the Vinaya collection of the Pāli canon, and the Vinaya texts provide concrete cases for handling encounters between snakes and monastic members.[24] Supplementing the Pāli Vinaya, I provide some cases from the Chinese
translations of the Vinaya. Although we have to separate metaphorical snakes and
natural snakes in early Buddhist literature, both the doctrines and disciplines of
early Buddhism advocated and enforced nonviolence and therefore were against
the killing of snakes. Reading the canonical texts, it is not difficult to find evidence that killing a living being is never an option in early Buddhism. The first
precept for any Buddhist is never to take the life of any sentient being.[25]

In early Buddhism, the most important rule while dealing with animals, no
matter how harmful they are, is not to kill them. James Stewart calls this the
notion of total pacifism: "Even killing a snake in self-defense is considered inap-
propriate. This pacifism is born from two causes. The first motive is the Buddhist
virtue of compassion; . . . the second motive for this extreme pacifism is more self-
interested, however, and is derived from a strange kind of self-preservation."[26] In
ancient South Asia, snakes appeared to be tremendously dangerous to human
beings, and Buddhist texts show numerous cases of this danger. In general, snakes
might bite monks, and protection against this danger was deemed necessary. In
the Vinaya collection of the Pāli canon, the Buddha was often consulted about
how to handle these issues. In the Cullavagga 3 (Khandha paritta), Gotama (Gautama, in Pāli) granted permission to the almsmen to make use of a safeguard for
their security and protection against snake bites.[27]

Killing snakes by accident and having the intention to kill snakes are both
counted as offenses in the Vinaya. In the Chinese Five-Part Vinaya, a group of
monks wearing wooden shoes in the monastic quarter were making noise that

disturbed other monks who were trying to meditate. Then one of the monks killed a snake with his sharp wooden shoes at night. In responding to this accident, the Buddha ordered a ban on wooden shoes for the minor offense of wrongdoing.[28] For a monk, according to the Chinese translation of the Five-Part Vinaya, even having the intention to kill a snake would be counted as an offense. When a monk who used a stone to try to strike a snake ended up killing a person accidentally, the Buddha said that in attempting to attack the snake this monk had committed the minor offense of wrongdoing.[29] Furthermore, the Pāli Vinaya does not allow monks to consume the meat of snakes because the snake was loathsome and disgusting. According to the Mahāvagga (VI), in ancient times, lay people had offered snake flesh to monks who made use of it. This behavior irritated some people who regarded the snake as a loathsome and disgusting animal.[30] This rule was attributed to the historical Buddha who maintained the position of preventing monks from consuming snake flesh because he was questioned by the serpent-king. Interestingly, the snake is often depicted as the symbolic animal of hatred (Skt. *dveṣa*), one of three poisons (Skt. *triviṣa*) in early Buddhism, and posing against Buddhist compassion and purity.

Some cases in the Vinaya texts show several methods taught by the Buddha to protect monks from the dangers of the snake, but this protection should not come at the cost of the snakes' lives. The Buddha instructed monks to make lamps, ropes, and canisters to keep snakes away or contain them and later release them. For example, a story in the Chinese translation of the Mūlasarvāstivāda Vinaya Kṣudrakavastu tells that the Buddha instructed monks to make lamps for reciting scriptures at night to prevent snakes from disturbing them.[31] In the Chinese translation of the Four-Part Vinaya, the Buddha taught those monks who did not detach from desires that they could use canisters to contain the snakes and tie the snakes up by ropes and then release them without harming them.[32] In the same chapter of the Four-Part Vinaya, after a venomous snake emerged from a hollow beam in the bathroom and killed a monk, the Buddha told the monks that if they had compassionate minds for all eight kinds of snake and all sentient beings, nobody would get killed by venomous snakes.[33] The Buddha's teaching here might have come from his own experience of cultivation yet did not apply to all monks. His cultivation as an enlightened teacher led him to develop a strong psychic power to control the snake, as the following discussion shows.

All the foregoing examples teach that, in the Vinaya texts, even a powerful man like the Buddha would not take the life of a fierce snake. Instead, the Buddha could use his psychic power to tame the snake. A story in the Mahāvagga (I) illustrates that the Buddha used his psychic power to battle with a serpent king in a fire room during his stay at Uruvelā. He controlled the serpent king without having destroyed its skin, flesh, or bones. Once he placed it in his bowl, he convinced the ascetic Uruvelakassapa to convert to Buddhism and offered him a constant supply of food.[34] In this story, the Buddha demonstrated his power of controlling the snake, without harming the snake. His power of controlling a dangerous animal from the Buddhist realm of beasts serves to demonstrate a Buddhist compassionate approach to dealing with the snake to attract lay patrons. This method of using psychic power to tame snakes echoes some of the narratives in the Avadāna literature. Reiko Ohnuma analyzes a story in the Avadānaśataka Sūtra (no. 52) about a black snake. In this story, a venomous black snake is pacified by the Buddha and dies after giving rise to faith (*prasāda*). Eventually, it is reborn as a deity in the Trayastriṃśa Heaven. Ohnuma argues that, in this story, the suicide of the snake was "a symbolic assertion of the total incompatibility of the animal state with moral agency, self-cultivation, or the final release from suffering."[35] Only if the very animality of the animals is eradicated can they be saved and reborn as deities in Trayastriṃśa Heaven. In the Chinese translation of the Avadānaśataka Sūtra, while the Buddha was staying in the Kāraṇḍa-veṇuvana near Rāja-gṛha, a wealthy elder was reborn as a snake because of his greed, envy, and selfishness. The Buddha went to visit the snake and tamed it with his compassionate power by shining five-colored lights from his five fingers.[36]

In general, modern and contemporary Theravāda Buddhists in South and Southeast Asia follow the principle of nonviolence.[37] In his study on Thai Buddhist masters, Kamala Tiyavanich notes that Thai Buddhists believed an old saying that those who make a living by killing snakes would die from a snake.[38] In Burmese Buddhism, some Buddhists still believe that a poisonous snake can be caught and released, but not killed, whenever it is found in a house or in the wilderness; even a person's self-defense cannot justify killing a snake. If a person attacks a poisonous snake but gets killed by this snake, it is karmic retribution. Poisonous snakes will not attack and kill the Buddhists who are ordained.[39]

The early Buddhist discourse on karmic retributions for killing animals, including snakes, continued in medieval Chinese Buddhism.[40] Many stories said that killing snakes would lead to nasty retribution. By avoiding the killing, a person can be spared from being harmed. If killing a snake is unavoidable, conversion to

Buddhism and constant practice of confession would ease the karma of killing. One story described the snake as a force bringing destructive power to the humans who killed it. Zheng Hui 鄭翬, a native of Gaoyou, said that his cousin Lu's village was near water, and several neighbors—but not Lu—killed a white snake. Soon after, there was tremendous lightning and rain, and the resulting flood sunk those families who were involved in executing the snake. Only the Lu family survived.[41] Another story took place in the early Yuanhe period (806–820). Five or six guests were studying on Mount Song 嵩山 in early autumn. While taking shelter from the heat under the Two-Emperor Pagoda, they saw a giant snake coiled in the center of the pagoda. After a discussion, most of the guests agreed to kill it, so the snake was killed and cooked in the kitchen. One guest who disagreed with killing the snake was unhappy and left. Soon after a heavy rainstorm arrived and killed several guests under the pagoda. The guest who argued against the killing went to an empty Buddhist chamber and prayed for his innocence to be recognized. He was the sole survivor of this storm.[42] This echoes a feature of the story about Miaoyin in the introductory section of this chapter. The snake, as the deity who controlled the rainstorm, could mobilize the overwhelmingly dangerous rainstorm with lightning and thunder that threatened human lives. The difference in this story is the message that killing a snake would lead to retribution, with punishment by death to the killer.

In medieval Chinese Buddhist discourse, it is possible to avoid karmic retribution from killing a snake by converting to Buddhism, practicing confession, and chanting the Buddha's name. Feng Min 馮珉 was a hunter from Shangyu 上虞. He answered the call to fight with a giant serpent that had often caused harm to local villagers. He brought a long spear but later killed the serpent by crushing it with a rock. Then he was worried about retribution from killing the snake, so he converted to Buddhism, practiced confession, and chanted the name of the Buddha. In ten years, he passed away peacefully.[43] In this story, the method of killing the snake that troubled the local community is the same as the one in the story of the monks on Southern Peak Mountain. Here, besides killing a serpent, Feng might have committed to many other killings. From a non-Buddhist perspective, killing a snake that threatened the safety of a local community may earn merit from shouldering social responsibility. In this case, Feng's killing of a snake clearly violated the first Buddhist precept, so he must be committed to confessions and chanting practice in order to purify his offense.

Furthermore, it seems that the Chinese Buddhist community inherited the idea that Buddhist psychic power could automatically drive snakes away, which shows that medieval Chinese Buddhists attempted to follow the historical Buddha's teaching and practice. When killing is not an option, a Buddhist monk should try to control a wild beast, including a snake, with the psychic power he cultivated from his Buddhist morality and practice. A monk called Yuanzhen 圓震 (705–790) from the Zhongshan 中山 region used to study the five Confucian classics, but after listening to the talk of a traveling monk hosted by his father he converted to Buddhism. Later, he received ordination from master Zhiyou 智幽 and studied the Chan method with master Shenhui (688–758). During his stay on Mount Wuya 烏牙山 in Nanyang 南陽, he resolved the problem of the snake disaster that bothered the local villagers by driving the snakes away without killing them. So his disciples preserved his whole body in a stupa to honor him.[44] In this story, Yuanzhen's eminence was manifested in his power to drive snakes away without hurting them. On the one hand, he extended his Buddhist power by controlling the behaviors and activities of snakes. On the other hand, he helped the local community by eliminating the threat of snakes.

Finally, there is also a legacy of taming rather than killing snakes in Chinese Buddhism. Buddhist monks could ordain the snake and convert it to Buddhism. For example, Huifu 惠符 (631?–730), a monk at the Tianzhu Temple 天柱寺 on Mount Huo 霍山, Qian County 潛縣 (modern Huoshan County, Anhui), confronted a giant snake on the mountain. He offered the snake two options, either to be swallowed or to receive Buddhist precepts. The snake suddenly appeared as a human body and requested to be ordained. So Huifu ordained it.[45] This legend tells that an eminent monk could use his psychic power to verbally communicate with a snake, and to convert the snake to Buddhism by ordaining it while it transformed into a human body. But it does show that all sentient beings including cold-blood snakes could receive ordination and live with Buddhist precepts. If a snake converted to Buddhism, it would purify its bad karmas from its previous lives.[46] Finally, this story reminds us that the body transformation would offer the inferior sentient being the chance to accelerate the path toward enlightenment in the Mahāyāna tradition as we see in the story of *nāga* girl in the Lotus Sutra.

With the rise of the Mahāyāna tradition, many doctrines and practices were transformed, revised, and reinvented. At first, snakes were associated with hell.

The Sutra Spoken by the Buddha on the Sea of Samādhi Attained through Contemplation of the Buddha (*Foshuo guan Fo Sanmei hai jing* 佛說觀佛三昧海經), translated by Buddhabhadra, has a graphic description of the Avīci Hell, in which three species of animals appeared. The Buddha told Ānanda that in this hell was an iron city with seven circles of walls. Four copper dogs guarded the four corners of this city. Fierce fires came out from their bodies, and the smoke was foul and disgusting. Within the city, there were eighteen sectors; in each sector there were 84,000 iron serpents. The serpents vomited poison and fire that spread throughout the entire city.[47] This passage describes the graphic scene of hell as a poisonous city where the dog and the serpent served as the source of fires that rendered the hellish city horrible for all sentient beings.

Although in the early Buddhist discourse, the snake was used to symbolize hatred, one of three poisons that produce all sufferings, the early Mahāyāna tradition further states that snakes have four poisons. For instance, in the Mahāyāna Mahāparinirvāṇa Sūtra, it states that snakes have the following four poisons: the seeing poison, the touching poison, the air poison, and the biting poison.[48] Apparently, these four poisons refer to visual, tactual, olfactory, and gustatory senses that cause suffering. This statement is different from the symbolic meaning of the snake in early Buddhist discourse specifying three poisons, but it makes the negative image of the snake even more visible. Mahāyāna tradition also developed the discourse against the poisonous snakes and other beasts. For instance, in the chapter on the universal gateway of Avalokiteśvara bodhisattva in the Lotus Sutra, commonly appearing as the "Scripture of Avalokiteśvara Bodhisattva" (*Guanyin jing* 觀音經), it says that "by virtue of one's constant mindfulness of Sound-Observer, [evil beings] would not dare to do one harm. Or, one may be surrounded by malicious beasts, sharp of tooth and with claws to be dreaded. By virtue of one's constant mindfulness of Sound-Observer, they shall quickly run off to immeasurable distance. There may be poisonous snakes and noxious insects, their breath deadly, smoking and flaming with fire. By virtue of one's constant mindfulness of Sound-Observer, at the sound of one's voice they will go away of themselves."[49] Here the Sound-Observer refers to Avalokiteśvara bodhisattva. The copy of this text has been found in the Dunhuang manuscripts (figure 5.1). In the meantime, this message was depicted in the mural on the east wall within Mogao Cave 112, Dunhuang, which was dated to the eighth century. In this painting, a Buddhist practitioner meditated with his palms jointed for praying to the bodhisattva. Various snakes, a scorpion, and two beasts including a tiger surrounded him (figure 5.2).[50]

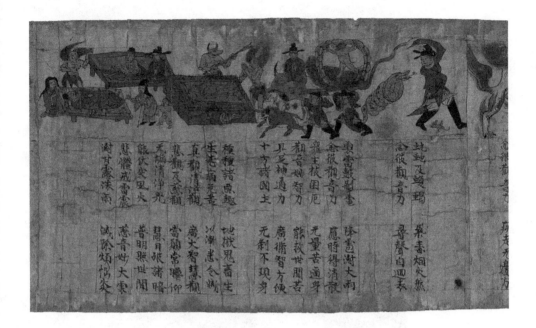

5.1 P. 4513, a copy of the *Guanyin jing* in the Dunhuang manuscripts from Mogao Cave 17, the library cave.
Picture from International Dunhuang Project website. © Bibliothèque nationale de France in Paris.

Furthermore, the snake metaphorically appeared as the power of the heretical teachings that the Buddha was in combat with. This metaphor seems to have been well received among Buddhists in early medieval China since it appeared in a popular Buddhist collection titled *Differentiated Manifestations of the Sutras and Vinayas* (*Jinglü yixiang*) compiled in 516. It tells a story in which a flood attacked a kingdom ruled by a king called Dāna, then an enormous snake circled the city and swallowed some of its residents. Two ascetics, Sahādeva and Mahādeva, came to tell the king that they could eliminate the problem of the snake. It turns out that once these two ascetics transformed, respectively, into a giant toad and a *garuda* (the supernatural eagle-like mount of Vishnu) the giant snake fled into the mountain. Then they revealed that they were the Buddha and Maitreya, and the giant snake was the Buddha's jealous cousin Devadatta. After Devadatta fled, two Buddhas bestowed five precepts to the king and the residents of his kingdom.[51] Three animals including a toad, a Garuda (a predatory bird with a rich mythological hisotry), and a snake appeared in this story. The snake appeared as the

5.2 A Buddhist surrounded by beasts. East Wall, Mogao Cave 112, Dunhuang.
© *Dunhuang shiku quanji*, 19, 2000.

heretic enemy of Buddhism but was defeated by the power of the Buddhas who did not kill the snake but drove it away. The departure of the defeated snake secured the kingdom in safety and tranquility, and most importantly, the conversion to Buddhism. These tropes can be seen in many stories in medieval Chinese Buddhism.

When Buddhism was introduced into China, the marginalized Mahāyāna tradition from South and Central Asia became dominant. Some of the Buddhist doctrines and practices were intermingled with local and indigenous ideas and practices in China. Unlike the Buddhist concept of hell, Buddhist ideas about animals were not exotic and foreign to Chinese Buddhists, though they did come across some fascinating new animals in Buddhism, such as lions, that they had never encountered in China. This was not the case with snakes. We see from the discussion above that, on the one hand, the poisonous and disgusting image of the snake continued its legacy in early medieval Chinese Buddhism, yet the Buddhist principle and precept of no killing sentient beings, including venomous snakes, also found its place in China. Furthermore, as I show in the following section, snakes were seen as wicked demons associated with women, and they became a favorite theme in the Buddhist narrative of karmic retribution in early medieval China.[52]

THE CONFLICT BETWEEN BUDDHIST PATRIARCHY AND FEMINIZED SNAKES

Discourses about women in early Buddhism and the Mahāyāna tradition are diverse and multidimensional;[53] even in the late imperial Chinese religious tradition, women were portrayed as Buddhist deities with some gendered qualities such as compassion, mercy, and nurturance.[54] But the misogynistic voice quickly earned its currency in Chinese Buddhism, drawing from the ancient patriarchal society. In this section I examine how this misogynistic discourse brought death to snakes in medieval Chinese Buddhism, paving the way toward redemption for both women and snakes as evil beings.

Buddhism and the pre-Buddhist Chinese tradition shared a common discourse that linked women and venomous snakes. The yin-yang theory in traditional Chinese cosmology played a pivotal role in associating animals with the energies that give rise to all materials, objects, and lives. Along with women, the snake is associated with the *yin* energy,[55] which is regarded as cold and dark in nature, in contrast to the warm and bright *yang* energy. In ancient China, the diviner interpreted dreams in which black and brown bears meant boy children, but snakes and serpents meant girl children.[56] Suspicion of the snake as the sign of women continued in court politics throughout the medieval period. In 634 in the Longyou 隴右 region (modern Gansu Province), a giant snake often appeared, which was regarded as the sign of femininity.[57] Many scholars have noted that early Buddhism metaphorically linked snakes with women. For example, women were likened to black snakes and accused of ensnaring men. Women were portrayed as monsters, demons, and venomous black snakes. Elizabeth J. Harris points to "the image of woman as temptress, the incarnation of evil. Here the woman appears as the witch, the serpent, and the siren. She is a danger to man's spiritual progress—a force that can lure a man with false promises of fulfillment, only to bring him to destruction."[58] Early Mahāyāna Buddhist literature further linked snakes with women. For example, snakes and dogs were compared with women as evil beings. "Tale of King Udayana of Vasta," contained within the Mahāyāna text Mahāratnakūṭa Sūtra (Collection of Jewels), stated: "As the filth and decay of a dead dog or dead snake are burned away, so all men should burn filth and detest evil. The dead snake and dog are detestable, but women are even more detestable than they are."[59]

Feminized snakes, more visible in Chinese Mahāyāna texts, are one of the most noticeable features of early medieval Chinese Buddhist narratives.[60] The feminized snake of early medieval China was manifested in a sixth-century story about the karmic demise of an empress who becomes a snake. The emperor Xiao Yan was one of the longest-reigning emperors in Chinese history, having reigned for forty-six of the eighty-five years he lived. He married Xi Hui, claimed in Confucian historical narratives to be a very jealous woman who often badmouthed other concubines and consorts in the court and so was viewed as a "venomous snake." Unhappy with the emperor's Buddhist beliefs and practices, she ripped up his copies of Buddhist scriptures. The emperor often hosted Buddhist monks at court and supported their monasteries, which irritated Xi Hui. She hatched an evil plot to harm the Buddhist monastic community by secretly putting green onion, garlic, chives, and even meat—ingredients prohibited in the Buddhist monastic code because they were thought to arouse an emotional response in the monks and disturb their concentration and mindfulness—into the vegetarian meals her husband offered to monks. But as it turned out, these monks were wise enough to discover her conspiracy and were quietly replacing Xi Hui's meals with their own. Xi Hui died unexpectedly at just thirty years of age; she fell into the realm of animals, only to be reborn as a snake tormented by hunger and plagued by venomous worms crawling on her body. She communicated with her husband for help. Drawing on his reserve of Buddhist compassion, the emperor composed a liturgy to perform the Buddhist confession ritual. After all these efforts, Xi Hui was released and reborn as an angel.[61]

This story indeed exemplifies the power of Buddhist compassion. The confession ritual allowed for the transfer of merits to his evil wife, even though she had been reborn as a snake. Why did she reincarnate as a snake? From the Confucian perspective she was seen as a woman who had treated other concubines and her attendants with cruelty, and from the Buddhist perspective she had violated its scriptures (dharma) by intending to add prohibited ingredients to the meals Buddhist monks (sangha) and causing them harm. This story explicitly portrays an evil woman's request for her compassionate husband to perform a confession ritual that would save her from torture in her snake-embodied afterlife.

The combination of Chinese misogyny and the Buddhist ophidiophobia that associated evil women with snakes appears in some medieval Chinese narratives.[62] If a woman did not fulfill her family obligations or treat her household well, she would be subject to Buddhist retribution by being transformed into a snake. One story about the older sister of the aide to Censor General Wei 御史中丞衛 explains how she became very ill and was eventually turned into a huge snake because she treated her servants so brutally that they had died. Her family was frightened and took her to the wilderness.[63] As a sister of a government official, she was a privileged woman who was expected to treat her servants nicely. But because beating and murdering them violated the Buddhist precept of not taking the lives of other sentient beings, she was kicked out from the realm of humans in this life, rather than through rebirth in her next life.

The punishment of being transformed into a snake is not limited to laywomen. Another story tells of a nun called Wang Sangu 王三姑 at Jingming Temple (Jingmingsi 靜明寺) in Xingyuan 興元. Before becoming a Buddhist nun, she was the wife of Du 杜. But she did not take care of her husband when he became old and fragile. She left him alone to die of cold and hunger.[64] Even though she converted to Buddhism and devoted herself to the monastic community, it did not purify her sin of treating her late husband with cruelty and in cold blood. After she died, she transformed into a snake while lying in her coffin, which meant that she would not be reborn as a human in her next lifetime but would be hunted as a troublesome beast.

A woman who converted to heretic teachings could also be reincarnated as a snake. A story from *A Record of Retributions* (*Baoying ji* 報應記) includes a very interesting account from the late Tang period about Mrs. Wang, the wife of Wu Kejiu 吳可久. During the couple's stay in Chang'an, they converted to Manichaeism. One year later, the wife suddenly died. After three years, she appeared in her husband's dream and told him she had become a snake because of her deviant belief in Manichaeism and was now trapped under the stupa of Huangzibei 皇子陂浮圖. She worried she was about be killed the next day. She begged her husband to invite monks to recite the Diamond Sutra to release her. Wu Kejiu asked monks to recite the scripture to release her; he then converted to Buddhism and venerated the Diamond Sutra.[65] This story demonstrates the Buddhist position that one's Manichean belief would result in reincarnation as a snake, but the Buddhist monks' recitation of the Diamond Sutra could release the bad karmic retribution. This story does not specify if Mrs. Wang was a cruel woman who harmed her husband or others but simply mentions her personal Manichean belief. Nevertheless, it illustrates that reincarnation into a snake was used in Buddhist apologetic literature against Manichaeism in the late Tang period.

In all these stories, Buddhism and the pre-Buddhist Chinese tradition portrayed women as callous, cruel, violent, and irritating sentient beings—physically and emotionally—and likened them to violent, poisonous, and cold-blooded snakes. When they were alive, they could rip up their husbands' Buddhist scriptures, sneak prohibited food into the meals of monks, and follow deviant teachings, such as Manichaeism. In short, they could be harmful to Buddhist dharma and sangha, just as the snake who appeared as the heretic teaching opposing and damaging Buddhism. In early medieval China, the Confucian community also developed a strong voice for denouncing women as dangerous forces against the patriarchy and hierarchy of Confucian family and society. It seems that, to take deep root in Chinese society, the Buddhist community quickly shared this sentiment and developed its own narrative against women by binding women and snakes together. This narrative teaches that both women and snakes could die in misery as a result of their evil karmic retributions, but they could be saved as long as these women/snakes converted to Buddhism, followed Buddhism, and respected Buddhism. Eventually their death was transformed into redemption.

CONFLICTS AMONG DIFFERENT RELIGIOUS PRACTICES

In the medieval period, religious competition between Daoism and Buddhism could be fierce, especially as Daoism weaponized snakes against Buddhism while vying for monastic property. Dealing with snakes is thus a fascinating aspect of the exchange between Buddhism and Daoism in medieval China. Meir Shahar suggests that the snake-like creature shows a connection between the Daoist god and Tantric Buddhism: "The equine deity is associated with snakes. His second-in-command is the Heaven-Blasting Silk-White Snake (Hongtian Sulian Bai She).

The associate of the Daoist god with the serpent-like creature likely derives from Tantric Buddhism. Dating from the Tang period, one esoteric scripture decrees writhing snakes for the adornment of the Horse-Headed Avalokiteśvara. The ultimate source of the ophidian motif might have been Śiva, who is similarly bejeweled by snakes."[66] I suggest that both Buddhist monks and Daoist priests used snakes for protecting lives and monastic property against danger. And both sides used snakes as weapons for killing each other.[67]

Before examining the conflict between Buddhism and Daoism in dealing with snakes, it is important to note that the Daoist attitudes toward snakes and Daoist methods of handling snakes evolved from ancient times to the medieval period. In the ancient era, the killing of a serpent was considered a praiseworthy act in the Daoist tradition, though the origin was not easy to trace. Later, the Daoist community developed narratives and ritual techniques for taming snakes. And in the medieval narratives, some Daoists claimed that they could mobilize snakes as their protectors to kill invading Buddhist monks. The medieval Daoist rhetoric sometimes traced its tradition of killing snakes back to the third century, centered on Xu Xun 许逊 (c. 239-292), one of the most important Daoist forerunners, who became famous for killing a giant snake. He was a disciple of Wu Meng 吴猛 (d. 274). The Daoist narratives said that, in the third century, the lower Yangtze River region suffered the disaster of snakes. Wu Meng selected about a hundred disciples to engage in battle with these snakes. Xu Xun used his sword to kill the snake king, claiming his reputation for resolving the snake problem in local communities.[68] This story mainly depicts how Daoists engaged in service with local communities by eliminating the so-called snake disaster.

In the early medieval period, Daoism developed a series of techniques and rituals for taming snakes, as Daoist priests realized that traveling deep in the mountains and forests was dangerous, and that beasts and reptiles might attack Daoist hermits. In his early fourth-century work *The Master Embracing Simplicity*, Ge Hong writes: "The most successful Daoist master is able to ascend mountains, to transgress water, to live hidden in the hills and swamps among snakes and tigers without being harmed by them. He feels no wind nor moisture nor heat nor frost."[69] In Ge's passage, the snake and the tiger represent the two most frequent animals one could encounter and be attacked by in the swamps and mountains respectively. The snake often hides itself in the swamp because of its humid environment. Yet the tiger was regarded as the fiercest beast in mountain areas. Later, in the Tang dynasty, Daoists often used talismans as protection to shield themselves from venomous snakes. During the reign of Baoli (825–827), Deng Jia 鄧甲 learned from Qiaoyan 峭岩, who resided on Mount Lao 嶗山, the methods of using talismans to summon demons and spirits, including snakes. His fame of controlling snakes reached the Kuaiji County where local people faced the disaster of venomous snakes. By setting up a Daoist ritual altar, Deng killed the snake king and also more than ten thousand snakes who followed the snake king.[70] This narrative seems to suggest that Deng followed Xu Xun's tradition. But the concrete killing method he used was not a sword but rather a Daoist ritual involving talismans on a ritual altar.

Although snakes often appeared as threats to Daoist communities, in medieval Daoist narratives, once snakes had been tamed they could also become the protectors of Daoist monastic property, defending Daoism from local governments and their military forces.[71] Many stories in the *Records of the Numinous Efficacy of the Taoist Teaching*, compiled by Du Guangting (850–933), show snakes serving as protectors of Daoist temples in the late Tang dynasty.[72] When the government officials and troops were about to burn down Daoist temples, snakes could kill the intruders and bring on rainstorms to protect the temples. Two stories indicate that the Daoist monastic community was armed with venomous snakes and that Daoists could use deadly force against invasion from a local government.

The first story tells of a giant snake serving as a protector for a Daoist temple in Xingyuan 興元. When Yang Shouliang 楊守亮 lost Xingyuan in 891, he went back to Liangcheng. But he found that the government office there was heavily damaged, so he ordered its restoration. One of his clerks suggested taking beams and bricks from the nearby Daoist temple of Lord Lao 老君觀. Local residents gathered a large sum of money to pay the government to spare the Daoist temple, but no deal was confirmed. While some workers ascended the temple under Yang's order, preparing to remove the beams and bricks, a giant snake appeared and frightened the workers, who fell and died. Yang was irritated, so he told his soldiers to burn the temple. But a sudden rainstorm with thunder and lightning prevented them from executing his orders, and the Daoist temple was saved.[73]

A second, similar story tells how snakes also mobilized a rainstorm with thunder and lightning to protect the Daoist temple Suling Gong 素靈宮 (Suling Palace) in Yangzhou 洋州 (modern Xixiang 西鄉縣, Shaanxi Province). In 784, Emperor Dezong visited Yangzhou and ordered a renovation of the government office. A local warlord Feng Xingxi 馮行襲 (?–910), commander of the Wuding

Military District 武定軍, told his son to order workers to take the necessary materials from the Suling Palace. As the workers started to carry out this task, they discovered innumerable snakes hidden under the bricks. Feng's son attempted to burn the temple down, but a rainstorm killed his clerks.[74] These two stories fall into the category of the medieval Chinese Daoist apologetic narrative, which illustrated how Daoist monastic communities weaponized the snake, whether by killing those committed to destroying Daoist building, or by bringing on a rainstorm to put out a fire, to protect their monastic property. Hence, once the snake is tamed it can play a decisive role in helping the Daoist monastic community to defend itself against the invasion of government and military forces.

More interestingly, not only could the tamed snakes help Daoist monastic communities against invasions, but the tamed snakes could also protect Daoist communities against Buddhist invasion. Some medieval Daoist narratives told how if Buddhist monks attempted to invade the Daoist realm and damage its property, snakes would come to assist the Daoists and kill Buddhist monks.[75] One story tells of more than thirty Buddhist monks who once occupied the Daoist Qiling Temple 啟靈觀 in Qin Prefecture during 880–885. As they attempted to damage the statue of the Celestial Honored One, putting into action a plan to use the Hall of the Celestial Honored One as their meditation space, a giant snake came out from the seat of the statue, spraying poisonous air. In the meantime, thunder and lightning scared the Buddhist monks, and they ran away. Several of them died. Later, the Daoist priest Zhang Faxiang came to reside there. Although the giant snake occasionally appeared in the local village, it did not harm any villagers.[76] In stating that the giant snake did not hurt local villagers, this story specifically targeted Buddhist monks who attempted to damage the statue of the Daoist deity, so they would receive the karmic retribution of death. All these stories show that the Daoist community could control the mystical power ruling these natural phenomena, in the form of rainstorms with thunder and lighting, and this power was brought on by a snake.[77]

Within the Buddhist community, various sub-traditions mobilized different strategies and approaches to deal with different species of snakes. In medieval China, the Tantric tradition, developing from early Mahāyāna Buddhism by following its principle of skillful means 方便, and perhaps also under the influence of Daoism, developed spells to cast on giant snakes and kill them. This new technology for handling the threatening snakes makes this tradition distinctive from the other Buddhist sub-traditions that developed in medieval China.

In the Tang dynasty, the biographies of two Esoteric Buddhist masters seem to link them with the tradition's ritualized snake killing.[78] The biography of Shanwuwei (Śubhakarasiṃha, 637–735) tells of a giant serpent appearing at Mount Mang. Worried this serpent would flood the city of Luoyang, Shanwuwei recited the Esoteric *dhāraṇī* of several hundred syllables in Sanskrit. A few days later the snake was found dead. (Contemporaneous audiences believed that this was the omen forecasting General An Lushan's rebellion against the established Tang leaders and his occupation of Luoyang, where he declared himself the emperor of Yan, his newly established state.)[79] A similar story also appeared in more detail in the biography of another Esoteric Buddhist master, Bukong (Amoghavajra).[80] It tells of a giant serpent frequently appearing to woodcutters on North Mang Mountain with its huge head like a hill. When the serpent saw Amoghavajra, it spoke in a human tongue and told him that it often wanted to stir up the water in the river to destroy the city of Luoyang so it received bad karma. Amoghavajra ordained the serpent with the Buddhist precepts and taught it about Buddhism. He told it that its serpent body could be abandoned. Soon after this the woodcutters saw the serpent dead in the valley.[81] In both stories serpents die, although neither explains in detail how the Esoteric ritual worked. Other sources state that Esoteric Buddhism introduced new ritual techniques for dealing with the danger of snakes.[82] In the biographies of two Esoteric masters, it seems that the killing of giant serpents was justified as an auspicious act to benefit the local community. Does this mean that the killing of an animal can be regarded as being auspicious in Chinese Esoteric Buddhism? Or was it a new development? Mahāyāna Buddhism appears to develop a new notion of auspicious killing. For example, Fujii Akira notes that the *Miscellaneous Collection of Dhāranis* (*Tuoluoni zaji* 陀羅尼雜集) and other commentaries on Tantric texts developed discourses that justified the killing of demons in Mahāyāna Buddhism.[83] David B. Gray suggests that "Despite their emphasis on universal compassion, some Mahāyāna Buddhists did not, and do not, unequivocally rule out the practice of violent actions such as killing."[84] He notes that, in their commentaries on the *Mahāvairocana-abhisambodhi Tantra*, Śubhakarasiṃha and Yixing endorsed subjugating evil teachings as expedience.

Stephen Jenkins points out that Candrakīrti's commentary on Āryadeva's verse suggested that since "any act that reverses the cycle of rebirth becomes auspicious, the possibility is opened that any action may be auspicious depending on a variety of factors. If an act of killing may make merit, then it is neither a necessary evil, nor merely value-free, but is clearly auspicious."[85] He uses an example of a bodhisattva having to cut off one of his fingers that had been bitten by a venomous snake. He also cites another example of a bodhisattva using the roar of the elephant to frighten a huge snake and thus save a group of people. Neither case directly involved killing a snake, but both show the ways in which violence was accepted and justified in Mahāyāna Buddhism.

According to W. Michael Kelsey in his study on the transformation of the image of snakes in Japan, initially Buddhists and other Japanese people regarded the snake as an evil and violent creature that often terrorized the populace but later considered it became a manifestation of Buddha.[86] Kelsey further categorizes five images of the snake in mythological and early sources: the mythical snake, the mythical snake as saved (defeated) by Buddhism, the Buddhist snake, the mytho-Buddhist hybrid, and the snake of salvation. In fact, in medieval Chinese Buddhism, Buddhists faced a similar situation. On the one hand, the snake cult was already developed, and the snake was regarded as a deity that controlled water and rain; similarly, in medieval Japan, Esoteric Buddhist monks also developed their rain-making skills.[87] On the other hand, snakes often terrorized local communities.

But in the medieval Chinese mind, snakes did not always deserve to die. For instance, they may have served monks as companions and protectors. In the early Tang dynasty, a monk called Huiyu 慧瑜 (563–641) moved to Jade Spring Mountain in Changsha. He stayed alone in a grass chamber, and occasionally visited a nearby spring. A huge snake occasionally showed himself there, protecting Huiyu against local bandits. When a group of bandits attempted to kill the snake, they fell ill as a result of confronting it, and seven of them died. Huiyu recited the Heart Sutra and the Scripture of the Great Vidyā Spells of Mahāprajñāpāramitā (*Mohe bore poluomi damingzhou jing* 摩訶般若波羅蜜大明呪經) to save three ill bandits.[88] In this story, the snake is cast as the monk's protector, and it kills seven bandits. On the one hand, these bandits might have died of their bad karma; on the other hand, they were deemed miserable sentient beings who deserved Buddhist compassion. So Huiyu appeared as a Buddhist preacher who could recite Buddhist spells to heal the bandits who were punished by the snake.

Another story in the *Collected Evidential Accounts of the Diamond Sutra* (*Jin'gang borejingjiyanji* 金剛般若經集驗記) compiled by Meng Xianzhong in 718 tells of a huge snake that acted as a protector of a Maitreya Pavilion 彌勒閣 in the Wuzhen Temple 悟真寺, located in the Chan Quarter on Southern Mountain in Lantian

藍田 County.[89] The pavilion, positioned in the upper section of the temple, was always locked to prevent monks from accessing it because many monks said that a huge black snake protected it. In 703, a monk called Qingxu 清虛 arrived at the temple for a summer retreat, and he told these monks that in southern China there was a lake deity who was also a huge snake and could bring on the rainstorm. Even though this snake deity was powerful, he had still tamed it, so he thought he could also tame the huge black snake in the Maitreya Pavilion. So he entered the pavilion and performed an invocation ritual in meditation and recited the Diamond Sutra for three days and nights. Eventually he found a spring in the Chan Quarter.[90] This story shows that a monk was able to tame a fierce snake and mobilize its power to identify the location where he could find water to benefit the monastic community. On the one hand, the snake was responsible for controlling the water. On the other hand, a monk could communicate with a snake by meditating and reciting the Diamond Sutra without being hurt. This is reminiscent of the story earlier in the chapter about the Buddha using his psychic power to tame the snake. So, literarily, this monk inherited the Buddha's legacy.

While Daoist priests took responsibility for resolving the violence of snakes and tigers in aid of local villages, later Buddhist literature portrayed eminent monks as heroes who could pacify snakes and tigers. While eminent Buddhist monks would never kill a tiger, they did kill snakes. Why did they treat snakes and tigers differently? In terms of Buddhist doctrine, it is commonly known that the serpent was the symbolic animal of greed, one of three poisons known to produce delusions. Furthermore, in early Buddhist literature, the snake was used as part of the metaphor of the four great elements, also called the four poisons. Therefore, removing or eliminating the serpent became a symbol for eliminating a poison. In addition, Daoist competition seems to have had an enormous impact, and Daoist narratives often use snakes as weapons against Buddhist monks.

CONCLUSION

In medieval Chinese Buddhism, the rules based on the traditional monastic code often could not cover all the issues monks confronted raised in daily monastic life; yet according to Daoxuan, who I discussed in chapter 1, they could be justified by doctrines. These textual rules and doctrinal principles, however, often differed from the daily experience of the monks who lived in their contemporaneous reality. In this chapter I demonstrate that dealing with snakes in early Buddhism followed the principle of nonviolence set forth in canonical texts. This legacy can also be found in medieval Chinese Buddhist texts. But medieval Chinese Buddhism faced many challenges while dealing with snakes. First, snakes and tigers posed the biggest threats toward both Buddhist and local communities. Chinese Buddhists often encountered snakes while traveling in the wilderness. Second, medieval Chinese Buddhists found that they had to engage with local communities by extending their Buddhist power to include eliminating snake disasters. Third, there was a conflict between Buddhist patriarchy and snakes in medieval China. The idea of an association between feminized snakes and women was manifested in many Chinese Buddhist narratives, especially those about miserable women whose greedy, jealous, and evil acts resulted in the karmic retribution of being reborn as snakes who would be tortured in the realm of animals. In offering confession rituals, medieval Chinese Buddhism attempted to save both women and snakes victimized by Chinese misogyny and Buddhist ophidiophobia. Fourth, medieval Chinese Buddhism faced competition from Daoism and local cultic practice.

One of the most distinctive new developments regarding the handling of snakes in medieval Chinese Buddhism was the killing of snakes to protect monks and monastic property. Although early Buddhism did not support the killing of any animal, including snakes, medieval Chinese Buddhist monks adapted the strategy of killing snakes to aid local communities, to heal illnesses in local villagers, and to compete with Daoist priests for religious power. In ancient times, Daoist priests had developed techniques and rituals for killing snakes—seen both as dangerous animals and as demons—by mobilizing spirits and deities. Meanwhile, in medieval China, Daoist priests transformed snakes from demons into protectors of monastic properties. Snakes in medieval Daoist narratives became weapons that were used against both political power and religious adversaries.

The killing of snakes in medieval Chinese Buddhism was a new development shaped by a number of factors. First, it seems that the evolving Mahāyāna teachings offered a doctrinal foundation for auspicious killing, with new traditions that authorized radical responses by a bodhisattva for the sake of sentient beings. Auspicious violence, such as self-immolation and killing evil sentient beings, became widely acceptable for medieval Chinese Buddhists, and sometimes even served as supportive evidence for the eminence of monastic members. Second, social and historical demands to kill snakes to benefit local communities and save local villagers drew the attention of, and a response from, Buddhist monks. Third, there were exchanges of ideas and practices between Buddhism and Daoism about how to handle venomous snakes. Buddhist monks developed techniques and rituals, and especially esoteric methods, for killing snakes to compete with Daoism. I view this new development as a challenge-response process. Doctrinal, historical, social, and religious challenges shaped the Buddhist acceptance of killing snakes in response to social, cultural, and religious crises in medieval China.

CHAPTER 6

Buddhists Enlightening Virtuous Birds

The Parrot as a Religious Agent

Chapter 5 might read like a case study of negative Buddhist attitudes toward the wicked reptile. But in this chapter, I attempt to offer some balance by focusing on a brighter Buddhist image: the parrot. To further illustrate the complexity of animal culture in general in medieval China, I examine the parrot's cultural significance across the history, literature, and religions of the period. As I briefly note in the introduction to this book, the parrot appeared as one of the most popular animals in Buddhism and Chinese traditions because it was thought to be a virtuous bird.

I have shown so far that Chinese Buddhism developed regionally and locally, in both thought and ritual practice, by negotiating among and incorporating numerous indigenous traditions across China. Although I echo some issues raised earlier in the book, here I reveal how tensions existed between the Chinese tradition and Buddhist tradition, and Buddhist doctrinal teachings and local Chan thoughts, by analyzing how a medieval Chinese author who had both political and Buddhist identities wrote about the parrot. I explore how the parrot played a role in fostering shared values, particularly virtue and benevolence, between the Chinese elite class and the Buddhists; in other words, how the parrot served as an agent for medieval Chinese Buddhists in their own community and beyond.

Although a certain species of parrot was native to the frontier regions of ancient China, its images and roles changed and transformed as the spread of Buddhism reintroduced the parrot in medieval Chinese literary, religious, and political culture. It is interesting to analyze how this bird was caught in numerous challenges from the perspectives of political sovereignty, dominant intellectual tradition, exotic religious culture, environmental contexts, and even the daily experiences of the medieval Chinese elite who were privileged to access this bird.

Many scholars have touched on historical sources that concern this bird.[1] As an animal with the capacity to mimic human speech,[2] the parrot was imbued with the power of moral transformation in medieval Chinese Buddhism, moving beyond the fashionable popularity of parrots in medieval Chinese literature. Parrots became a desirable choice of pet for the upper class, due to their astonishing beauty and apparent ability to understand human emotions and feelings. After all, raising parrots reflected the lifestyle and fashions of the elite. Many poems and texts left by literati and officials can tell us about the rich history and culture of parrots in medieval China.[3]

One such high-ranking literati official was Wei Gao 韋皋 (745–805), a lay Buddhist who was also a well-versed military general ruling the southwestern region of the Tang Empire, defending it from Tibetans and other local powers. Wei Gao wrote a powerful essay titled "Record of the Stupa for a Parrot's Relics in the Xichuan Area" (Xichuan yingwu sheli ta ji 西川鸚鵡舍利塔記); with this essay he developed a Buddhist rhetoric in which an enlightened parrot is analogous to Chinese sages in terms of body and virtue. The images of the parrot in Wei Gao's writing take shape under the influence of literary traditions and allusions, historical conditions, religious doctrines and practices, politics, and his personal experiences.

In this chapter, as I contextualize the Buddhist rhetoric of writing about the enlightened parrot in medieval Chinese literary and cultural history, I also demonstrate that in the Tang dynasty, cultural elites could accept the notion of an enlightened parrot and attach considerable social importance to it. In presenting parrots as previous incarnations of the Buddha, it seems that Wei Gao attempted to transform this bird, viewed as imbued with the capacity for human language, virtue, and intelligence, as a plausible advocate of Buddhist teachings.

In particular, this piece of writing by Wei Gao is a religious text serving its Buddhist rhetorical purpose to instruct how a bird could receive salvation by its Pure Land cultivation and practice. I intend to reveal the author's intellectual and religious world by analyzing the interconnected historical allusions (*gudian* 古典) and contemporary allusions (*jindian* 今典) as well as the Buddhist concepts and practices. Wei's ninth-century text not only drew upon some earlier literary traditions by using historical allusions in early medieval Chinese literature, but it also indexed experiences from his personal life.

When referring to Wei's personal experiences I include as well the emotions those experiences generated. For instance, in his writing on the parrot he does not explicitly express the bitter recollection of a romance during his youth, but the historical allusions he used in this writing refer to where he was during a specific religious or romantic experience. I suggest that this interconnectedness between the historical and contemporary allusions in Wei's parrot text served Buddhist rhetoric concerning karmic retribution. Wei was a highly educated literati-official, so his writing illustrated his training, typical at the time, in classical literature, history, and intellectual thoughts. The historical allusions he used show that he knew the literary and intellectual traditions that could contribute to his commemorative inscriptional text for the parrot. In the meantime, as a high-ranking official in the Tang dynasty, he was familiar with many legendary and factual historical events and accounts that circulated about the parrot. In other words, his knowledge about the parrot was conditioned by the historical context of his era. Furthermore, I also explore how Wei brings traditional Chinese thoughts and Buddhist doctrines and practices together to develop a plausible case for the salvation of the parrot for the acceptance of his contemporary Buddhist readers.

In the first section, I analyze the classical allusions used in Wei's parrot text and demonstrate how the historical allusions from the *Selections of Refined Literature* (*Wenxuan* 文選) that appeared in it can be connected with his personal experiences to show a Buddhist teaching of karmic retribution. I also examine the gap between the historical image of the parrot as a bird from the Western Regions and the historical knowledge about parrots in the Tang dynasty. In addition, I analyze the religious implications of Wei Gao's writing on the parrot, with a focus on the Pure Land thought and practice.

In the second section I analyze the body and virtue discourse in Wei Gao's text on the enlightened parrot. Wei's apologetic strategy seems to compare the parrot's physiological characteristics as a bird with the exotic body features of ancient Chinese sages as commonly known to readers at that time. Therefore, the parrot not only shared the same virtues and qualities of compassion and wisdom of the ancient Chinese sages, but also shared similar physiological features.

In the third section I trace the images and roles of the parrot in early medieval Chinese Buddhist literature and political culture. I suggest that early medieval Chinese Buddhist literature gradually portrayed the parrot as a virtuous and intelligent bird with the capability of human speech. This lays a doctrinal and intellectual foundation for the cultural use of the parrot in medieval Chinese political and religious culture.

BUDDHIST RHETORIC IN LITERARY, HISTORICAL, AND CULTURAL CONTEXTS

One of the most interesting texts on Buddhist animals in medieval China is Wei Gao's essay "Record of the Stupa for a Parrot's Relics in the Xichuan Area." This epigraphic piece was carved on the stupa dedicated to a deceased parrot. The original stupa no longer exists, although local records indicate it was in Sanxue Temple 三學寺 in Jintang County, near Chengdu. Jintang County 金堂縣 was established in the second year of the Xianheng period (671), taking its name from the nearby Mount Jintang 金堂山. A local gazetteer compiled in 1733 by Zhang Jinsheng 張晉生 and his group under the supervision of Huang Tinggui 黃廷桂 gives the site of the stupa as Mount Sanxue 三學山.[4] It is unclear when and how the original stupa disappeared. Nevertheless, the stupa's inscription survived in the *Selected Literary Works of the Tang Dynasty* (*Tang wen cui* 唐文粹), a collection compiled in 1011 by Yao Xuan 姚鉉 (967–1020).[5] In this section, I will contextualize Wei's inscription from literary, social, cultural, and religious perspectives.[6]

The author Wei Gao was born into the influential Wei family, near Chang'an, the capital city. He later became a talented and accomplished general in the late eighth century, serving as the military governor of the Xichuan Circuit for a long time. He repeatedly defeated the Tibetan forces and secured the southwestern borders of the Tang Empire. In addition to his remarkable political and military career, Wei was "instrumental to the development of Chan in Sichuan and the Nanzhao Kingdom."[7] He wrote many essays for the Buddhist communities in the regions he governed, including an inscription for a giant stone Buddha,[8] an epitaph for the monk Shenhui, and this inscription for the parrot. The latter caught my attention for its rich information bridging traditional Chinese views on animals, sages, and Buddhist views of animals and Buddhahood.

According to the colophon, Wei Gao wrote this record on the fourteenth day of the eighth month of the nineteenth year of the Zhenyuan period (September 3, 803) during the reign of Emperor Dezong. Wei was then at the peak of his political and military career and had received numerous honors from the emperor. He resided in Chengdu as a high-ranking administrative and military official and met many Buddhist monks and lay devotees.[9] Wei's manuscript, like the engraved stupa, no longer survives. It is unclear whether the text may have circulated among

Wei Gao's lay and monastic friends. It was recorded in both Buddhist and non-Buddhist literary collections from the Song dynasty onward.

A close reading of Wei Gao's epitaph for a parrot raises interesting questions. Like many Tang writings, it frequently alludes to earlier works, following a convention to show that its author was well versed in older Chinese literary traditions. The literary allusions reflected in the parrot inscription come from various writings included in the *Selections of Refined Literature*, compiled by Xiao Tong (501–531), especially "Rhapsody on the Parrot" (Yingwu fu 鸚鵡賦) by Mi Heng 禰衡 (173–198), so popular that the Island of the Parrot (Yingwu zhou) was named in its honor, and allegedly "Stele of the Dhūta Monastery" (Toutuosi bei 頭陀寺 碑) by Wang Jin 王巾 (?–505).[10] Both texts were well known to Tang dynasty literati, but for Wei Gao they had special importance: he had actually stayed in the Dhūta Temple when he was young; and the number of allusions he made to "Rhapsody on the Parrot" measure the tremendous impact of Mi Heng on his writings.[11]

Wei's inscription said that the parrot came from the Western Regions and was endowed with beauty and the capacity for speech; such comments were also found in Mi's text: "A Marvelous bird from the Western Regions," Mi exclaimed. "Manifests a wondrous natural beauty. It embodies the sublime substance of the metal essence, embodies the shining brilliance of the fire's power."[12] Wei similarly wrote: "The primal essence gave form to the myriad species by means of the five elemental energies. Even though some creatures may have scales, and others shell, fur, or feathers, there are sure to be some whose [sentient] endowments are keen and pure. Whether resplendent like fire or an unusual pure green in color, all respond to human culture."[13] Wei not only followed the literary allusion from Mi Heng's poem, but also attempted to build a strong karmic connection between the parrot and Buddhism, as I show below. For Wei Gao, a lay Buddhist in the medieval period, both the parrot and Buddhism came from the Western Regions.[14]

The Dhūta Temple's role in Wei Gao's personal life may indicate that he felt a karmic connection to the parrot's Buddhist affinity. When he was young, he traveled to Jiangxia 江夏 and stayed in the mansion of Prefect Jiang 姜郡守. Jiang's son Jingbao 荊寶 became a good friend to Wei Gao. Although Jingbao addressed Wei Gao as his older brother, he respected him like an uncle. Jingbao asked his female servant Yuxiao 玉簫, who was ten years old, to serve Wei Gao. Two years later, Wei Gao left Prefect Jiang's mansion to dwell in the Dhuta Temple. Yuxiao was again dispatched by Jingbao to serve Wei Gao. After Yuxiao grew up, she fell in love with Wei.

When Wei's uncle wrote a letter summoning him to return home, Wei prepared to embark on his journey and sent a letter to Jingbao, informing him of his departure. Jingbao and Yuxiao came to visit Wei. Although Wei said that he was unable to take Yuxiao with him, he promised to marry her in five to seven years. He gave Yuxiao a jade ring and a poem. After five years, Yuxiao had still not heard from Wei, so she went to the Island of the Parrot for quiet prayer. Two years later, Yuxiao lamented that Wei Gao might never reappear. Out of disappointment, she committed suicide by starvation. Jingbao was so moved by her love for Wei Gao that he buried her with the jade ring.

Later Wei became the military governor of Chengdu and met a prisoner who claimed to be Jingbao. Jingbao told him that Yuxiao had killed herself. Wei Gao felt guilty and started supporting Buddhism by making images and copying scriptures. He often thought of Yuxiao and regretted that he would never meet her again. But a local diviner who had a skill for summoning the souls of the deceased instructed Wei Gao to fast for seven days. At midnight one moonlit night, Yuxiao came to meet Wei Gao. She told Wei that because of his devoted copying of scriptures and making images, she would be reborn in ten days, and in sixteen years would serve Wei Gao again. Wei Gao built a career as a successful statesman, ruling the southwestern borderland of the Tang Empire. Sixteen years after his encounter with Yuxiao's soul, while celebrating his birthday, he saw a dancer who looked exactly like her. He realized that Yuxiao's wish had been fulfilled.[15] This story is rhetorical rather than factual. It was perhaps created by later generations as an attempt to build karmic connections among several events in Wei Gao's life.

Another story about Wei Gao's karmic connection with Buddhism is related to his birth. It is said that when he was born, his family invited some monks for a vegetarian feast. An ugly "barbarian" (non-Han) monk showed up without invitation. When he saw the baby, he greeted it as if they had met before. All of the guests were surprised. Wei Gao's father questioned the "barbarian" monk. He answered that this baby was the reincarnation of Zhuge Liang of the late Han dynasty, and he foretold that Wei Gao would later become a military governor. Wei Gao indeed became a military governor, ruling the Shu 蜀 region for eighteen years. This story was collected in a volume of tales in the Tang dynasty compiled by Zhang Du (around the ninth century),[16] but it is not repeated in any other sources.

Many Buddhist sources have portrayed Wei Gao as a major patron of the religion in the Shu region.[17] For instance, he became the disciple of the Chan master Shenhui 神會 and studied meditation with him. He supported the Jingzhong Temple (Jingzhongsi 淨眾寺), where Shenhui resided. After Shenhui passed away, Wei Gao erected a tomb monument for him and composed an inscription for it.[18] Wei Gao also patronized the local Buddhist community by writing many essays for local monasteries. One of the more important of these is the "Record of the Transmission of the New Commentary on the Vinaya at Baoyuan Temple" (Baoyuansi chuanshou pini xinshu ji 寶圜寺傳授毘尼新疏記). It was inscribed on a stele at this temple. He donated money for copying this new commentary and invited the Vinaya master Guangyi 光翌 to teach it to a select group of monks.[19] Wei Gao's most important act of patronage was probably his ongoing support for the construction of a giant statue of Maitreya Buddha at Lingyun Temple (Lingyunsi 凌雲寺) in Jiazhou 嘉州 (present-day Leshan 樂山) between 789 and 803. After its completion, Wei composed a commemorative record for the statue.[20] In addition, he renovated the statue of Samantabhadra Bodhisattva at Daci Temple 大慈寺 and rebuilt Baoli Temple 寶歷寺.

Wei Gao's inscription about the parrot reveals a gap between literary and religious rhetoric and historical reality. The statement that the parrot was a bird of the Western Regions, and that its name appeared in the Sanskrit scriptures, seems to mirror the description in Mi Heng's second-century rhapsody, but does not correspond with the knowledge of Wei's Tang contemporaries, whether court officials or Buddhist monks. Many of them were aware that parrots came also from the southwestern regions of the Tang Empire and especially from the small kingdoms south of Jiao Prefecture (Jiaozhou 交州, extending into modern Vietnam). Many different genres of writings in the Tang dynasty and various historical sources attest to this knowledge about the native lands of parrots. For instance, on November 30, 631, the Kingdom of Linyi 林邑 paid a tribute of a five-color parrot to the Tang court. On December 10, 631, Silla paid a tribute of two beautiful courtesans to the Tang court. Wei Zhen advised the emperor not to accept the women as tributes, and the emperor observed that the parrot was complaining about the cold weather and missing its homeland. The emperor sent both the parrot and the courtesans back with the envoys.[21]

According to Edward H. Schafer, Chinese sources mentioned parrots from the Long Mountains (in the modern Shaanxi-Gansu border region) from as early as the third century BCE, and people in central China regarded the parrot as a sacred bird from the Western Regions for their miraculous gift of speech.[22] In the early medieval period, parrots from this area must have been sought out for capture. Parrots from the tropical South became known in the Han dynasty. He noted that parrots of different colors came from many southern regions within or beyond the borders of the Tang Empire. He argues that parrots in the Tang dynasty were reputed to be refined in understanding, discriminating in intelligence, and excellent at answering questions.[23] Schafer suggested that the parrots in the area of the Long Mountains survived until the Song era. Green parrots from the forested eastern slopes of the Tibetan massif appeared in Chinese literature in the second century. The reputation of both these native parrots from the Long Mountains and the Tibetan region was eclipsed in the Tang dynasty by that of the supposedly more auspicious "five-colored parrots," "white parrots," and "red parrots" from Southeast Asia and even further afield, such as Australia. Schafer highlighted that "five-colored" denotes "polychromatic and rainbow-hued things." Many neighboring states offered splendid parrots as auspicious tributes to Chinese imperial courts.[24]

Aside from its literary implications, a close of reading of Wei's parrot inscription reveals religious and sociocultural implications. Wei indicates that keeping parrots as pets was a widespread custom among the upper classes. Mr. Pei, the original owner of the parrot, was from a reputable aristocratic clan. Parrots were still exotic to most people from lower classes; they could not own parrots and so had no context for them in their daily lives, though they must have known about parrots from literature or art, especially Buddhist sources. The parrot was also one of the most common animals depicted in medieval Buddhist art. For example, various parrots appeared in the murals of medieval Buddhist caves in Dunhuang (figure 6.1, figure 6.2).[25] Schafer points out that Chinese writers developed a particular trope by which the parrot adopted the role of "the wise talking bird as guardian of the household, especially a proxy for the husband in watching over his wife's fidelity."[26]

In a religious context, the parrot became significant in Buddhism in the Tang dynasty. Wei Gao's parrot text stated that, "When Pei had struck the stone ten times and the bird had completed ten recitations, it smoothed its feather, tucked up its feet, and, without wavering or fidgeting, serenely ended it life. According

6.1 A green parrot sitting on a lotus flower, Mogao Cave 45, Dunhuang. c. 7th century. © *Dunhuang shiku quanji*, 2000.

to the Buddhist scriptures, with the completion of ten recollections or recitations [of the Buddha's name] one may achieve rebirth in the western [pure land]. It is also said that one who has acquired the wisdom of a Buddha will leave Śarīra relics when he dies. One who really understands this concept certainly will not make [a] distinction based on species."[27] The parrot who recited the name of the Amitābha Buddha ten times would eventually be reborn in the Western Paradise, which was the Chinese understanding of the Sukhāvatī in Pure Land tradition.[28] In other words, this parrot received salvation from the Amitābha Buddha for being reborn in the Pure Land, and this salvation was verified by the relics remaining after its cremation. The parrot is not infrequently encountered in early Buddhist literature. But as Reiko Ohnuma notes in her reading of the Śuka Avadāna (Avadānaśataka Sūtra no. 56), "even a parrot endowed with human

6.2 Two green parrots depicted in Yulin Cave 25, Dunhuang, c. 8th century.
© *Dunhuang shiku quanji*, 2000.

speech is ultimately limited in what he can achieve within an animal's body—and even that comes about not through his own agency, but through the agency of the Buddha."[29] She points out that the human prerogative to engage in intentional self-cultivation is unique. In the Śuka Avadāna, the parrot saw the Buddha, gave rise to faith, and was reborn as a god in the Trāyastriṃśa heavenly realm.

Yet Wei's text states that the parrot he met could practice self-cultivation by chanting Amitābha Buddha's name. Eventually the parrot was reborn in the Western Paradise, which is different from way it was reborn in the early Buddhist tradition. In fact, Wei's inscriptional text shows a more sophisticated rhetoric for the parrot's path toward salvation. First, Wei noted that the parrot had recited Amitābha ten times and died but he did not explicitly say that the parrot was enlightened or was reborn in the Pure Land. Instead, he cited a Buddhist canonical text without giving the title and claimed that a sentient being who recited the name of the Amitābha Buddha ten times would be reborn in the Western Paradise. Then he cited another canonical text again without the title and claimed that a sentient being who obtained the Buddha's wisdom would leave relics behind.

Second, he continued to claim that there would be no different outcome between humans and animals for their practice of reciting Amitābha ten times and obtaining the Buddha's wisdom. The parrot was tested with cremation and indeed its relics were recovered, which was verified by observers and listeners. Third, Wei used a rhetorical question asking why the parrot was not the manifestation of a Bodhisattva. In the Amitāyurdhyāna Sūtra (*Guang Wuliangshoufo jing* 觀無量壽佛經), reciting Amitābha ten times is designed for practitioners of the lowest grade (*xia pin xia sheng* 下品下生). For a more severe case of bad karma, they would experience numerous kalpas and immeasurable hardship, and so they should recite Amitābha ten times. By reciting the name of the Amitābha Buddha, they could eliminate their evil karma from eight billion kalpas. When their life journeys come to an end, they would see the golden lotus flower. Then they would instantly be reborn in the extremely joyful world sphere.[30] The parrot is a sentient being from the animal realm, which is hardly the lowest grade practitioner. But this might be Wei's strategy of using the lowest grade practitioners to persuade others that, even though the parrot was a bird, in comparison with those lowest practitioners, the parrot would have no problem being reborn in the Pure Land.

Furthermore, Wei described how the parrot was treated after its death, depicting its salvation. Wei wrote, "Pei ordered a fire to be built and immolated [the bird] according to standard cremation procedure. When the blaze finally died out, lo and behold, there were more than ten beads of Śarīra relics. They glistened brightly before the eye and felt smooth to the palm, like fine jade. Those who saw them gaped in amazement. Whoever heard about them listened with alarm. Everyone agreed that if the bird was able to entice the wayward and bring benefit to the world [like this], how could it not have been the manifestation of a Bodhisattva?"[31] Since Wei indicates that the parrot could be the manifestation of a bodhisattva, it would be very close to eventually becoming a Buddha. According to Gregory Schopen's study of some early Mahāyāna texts preserved in the Gilgit manuscripts, being reborn in the world sphere of Sukhāvatī might be a generalized goal for Mahāyāna practitioners but it was reserved for the advanced bodhisattva who regarded Sukhāvatī as their buddhafield.[32] Wei's text clearly described the deathbed moment of the parrot. When the parrot became ill and was about to die, its master told it that it should practice visualization and chanting. These two practices refer to visualizing the vision of Amitābha's welcoming descent and chanting the name of Amitābha. In his commentary on the Amitāyurdhyāna Sūtra, Shandao (613-681) provides systematic instructions on the practice of visualization and recitation centered on Amitābha. While chanting the name of Amitābha with the thought of receiving the welcoming of Amitābha, one could be reborn in the Pure Land.[33] So the parrot indeed followed the instructions, chanting the name of Amitābha ten times while its master was striking the chime. The bird focused its mind on the *samādhi*, the thoughtful recollection of the Buddha. When the recitation stops, the parrot should be in the state of non-thought, as it has practiced before. Wei's text points out that this non-thought visualization of Amitābha led to the realization of the Buddhist truth. In his text, Wei notes the progress of cultivation from the thought to the non-thought (*wunian* 無念, also "no-thought"), which illustrates his understanding of Buddhist thoughts. He points out that being in non-thought is the Buddhist truth and it is empty. Wei actually indicates that non-thought should be regarded as the state of enlightenment, which was empty. Therefore, when the parrot reached the state of non-thought, it reached enlightenment.

Wendi Adamek's study helps us understand the historical and religious context in which Wei Gao discussed non-thought in his text for the parrot. Wei Gao has a close connection with the Jingzhong Temple in Chengdu, which was primarily associated with both Pure Land and Chan practices in the ninth century. According to the *Song Biographies of Eminent Monks*, Wei once learned the method of cultivating mind with the master Shenhui 神會 (720–794) of the South School of the Chan tradition at Jingzhong Monastery in Chengdu. As a major patron of Shenhui, Wei wrote a text carved on Shenhui's stele after his death.[34] Shenhui was a dharma heir of a Korean Chan master named Wuxiang 無相 (Korean Musang, 684–762) who was regarded as the founder of the Jingzhong School of the early Chan tradition. Adamek points out that Wuxiang developed a special style of vocal *nianfo*. After Wuxiang expounded the dharma on a high seat, he led a vocal recollection of the Buddha. When the recitation ended, he taught the "no-recollection, no-thought, and do not be deluded" premise. He would also remind the audience that no-thought is *samādhi*. For Adamek, Wuxiang's *nianfo* practice indicates that there was a lack of concern over the boundary between Pure Land and Chan. She suggests that Wuxiang's practice was influenced by Fazhao (d. 820?) who developed the chanting practice in the Pure Land tradition that was linked with visualization of Amitābha.[35] Early Chan shared some similar ideas about the *nianfo* practice in the Pure Land tradition that was centered on the no-thought and invocation of the Buddha.[36] As John McRae points out, no-thought means the state of enlightenment in the Northern School of early Chan tradition. While discussing Shenxiu's 神秀 (606–706) "Five Expedient Means" (Ch. *Wufangbian* 五方便) from early Chan works discovered in Dunhuang, McRae notes that in the context of constructing Five Expedient means, the "non-thought (*wunian*)" should be understood as referring to "the moment at which this achievement (thoughts have been transcended) occurs and to the fundamental mind or enlightenment itself, which is like an ocean with no waves."[37] In this sense, the state of so-called non-thought might indicate the state of the enlightenment.

Wei wrote one more thing about the monumental success of the parrot's rebirth which emphasized the importance of monastic witness and endorsement: "At that time, an eminent monk Huiguan 慧觀 once visited Mount Wutai 五台山 for a pilgrimage of paying homage to holy traces. He heard about this bird and cried with tears. He begged for the relics of this parrot and housed it with tile earthenware on the Mountain Ling 靈, constructing a pagoda for honoring this marvelous thing." Although the salvation of this parrot was supervised by a lay Buddhist and witnessed by a lay Buddhist, Wei's reference to Huiguan's honoring activities associated with the post-cremation of the parrot might indicate that the salvation of the parrot deserved a crucial monastic endorsement. For Wei, the relics it left after cremation indeed verified its eventual rebirth in the Pure Land.[38] And Wei's statement about the relics left by the parrot aims to persuade readers that the parrot was indeed reborn in the Pure Land. But neither the parrot nor the funeral ceremony participants were monastic members. They were lay Buddhists. So Wei continued to introduce the support of a monastic member.[39] He said that the eminent monk Huiguan, who was on his pilgrimage journey to Mount Wutai, heard this story and requested to honor this parrot's relics with a stupa. This development should be regarded as recognition and honor from the monastic community. In other words, though the parrot was a bird and its owner was a lay Buddhist, its rebirth in the Pure Land has been recognized by the monastic community, which was represented by Huiguan, an eminent monk and pilgrim.

THE ENLIGHTENED PARROTS AND CHINESE SAGE-KINGS

Medieval Chinese Buddhists always attempted to build up the parallelism between the Buddha and Chinese sages.[40] For example, the *Pearl Forest of the Dharma Grove*, compiled by Daoshi, claimed that Confucius profoundly understood the Buddha to be a great sage (*dasheng* 大聖).[41] In medieval Chinese Buddhist literature, the Buddha was not only called the "World Honored One" (*shizun* 世尊), he was also often called the "great sage."[42] Wei Gao indicated that he too believed the parrot to be enlightened by its Pure Land practice, and he also connected the enlightened parrot with ancient sages, writing: "In ancient times, beings that penetrated the level of the sages and worthies and appeared as manifestations include Nüwa 女媧 who came with a serpent's body to instruct the emperor [Fuxi], and Zhongyan 中衍 who had the body of a bird and came to establish the marquise [of Qin]. They are recorded in the books of [bamboo] slips. Who says that these tales are strange? How much the less should it be so when this bird spread the way and left so much clear proof of its sagehood."[43] So he paid particular attention to the shared physiological features of the parrot as a bird and the ancient sage-kings as cultural heroes who laid the foundation for Chinese civilizations. It seems that he attempted to persuade his readers not to be surprised that the parrot, being a bird, could be reborn in the Western Paradise since those ancient sages and sage-kings who had animal bodies or animal body parts achieved sagehood. For Wei Gao, a devoted Buddhist layperson, the body became the focus of the Buddhist apologetic discourse.

Confucian discourse on the parrot, however, stated that animals were inferior to human beings, morally and spiritually. Citing *Liji* 禮記 and *Huainanzi* 淮南子, Roel Sterckx points out that in traditional Chinese culture the ability of parrots and apes to speak did not make them equal to human beings. The sage "wields an indirect, non-physical, and moral authority over the beasts through the medium of music and the cultivation of virtue."[44]

Wei Gao offered an alternative viewpoint in the belief that animals are not inferior to human beings and can receive ultimate salvation. In medieval China, it was widely accepted that some ancient sages or cultural heroes had the body parts of animals. Examples in the paragraph above from Wei's writing indicate that Nüwa 女媧 had a serpent's body, while Zhongyan 中衍 had a bird's body. According to the *Basic Annals of the Qin* in the *Records of the Grand Historian* (史記 秦本紀), one of the ancestors of the Qin was Dafei, who assisted the sage ruler Yu to pacify the waters and the land. Later he assisted the ruler Shun to tame birds and beasts. Dafei had two sons. One, Dalian, became the founder of the bird-custom family. Dalian had two great-great-grandsons, Mengxi and Zhongyan, who both had a bird body and spoke the language of men.[45] The rulers of the Xia dynasty hired Mengxi to tame beasts. Such legends were common knowledge among many medieval Chinese writers, including Buddhist scholars and officials. It was not surprising to see that Wei Gao also wrote about such legends while discussing the salvation of the parrot in Pei's family.

A debate between Buddhists and Daoists in the early Tang dynasty reflects the attempt of some Buddhists to link the birthplace and status of the Buddha as a "foreigner" and "barbarian" to the situation of some sage kings in ancient China. The Daoist Fu Yi 傅弈 (555-639) submitted a memorial to Emperor Taizong (Li Shimin, 598-649, r. 626-649) attacking foreign Buddhist monks as "barbarians" with human faces but the minds of beasts. For Fu Yi, the Buddha was a "barbarian" from the Western Regions who had been born from evil mud. In his eyes, because the Buddha often dealt with mud and bricks, he was malodorous. His followers were like donkeys, an evil, greedy, and deviant species. In short, Fu Yi argued that the Buddha was born as a "barbarian" in a foreign land and he did not look like a Chinese man.[46] On the Buddhist side, one of the leaders of the Buddhist community, Falin 法琳 (572-640), offered counterarguments to these two points. Buddhist apologists cited three traditional Chinese sources: *Record of the Grand Historian* by Sima Qian 司馬遷; a catalogue (*Qizhi* 七誌, *Seven Bibliographic Treatises*) of Wang Jian 王儉 (452-489); and chronicles (*Diwang nianli* 帝王年曆, *Chronicles of the Rulers*) by Tao Hongjing 陶弘景 (456-536).[47] These sources, the apologists claimed, showed that both Emperor Fuxi and his instructor Nüwa had a snake's body and a human head, that Dalian 大廉 had a human body and an ox's head, and that Zhongyan 中衍—who like Fuxi and Nüwa figures in Wei Gao's writing—had a bird's body and a human face. So they all had bodies that were partially bestial in nature.

Furthermore, Falin noted, many ancient Chinese sages and rulers had been either born to "barbarians," like King Wen of the Zhou dynasty who was born among the Western Qiang tribes, or to be connected with animals, Jiandi 簡狄 gave birth to Qi, the early ruler of the Shang, after eating the eggs of a swallow.[48] Yu 禹 of the Xia dynasty, also born among the Western Qiang, came out by cutting through his mother's body. Yu's story is very similar to the legendary birth of the prince Siddhartha who came out from his mother's right side. Yiyin 伊尹, who served King Tang 湯 of the Shang dynasty and helped defeat King Jie 桀 of the Xia dynasty, was said to have been found in a hollow mulberry tree (*kongsang* 空桑).[49] The Yuan family, founders of the Northern Wei dynasty (386-535), were also born as so-called barbarians. They all responded to the call of Heaven or even obtained the mandate of Heaven to become rulers. Although they were born in remote and vulgar lands and their bodies and appearances were rustic, they were endowed with heavenly dignity and embraced sagely virtue. Even Laozi was said to have been born from a herdswoman. Falin concluded that such humble origins were by no means a barrier to sagehood, and cited Confucius's observation on settling among nine "barbarian" tribes in the east: "Once a gentleman settles amongst them, what uncouthness will there be?"[50] Essentially, Falin argued that whoever has the Way should be respected and honored.

Falin also argued that the Buddha could manifest himself anywhere in accord with the needs of sentient beings. But he still attempted to link the Buddha to the royal lineage in ancient South Asia, claiming that the Buddha was the grandson of the thousand-generation wheel king—one who rules with justice and brings tranquility to his people—and the crown prince of the Kshatriya king. The place where he was born was the center of the three-thousand realm and the great kingdom of Jambudvīpa.

Moreover, Falin took issue with some contemporaneous claims that people born among the Qiang "barbarians" (Qianghu 羌胡) in the west or among the Rong "caitiffs" (Ronglu 戎虜) in the north, rather than in central China, were evil. Finally, he raised a geographical issue to refute Fu Yi. He cited the chapter on geography in the *History of the Han Dynasty* (*Hanshu*) to say that the so-called western barbarian regions were limited to thirty-six states on the eastern side of the Pamir mountain ranges, and India was not one of these "barbarian" regions.[51] An official Tang historian, Sima Zhen 司馬貞 (679–732), compiled a book titled the *Basic Annals of Three Sovereigns* (*Sanhuang benji* 三皇本紀) in the early eighth century, which illustrated some ideas about early Chinese cultural heroes appearing in the *Records of Grand Historians* (*Shiji*). This book recounts a legend about Fuxi as a founder of Chinese civilization. It states that that Taihao 太皞 (also known as Paoxi shi 庖犧氏 or Fuxi 伏羲, "animal-tamer") replaced Suiren 燧人 ("fire-maker") as sovereign. His mother became pregnant after stepping in the footprint of a giant. Born with the body of a snake and a human head, he possessed divine virtue and created diagrams (*bagua* 八卦) based on his observations of heaven and earth. Despite being part-beast, both Fuxi and Nüwa had divine virtues that legitimated their sovereignty.

For Falin and his fellow Buddhists who developed the Han-centric thinking from their education, some sage kings of ancient China may have born among so-called barbarians and some may have been captives, but they were still sage kings. So even though the Buddha was not born in the civilized realm of China and was not a member of a noble family from central China, he was still a sage. In any case, because the Buddha was born to a noble South Asian caste, and he left his brilliant teachings to his followers; he was no different from the Chinese sages.

Legends of ancient Chinese sages with animal bodies also appeared in many medieval Daoist scriptures. One text dated to the Tang dynasty, Luminous Scripture of the Karmic Causality in Former Lives, from the Canon of the Numinous Treasure of Cavern Mystery of the Most High (Taishang dongxuan lingbao suming yinyuan ming jing 太上洞玄靈寶宿命因緣明經), discusses the origins of Chinese civilization in terms of Daoist cosmology. According to this text, the Lord of the Way of the Most High (Taishang daojun 太上道君) told his attendants that there were three Ways: The Way of the Origin (*yuandao* 元道), the Way of the Beginning (*shidao* 始道), and the Way of the Humanity (*rendao* 人道). The Way of the Origin was the great virtue of heaven and earth, the Way of the Beginning was the treasury virtue of heaven and earth, and the Way of the Humanity was the connection virtue of heaven and earth. These three Ways combined to form Virtue, which was the origin of the void. At the beginning of the royal transformation, Nüwa, with the body of a snake, and Fuxi, in this telling, with the body of hoofed chimera called a qilin 麒麟, were intermingled, and yin and yang were in a state of chaos. Then the Three Sages (*sansheng* 三聖, also known as the Three August Ones, Sanhuang 三皇) ruled and abdicated in succession and the Five Thearchs (*wudi* 五帝) began their rule. It then goes on to the accomplishments of the Great Yu and Shun for their efforts of serving people.[52] The virtue of these figures such as Three August Ones and Five Thearchs led to their veneration as rulers, despite their animal bodies.

In his *Treatise on Discerning the Truth* (Bianzheng lun 辯正論), Falin refutes Daoist claims regarding the appearance of the Buddha and emphasizes the Buddha's characteristic bodily marks as a testament to his being a superior man. Daoists declared that sages have wondrous appearances, different from those of common men. Some were described as having eight-color double pupils or river eyes and sea mouths. Others have dragon faces, and pace like cranes, or have sunken fontanels or exotic hair. "Barbarians," by contrast, often have curly hair, green eyeballs, high snouts, and deep-set eyes, marking them as distinct from Chinese sages. Falin begins by admitting that Chinese sages indeed manifest wondrous physical traits, such as snake bodies, dragon heads, double pupils, or quadruple nipples. Duke Zhou and Yu the Great both looked different from common people. Yet

for Falin, the Buddha was no different, being able to transform his body in resonance with myriad things. So he had white curls, violet eyebrows, lips like fruit,
eyes like flowers, and a swastika mark with thousand-spoke wheels.[53]

According to medieval Chinese physiognomic discourses, noble people often
had dragon eyeballs and phoenix eyes, and they walked like dragons, tigers, or
phoenixes.[54] If a man's neck looked like that of a lion, he was destined to become
a marquis.[55] Since the late Han dynasty, it seems that there was a widespread concept that ancient sages often had the body parts of animals. The following story
illustrates this popular concept. Zhou Xie 周燮, a native of Runan who lived in
the second century, had been an ugly baby with an underhung jaw and a curved
snout 欽頤折頞. His mother thought his appearance was frightening and planned
to abandon him. But his father argued that the sages often have exotic appearances. He offered some examples, including Fuxi with an ox's head, Nüwa with a
snake's body, Gaoyao 皋繇 with a bird-beak mouth, and Confucius with lips like
those of an ox. He concluded, "So the sages were exotic in appearance. Moreover,
Cai Ze 蔡澤 had a concave chin and a shrunken snout. This baby will bring prosperity to our lineage."[56]

The relationship between the spirit and the body became a focus of debate
between some Buddhists and their critics. In a major sixth-century exchange,
some Chinese Buddhists strongly rejected the contention of Fan Zhen 范縝 (450–
515) that the body can be separated from the spirit, concluding that having an
animal's body does not prevent a sentient being from receiving salvation. In his
essay "On the Extinction of Spirit" (Shenmie lun 神滅論), Fan argued that the
spirit and body cannot be separated, and that when people die, their spirits also
perish: "The soul and the body are identical. Therefore, while the body survives
the soul survives, and when the body perishes the soul is extinguished."[57] This is
because "the body is the soul's material basis; the soul is the functioning of the
body."[58] So the body and the soul cannot be regarded as separate. Fan also stated:
"We know that certain parts of the bodies of sages are quite out of the ordinary,
and that sages are not only superior to ordinary human beings, but also surpass
all other creatures in bodily form. Whether or not ordinary men and sages are
made of the same substance is a question I would not dare to attempt to answer."
According to Fan, Xiang Yu (Xiang Ji) and Yang Huo "had an outward resem-
blance, but not an inner one. If the inner organs are not the same, outward resemblances are meaningless."[59]

In contrast, the Buddhist apologists argued that the spirit and the body can indeed be separated, hence a sage can be born in the body of a common person or even an animal. Fan's cousin Xiao Chen 蕭琛 (479–529) composed an essay questioning Fan's argument.[60] Xiao drew on many historical cases to propose that the body is the mere vessel of the spirit, and the spirit does not perish with the body. In their bodily constitutions, sages do not differ from common people. Their bodies may vary in degrees of solidity or fragility, but they are not inherently different from those of common people.

For Xiao Chen, common people may be indistinguishable from sages and worthies in terms of physical constitution, but they have different spirits, supporting the Buddhist idea that the body was merely a vessel in which the spirit dwelt. Yang Huo did not differ physically from Confucius, though he was not a respected gentleman in Confucius's eyes. Xiang Ji (Xiang Yu) looked like the sage Shun. The common spirits of Yang Huo 陽貨 and Xiang Ji occupied sage-like bodies. Both Shun and Xiang Yu had double pupils in their eyes. Nüwa had a serpent's body, and Gaotao 皋陶 had a horse's mouth. So the spirits of these sages were temporarily dwelling within the bodies of beasts. In early medieval China, Confucius, Shun, Nüwa, and Gaoyao were regarded as cultural heroes who had laid the foundations of Chinese civilization. They shared bodily features with beasts. Xiao Chen interpreted these phenomena by proposing the separation of body and spirit: a sage's spirit can dwell in the body of a beast. Similarly, an enlightened spirit can dwell in the body of a parrot.

In a chapter titled "The Yellow Emperor" 黃帝篇 in the *Book of Liezi* 列子, while discussing the Daoist principle of action, one section focuses on the distinctions between sages and common people and between human beings and beasts. It claims that while a man may be six-*chi* tall and have hands that are different from his feet, he may still have the mind of a beast. Species with wings at their sides and with horns on their heads, or with widely splayed teeth and nails, are called beasts and birds, but they may have the mind of a man. Sages such as Fuxi, Nüwa, Shennong 神農, and the emperors of the Xia dynasty 夏后氏 had snakes' bodies and human faces, or heads of oxen and tigers' snouts. They apparently did not look like men, but they still had the virtues of great sages. In contrast, Jie of the Xia dynasty, Zhou of the Shang dynasty, Duke Huan of Lu 魯桓, and King Mu of Chu 楚穆 had seven orifices in their heads, and in all respects looked like humans, but all had the minds of beasts. For Liezi, sages such as the Yellow Emperor could mobilize beasts and birds. When the Yellow Emperor fought with the Yan Emperor 炎帝, he commanded bears, wolves, leopards, and tigers as his vanguard, and eagles, pheasants, falcons, and kites as his standard-bearers. The sage Yao 堯 attracted beasts and birds by his music. This is because sages know everything and understand everything. They can comprehend the speech of domestic animals. They know the habits of all the myriad things and can comprehend the cries of all the different species. They meet the spirits and goblins first, human beings second, and beasts and birds last.[61]

In early medieval China, Daoists also acknowledged that both humans and animals have the capacity and potential for moral benevolence. As Michael Puett remarks, the capacity and potential of humans, spirits, sages, and also animals in Ge Hong's *Master Who Embraces Simplicity* (*Baopuzi* 抱樸子) are the same. For Ge Hong, both humans and animals are earthly things and therefore they are capable of benevolence. But most humans and animals lack clarity. The few humans who are endowed with clarity are called sages. Sages and spirits are heavenly things so they have clarity.[62]

VIRTUOUS AND INTELLIGENT PARROTS IN MEDIEVAL CHINESE BUDDHIST AND POLITICAL CULTURE

Exploring a broader context of medieval Chinese Buddhist and political culture, it is not surprising to notice that the parrot was connected with the virtuous and wise sage. In this section, I first focus on the changing images of the parrot in medieval Chinese Buddhist literature from a wicked bird destined to be reborn in the animal realm to a wise bird that could benefit sentient beings. Then I discuss how the parrot became a symbolic animal and auspicious bird for monarchs, and a righteous witness for ensuring court justice in medieval Chinese political culture.

The tradition of the parrot appearing as a virtuous and intelligent bird has its doctrinal foundation in Buddhist literature. It can be traced back to early Indian and Buddhist literature. The parrot appeared as an animal of virtuosity, generosity, and compassion in Book 13 Anusasana Parva of the Indian epic *Mahābhārata*, and this literary tradition seems to have an impact on some tales in early Buddhist Jātaka literature, especially Jātaka 429, "Mahāsuka-Jātaka" and Jātaka 430, "Cullasuka-Jātaka."[63] Nevertheless, early Buddhism developed a very diverse literary tradition for portraying the parrot in different contexts, and in different images and roles, as the references in this note reveal.[64] And in early Buddhist cosmology, as many Buddhist texts and Jātaka tales reveal, parrots appear as beings of the animal realm, as previous incarnations of the Buddha, and as preaching assistants to the Buddha in his previous lives. Medieval Chinese Buddhist readers were not unfamiliar with these images and roles because there were numerous Chinese translations of early Buddhist texts available from the early medieval period.

The images of the parrot underwent a long process of change as its legacy in early Buddhism continued in medieval China. The parrot did not appear as a virtuous and intelligent bird in early Buddhist scriptures. In these, the parrot was a bird, an animal, and a sentient being born in the realm of animals, which is lower than humans, demigods (asuras), and gods (devas). Was it possible for a parrot to receive salvation? Yes, it was. Could a parrot become an arhat, a bodhisattva, or a Buddha? No, it could not. Why would a sentient being be reborn as a parrot in the realm of animals? Some early texts translated into Chinese described the parrot as the product of bad rebirth. For instance, a scripture on Dharma-vardhana, the son of King Asoka, offered a brief explanation. It noted that sentient beings who were lustful, talkative, favored by relatives, as well as spoiled by relatives and others, would be reborn as a parrot.[65]

A similarly negative image of the parrot, in this case associated with a woman with bad karma, can be found in an early text titled *Foshuo mayi jing* 佛說罵意經, translated by An Shigao in the first century.[66] It discusses why a person, and particularly a woman, would be reborn as a parrot. It says that a parrot has red lips and red feet because in its previous life it enjoyed colorful clothes and painted its lips red. If a woman enjoyed wearing long skirts, then she would be reborn as a bird with a long tail. It concludes that a sentient being would receive what he or she enjoyed in his or her previous lives.[67]

Some Buddhist texts even indicated that the parrot's capacity for language would impede a good rebirth. A text from Dunhuang titled The Scripture Spoken by the Buddha on the Causes and Effects of Good and Evil Actions (*Foshuo shan'e yinguo jing* 佛說善惡因果經) says that one who imitated others' words would be reborn as a parrot.[68] This text was not incorporated into the Buddhist canon but was very popular in East Asia. Sogdian and Tibetan versions were also found at Dunhuang. The Sogdian text (P. Sogh. 4) was apparently translated from the Chinese version, as shown by the inscription on the Dunhuang manuscript of the

Chinese title.⁶⁹ The textual materials in Chinese, Sogdian, and Tibetan from Dunhuang and Central Asia indicate the popularity of this text among Chinese and Central Asian Buddhists.

Early Mahāyāna texts, however, do offer the parrot hope of salvation. What is a parrot's best path for salvation from *dukkha* (suffering)? A parrot can be reborn in the Trāyastriṃśa heavenly realm. According to the *Scripture of the Wise and Foolish* (*Xianyu jing*), an elder Sudatta had two parrots. The Buddha once preached in the Jetavana Garden at the invitation of the Sudatta. The Buddha's disciple Ananda taught these two parrots the four noble truths. Later they were killed by a fox. The Buddha told Ananda that because the parrots had received the teaching of four noble truths, they would be reborn in the Trāyastriṃśa heavenly realm.⁷⁰

The positive image of the parrot appeared in early Jātaka stories, in which the parrots often appear as previous incarnations of the Buddha. An early translation of the Buddhist text *Foshuo zhangzhe Yinyue jing* 佛說長者音悅經, by Zhiqian 支謙, tells a cause-and-effect story about the Buddha's previous life as a parrot. A king called Yinyue was in his palace when he heard the wondrous sound of a parrot. He ordered that the parrot be brought to him, and decorated its body with various precious jewels, after which he would watch it tirelessly. Additionally, a bald eagle came to the palace and saw the parrot and asked how it had earned such rich favor from the king. The parrot told the eagle that his wondrous sound had attracted the king, who then decorated its body with five-color jewels. At this, the eagle became jealous and also began to make a sound. But the eagle's sound served only to frighten the king. The king ordered that the eagle be captured and its feathers removed. Having endured the loss of its feathers, the eagle left for the wild. Other birds asked it why it had suffered like this. The parrot, it explained, should be held responsible for its suffering. The Buddha commented that good sounds invoked blessings, while bad sounds brought disaster. The eagle was jealous of the parrot so received retribution. It turned out that the parrot was the Buddha in a previous life.⁷¹

Some narratives began to portray the parrot as a passionate advocate of the Buddha's teachings, whose eloquence transformed kings to the Buddhist conversion. One story in the Samyuktaratnapitka Sūtra (*Za baozang jing* 雜寶藏經 (fifth century) tells how a parrot taught a king to follow Buddhist teachings and to behave as a good king.⁷² In Kauśāmbī, a Brahman prime minister was quick-tempered and violent and his wife was deviant and adulterous. The Brahman told his wife to drive Śramaṇa Gautama (the title of the Buddha while being an ascetic practitioner) away from begging in front of their door. Then the Buddha came to visit the couple and scolded them for their disgraceful and deviant thoughts. The next day, the Brahman tried to attack the Buddha with a sword but failed. Eventually the Buddha converted the couple and they obtained the fruit of Srotāpanna. Following this conversion, the Buddha told a story about his previous life as a parrot king who transformed the deviant couple into Buddhists. In the *Mūlasarvāstivāda Vinaya Kṣudrakavastu*, there is another story about how a parrot helped his lord Daoyao to defeat the King and shows the loyalty of the parrot toward his lord. Through its actions, the parrot became involved in political and military affairs and made a tremendous contribution to the accomplishments of his lord.

Similarly, in the *Collection of Scriptures on the Six Pāramitās* (*Liudu jijing* 六度集 經), there are several Jātaka stories about the Buddha's previous lives as parrot kings. These stories shared common features. First, the bodhisattva was the king of a group of parrots. Second, he was wise and passionate, knew Buddhist principles and teachings, cultivated himself with Buddhist practices, and instructed his fellow parrots to do the same. Third, the bodhisattva endured physical sufferings, like those of other parrots, at the hands of human kings. Hence, he understood the sufferings of his fellow parrots, knew its causes, and would do his best to help eliminate it. One story from chapter 4 of the *Collection of Scriptures* relates that the Buddha, in a previous life as parrot king, taught other parrots to eliminate the desire for survival. He often taught other parrots six perfections. The human king of the area liked eating parrots, hence hunters competed to please the king by hunting parrots. They used a net to capture a number of parrots, from which the king's chefs chose fat specimens for cooking. The parrot king pitied his fellow parrots and lamented that they should be killed and consumed by the human king. The parrot king taught that one should eliminate desires for food and other worldly pleasures; desire was the poison that produced suffering.[73] A similar story can be also found in chapter 6, in which the bodhisattva appears as the parrot king who leads a community of six thousand parrots. He told his fellow parrots that they should cultivate themselves, rather than indulging in entertainment.[74]

Filial piety was another important moral quality of the parrot according to many Buddhist narratives. While discussing a sixteenth-century text on Guanyin of the South Sea (Nanhai guanyin), the *Shancai longnü baojuan* 善財龍女寶卷, Yü Chün-fang notes how Guanyin recruited a white parrot as her attendant. She traces this back to the older tradition that the Tang dynasty parrots and *kalavinka* birds were prized novelties. Yü also analyzes a scene in the tableau of didactic sculptures at the Great Buddha Creek at Baodingshan, Dazu, Sichuan. This scene depicts a Jātaka story of the Buddha's previous life as a filial parrot who carries a grain of rice in its mouth to serve his parents. The story was recorded in the *Za baozang jing*. Another Jātaka story from the *Liudu jijing* recounts a parrot's escape from his captor by feigning death. Yü notes that parrots appear as protagonists in Buddhist scriptures and that these in turn serve as sources for the *baojuan* of folk tradition. Yü suggests that the *Shancai longnü baojuan* condenses a story from the *Newly Printed and Completely Illustrated Tale of the Filial and Righteous Brother Parrot* (*Xinkan quanxiang yingge xiaoyi zhuan* 新刊全像鸚哥孝義傳). The latter relates the tale of a filial parrot who helped his parents achieve rebirth in the Pure Land. Later the filial and righteous parrot became the attendant of Nanhai Guanyin.[75]

Aside from the parrot's role as a crucial symbolic bird in medieval Chinese Buddhism, it also appeared as an important bird associated with some emperors as sage-kings in medieval Chinese political culture. As I show in this section, the medieval Chinese understanding and imagination of kingship bridged the gap between parrot and rulers. According to Buddhist Jātaka narratives, the parrot began as a common bird but later became the king of birds. Some Chinese Buddhists like Wei Gao would have been familiar with this image of the parrot in Buddhist narratives. The parrot's anointment in Buddhist literature as king of the birds seems to correspond with its appearance in an early medieval Chinese political ideology centered on the prophecy of a new ruler.

The first instance in which the parrot served as a symbol of divine rule relates to Gao Huan 高歡 (496–547). In the Eastern Wei dynasty (534–550), Gao Huan was the prime minister serving Emperor Xiaojing 孝靜帝 (Yuan Shanjian 元善見, 524–555, r. 534–550). He advised the emperor to move the capital to Ye 鄴, while he would be commanding the troops stationed in Jinyang and exerting real dynastic authority. At that time, a children's ballad prophet in the capital city was singing a song about how a green vulture moved to the capital city Ye, but the power fell into the hands of the parrot. After Gao Huan died, his son Gao Yang 高洋 (526–559, r. 550–559) took the throne from Yuan Shanjian and founded the Northern Qi dynasty. Gao Yang honored his father Gao Huan with the title Emperor Shenwu 神武 (divine martial ability). Then his contemporaries realized that the "parrot" (*yingwu* 鸚鵡) in the earlier children's ballad referred to Gao

Huan,[76] because the second syllable of *yingwu* was homophonous with the second syllable of Shenwu, his title.

In the Tang dynasty, the parrot prophecy was connected with Wu Zetian 武則天 (624–705), the only female emperor in Chinese history, due to homophony between her surname and the second syllable of *yingwu*. As recent scholarship suggests, it appears that Wu Zetian manipulated the image of the parrot to legitimize her claims to divine sovereignty. She ordered her attendants to write a commentary on the Great Cloud Sutra, which was titled *Commentary on the Meaning of Predicating the Divine Empress in the Great Cloud Sutra*.[77] Some manuscripts of this commentary have been found in Dunhuang. This became the major textual foundation for Wu Zetian's construction of political legitimacy. It argued that the prophecy for a woman as a new ruler came from Confucius, from the divine dragon, and from the mandate of heaven. It also developed prophecy discourses based on various animals, including the parrot, which was portrayed as a divine bird endowed with the capacity for human language. This commentary stated that *yingwu* corresponded to the surname of an incoming sage and divine empress. After Wu Zetian took the throne and was about to appoint a crown prince, she consulted with her prime minister, Di Renjie 狄仁傑, and told him that in her dream, a large parrot folded its two wings. Di informed her that this parrot represented her, due to the phonetic correspondence with her surname, and that its wings represented her two sons: she must elevate their political positions so that they could serve as wings. This story shows that Wu Zetian also used the parrot as a symbol to legitimize her reign.[78] In the eyes of contemporaries, the parrot had become an auspicious bird symbolic of the imperial ruler.

The parrot prophecy had a broader context in medieval Chinese political culture. When Buddhism came to China around the first century, there was a culture of political prophecy that had flourished among intellectual and cultural elites since Dong Zhongshu (179–104 BCE) had incorporated it into Confucian political thought. Rulers legitimated their power and authority by recognizing correspondences between auspicious signs and political and social changes. To accumulate social and cultural capital to promote Buddhism, many Buddhist monks claimed that they had the ability to interpret auspicious signs and predict political and social changes. In the Southern and Northern Dynasties, Chinese Buddhists gradually adopted indigenous prophecy practices to make Buddhist beliefs, rituals, and symbolism more accessible to Chinese audiences.[79] Thus, it is not surprising that later in the early Tang era, Chinese Buddhists, integrating Buddhism with prophecy traditions dating from the Eastern Han dynasty, sought to portray the Western Regions culture of Buddhism as a manifestation of a ruler's virtuous governance. Therefore, the existence and prosperity of Buddhism in the Central Plain became an endorsement of the virtuous political culture of a ruler.

In the early Tang dynasty, such rhetoric of connecting auspicious signs with rulers continued to appear in the writings of Chinese Buddhist monks. When Fu Yi attacked Buddhism at the court, a Buddhist monk Minggai 明槩 penned a petition responding to Fu. He first praised the way and virtue of the Three Sovereigns and Five Thearchs, noting the benefits brought by their universal embracement, compassionate teachings, and benevolent minds. He then offered a narrative of the early history of Buddhism in China. According to this, the Han emperor Mingdi 漢明帝 had dreamed of the auspicious sign of a giant golden figure in the Palace of Sweet Springs (Ganquan gong), so he dispatched Qin Jingxian to the Western Regions in search of this figure. Subsequently, Minggai praised the founders of the Tang dynasty, to whom auspicious signs were similarly manifested, and who turned their minds to the protection of Buddhism.[80]

CONCLUSION

Parrots played crucial roles in medieval Chinese literary, cultural, and religious life. Their roles in both Buddhist and non-Buddhist writings are manifold and complex. By the Tang dynasty, the Buddhist view of parrots was culturally assimilated, bringing together both traditional Chinese views of parrots and newly developed Chinese Buddhist ideas on enlightened animals. Chinese literati-officials, such as Wei Gao, were familiar both with Confucian attitudes toward animals and sages and with the literary masterpieces of the *Collections of Refined Literature*. Even if equipped with up-to-date knowledge of the history and geography of parrots, they might have reverted to earlier literary conventions. While dealing with parrots as enlightened animals in the Tang dynasty, it is important to consider the diverse images and roles of these birds by taking historical, literary, cultural, and religious elements into account.

As a highly educated literati-official and a lay Buddhist, Wei Gao developed a strong Buddhist rhetoric claiming that the parrot received salvation by practicing the Pure Land tradition, such as reciting the name of the Amitābha Buddha. First, he recognized the importance of the parrot's ability to mimic human speech, which set a precedent for this bird cultivation by teaching it to recite the name of the Amitābha Buddha. The linguistic ability of the parrot could serve as a tool for the ritual practice of Buddhism as a social and cultural tradition developed by humans.

Second, in applying the historical allusions of the Island of the Parrot and the Dhuta Temple, Wei Gao's inscription suggests an obscure Buddhist karmic connection between the parrot and his personal life. Karmic connection and retribution, as a new concept introduced by Buddhism into China, played an important role in helping Buddhism take root in Chinese society.

Third, in the late Tang dynasty, many people acknowledged that various species of parrots did not come exclusively from the Western Regions. Wei Gao attempted to build up the connection between the enlightened parrot and the Buddha by claiming that the parrot came from the Western Regions, the same place where the enlightened Buddha lived, as most Tang Buddhists understood and imagined.

Fourth, Wei Gao also indicated that the parrot could practice reciting the Amitābha Buddha's name until reaching the status of non-thought. Wei Gao's parrot text shows his acceptance of the Chan idea of non-thought, which he learned from the Chan monks who lived in Chengdu where he governed and sponsored many Buddhist projects. Fifth, Wei Gao introduces a parallel between the parrot in medieval Chinese Buddhism and the sage-kings in ancient China by stating that they share the same animal bodies and virtues. Wei's statement was a powerful apologetic response against the long-term challenge from the non-Buddhist side in medieval China.

In this chapter I analyzed that statement within a broader context of political culture in which the parrot was a bird symbolizing the divine power serving the political legitimacy of several emperors, particularly Gao Huan in the Northern Qi dynasty and Wu Zetian in the Tang dynasty. It is important to note that Wei Gao's writing adds a new dimension to medieval Chinese Buddhist apologetic literature by building up the parallel between the enlightened parrot and ancient sages in terms of their shared exotic bodies and high virtues. It reveals that both lasting political discourse and ethical concerns shaped the Buddhist writing about the animals. In sum, literary tradition, religious tradition, and political tradition together shaped medieval Chinese understanding and interpretation of animals.

Epilogue

Instead of offering further implications of my current research, which I hope will inspire readers and writers to move forward with their own contributions, let me briefly reflect on the connections between the past and present, as well as future, and between religions and science and technology in a contemporary context. Within a framework of human-animal studies, my discussion has highlighted three major issues that played crucial roles in the question of the animal in traditional China. These three issues, though principally arising during the Chinese medieval period, are still of great relevance today. They refer to the relationships between animals and the state, between animals and religion, and among the religions themselves. With escalating conflicts between animals and humans, the state attempted to understand what animals meant for its political, economic, and cultural interests, and how it could benefit from objectifying animals. Buddhist and Daoist clergies also tried to objectify animals for their own interests by engaging with society through spiritual arguments and often by detailing approaches for dealing with animal issues that differed from those of the state. Furthermore, questions of animal-human relations became a domain for rhetorical sparring among different religions. In China, Buddhism and Daoism learned from each other in an evolving way while handling problems with animal husbandry and exploitation. Today, the political, social, and cultural agents of the state, local communities, and religious organizations that deal with questions concerning the environment and animal rights remain as active as they were in the past.

In medieval China, local cultic practices, intellectual discourse, and political ideologies joined together to create multiple layers of knowledge and practice in interacting with domestic as well as wild animals. The state offered domestic animals as seasonal sacrifices to gods and deities, while the ruling class enjoyed hunting wild animals. Animals were a significant source of consumable meat and clothing, as well as being useful for providing labor and transporting goods and people. They could be both symbols of divine beings and objects of entertainment, the subjects of literary allegories, and topics of intellectual and political writings. Human settlements were often surrounded by wilderness inhabited by predatory animals, and both Buddhism and Daoism regarded dealing with wild animals as a pressing issue. Consequently they developed a panoply of doctrinal teachings, ritual performances, and practical techniques for handling the animals that crossed their paths.

Today, these teachings appear especially relevant given the rising concern for animal rights among the public. Over the past decade, the influence of the animal turn in the discipline of religious studies has led many scholars to expand their traditional approach and explore the very rich sociocultural implications of Buddhist attitudes toward animals in their narratives and rituals. Animal-human relations have gradually become a major subject of contemporary scholarship in Chinese religious studies. Nowadays, policy makers, religious community leaders, and environmental and ecological activists often mobilize various political, intellectual, cultural, social, and religious resources for resolving contemporary problems. In the process, all agents actively engaged with conflicts between animals and humans at the local level. Yet beyond the issues I have discussed in this book, one of the most intriguing issues is the relationship between traditional religious traditions and modern science and technology in terms of handling animal-human relations, given that we are living in a biotechnology-dominated society.

Contemporary society faces some unprecedented challenges, including a number related to ecological and environmental crises across the globe. The grave implications of our actions or inactions draw the attention of scholars from various disciplines to examine the complex relations between nature and society, between humans and animals, between tradition and modernity, and between ethics and scientific and technological advancement. In 1967, the historian Lynn White Jr. published his revelatory essay declaring Christianity's responsibility for our current ecological crisis. For him, Christianity in its Western form was the most anthropocentric religion in the world. Its creation theory laid the dogmatic foundation for human dominance over nature and animals. As White Jr. stated: "Man named all the animals, thus establishing his dominance over them. God planned all of this explicitly for man's benefit and rule: no item in the physical creation had any purpose save to serve man's purposes."[1] But he does also indicate that in Western Christian tradition, St. Francis of Assisi demonstrated the virtue of humanity toward nonhuman species. Other scholars have attempted to find alternative ideas in non-Christian/Western traditions expressing a more empathic attitude toward nature and other species.[2] Aaron Gross further examined how Judeo-Christian traditions as well as philosophical conjectures from the Enlightenment to the present era promoted the ascendency of humans over animals, the disavowal of responsibility, and the unethical treatment of animals in the food industry.[3] The attitudes of religions toward the treatment of animals should be addressed more broadly to include discussion of Chinese religious traditions on the question of human-animal relationships. As this book indicates, the historical experience of animals in China in state authority, religious community, and local community contexts might provide some intellectual resources with contemporary practical implications.

My discussions show that Buddhism and Daoism in the medieval period developed ambivalent approaches to the common issue of attacks by wild beasts. In considering this phenomenon, we should first consider that Buddhism and Daoism normally preferred not to harm animals but extended their compassion even to the taming of dangerous tigers, wolves, and snakes. This nonviolent approach is consonant with the doctrines and ethical values of Buddhism and Daoism, and it helps Buddhist and Daoist communities create cultural and spiritual capital for persuading local community members to give up cultic blood sacrifices to the beasts in favor of organized religion. These doctrines may pose a conflict for state authorities in some regions where the local government has taken control of resolving the problem. But in areas where state power is weak, the religious handling of beast terror might serve as the most effective solution. The nonviolent religious approach has its counterpart in official government policy promoting virtuous governance by trapping and relocating animals without killing them.

We should also note that in traditional China neither Buddhism nor Daoism had a universal presence across the empire. In other words, there was no headquarters for coordinating the responses of local Buddhist and Daoist communities to respond to the challenges of tiger terror and snake disaster. Local communities would have to come up with their own plans and their governments did not direct the animal question to the religious communities. Government officials did not ask monks and masters to eliminate the so-called terror or the disaster, though occasionally eminent monks and celestial masters might receive honorific titles from the state. Community members including both clergy and lay people often made their own choices for responding to the beast issue. While confronting the ferocious tiger and the poisonous snake, their choices concerning killing or taming beasts mostly depended on how they and their religious communities could benefit from these choices. If taming a tiger could bring cultural and religious capital to the monk or the master and his religious community, they would use this strategy. The traditions of religious legend, the doctrinal foundation, personal experience and ability, and community interest all played roles in driving the clergy to make a particular choice. Buddhism and Daoism developed a fierce competition over the issue of handling beasts and reptiles. Both religious philosophies evolved ways to justify killing certain animals, which also seemed to echo the legalistic approach of the official ideology. Thus, the religious communities transformed their approaches to address the conflicts between humans and beasts based on their religious and cultural interests. Choosing to tame harmful animals rather than kill them helped Buddhism and Daoism build their cultural capital for attracting followers and competing with the state authorities.

These historical transformations have contemporary relevance with regard to issues like how to approach the relationship between humans and animals, the relative power of state-supported and religious communities, the conflict between society and nature, and the differences in dealing with problems on a domestic compared to an international level. We are living in an era of globalization, and religious organizations can be instrumental in promoting environmentalism and animal rights internationally. As legally established nongovernmental organizations, they could accomplish much more by collaborating with state authorities instead of competing with them. In medieval China, Buddhism and Daoism learned from each other and developed ideas, rituals, and practices based on mutual agreement. Facing new challenges in the contemporary time, Buddhism and Daoism can continue learning from other religious traditions and practices such as Judaism, Christianity, and Islam. Engaging in dialogue with scholars who hold different beliefs can enhance and enrich Buddhism and Daoism in terms of approaches to contemporary environmental and ecological problems because no single group has all the answers. Buddhism has transformed from competition and dialogue with Daoism to competition and dialogue with Christianity. Buddhist communities in North America have been developing Buddhist chaplaincy programs for serving the military and health care sectors, offering deathbed liturgies for both humans and animals.

Buddhism and Daoism also have to reconcile their belief systems with the latest findings and discoveries in science and technology. For example, agriculture and food production has changed dramatically since the 1950s and 1960s. Traditional agriculture was once considered to be a contract between humans and nature.[4] Under this contract, farmers waited for crops and animals to grow. There was an unambiguous seasonal dependency and an understanding of the importance of maintaining ecological balance to ensure the long-term sustainability of farming. Now, in most developed countries, cereal crops, vegetables, fruit, and animals that serve human needs are no longer naturally fostered, they are technologically assisted. Under the modern, industrialized mode of production, technology is used to maximize productivity by modifying the genes of plants and animals. The modern state of biotechnology has altered the traditional contract between humans and nature. Most crop plants and food animals are cultivated and reared in human-created or modified environments. Animals are no longer aware of nature's rhythms when they do not witness the sun rise and set. Scientists have documented numerous ways that animals transform nature and the environment. According to Oswald J. Schmitz and his colleagues, "Animals can mediate net carbon sequestration by plants (net primary productivity, NPP) by altering CO_2 uptake into and from ecosystems. Herbivore grazing and tree browsing can alter the spatial distribution of plant biomass. Predators can modify herbivore impacts via predation and predator-avoidance behavior. Animal trampling compacts soils and alters soil temperatures by changing the amount of solar radiation reaching soil surfaces. Animals also change the chemical quality of organic matter that enters the soil pool."[5] Some ethicists and religious scholars are concerned that the animality of these unnaturally reared animals is underdeveloped because they now live in a human-made environment that is totally estranged from their natural ecosystem. These animals will never be able to develop their sensory, perceptive, and cognitive abilities from constant contact with sunshine, air, water, earth, grass, minerals, and other elements in nature. In other words, technology has redefined human-animal relations by disconnecting them from mutual reliance on each other and the benefits of traditional agriculture and husbandry. A full-length discussion of these issues is beyond the scope of this book, but our future depends on our continued awareness of (and actions regarding) them.

Notes

INTRODUCTION

1. Peter Holley, "Foul-Mouthed Parrot May Be Used as Evidence in Murder Trial, Prosecutors Say," *Washington Post*, June 26, 2016; see also Kenza Bryan, "Woman Convicted of Husband's Murder . . . ," *Independent*, July 21, 2017.

2. Wang Renyu, *Kaiyuan Tianbao yishi*, in *Tang Wudai birking together, ji xiaoshuo daguan*, ed. Ding Ruming (Shanghai: Shanghai guji chubanshe, 2000), 1720. On the textual history of this collection, see Glen Dudbridge, *A Portrait of Five Dynasties China: From the Memoirs of Wang Renyu (880–956)* (Oxford: Oxford University Press, 2013), 33-35; Manling Luo, "Remembering Kaiyuan and Tianbao: The Construction of Mosaic Memory in Medieval Historical Miscellanies," *T'oung Pao* 97, no. 4/5 (2011): 290-95.

3. Clifford Geertz, "Centers, Kings, and Charisma: Reflections on the Symbolics of Power," in *Local Knowledge: Further Essays in Interpretive Anthropology* (New York: Basic Books, 2000), 121-46; Robert Wessing, "Symbolic Animals in the Land between the Waters: Markers of Place and Transition," *Asian Folklore Studies* 65, no. 2 (2006): 205-39.

4. Chen Huaiyu, *Dongwu yu zhonggu zhengzhi zongjiao zhixu* (Shanghai: Shanghai guji chubanshe, 2012).

5. For tigers in the Sundarban forests, see Michael Lewis, "Indian Science for Indian Tigers? Conservation Biology and the Question of Cultural Values," *Journal of the History of Biology* 38, no. 2 (2005): 185-207.

6. Anna Peterson, "Review: Religious Studies and the Animal Turn," *History of Religions* 56, no. 2 (2016): 232-45; Donovan Schaefer, *Religious Affects: Animality, Evolution, and Power* (Durham, NC: Duke University Press, 2015).

7. Reiko Ohnuma, *Unfortunate Destiny: Animals in the Indian Buddhist Imagination* (New York: Oxford University Press, 2017).

8. Alan Bleakley, *The Animalizing Imagination: Totemism, Textuality and Ecocriticism* (New York: St. Martin's Press, 2000), 38-40.

9. Chen Huaiyu, *Dongwu yu zhonggu zhengzhi zongjiao zhixu*, 314-66.

10. Stephen F. Teiser, *Reinventing the Wheel: Paintings of Rebirth in Medieval Buddhist Temples* (Seattle: University of Washington Press, 2006); Stephen F. Teiser, *The Scripture on the Ten Kings and the Making of Purgatory in Medieval Chinese Buddhism* (Honolulu: University of

Hawai'i Press, 1994); Stephen F. Teiser, *Ghost Festival in Medieval China* (Princeton, NJ: Princeton University Press, 1988).

11. Edward H. Schafer, "Cultural History of the Elaphure," *Sinologica* 4 (1956): 251-74; Edward H. Schafer, "Parrots in Medieval China," in *Studia Serica Bernhard Karlgren Dedicata: Sinological Studies Dedicated to Bernhard Karlgren on His Seventieth Birthday*, ed. Søren Egerod et Else Glahn (Copenhagen: Ejnar Munksgaard, 1959), 271-82; Edward H. Schafer, *The Vermilion Bird: T'ang Images of the South* (Berkeley: University of California Press, 1967); Edward H. Schafer, "Hunting Parks and Animal Enclosures in Ancient China," *Journal of the Economic and Social History of the Orient* 11 (1968): 318-43.

12. Madeline K. Spring, *Animal Allegories in T'ang China* (New Haven, CT: American Oriental Society, 1993).

13. Sung Hou-mei, *Decoded Messages: The Symbolic Language of Chinese Animal Painting* (New Haven, CT: Yale University Press, 2009).

14. Rania Huntington, *Alien Kind: Foxes and Late Imperial Chinese Narrative* (Cambridge, MA: Harvard University Press, 2004).

15. Wilt L. Idema, *Insects in Chinese Literature: A Study and Anthology* (Amherst, NY: Cambria Press, 2019); Wilt L. Idema, *Mouse vs. Cat in Chinese Literature: Tales and Commentary* (Seattle: University of Washington Press, 2019).

16. Roel Sterckx, *The Animal and the Daemon in Ancient China* (Albany: State University of New York Press, 2002); Roel Sterckx, Martina Siebert, and Dagmar Schäfer, eds., *Animals Through Chinese History. Earliest Times to 1911* (Cambridge: Cambridge University Press, 2019).

17. Keith Knapp, "The Use and Understanding of Domestic Animals in Medieval Northern China," *Early Medieval China* 25 (2019): 85-99; Keith Knapp, "The Meaning of Birds on Hunping (Spirit Jars): The Religious Imagination of Second to Fourth century Jiangnan," *Azjiske študije/ Asian Studies* 7, no. 2 (2019): 153-72; Keith Knapp, "Noble Creatures: Filial and Righteous Animals in Early Medieval Confucian Thought," in *Animals through Chinese History: Earliest Times to 1911* (Cambridge: Cambridge University Press, 2019), 64-83.

18. Kang Xiaofei, *The Cult of the Fox: Power, Gender, and Popular Religion in Late Imperial and Modern China* (New York: Columbia University Press, 2006).

19. Vincent Goossaert, *L'interdit du bœuf en Chine. Agriculture, Éthique et sacrifice.* Bibliothèque de l'Institut des hautes études Chinoises, vol. 34 (Paris: Collège de France, Institut des hautes études Chinoises, 2005).

20. Tony Page, *What Does Buddhism Say About Animals* (London: UVAKIS Publications, 1998); Page, *Buddhism and Animals: A Buddhist Vision of Humanity's Rightful Relationship with the Animal Kingdom* (London: UVAKIS Publications, 1999); Christopher Key Chapple, *Nonviolence to Animals, Earth and Self in Asian Traditions* (Albany: State University of New York Press, 1993); Norm Phelps, *The Great Compassion: Buddhism and Animal Rights* (New York: Lantern Books, 2004); Pu Chengzhong, *Ethical Treatment of Animals in Early Chinese Buddhism: Beliefs and Practices* (Newcastle upon Tyne: Cambridge Scholars Publishing, 2014); James Stewart, *Vegetarianism and Animal Ethics in Contemporary Buddhism* (London: Routledge, 2015).

21. Timothy H. Barrett, *The Religious Affiliation of the Chinese Cat: An Essay Towards an Anthropozoological Approach to Comparative Religion.* London: School of Oriental & African Studies,

University of London, 1998; Timothy H. Barrett, "The Monastery Cat in Cross-Cultural Perspective: Cat Poems of the Zen Masters," in *Buddhist Monasticism in East Asia: Places of Practice*, ed. James A. Benn, Lori Meeks, and James Robson (London: Routledge, 2009), 107–24; Chen Huaiyu, *Dongwu yu zhonggu zhengzhi zongjiao zhixu*; Meir Shahar, "The Chinese Cult of the Horse King: Divine Protector of Equines," in *Animals and Human Society in Asia: Historical and Ethical Perspectives*, ed. Rotem Rosen, Michal Biran, Meir Shahar, and Gideon Shelach (Basingstoke: Palgrave Macmillan, 2019), 355–90; Meir Shahar, "The Tantric Origins of the Horse King: Haayagrīva and the Chinese Horse Cult," in *Chinese and Tibetan Esoteric Buddhism*, ed. Yael Bentor and Meir Shahar (Leiden: Brill, 2017), 147–90.

22. Chen Huaiyu, *Dongwu yu zhonggu zhengzhi zongjiao zhixu*, 99–150.

23. Lynn White Jr., "The Historical Roots of Our Ecological Crisis," *Science* 155 (1967): 1203–07; Aaron Gross, *The Question of the Animal and Religion: Theoretical Stakes, Practical Implications* (New York: Columbia University Press, 2015); Bron Taylor, "The Greening of Religion Hypothesis (Part One): From Lynn White Jr. and Claims that Religions Can Promote Environmentally Destructive Attitudes and Behaviors to Assertions They Are Becoming Environmentally Friendly," *Journal for the Study of Religion, Nature and Culture* 10, no. 3 (2016): 268–305; Bron Taylor, Gretel Van Wieren, and Bernard Zaleha, "The Greening of Religion Hypothesis (Part Two): Assessing the Data from Lynn White Jr. to Pope Francis," *Journal for the Study of Religion, Nature and Culture* 10, no. 3 (2016): 306–78.

24. Chris Coggins, *The Tiger and the Pangolin: Nature, Culture, and Conservation in China* (Honolulu: University of Hawaiʻi Press, 2003); Mark Elvin, *The Retreat of the Elephants: An Environmental History of China* (New Haven, CT: Yale University Press, 2004); Mary Evelyn Tucker and Duncan Williams, eds., *Buddhism and Ecology: The Interconnection of Dharma and Deeds* (Cambridge, MA: Harvard University Center for the Study of World Religions, 1998).

25. Jan Jakob de Groot, *The Religious System of China*, vol. 4 (Leiden: Brill, 1901), 162–81; Charles Hammond, "An Excursion in Tiger Lore," *Asia Major* 3rd series 4, no. 1 (1991): 87–100; Charles Hammond, "The Righteous Tiger and the Grateful Lion," *Monumenta Serica* 43 (1996): 191–211; Huaiyu Chen, "Yazhou huren chuanshuo zhi wenhuashi bijiao yanjiu," *Chengda lishi xuebao* 58 (2020): 21–55; the last section deals with a comparison with the were-tigers in India.

1. BUDDHISTS CATEGORIZING ANIMALS

1. Geoffrey E. R. Lloyd, *Ancient Worlds, Modern Reflections: Philosophical Perspectives on Greek and China* (Oxford: Oxford University Press, 2006), 93–117.

2. David Clough, "Putting Animals in Their Place: On the Theological Classification of Animals," in *Animals as Religious Subjects: Transdisciplinary Perspectives*, ed. Celia Deane-Drummond, David L. Clough, and Rebecca Artinian-Kaiser (London: Bloomsbury, 2013), 212.

3. Darrell Posey and William Leslie Overal, eds., *Ethnobiology: Implications and Applications. Proceedings of the First International Congress of Ethnobiology* (Belém: Museu Paraense Emílio Goeldi, 1990); Brent Berlin, *Ethnobiological Classification: Principles of Categorization of*

Plants and Animals in Traditional Societies (Princeton, NJ: Princeton University Press, 1992); Roy Ellen, *The Cultural Relations of Classification: An Analysis of Nuaulu Animal Categories from Central Seram* (Cambridge: Cambridge University Press, 1993); Paul Sillitoe, "Ethnobiology and Applied Anthropology: Rapprochement of the Academic with the Practical," *Journal of the Royal Anthropological Institute* 12 (2006): S119–42.

4.   Daoxuan, *Liangchu qingzhong yi*, T. 45, no. 1895, 841a.

5.   Daoxuan, *Liangchu qingzhong yi*, T. 45, no. 1895, 845b.

6.   See Huaiyu Chen, *The Revival of Buddhist Monasticism in Medieval China* (New York: Peter Lang, 2007), 148–51.

7.   See Huaiyu Chen, "Yi *Liangchu qingzhong yi* weili lueshuo Daoxuan lüshi zhi yixue [Notes on Daoxuan's doctrinal exegesis with special references to *Ritual of Measuring and Handling Light and Heavy Property*]," *Fudan zhexue pinglun* [Fudan review of philosophy] 3 (2006): 78–90.

8.   For the explanation of this term referring to nonhuman animals in early Buddhist context, see Reiko Ohnuma, *Unfortunate Destiny: Animals in the Indian Buddhist Imagination* (New York: Oxford University Press, 2017), 1–2.

9.   Daoxuan, *Guanzhong chuangli jietan tujing*; T. 45, no. 1899, 882c.

10. Huaiyu Chen, *The Revival of Buddhist Monasticism in Medieval China*, 132–79.

11. For a general survey of Buddhist attitude toward the natural world, see Peter Harvey, *An Introduction to Buddhist Ethics* (Cambridge: Cambridge University Press, 2000), 150–86.

12. Guo Fu, Li Yuese (Joseph Needham), and Cheng Qingtai, *Zhongguo gudai dongwuxue shi* (Beijing: Kexue chubanshe, 1999), 131–41; Guo Fu summarizes the systems of animal classification in *Erya, Guanzi, Liji, Lüshi chunqiu, Kaogongji,* and *Bencao gangmu*; Gou Cuihua, "Zhongguo gudai de dongzhiwu fenlei," *Kejishi wenji* 4 (1980): 43; Gou Cuihua et al., "Ye tan Zhongguo gudai de shengwu fenleixue sixiang," *Ziran kexueshi yanjiu* 1, no. 4 (1982): 167; Gou Cuihua et al., *Zhongguo gudai shengwuxue shi* (Beijing: Kexue chubanshe, 1989); 12.

13. Padmanabh S. Jaini, "Indian Perspectives on the Spirituality of Animals," in *Buddhist Philosophy and Culture: Essays in Honour of N. A. Jayawickrema*, ed. David J. Kalupahana and W. G. Weeraratne (Colombo, Sri Lanka: N. A. Jayawickrema Felicitation Volume Committee, 1987), 169–78; Sakya Trizin, *A Buddhist View on Befriending and Defending Animals* (Portland, OR: Orgyan Chogye Chonzo Ling, 1989); Christopher Key Chapple, *Karma and Creativity; Nonviolence to Animals, Earth, and Self in Asian Traditions* (Albany: State University of New York Press, 1993); Mary Evelyn Tucker and Duncan Ryūken Williams, eds., *Buddhism and Ecology: The Interconnection of Dharma and Deeds* (Cambridge, MA: Harvard University Press, 1997), 131–48; Eric Reinders, "Animals, Attitude Toward: Buddhist Perspective," in *Encyclopedia of Monasticism*, ed. William M. Johnston (Chicago: Fitzroy Dearborn, 2000), 30–31.

14. Robert Grant, *Early Christians and Animals* (London: Routledge, 1999).

15. Joyce E. Salisbury, *The Beast Within: Animals in the Middle Ages* (London: Routledge, 1994).

16. Kristina Jennbert, "Sheep and Goats in Norse Paganism," in *PECUS. Man and Animal in Antiquity. Proceedings of the Conference at the Swedish Institute in Rome, September 9–12, 2002*, ed. Barbro Santillo Frizell (Rome: The Swedish Institute in Rome, 2004), 160–66.

17.   Auli Tourunen, "A Zooarchaeological Study of the Medieval and Post-medieval Town of Turku," PhD thesis, Humanistic Faculty of the University of Turku, Turku, 2008, 82–124.

18.   Lambert Schmithausen, *Buddhism and Nature: The Lecture Delivered on the Occasion of the EXPO 1990. An Enlarged Version with Notes* (Tokyo: International Institute for Buddhist Studies, 1991); Lambert Schmithausen, "The Early Buddhist Tradition and Ethics: VI. The Status of Animals," *Journal of Buddhist Ethics* 4 (1997): 1–74; James P. McDermott, "Animals and Humans in Early Buddhism," *Indo-Iranian Journal* 32, no. 2 (1989): 269–80; Bimal Churn Law, "Animals in Early Jain and Buddhist Literature," *Indian Culture* 12, no. 1 (1945): 1–13.

19.   Lambert Schmithausen, *Buddhism and Nature*, 16.

20.   According to transmigration theory, humans could be reborn as animals and animals could be reborn as humans, a concept rooted in Vedic religion; see Hermann Oldenberg, *Die Religion des Veda* (Berlin: Verlag von Wilhelm Hertz, 1894), 562–64; English version, *The Religion of the Veda*, trans, Shridhar B. Shrotri (Delhi: Motilal Banarsidass, 1988), 322–23.

21.   Daoshi, *Fayuan zhulin, T.* 53, no. 2122, 317b.

22.   Paul Waldau, *The Specter of Speciesism: Buddhist and Christian Views of Animals* (New York: Oxford University Press, 2001), chaps. 6 and 7; Paul Waldau, "Buddhism and Animals Rights," in *Contemporary Buddhist Ethics*, ed. Damien Keown. The Curzon Critical Studies in Buddhism Series. (Richmond, Surrey, England: Curzon Press, 2000), 81–112; Paul J. Waldau and Kimberley Patton, eds., *A Communion of Subjects: Animals in Religion, Science and Ethics* (New York: Oxford University Press, 2004).

23.   Paul Waldau, "Buddhism and Animals Rights," 85–86.

24.   Mahnaz Moazami, "Evil Animals in the Zoroastrian Religion," *History of Religions* 44, no. 4 (2005): 300–17.

25.   George Sarton, *Introduction to the History of Science* (Baltimore, MD: Williams & Wilkins Co., 1927), 333.

26.   Hans-Peter Schmidt, "Ancient Iranian Animal Classification," *Studien zur Indologie und Iranistik* 5/6 (1980): 231–32.

27.   *Bencao gangmu* also lists human beings and animals together, see Guo Fu, "Dongwu de fenlei," in Guo Fu, Li Yuese (Joseph Needham), and Cheng Qintai, eds., *Zhongguo gudai dongwuxue shi*, 137.

28.   Jñānagupta, *Fo benxing ji jing, T.* 3, no. 190, 825a.

29.   George G. Simpson, *Principles of Animal Taxonomy* (New York: Columbia University Press, 1962).

30.   Jacques Gernet, *Buddhism in Chinese Society: An Economic History from the Fifth to the Tenth Centuries* (New York: Columbia University Press, 1995), 60, 83, 316.

31.   Brian K. Smith, "Classifying Animals and Humans in Ancient India," *Man* 26, no. 3 (1991): 527–48; Brian K. Smith, *Classifying the Universe: The Ancient Indian Varna System and the Origins of Caste* (New York: Oxford University Press, 1994), 241. In ancient Iran, there were several classification systems of animals. In *Yašt* (13.74) the animals were grouped into two divisions: *pasuka* (domestic) and *daitika* (wild). See Hans-Peter Schmidt, "Ancient Iranian Animal Classification," 214–15. Schmidt also notices that in Rgveda, animals had been classified as wild and domesticated (233).

32.   Brian K. Smith, *Classifying the Universe*, 248.

33.   Francis Zimmermann, *The Jungle and the Aroma of Meats: An Ecological Theme in Hindu Medicine* (Delhi: Motilal Banaesidaa Publishers, 1999), 96–124, 195–96, 210–17. This book was first published in French as *La Jungle et le fumet des viands. Un theme écologique dans la medicine hindoue* (Paris: Éditions du Seuil, 1982).

34.   Roswith Conard, "The Domestic Animals in the Cultures of India," *Journal of Indian History* 52 (1974): 76–78.

35.   Herbert P. Sullivan, "A Re-examination of the Religion of the Indus Civilization," *History of Religions* 4, no. 1 (1964): 118–19. For the discussion of cattle as sacred animals, see Marvin Harris, "The Cultural Ecology of India's Sacred Cattle," *Current Anthropology* 33, no. 1, Supplement: Inquiry and Debate in the Human Sciences: Contributions from Current Anthropology, 1960–1990 (1992): 261–76.

36.   Trilok Chandra Majupuria, *Sacred and Symbolic Animals of Nepal: Animals in the Art, Culture, Myths and Legends of the Hindus and Buddhists* (Kathmandu: Sahayogi Prakashan Tripureswar, 1977), 7–38. This book discussed about fifty natural, imagined, and mystical animals, but no tiger. Also see Trilok Chandra Majupuria, *Sacred Animals of Nepal and India* (Lashkar: M. Devi, 2000). For lion and tiger as the vahana of the Goddess Durgā, see Stephanie Tawa Lama, "The Hindu Goddess and Women's Political Representation in South Asia: Symbolic Resource or Feminine Mystique?" *Revue Internationale de Sociologie* 11, no. 1 (2001): 5–20.

37.   Hermann Oldenberg, *Die Religion des Veda* 68–87; also see English translation, *The Religion of the Veda*, trans. Shridhar B. Shrotri (Dehli: Motilal Banarsidass, 1988), 36–43.

38.   O. P. Dwivedi, "Satyagraha for Conservation: Awakening the Spirit of Hinduism," in *This Sacred Earth: Religion, Nature, Environment*, ed. Roger S. Gottlieb (New York: Routledge, 1996), 155–56.

39.   Kumārajīva, *Shizhu piposha lun T.* 26, no. 1521, 21b.

40.   Buddhabhadra, *Mohe sengqi lü, T.* 22, no. 1425, 495b–c.

41.   Puṇyatāra and Kumārajīva, *Shisong lü, T.* 23, no. 1435, 424c.

42.   Yijing, *Genben shuo yiqieyou bu pinaiye, T.* 23, no. 1442, 464c.

43.   Saṃghabhadra, *Shanjian lü piposha, T.* 24, no. 1462, 715b.

44.   *Taishang dongxuan lingbao yebao yinyuan jing*, juan 2; see John Lagerwey's introduction to this text, in Kristopher Schipper and Franciscus Verellen eds., *The Taoist Canon: A Historical Companion to the Daozang* (Chicago: University of Chicago Press, 2004), 518–20; for a detailed study, see Livia Kohn, "Steel Holy Food and Come Back as a Viper: Conceptions of Karma and Rebirth in Medieval Daoism," *Early Medieval China* 4 (1998): 1–48.

45.   Interestingly, in some areas of Thailand, local people sometimes also categorized animals into four groups: birds, worms, beasts, and exotic animals; see Stanley Jeyaraja Tambiah, "Animals Are Good to Think and Good to Prohibit," in *Culture, Thought, and Social Action: An Anthropological Perspective* (Cambridge, MA: Harvard University Press, 1985), 192–211.

46.   For a natural history perspective on camels in ancient China, see Stanley J. Olsen, "The Camel in Ancient China and Osteology of the Camel," *Proceedings of the Academy of Natural Sciences of Philadelphia* 140, no. 1 (1988): 18–58. Originally, the camel appeared in North America; later in the Pleistocene epoch it entered South America and Asia. By the end of Pleistocene epoch, it disappeared in North America. In the Zhou dynasty,

people in China already knew the camel as a domesticated animal. In the Han dynasty, in northern regions the use of camels was well known.

47. Edward H. Schafer lists as domestic animals: horses, cattle, camels, sheep and goats, asses, mules, onagers, and dogs. See Edward H. Schafer, *The Golden Peach of Samarkand: A Study of T'ang Exotics* (Berkeley: University of California Press, 1963), 58–78. Schafer also lists some wild animals (79–91).

48. Lambert Schmithausen, *Buddhism and Nature*, 16.

49. Vincent Goossaert examined the taboo in Chinese religions on eating beef from the perspective of agriculture, morality, and sacrifice, and also noted the Buddhist attitude toward cows; see Vincent Goossaert, *L'interdit du bœuf en Chine. Agriculture, éthique et sacrifice*. Bibliothèque de l'Institut des hautes études Chinoises, vol. 34 (Paris: Collège de France, Institut des hautes études Chinoises, 2005), 51–61.

50. Saṃghadeva, *Zengyi Ahan jing*, T. 2, no. 125, 587b.

51. Zhiqian, *Zhuanji baiyuan jing*, juan 3, T. 4, no. 200, 213a. Jan Nattier is suspicious that Zhiqian was really the translator of this text; see Jan Nattier, *A Guide to the Earliest Chinese Buddhist Translations: Texts from the Eastern Han and Three Kingdoms Periods* (Tokyo: The International Research Institute for Advanced Buddhology, Soka University, 2008), 116–48.

52. Zhu Fonian, *Chuyao jing*, juan 22, T. 4, no. 212, 725a. The passage says that some people enjoyed their longevity yet did not have wisdom and concentration, without humility, and they were not different from the "six animals" classification, e.g., camel, mule, donkey, elephant, horse, pig, and dog. Apparently, the term "six animals" refers here to animals in general.

53. Brian K. Smith, *Classifying the Universe*, 248.

54. For the study on releasing lives, see Huang I-mei, "Kaisatu Hōjō to Jin no shiso," *Oryō shigaku* 13 (1987): 29–55; Kuwatani Yuken, "Hōjō shisō ni okeru kyōsei " *Nihon bukkyō gakkai nenhō* 64 (1999): 213–227; Chiba Shokan, "Chūgoku ni okeru hōjō shisō no tenkai: seshoku shisō no kannen o chūshin ni," *Tendai gakuhō* 36 (1993): 89–95; Namura Takatsuna, "Chigi daishi no hōjōchi ni tsuite," *Shūgakuin ronjū* 22 (1976): 72–85. On the relationship between Zhiyi and *Fanwang jing*, see Fujii Kyoko, "Tendai Chigi to bonmōkyō," *Indogaku bukkyōgaku kenkyū* 90 (1997): 241–47. For a later development of the idea of releasing life, see Chün-fang Yu, *Renewal of Buddhism in China: Chu-Hung and the Late Ming Synthesis* (New York: Columbia University Press, 1981); Joanna F. Handlin Smith, "Liberating Animals in Ming-Qing China: Buddhist Inspiration and Elite Imagination," *Journal of Asian Studies* 58, no. 1 (1999): 51–84. For an examination of how this practice was carried out in medieval Japan, see Duncan Williams, "Animal Liberation, Death, and the State: Rites to Release Animals in Medieval Japan," in *Buddhism and Ecology: The Interconnection of Dharma and Deed*, ed. Mary Evelyn Tucker and Duncan Ryūken Williams (Cambridge, MA: Harvard University Press, 1997), 149–64.

55. P. 2940: *Zhaiwan wen*; for the transcription and modern edition, see Huang Zheng and Wu Wei, eds., *Dunhuang yuanwen ji* (Changsha: Yuelu shushe, 1995), 67; for a study on this genre, see Paul Magnin, "Donateurs et joueurs en l'honneur de Buddha," in *De Dunhuang au Japon, Études chinoises et bouddhiques offertes à Michel Soymié*, ed. Jean-Pierre Drège (Genève: Librairie Droz, 1996), 103–38.

56. S. 5637: *Jima wen*; for an edited version see Huang Zheng and Wu Wei, eds., *Dunhuang yuanwen ji*, 242–43.

57. Huijiao, *Gaoseng zhuan*, T. 50, no. 2059, 406c.

58. Daoxuan, *Xu gaoseng zhuan*, T. 50, no. 2060, 477c.

59. John Brough, "Buddhist Chinese Etymological Notes," *Bulletin of the School of Oriental and African Studies* 38, no. 3 (1975): 581–85; Ohnuma, *Unfortunate Destiny*, 175–76.

60. Later the cult of fox became more visible in popular religion; for an excellent study, see Xiaofei Kang, *The Cult of the Fox: Power, Gender, and Popular Religion in Late Imperial and Modern China* (New York: Columbia University Press, 2006).

61. Edward H. Schafer, *The Golden Peaches of Samarkand*, 84–87.

62. Fayun, *Fanyi mingyi ji*, juan 2, T. 54, no. 2131, 1088c.

63. Huilin, *Yiqiejing yinyi*, juan 19, T. 54, no. 2028, 424b.

64. Daoxuan, *Xu gaoseng zhuan*, juan 17, T. 50, no. 2060, 563c.

65. The rhinoceros or rhinoceros horn as a symbol of solitary living is still a controversial issue in the field; for the debates, see K. R. Norman, "Middle Indo-Aryan," in *Indo-European Numerals*, ed. Jadranka Gvozdanovich (Berlin: Mouton de Gruyter, 1992), 199–241; K. R. Norman, "Solitary as Rhinoceros Horn," *Buddhist Studies Review* 13 (1996): 133–42; and Richard Salomon, *A Gandhārī Version of the Rhinoceros Sūtra* (Seattle: University of Washington Press, 2000). Looking at the Chinese translations, both rhinoceros and rhinoceros horn were used to indicate the loneliness of a bodhisattva.

66. Daniel Boucher, *Bodhisattvas of the Forest and the Formation of the Mahāyāna: A Study and Translation of the Rāṣṭrapālaparipṛcchā-Sūtra* (Honolulu: University of Hawai'i Press, 2008), 123, 126.

67. Xu Tingyun, "Sui Tang wudai shiqi de shengtai huanjing," *Guoxue yanjiu* 8 (2001): 209–44, especially 215–16.

68. But Daoxuan does not mention how to deal with birds. Birds were important to medieval Chinese society, at least in Dunhuang. See Lewis Mayo, "The Order of Birds in Guiyi jun Dunhuang," *East Asian History* 20 (2000): 1–59.

69. Buddhayaśas and Zhu Fonian, *Sifen lü*, T. 22, no. 1428, 961a19. Most cases in monastic code pertained to the animals' disturbance of spiritual, intellectual, and daily life of monks. For example, another accident happened to the monks in T. 22, no. 1428, 961a21: some brown bears damaged the robes, sitting mats, bottles containing needles used in traditional medicine, and even the bodies of monks, so brown bear were also prohibited by the Buddha. These damaged materials were essential in sustaining monastic life.

70. There are some debates on the definitions of pets from the perspective of animal history. On the pets in medieval Europe, see Richard Thomas, "Perceptions versus Reality: Changing Attitudes Towards Pets in Medieval and Post-Medieval England," in *Just Skin and Bones? New Perspectives on Human-Animal Relations in the Historical Past*, ed. Aleksander Pluskowski (Oxford: Archaeopress, 2005), 95–104. According to some scholars, this approach appeared in the study of urban history and urban culture, because pets were regarded as the underrepresented minority group that has been ignored by traditional historians; see Charles Phineas, "Household Pets and Urban Alienation," *Journal of Social History* 7, no. 3 (1974): 338–43, concerning the rise of animal history as a field of study. On an overview of the scholarship on the history of animals, also see Erica Fudge, "A Left-Handed Blow: Writing the History of Animals," in *Representing Animals*, ed. Nigel

Rothfels (Bloomington: Indiana University Press, 2002), 3–18; especially 4–5. On the study of dogs in Europe, see Teresa Mangum, "Dog Years, Human Fears," in *Representing Animals*, ed. Nigel Rothfels (Bloomington: Indiana University Press, 2002), 35–47.

71. *Da fangbian Fo bao'en jing*, juan 6, *T.* 3, no. 156, 161a.

72. Dharmarakṣa, *Daban niepan jing*, juan 29, *T.* 12, no. 374, 538b.

73. Huiyuan, *Dasheng yizhang*, juan 7, *T.* 44, no. 1851, 615a.

74. Lambert Schmithausen, *Buddhism and Nature*, 5.

75. Daoxuan, *Liangchu qingzhong yi*, *T.* 45, no. 1895, 845c.

76. In my earlier book I mentioned that during the ceremony of venerating the Buddha's relics, some Buddhists sacrificed their bodies. See Huaiyu Chen, *The Revival of Buddhist Monasticism in Medieval China* (chap. 2). But the Buddhist never sacrificed the bodies of the animals to venerate the relics of the Buddha. In some Jātaka stories, we can even find that the Prince of Bodhisattva even donated his body to feed the hungry tigress. See "Vyaghri Jataka," *Jatakamala* no. 1, in Āryaśūra, *Jātakamālā: Or, A Garland of Birth Stories*, trans. Jacob Samuel Speyer (Delhi: Sri Satguru Publications, 1988), 4–12. This story does not occur in the Pali Jātaka.

77. In South Asian tradition, some animals were also viewed as sacred. See Trilok Chandra Majupuria, *Sacred Animals of Nepal and India*.

78. Donald N. Blakeley, "Listening to the Animals: The Confucian View of Animal Welfare," *Journal of Chinese Philosophy* 30, no. 2 (2003): 137–57. Blakeley bases his article on the works of Confucius, Mencius, Zhu Xi, and Wang Yangming. He does not examine the later sources from the Han to the Tang periods.

79. Christopher Key Chapple, "Animals and Environment in the Buddhist Birth Stories," in *Buddhism and Ecology*, 131–48, esp. 140.

80. Roel Sterckx, "Animal Classification in Ancient China," *East Asian Science, Technology and Medicine* 23 (2005): 96–123; Sterckx analyzes animal classification in ancient China centered on *Erya*. In *Erya*, animals were classified into four categories: insects, fish, birds, and beasts. Also see chapter 3 in Roel Sterckx, *The Animal and Daemon in Early China* (Albany: State University of New York Press, 2002); and Roel Sterckx, "Transforming the Beasts: Animals and Music in Early China," *T'oung Pao* 2nd Series 86, no. 1/3 (2000): 1–46.

81. Very few works have touched on the issue of the taxonomy of animals in medieval China. For an early attempt see Zhang Mengwen, "Zhongguo shengwu fenleixue shi shulun" (originally published in 1942); reprinted in *Zhongguo keji shiliao*, no. 6 (1987): 3–27. Zou Shuwen, "Zhongguo gudai de dongwu fenleixue," in *Zhongguo kejishi tantao*, eds. by Li Guohao, Zhang Mengwen, Cao Tianqin (Hongkong: Zhonghua shuju xianggang fenju, 1986), 511–24.

82. Hans-Peter Schmidt, "Ancient Iranian Animal Classification," 209–44. Schmidt notes: "Manichaeism differs from Zoroastrianism by considering all animals as demonic creatures. They must however be protected because they contain incarcerated particles of light" (232).

83. This chapter is a revised version based on the first part of my earlier article; see Huaiyu Chen, "A Buddhist Classification of Plants and Animals in Early Tang China," *Journal of Asian History* 43, no. 1 (2009): 31–51. In this article, I also discuss that Daoxuan's classification of plants is more influenced by Chinese botanical tradition than by Buddhist tradition, for he classifies them into three principal groups: grains, fruits, and trees.

84. See my discussion in Huaiyu Chen, *The Revival of Buddhist Monasticism in Medieval China*, 24–43.

2. CONFUCIANS CIVILIZING UNRULY BEASTS

1. Yan Juanying, ed., *Beichao fojiao shike tapian baipin* (Taipei: Academica Sinica, 2008), plate no. 023.
2. Lin Fu-shih, "The Images and Status of Shamans in Ancient China," in *Early Chinese Religion*, Part 1, ed. John Lagerwey and Marc Kalinowski (Leiden: Brill, 2009), 418–19.
3. These groups only appeared as marginal and "barbaric" in the eyes of the imperial court centered on the Han civilization because the court, of course, regarded itself and its worldview as part of a civilized cultural system.
4. Wu Gang et al., *Quan Tang wen buyi* [*Qian Tang zhi zhai xinji*] (Xi'an: Sanqin chubanshe, 2006), 24.
5. Wu Gang et al., *Quan Tang wen buyi*, 55.
6. Qiao Dong, Li Xianqi, and Shi jiazhen, Luoyang di'er wenwu gongzuodui eds., *Luoyang xinhuo muzhi xubian* (Beijing: Kexue chubanshe, 2008), 52.
7. Zhao Chao, ed., *Han Wei Liang Jin Nanbeichao muzhi huibian* (Tianjin: Tianjin guji chubanshe, 1992), 159.
8. Zhao Chao, ed., *Han Wei Liang Jin Nanbeichao muzhi huibian*, 220.
9. Zhao Chao, ed., *Han Wei Liang Jin Nanbeichao muzhi huibian*, 208.
10. Zhao Chao, ed., *Han Wei Liang Jin Nanbeichao muzhi huibian*, 275–76.
11. Zhao Chao, ed., *Han Wei Liang Jin Nanbeichao muzhi huibian*, 444.
12. Zhou Shaoliang and Zhao Chao, eds., *Tangdai muzhi huibian* (Shanghai: Shanghai guji chubanshe, 1992), 910.
13. Dugu Ji, "Chou Changmei xian jianzeng 酬常郿縣見贈," in *Quan Tang shi*, juan 247 (Beijing: Zhonghua shuju, 1979), 2776.
14. Liu Zongyuan, "Zhashuo 䄍説," in *Quang Tan wen*, juan 584 (Beijing: Zhonghua shuju, 1983), 5898–99.
15. Yao Silian, *Liang shu*, juan 23 (Beijing: Zhonghua shuju, 1973), 364.
16. Yao Silian, *Liang shu*, juan 47, 650.
17. Yao Silian, *Liang shu*, juan 53, 773.
18. Ouyang Xiu et al., *Xin Tang shu*, juan 181 (Beijing: Zhonghua shuju, 1975), 5349.
19. Ikeda On, "Chūgoku kodai mōjū taisaku hōgi," in *Ritsuryōsei no shomondai: Takikawa Masajirō Hakushi beiju kinen ronshū*, ed. Masajirō Takikawa and Masao Shimada (Tokyo: Kyūko Shoin, 1984), 611–37.
20. Li Ximi and Mao Huaxuan, eds., *Tang dazhaoling ji bubian* (Shanghai: Shanghai guji chubanshe, 2003), 807.
21. Li Daoping, ed., *Zhouyi jijie cuanshu* (Beijing: Zhonghua shuju, 2004), 702; Ma Xinmin and Li Xueqin, eds., *Erya zhushu* (Beijing: Beijing daxue chubanshe, 2000), 354.
22. Liu Xu et al., *Jiu Tang shu*, juan 45 (Beijing: Zhonghua shuju, 1975), 1947.
23. Ma Xinmin, ed., *Chunqiu Zuozhuan zhengyi* (Beijing: Beijing daxue chubanshe, 1999), 1498.
24. Zhou Yiliang, *Wei Jin Nanbeichao shi zhazhi* (Beijing: Zhonghua shuju, 1985), 220–23, notes on shooting pheasants.

25. Sima Guang et al., *Zizhi tongjian*, juan 129 (Beijing: Zhonghua shuju, 1996.)

26. Liu Yiqing, *Shishuo xinyu*, trans. Richard Mather, *A New Account of Tales of the World* [*Shih-Shuo Hsin-Yü*] (Ann Arbor: Center for Chinese Studies, University of Michigan, 2002), 297.

27. Li Yanshou, *History of Southern Dynasties* [Nan shi], juan 5 (Beijing: Zhonghua shuju, 1975), 151.

28. Pan Anren, "Shezhi fu," in *Wenxuan*, juan 9, ed. Xiao Tong, ann. Li Shan (Shanghai: Shanghai guji chubanshe, 1986), 415–23.

29. Han Yu, "Zhi Dai jian," in *Quan Tang shi*, juan 338, ed. Peng Dingqiu (Beijing: Zhonghua shuju, 1979), 3786–87.

30. Liu Zhen et al., *Dongguan Han ji*, ann. Wu Shuping (Zhengzhou: Zhongzhou guji chubanshe, 1987), juan 13, 465–66; Fan Ye, *Hou Han shu* (Beijing: Zhonghua shuju, 1965), juan 25, 874. For commentary on how this mode of writing is designed for portraying good officials, see Sun Zhengjun, "Zhonggu liangli shuxie de liangzhong moshi," *Lishi yanjiu* 3 (2014): 4–21.

31. Liu Zhen et al., *Dongguan Han ji*, juan 13, 500. This passage was preserved in *Taiping yulan*, juan 267. As Wu Shuping noted, there is no biography of Wang Fu in Fan Ye's *Hou Han shu*. But his story briefly appeared in "Xinanyi luezhuan"; it was also preserved in Xie Cheng, *Hou Han shu*, comp. and ed. Wang Wentai, juan 5; and *Huayang guozhi*, juan 10, "Xianxian shinü zongzan."

32. Fan, *Hou Han shu*, juan 79, 2550.

33. Fan, *Hou Han shu*, juan 41, 1413.

34. Hou-mei Sung, *Decoded Messages: The Symbolic Language of Chinese Animal Painting* (New Haven, CT: Yale University Press, 2009), 137, 141, 166.

35. Deborah Cao, *Animals in China: Law and Society* (Basingstoke: Palgrave Macmillan, 2015), 11–18.

36. For a brief discussion on the good omens as the expressions of the righteous conduct of the emperor, see Tiziana Lippiello, *Auspicious Omens and Miracles in Ancient China: Han, Three Kingdoms and Six Dynasties* (Sankt Augustin: Monumenta Serica Institute, 2001), 31.

37. Wang Meng'ou, ed, *Liji jinzhu jinyi* (Taipei: Taiwan shangwu yinshuguan, 1979), 150.

38. Sarah A. Queen, *From Chronicle to Canon: The Hermeneutics of the Spring and Autumn, According to Tung Chung-shu* (Cambridge: Cambridge University Press, 1996); Keith Knapp, *Selfless Offspring: Filial Children and Social Order in Medieval China* (Honolulu: University of Hawai'i Press, 2005), 83. Some scholars have suggested that correlative thought could be also found in ancient India and other parts of the world; see Steve Farmer, John B. Henderson, and Michael Witzel, "Neurobiology, Layered Texts, and Correlative Cosmologies: A Cross-Cultural Framework for Premodern History," *Bulletin of the Museum of Far Eastern Antiquities* 72 (2000): 48–90.

39. Charles Holcombe, *In the Shadow of the Han: Literati Thought and Society at the Beginning of the Southern Dynasties* (Honolulu: University of Hawai'i Press, 1994), 131.

40. Roel Sterckx, *The Animal and the Daemon in Ancient China* (Albany: State University of New York Press, 2002), 123–63; For a Confucian perspective on animals, see Rodney Taylor, "Of Animals and Humans: The Confucian Perspective," in *A Communion of Subjects: Animals in Religion, Science, and Ethics*, ed. Paul Waldau and Kimberley Patton (New York: Columbia University Press, 2006), 293–307.

41.   Roel Sterckx, "Transforming the Beasts: Animals and Music in Early China," *T'oung Pao*, 2nd series 86, no. 1/3 (2000): 5.

42.   Thomas T. Allsen, *The Royal Hunt in Eurasian History* (Philadelphia: University of Pennsylvania Press, 2006), 183.

43.   For a discussion of this phrase see Keith Knapp, *Selfless Offspring*, 91; more recently, he again discussed the animals as moral exemplars in early medieval Confucian tradition, see Keith Knapp, "Noble Creatures: Filial and Righteous Animals in Early Medieval Confucian Thought," 64–83.

44.   Thomas K. Allsen, *The Royal Hunt in Eurasian History*, 146–65.

45.   Readers may recall a famous case in the Tang dynasty. When the locust disaster reached the capital city, Emperor Taizong ate a handful of locusts show his concern over his depredations; see Sima Guang et al., *Zizhi tongjian*, juan 192, 6053–54; Howard J. Wechsler, *Mirror to the Son of Heaven: Wei Cheng at the Court of T'ang T'ai-tsung* (New Haven, CT: Yale University Press, 1974), 82.

46.   Miranda Brown, *The Politics of Mourning in Early China* (Albany: State University of New York Press, 2007), 69; she also noted that in the later Han the ultimate expression of filial devotion was so powerful that it could influence the natural realm, bring up auspicious omens, such as phoenix and white hare, and so forth (80–81).

47.   Norman Kutcher, *Mourning in Late Imperial China* (Cambridge: Cambridge University Press, 1999), 2.

48.   In the Northern Song dynasty, Huang Tingjian wrote a poem describing Li Ling as "the filial and compassionate parents of people, so tiger went away and locusts withdraw and flew away." See Beijing daxue guwenxian yanjiusuo, ed., *Quan Song shi*, juan 1009 (Beijing: Beijing daxue chubanshe, 1998: 11531).

49.   Interestingly, in Enlightenment France, the "enlightened" thinkers also viewed "Oriental" people as "barbarians or children." See Denis Diderot and Jean Le Rond D'Alembert, eds., *Encyclopédie, ou Dictionnaire raisonné des arts, des sciences, et des métiers, par une société de gens de letters*, vol. 7 (Paris and Amsterdam: Andre le Bretonne et al., 1751–1780), 455.

50.   Zhou Shaoliang and Zhao Chao, *Tangdai muzhi huibian*, 165.

51.   Zhou Shaoliang and Zhao Chao, *Tangdai muzhi huibian*, 275.

52.   Hou Xudong, *Beichao cunmin de shenghuo shijie: Chaoting, Zhouxian yu cunli* (Beijing: Shangwu yinshuguan, 2005), 295.

53.   Hou Xudong, *Beichao cunmin de shenghuo shijie*, 299–300.

54.   Anne Cheng, "Filial Piety with a Vengeance: The Tension between Rites and Law in the Han," in *Filial Piety in Chinese Thought and History*, ed. Alan K. L. Chan and Sor-Hoon Tan (London: Routledge, 2004), 29–43, esp. 35. For the discussions on the mutual relationship between the ritual and rules in the Han dynasty, see A. F. P. Hulsewé, *Remnants of Han Law* (Leiden: Brill, 1955), 80; Léon Vandermeersch, "Ritualisme et juridisme," in *Essais sur le rituel, Colloque du centenaire de la Section des Sciences religieuses de l'Ecole Practique des Hautes Etudes*, vol. 2, A. Blondeau and K. Schipper eds. (Louvain and Paris: Peeters, 1990; reprinted in *Etudes sinologiques*, Paris: Presses Universitaires de France, 1994), 209–20; Michael Nylan, "Confucian Piety and Individualism in Han China," *Journal of American Oriental Society* 116 (1996): 1–27. Ch'u T'ung-tsu (Qu Tongzu) provides an image of the comparison and interaction between Confucianism and Legalism focusing on their viewpoints of moral teaching and lawful regulations in

ancient China, especially in pre-Qin period; see Ch'u T'ung-tsu, *Law and Society in Traditional China* (Paris: Mouton, 1961); and Ch'u T'ung-tsu, *Zhongguo falü yu zhongguo shehui* (Beijing: Zhonghua shuju, 1981), 270-325.

55. Masubuchi Tatsuo, *Chūgoku kodai no shakai to kokka* (*Society and State in Ancient China*) (Tokyo: Iwanami Shoten, 1996), 225-95.

56. *Tang liu dian*, juan 30, lists all major officials from grand protector to county magistrate. According to *Tang liu dian*, all county magistrates were required to guide and expand transforming traditions and customs and comfort local people. Liu Houbin's study suggested that in the Tang dynasty, Confucian moral transformation played a pivotal role in the governance evaluation of a magistrate's political career; see Liu Houbin, "Tangdai xianling de xuanshou," in *Zhongguo lishi bowuguan guankan* 3 (2007): 51-58; a more recent study on the Tang county magistrates, see Lai Ruihe, *Tangdai zhongceng wenguan* (Taipei: Lianjing chuban gongsi, 2008), chap. 4.

57. William Theodore de Bary et al., *Sources of Chinese Tradition: Volume 1: From Earliest Times to 1600* (New York: Columbia University Press, 2013), 43.

58. Ye Wei, *Nanbeichao Sui Tang guanli fentu yanjiu* (Beijing: Beijing daxue chubanshe, 2009), 199-226.

59. Zhou Shaoliang and Zhao Chao, *Tangdai muzhi huibian*, 181.

60. Qiao Dong, Li Xiangi, and Shi Jiazhen, eds., "Luoyang di'er wenwu gongzuodui," in *Luoyang xinhuo muzhi xubian*, no. 68 (Beijing: Kexue chubanshe, 2008).

61. Qiao Dong, Li Xiangi, and Shi Jiazhen, eds., *Luoyang xinhuo muzhi xubian*, no. 383.

62. Thomas A. Metzger, "Was Neo-Confucianism 'Tangential' to the Elite Culture of Late Imperial China?" *The American Asian Review* 4, no. 1 (1986): 2-3.

63. P. Steven Sangren, *History and Magical Power in a Chinese Community* (Stanford, CA: Stanford University Press, 1987), 142.

64. Ogata Isamu, *Chūgoku kodai no ie, to kokka: Kōtei shihaika no chitsujo kōzō* (Tokyo: Iwanami Shoten, 1979), 187-214, esp. 198-214.

65. Ogata Isamu, *Chūgoku kodai no ie, to kokka*, 222-23.

66. Howard J. Wechsler, *Offerings of Jade and Silk: Ritual and Symbol in the Legitimation of the T'ang Dynasty* (New Haven, CT: Yale University Press, 1985), 94, 102-04.

67. C. K. Yang, *Religion in Chinese Society: A Study of Contemporary Social Functions of Religion and Some of Their Historical Factors* (Berkeley: University of California Press, 1961), 140.

68. For the discussion on how immoral cults implied a forbidden social promiscuity and a forbidden religious promiscuity, as well as divinities incarnating and mixing with them; see Maurice Freedman, "On the Sociological Study of Chinese Religion," in *Religion and Ritual in Chinese Society*, ed. Arthur P. Wolf (Stanford, CA: Stanford University Press, 1974), 36. Valerie Hansen notes it as the unauthorized cults; see Valerie Hansen, *Changing Gods in Medieval China, 1127–1276* (Princeton, NJ: Princeton University Press, 1990).

69. Sima Qian, *Shiji*, juan 66 (Beijing: Zhonghua shuju, 1959), 3211. When the Wen Marquise of Wei 魏文侯 was the ruler, Ximen Bao 西門豹 became the county magistrate of Ye 鄴令. He ordered an end to the practice of marrying women to the deity of the river.

70. For a concise study of these five rites in Tang code, see David McMullen, "Bureaucrats and Cosmology: The Ritual Code of T'ang China," in *Rituals of Royalty: Power and Ceremonial in Traditional Societies*, ed. David Cannadine and Simon Price (Cambridge: Cambridge University Press, 1987), 181-236.

71.   For a general introduction to the five rites in the Tang dynasty, see Ren Shuang, *Tang-dai lizhi yanjiu* (Shenyang: Dongbei shifan daxue chubanshe, 1999).

72.   For an examination of the role of this genre in late and mid-Tang political culture. see Qiu Luming, "Quanli yu guanzhong: Dezhengbei suojian Tangdai de zhongyang yu difang," in *Chang'an yu Hebei zhijian: Zhongwan Tang de zhengzhi yu wenhua* (Beijing: Beijing shifan daxue chubanshe, 2018), 124–73.

73.   "Tang Li Mingfu dezheng bei 唐李明府德政碑," see Chen Shangjun, ed., *Quan Tang wen bubian*, vol. 2 (Beijing: Zhonghua shuju, 2005), 1770.

74.   Miranda Brown, *The Politics of Mourning in Ancient China*, 118–119, 136.

75.   Gilbert Lewis, *Day of Shining Red: An Essay on Understanding Ritual* (Cambridge: Cambridge University Press, 1980), 19.

76.   James L. Watson, "The Structure of Chinese Funerary Rites: Elementary Forms, Ritual Sequence, and the Primacy of Performance," in *Death Ritual in Late Imperial and Modern China*, ed. James L. Watson and Evelyn S. Rawski (Berkeley: University of California Press, 1988), 5.

77.   The regional shift of economic gravity, however, might be an element. In the medieval period, with the construction of the canal system and the expansion of transportation, the population booming in the southern region might lead to increasing confrontations between humans and tigers. For the development of transportation system and the southward of economy and population in the Tang period, see Denis Twitchett, *Financial Administration Under the T'ang*, 2nd edition (Cambridge: Cambridge University Press, 1970), 84–96.

78.   Li Yanshou, *Nan shi*, juan 23, 636.

79.   Daoxuan, *Xu gaoseng zhuan*, T. 50, no. 2060: 657a.

80.   Daoxuan, *Xu gaoseng zhuan*, T. 50, no. 2060: 547b.

81.   Daoxuan, *Xu gaoseng zhuan*, T. 50, no. 2060: 506c.

82.   Ming Sengshao, *Zheng erjiao lun*, T. 52, no. 2102, 38b.

83.   Ming Sengshao, *Zheng erjiao lun*, T. 52, no. 2102, 19a; Zongbing, *Hongmingji*, juan 2, *Treatise on Understanding Buddhism* [*Mingfo lun*].

84.   Zhang Jiyu, ed., *Zhonghua daozang*, vol. 2 (Beijing: Huaxia chubanshe, 2004), 2.

85.   Zhang Jiyu, ed., *Zhonghua daozang*, vol. 8, 643.

3. BUDDHISTS TAMING FELINES

1.   Hagiographical sources in medieval Chinese Buddhism refer to the biographies of eminent monks compiled by Huijiao (497–554), Daoxuan (596–667), and Zanning (919–1001). For the study of these biographies as hagiographies in Chinese Buddhism; see John Kieschnick, *The Eminent Monk: Buddhist Ideals in Medieval Chinese Hagiography* (Honolulu: University of Hawai'i Press, 1997); Koichi Shinohara, "Animals in Medieval Chinese Biographies of Buddhist Monks," *Religions* 10, no. 6 (2019): 348.

2.   On the tigers in Chinese history, see Guo Fu, Li Yuese (Joseph Needham), and Cheng Qingtai, *Zhongguo gudai dongwuxue shi* (Beijing: Kexue chubanshe, 1999); Weng Junxiong, "Tangdai hu xiang de xingzong: Jianlun Tangdai hu xiang jizai zengduo de yuanyin," *Tang Yanjiu* 3 (1997): 381–94; on the living environment of animals in medieval China, see Xu Tingyun, "Sui Tang Wudai shiqi de shengtai huangjin," *Guoxue yanjiu* 8 (2001): 209–44.

3. In general, the *dhuta* cultivation refers to ascetic practices for eliminating defilements, purifying impurities through detaching from worldly life. For the Buddhist practice in the forest, see Daniel Boucher, *Bodhisattvas of the Forest and the Formation of the Mahāyāna: A Study and Translation of the Rāṣṭrapālaparipṛcchā-sūtra* (Honolulu: University of Hawai'i Press, 2008), 40–63; Paul M. Harrison, "Searching for the Origins of the Mahāyāna: What Are We Looking For?" *Eastern Buddhist* 28, no. 1 (1995): 48–69.

4. Daoxuan, in "Fazang," *Xu gaoseng zhuan*, juan 19, *T.* 50, no. 2060: 581a.

5. Robert B. Marks clearly demonstrated that in the modern-day Lingnan region tiger attacks resulted from the humans' deforestation, which led to the destruction of the tiger habitat. See Robert B. Marks, *Tigers, Rice, Silk, and Silt: Environment and Economy in Late Imperial South China* (Cambridge: Cambridge University Press, 1998), 323–27.

6. Tiger violence was depicted in the Dunhuang cave wall paintings. Dunhuang yanjiuyuan [Dunhuang Academy], ed., *Dunhuang shiku quanji* [A complete collection of Dunhuang caves], juan 19, "dongwuhua juan [volume of animal paintings]" (Shanghai: Shanghai renmin chubanshe, 2000), 107.

7. Tigers are more prominent in China. Ancient Near East and Middle East were beyond the historical range of the tiger. Tigers rarely appeared in Egyptian, Hittite, Akkadian, and Hebrew literature. Other animals such as ox, horse, sheep, and falcon figured more prominently in their religious life, either appearing as the symbols of many deities, or playing various roles in sacrificial rites and divination. See Billie Jean Collins, ed., *A History of the Animal World in the Ancient Near East* (Leiden: Brill, 2002), 307–424.

8. Earlier scholarship exists from the perspective of literary studies; see Edward H. Schafer, *The Vermilion Bird: T'ang Images of the South* (Berkeley: University of California Press, 1967), 228; Charles Hammond, "An Excursion in Tiger Lore," *Asia Major* (3rd series) 4, no. 1 (1991): 87–100; Charles Hammond, "The Righteous Tiger and the Grateful Lion," *Monumenta Serica* 43 (1996): 191–211.

9. The roles and images of animals in Chinese religions have been examined in many works, such as Roel Sterckx, *The Animal and the Daemon in Ancient China* (Albany: State University of New York Press, 2002); Rodney Taylor, "Of Animals and Humans: The Confucian Perspective," in *A Communion of Subjects: Animals in Religion, Science, and Ethics*, ed. Paul Waldau and Kimberley Patton (New York: Columbia University Press, 2006), 293–307. Timothy H. Barrett briefly mentioned the roles and status of tigers in medieval Chinese Buddhism and suggested that tiger in medieval Chinese Buddhism played similar roles as lion in medieval Christianity; see Timothy H. Barrett, "The Monastery Cat in Cross-Cultural Perspective: Cat Poems of the Zen Masters," in *Buddhist Monasticism in East Asia: Places of Practice*, ed. James A. Benn, Lori Meeks, and James Robson (London: Routledge, 2009), 116–17.

10. Alan Bleakley, *The Animalizing Imagination: Totemism, Textuality and Ecocriticism* (New York: St. Martin Press, 2000), 38–40.

11. As Lambert Schmithausen points out, the attitudes of many religious traditions are diverse, and these religions acknowledged that there were tensions between human beings and the nature; see *Maitrī and Magic: Aspects of the Buddhist Attitude Toward the Dangerous in Nature* (Wien: Verlag der Österreichischen Akademie der Wissenschaften, 1997), 9.

12. For the taxonomy, see Don E. Wilson and DeeAnn M. Reeder, eds., *Mammal Species of the World: A Taxonomic and Geographic Reference*, 3rd edition (Baltimore, MD: John

Hopkins University Press, 2005), 546–47; Eduardo Eizirik, Jae-Heup Kim, Marilyn Menotti-Raymond, et al., "Phylogeography, Population History and Conservation Genetics of Jaguars (*Panthera onca*, Mammalia, Felidae)," *Molecular Ecology* 10, no. 1 (2001): 65–79.

13. Clifford Geertz, "Centers, Kings, and Charisma: Reflections on the Symbolics of Power," in *Local Knowledge: Further Essays in Interpretive Anthropology* (New York: Basic Books, 2000), 121–46; Robert Wessing, "Symbolic Animals in the Land between the Waters: Markers of Place and Transition," *Asian Folklore Studies* 65, no. 2 (2006): 205–39.

14. More than 100,000 years ago, some Siberian tigers might have migrated to Alaska; see Sandra Herrington, "Subspecies and the Conservation of *Panther tigris*: Preserving Genetic Heterogeneity," in *Tigers of the World: The Biology, Biopolitics, Management and Conservation of an Endangered Species*, ed. Ronald L. Tilson and Ulysses S. Seal (Park Ridge, NJ: Notes Publications, 1987), 512–60.

15. Carlos Carroll and Dale G. Miquelle, "Spatial Viability Analysis of Amur Tiger *Panthera tigris altaica* in the Russian Far East: The Role of Protected Areas and Landscape Matrix in Population Persistence," *Journal of Applied Ecology* 43, no. 6 (2006): 1056–68; Gregory D. Hayward, Dale G. Miquelle, Evgeny N. Smirnov, Chris Nations, "Monitoring Amur Tiger Populations: Characteristics of Track Surveys in Snow," *Wildlife Society Bulletin* 30, no. 4 (2002): 1150–59.

16. Susan A. Mainka and Judy A. Mills, "Wildlife and Traditional Chinese Medicine: Supply and Demand for Wildlife Species," *Journal of Zoo and Wildlife Medicine* 26, no. 2 (1995): 193–200, esp. 194–195; Chris Coggins, *The Tiger and the Pangolin: Nature, Culture, and Conservation in China* (Honolulu: University of Hawai'i Press, 2003).

17. Eric Dinerstein et al., "The Fate of Wild Tigers," *BioSciene* 7, no. 6 (2007): 508–14; John Seidensticker, Sarah Christie, and Peter Jackson, eds., *Riding the Tiger: Tiger Conservation in Human-Dominated Landscapes* (Cambridge: Cambridge University Press, 1999); Susan A. Mainka and Judy A. Mills, "Wildlife and Traditional Chinese Medicine: Supply and Demand for Wildlife Species."

18. Trilok Chandra Majupuria, *Sacred and Symbolic Animals of Nepal: Animals in the Art, Culture, Myths and Legends of the Hindus and Buddhists* (Kathmandu: Sahayogi Prakashan Tripureswar, 1977), 102. For an art history perspective, see Heinrich Zimmer, *Myths and Symbols in Indian Art and Civilization*. Bollingen Series XI. (Princeton, NJ: Princeton University Press, 1972).

19. Manorama Upadhyaya, *Royal Authority in Ancient India* (Jodhpur: Books Treasure, 2007), 53–54; Asheem Srivastav and Suvira Srivastav, *Asiatic Lion on the Brink* (Dehra Dun: Beshen Singh Mahendra Pal Singh, 1999), 90–93; Prasanna Kumar Acharya, *Architecture of Mānasāra* (New Delhi: Munshiram Manoharlel Publishers Pvt. Ltd., 1994, reprinted edition), 597–599; Nancy Falk, "Wilderness and Kingship in Ancient South Asia," *History of Religions* 13, no. 1 (1973): 1–15.

20. Trilok Chandra Majupuria, *Sacred and Symbolic Animals of Nepal*, 107.

21. Koichi Hokazono, "Butten toshite no Śākyasiṃhajātaka nitsuite." *Indogaku bukkyōgaku kenkyū* 36, no. 1 (1987): 403–401 (L).

22. This is the name that appeared in Tocharian A vocabulary as śiśäk śanwem, which is used to describe the twenty-fifth mark of the thirty-two marks in the Tocharian drama

Maitreyasamiti-Nāṭaka; see Ji Xianlin, with Werner Winter and Georges-Jean Pinault eds., *Fragments of the Tocharian A Maitreyasamiti-Nāṭaka of the Xinjiang Museum, China* (Berlin: Mouton de Gruyter, 1998), 83–87; the Sanskrit name can be found in Franklin Edgerton, *Buddhist Hybrid Sanskrit Grammar and Dictionary*, 2 vols. (New Delhi: Motilal Banarsidass, 1985), 595; according to Edgerton, this is also the title of the Buddha of the East and sometimes the Buddha's disciples also used this title; Gerd Carling, with Georges-Jean Pinault and Werner Winter, eds., *Dictionary and Thesaurus of Tocharian A, Vol. 1: A–J* (Wiesbaden: Harrassowitz Verlag, 2009), 13b.

23. Jñānagupta, *Qishi jing*, T. 1, no. 24, 364a–b.

24. Monier Monier-Williams, *A Sanskrit-English Dictionary* (New Delhi: Asian Educational Services, 2009), 1213.

25. Y-Liang Chou (Zhou Yiliang), "Tantrism in China," *Harvard Journal of Asiatic Studies* 8, no. 3–4 (1945): 317.

26. Buddhayaśas, *Wufen lü*, T. 22, no. 1421, 18b–c.

27. There are two main discourses on sacrifices in ancient South Asia. One concerns animal sacrifice, which was practiced by Brahmanism, although Buddhism was against this practice. The other is the sacrifice of Buddhist saints, for the sake of all sentient beings, as often appeared to be the practice of the Buddha's Bodhisattva in his previous lives; see Reiko Ohnuma, *Unfortunate Destiny: Animals in the Indian Buddhist Imagination* (New York: Oxford University Press, 2017), 65–69.

28. Huijue, *Xianyu jing*, T. 4, no. 202, 438a–c.

29. Herbert Härtel, ed., *Along the Ancient Silk Routes: Central Asian Art from the Western Berlin State Museums, An Exhibition Lent by the Museum für Indische Kunst, Staatliche Museen Preussicher Kulturebesitz* (New York: Harry N. Abrams, 1982), 100–101, 34 (Jātaka scenes); Albert Grünwedel, *Alt-Kutscha* (Berlin: D. Reimer, 1920), vol. 2, 57, figs. 42, 44; Albert von Le Coq, *Die buddhistieche Spätantike in Mittelasien* (Berlin: D. Reimer, 1922–1926), vol. 4, 17, pl. 10; Albert von Le Coq and Ernst Waldschmidt, eds., "Neue Bildwerke II," in *Die buddhistische Spätantike in Mittelasien*, vol. 6 (Berlin: D. Reimer, 1928), 9ff.

30. Saṃghadeva, *Zengyi Ahan jing*, T. 2, no. 125, 640a.

31. Étienne Lamotte, *History of Indian Buddhism: From the Origins to the Śaka Era*, trans. Sara Webb-Boin (Louvain: Université Catholique de Louvain, Institut Orientaliste, 1988), 649.

32. Dharmarakṣa, *Daban niepan jing*, T. 12, no. 374, 522b–c.

33. For the discussions on the roaring analogue of the Buddha and his disciples, see Sylvain Lévi and E. Chavannes, "Les seize arhat protecteurs de la Loi," *Journal Asiatique* 2, no. 8 (1900): 89–304, 250; John Strong, "The Legend of the Lion-Roarer: A Study of the Buddhist Arhat Piṇḍola Bhāradvāja," *Numen* 26, no. 1 (1979): 68–71.

34. See the biography of Kumārajīva in Huijiao, *Gaoseng zhuan*, juan 2, T. 50, no. 2059, 331a.

35. Edwin G. Pulleyblank, "Why Tocharians?" *Journal of Indo-European Studies* 23 (1995): 427–28; Douglas Q. Adams, *A Dictionary of Tocharian B* (Amsterdam: Rodopi, 1999), 660; Harold W. Bailey, *The Culture of the Sakas in Ancient Iranian Khotan* (Del Mar, CA: Caravan Books, 1982), 35.

36. For the discussion on Rouzhi (I followed conventional Chinese pronunciation for Yuezhi), see Craig Benjamin, *The Yuezhi: Origin, Migration and the Conquest of Northern Bactria* (Turnhout: Brepols, 2007).

37.   Susie Green, *Tiger* (London: Reaktion Books, 2006); Don E. Wilson and DeeAnn M. Reeder eds., *Mammal Species of the World: A Taxonomic and Geographic Reference*, 3rd edition (Baltimore, MD: The John Hopkins University Press, 2005), 548; Peter Boomgaard, *Frontiers of Fear: Tigers and People in the Malay World, 1800–1950* (New Haven, CT: Yale University Press, 2001); Fanny Eden, *Tigers, Durbars and Kings: Fanny Eden's Indian Journals, 1837–1838*, ed. Janet Durbar (London: John Murray Publishers, 1989); George B. Schaller, *The Deer and the Tiger: A Study of Wildlife in India* (Chicago: University of Chicago Press, 1967).

38.   It should be noted, however, that in Orissa—among the Kondhs, the Indian minority ethnic community—tigers are regarded as "the personification of the forest and the power of the goddess that helps shamans in their fight against demons and evil spirits." See Stefano Beggiora, "Tigers, Tiger Spirits and Were-tigers in Tribal Orissa," in *Charming Beauties and Frightful Beasts: Non-human Animals in South Asian Myth, Ritual and Folklore*, ed. Fabrizio M. Ferrari and Thomas Dähnhardt (Sheffield: Equinox Press, 2013), 82–95.

39.   Christian missionaries had already noted the significant role of the tiger in the symbolism of Chinese culture; see "Art. IV: Notices in Chinese History," *The Chinese Repository* 7, no. 11 (March 1839): 596–97; C. A. S. Williams, *Chinese Symbolism and Art Motifs: A Comprehensive Handbook on Symbolism in Chinese Art through the Ages* (Tokyo: Tuttle Publishing, 1974), 377.

40.   Charles E. Hammond, "An Excursion in Tiger Lore"; Werner Eichhorn, "Das Kapitel *Tiger* im T'ai-P'ing Kuang-Chi," *Zeitschrift der Deutschen Morgenländischen Gesellschaft* 104, no. 9 (1954): 140–62.

41.   Wei Shou, *Wei shu* (Beijing: Zhonghua shuju, 1974), juan 3, 60.

42.   Wang Meng'ou, ed., *Liji jinzhu jinyi* (Taipei: Taiwan shangwu yinshuguan, 1979), 150.

43.   For the English version of the Book of Five Sections, see Franklin Edgerton, *The Pañchatantra Reconstructed*, vol. 2 (New Haven, CT: American Oriental Society, 1924); however, it does not have this story translated. The old Uyghur fragments have been found in Xinjiang, see Friedmar Geissler and Peter Zieme, "Uigurische *Pañchatantra*-Fragmente," *Turcica*, vol. 2 (1970): 32–70; M. Ölmez, "Ein weiteres alttürkischen *Pañchatantra*-Fragment," *Ural-Altaische Jahrbücher* N. F. 12 (1993): 179–91.

44.   Boris I. Marshak, "The Tiger, Raised from the Dead: Two Murals from Panjikent," *Bulletin of the Asia Institute*, New Series 10 (1996): 207–17; Boris I. Marshak, *Legends, Tales, and Fables in the Art of Sogdiana* (New York: Bibliotheca Persica Press, 2002), 130; Boris I. Marshak and Franz Grenet, "L'arte sogdiana (IV–IX secolo)," in *Le arti in Asia Centrale*, ed. Pierre Chuvin (Milano: Garzanti, 2002), 114–163.

45.   D. N. MacKenzie, "Buddhist Terminology in Sogdian: A Glossary," *Asia Major* 18, no. 1 (1971): 28–89; Nicholas Sims-Williams, "Indian Elements in Parthian and Sogdian," in *Sprachen des Buddhismus in Zentralasien*, ed. K. Röhborn and W. Veenker (Wiesbaden: Otto Harrassowitz, 1983), 132–41; Xavier Tremblay, *Pour une histoire de la Sérinde: Le Manicheisme parmi les peuples et religions d'Asie Centrale a'apres les sources primaires* (Wien: Verlag der Österreichischen Akademie der Wissenschaften, 2001), 69–71, 203–06.

46.   Wilt L. Idema trans., *Personal Salvation and Filial Piety: Two Precious Scroll Narratives of Guanyin and Her Acolytes* (Honolulu: University of Hawai'i Press, 2008), 35–37.

47.   Dharmarakṣa, *Dafangdeng daji jing*, juan 23, *T*. 13, no. 397, 167b–168b.

48. Zhiyi, *Mohe zhiguan*, juan 8, *T.* 46, no. 1911, 115a-b.

49. Daoxuan, *Xu gaoseng zhuan*, juan 2, *T.* 50, no. 2060, 610a-b.

50. Lu Changyuan 陸長源, "Tang gu Lingquansi Yuanlin chanshi shendaobei bingxu 唐故靈泉寺元林禪師神道碑並序," in *Quan Tang wen*, juan 510 (Beijing: Zhonghua shuju, 1983), 5186.

51. Zanning, *Song gaoseng zhuan*, juan 6, *T.* 50, no. 2061, 740c.

52. John Kieschnick, *The Eminent Monk*.

53. In contrast, in ancient Khotan, kings were called the "lion king" (Tibetan: *rgyal po seng 'ge*, or *seng 'ge rgyal po*), which can be traced back to the legendary story of a king named Sang gra ma who killed a lion that attacked his soldiers. See Ronald E. Emmerick, *Tibetan Texts Concerning Khotan* (London: Oxford University Press, 1967), 48–49. This legend might have some historical base, since lions were indeed active in ancient Central Asia. But apparently it would be impossible for a ruler in Central China to encounter and kill a lion in the wilderness.

54. On the legends of offering bodies as gifts in early Buddhist literature, see Reiko Ohnuma, "The Gift of the Body and the Gift of Dharma," *History of Religions* 37, no. 4 (1998): 323–59; on the analysis of the tigress story, see Reiko Ohnuma, *Head, Eyes, Flesh, and Blood: Giving Away the Body in Indian Buddhist Literature* (New York: Columbia University Press, 2007), 9–14. Numerous Jātaka stories have appeared in Buddhist caves along the Silk Route, in Kizil (caves 8, 13, 17, 34, 38, 47, 114, 184), Dunhuang (caves 254, 428, 301, 302, 419, 85, 72), and some other places; see Alexander Peter Bell, *Didactic Narration: Jataka Iconography in Dunhuang with a Catalogue of Jataka Representations in China* (Münster: LIT Verlag, 2000), 141–43. The story of the tigress was also found in the old Uyghur literature; see Simone-Christine Raschmann and Ablet Semet, "Neues zur alttürkischen 'Geschichte von der hungrigen Tigerin,'" in: *Aspects of Research into Central Asian Buddhism: In Memoriam Kōgi Kudara*, ed. Peter Zieme (Turnhout, Belgium: Brepols, 2008), 237–75.

55. Buddhabhadra, *Mohe sengqi lü*, *T.* 22, no. 1425, 257a.

56. *Foshuo shan'e yinguo jing*, *T.* 85, no. 2881, 1382a. This version is based on the manuscript in the Japanese collection, which was dated in 713. Some fragments of this text also appeared in S. 714, 2207, 3400, 4911, 4917, 4978, 5458, 5602, 5610, 6311, and 6960 in the Stein collection, and P. 2055, 2922 in the Pelliot collection, and some other manuscripts in the Beijing collection.

57. Zanning, *Song gaoseng zhuan*, *T.* 50, no. 2061, 857b.

58. Zanning, *Song gaoseng zhuan*, *T.* 50, no. 2061, 857c.

59. Li Fang et al., *Taiping guangji*, juan 426 (Beijing: *Zhonghua shuju*, 1961), 3467–68.

60. In these narratives, tigers were still regarded as the sentient beings in the animal realm in Buddhist sense and they were inferior to human beings. The tigers have no spiritual dimensions and they could not communicate with human beings spiritually. Paul Waldau suggests that in early Buddhism, the animals were still inferior to human beings, which reflects a typical anthropocentrism; see Paul Waldau, *The Specter of Speciesism: Buddhist and Christian Views of Animals*, chap. 6 and 7 (New York: Oxford University Press, 2001); Paul Waldau, "Buddhism and Animals Rights," in *Contemporary Buddhist Ethics*, ed. Damien Keown (Richmond, Surrey, England: Curzon Press, 2000), 85–105.

61. Sengyou, *Chu sanzang jiji*, *T.* 55, no. 2145, 102a.

62. Sengyou, *Chu sanzang jiji*, T. 55, no. 2145, 104b.

63. Huijiao, *Gaoseng zhuan*, T. 50, no. 2059, 399c.

64. Huijiao, *Gaoseng zhuan*, T. 50, no. 2059, 396c.

65. Huijiao, *Gaoseng zhuan*, T. 50, no. 2059, 408c.

66. Huijiao, *Gaoseng zhuan*, T. 50, no. 2060, 682b.

67. For a brief discussion on the encounters between humans and tigers in Southeast China, see Chris Coggins, *The Tiger and the Pangolin*, 51–86.

68. A mural in Mogao Cave 74 depicted a monk surrounded by a herd of beasts including a tiger; see Dunhuang yanjiuyuan ed., *Dunhuang shiku quanji*, juan 19, 97.

69. Fazang, *Huayanjing zhuanji*, T. 51, no. 2073, 165b.

70. Daoxuan, *Xu gaoseng zhuan*, T. 50, no. 2060, 681a.

71. Zanning, *Song gaoseng zhuan*, T. 50, no. 2061, 832b.

72. Huijiao, *Gaoseng zhuan*, T. 50, no. 2059, 340.

73. Huijiao, *Gaoseng zhuan*, T. 50, no. 2059, 404a.

74. The ritual of circumambulation has a long history in ancient South Asia. In Buddhism, generally it "consists of an individual walking around a stupa, accumulating merit to speed his or her path to nirvana." See Lars Fogelin, *An Archaeological History of Indian Buddhism* (Oxford: Oxford University Press, 2015), 96. In medieval Chinese Buddhism, this ritual also refers to walking around the image of the Buddha.

75. Daoxuan, *Xu gaoseng zhuan*, T. 50, no. 2060, 543b.

76. Daoxuan, *Xu gaoseng zhuan*, T. 50, no. 2060, 607b.

77. Huijiao, *Gaoseng zhuan*, T. 50, no. 2059, 408a.

78. The mountain spirit is sometimes also called mountain demon; see Richard von Glahn, *The Sinister Way: The Divine and the Demonic in Chinese Religious Culture* (Berkeley: University of California Press, 2004), 78–97. He cites Dai Fu's 戴孚 *Guanyi ji* 廣異記 and suggests that the mountain spirits often were friends of tigers and other beasts. The discussion on the legends about the tiger in *Guangyi ji* can be found in Glen Dudbridge, *Religious Experience and Lay Society in T'ang China: A Reading of Tai Fu's Kuang-I Chi* (Cambridge: Cambridge University Press, 2002), 219–20. The interactions between mountain spirits and tigers can be found in Li Fang et al., *Taiping guangji*, vol. 4 (Beijing: Zhonghua shuju, 1961), 3480–83.

79. Regarding eminent monks who could communicate with spirits, see John Kieschnick *The Eminent Monk*, 96–109.

80. Huijiao, *Gaoseng zhuan*, T. 50, no. 2059, 350a.

81. Zanning, *Song gaoseng zhuan*, T. 50, no. 2061, 768a.

82. David A. Mason, *The Spirit of the Mountain: Korea's San-Shin and Traditions of Mountain Worship* (Seoul: Hollym, 1999).

83. Huijiao, *Gaoseng zhuan*, T. 50, no. 2059, 522c–523a.

84. Daoxuan, *Guang hongmingji*, T. 52, no. 2103, 231b.

85. For the discussion on the dharma scepter, see John Kieschnick, *The Impact of Buddhism on Chinese Material Culture* (Princeton, NJ: Princeton University Press, 2003), 113–15; Meir Shahar, *The Shaolin Monastery: History, Religion, and the Chinese Martial Arts* (Honolulu: University of Hawai'i Press, 2008), 105–07.

86. Zhipan, *Fozu tongji*, T. 49, no. 2035, 553.

87. Zhipan, *Fozu tongji*, T. 49, no. 2035, 199a.

88. Zanning, *Song gaoseng zhuan*, T. 50, no. 2061, 847c; a layperson named Li Tongxuan 李通
玄 could do the same thing, according to his biography; T. 50, no. 2061, 853a.

89. Daoxuan, *Xu gaoseng zhuan*, T. 50, no. 2060, 555b.

90. Huixiang, *Hongzan fahua zhuan*, T. 51, no. 2067, 27b. According to *Records of Miraculous
Retribution* (*Mingbao ji* 冥報記), a layperson could also attract tigers to listen to the recitation of the sutra. Wei Zhonggui 韋仲珪 (c. sixth and seventh centuries) was a lay Buddhist. He was also a filial son and was well respected in his hometown. After his father
had passed away, he sent his wife and concubine away and resided alone, beside his
father's tomb. He often recited the Lotus Sutra. One night a tiger came to listen to his
recitation; see Tang Lin, *Mingbao ji* (Beijing: Zhonghua shuju, 1992), 21.

91. Huijiao, *Gaoseng zhuan*, T. 50, no. 2059, 337.

92. Zanning, *Song gaoseng zhuan*, T. 50, no. 2061, 871b.

93. Huijiao, *Gaoseng zhuan*, T. 50, no. 2059, 387c.

94. Daoxuan, *Xu gaoseng zhuan*, T. 50, no. 2060, 663c.

95. Daoxuan, *Xu gaoseng zhuan*, T. 50, no. 2060, 666a.

96. Zanning, *Song gaoseng zhuan*, T. 50, no. 2061, 806b.

97. In ancient Egypt, some animals were thought to speak and understand the human language and even react based on their understanding of human commands; see Billie Jean
Collins, ed., *A History of the Animal World in the Ancient Near East*, 253-55.

98. Baochang, *Biqiuni zhuan*, T. 50, no. 2063, 935c.

99. Baochang, *Biqiuni zhuan*, T. 50, no. 2063, 940a.

100. Nianchang, *Fozu lidai tongzai*, T. 49, no. 2036, 601c.

101. Nianchang, *Fozu lidai tongzai*, T. 49, no. 2036: 687b; Nianchang, ed., *Fozu lidai tongzai*, juan
20; X. vol. 79, no. 1559: 391a-b, Zhengshou, ed., *Jiatai pudenglu*, juan 16, Fazhong chanshi
法忠禪師; T. vol. 50, no. 2062: 920a.

102. One of the most popular legends about riding the tiger in medieval Buddhist hagiographies was that of Fenggan 封幹, who was a Chan monk living the Guoqing Temple 國清
寺 on Tiantai Mountain; his biography appeared in chapter 19 of the *Song gaosengzhuan*
(T. 50, no. 2061, 831b). His story is often depicted in the paintings of the Song and later
dynasties; see Hou-mei Sung, *Decoded Messages: The Symbolic Language of Chinese Animal
Painting* (New Haven, CT: Yale University Press, 2009), 137, 142.

103. Walter Scheidel, "Comparing Comparisons: Ancient East and West," in *Ancient Greece
and China Compared*, ed. G. E. R. Lloyd and Jingyi Jenny Zhao (Cambridge: Cambridge
University Press, 2018), 43.

104. Similar to early medieval Chinese narratives, this story seems to be legend rather than
fact; it appeared in Christian literature more than one century after St. Francis's death
in Ugolino di Monte Santa Maria, *Actus Beati Francisci et Sociorum Eius* (*The Acts of Blessed
Flowers and His Companions*) and its expanded version in Italian titled *I Fioretti di San Fran-
cesco* (*The Little Flowers of St Francis*). For modern studies on this story, see Lynn White Jr.,
"The Historical Roots of Our Ecological Crisis," *Science* 155 (1967): 1203-07; David Salter,
Holy and Noble Beasts: Encounters with Animals in Medieval Literature (Cambridge, UK: D.
S. Brewer, 2001), 25-32.

105. For example, E. Gordon Whatley, Anne B. Thompson, and Robert K. Upchurch, eds.,
Saints' Lives in Middle English Collections (Kalamazoo, MI: Medieval Institute Publications,
2004).

106. For the story, see Jacobus de Voragine, *The Golden Legend Readings on the Saints*, vol. 1 (Princeton, NJ: Princeton University Press, 1993), 84–85; for the study of this story, see Laura Hobgood-Oster, *Holy Dogs and Asses: Animals in the Christian Tradition* (Urbana: University of Illinois Press, 2008), 63.

107. Dag Øistein Endsjø, *Primordial Landscapes, Incorruptible Bodies Desert Asceticism and the Christian Appropriation of Greek Ideas on Geography, Bodies, and Immortality* (New York: Peter Lang, 2008).

108. Clarence J. Glacken, *Traces on the Rhodian Shore: Nature and Culture in Western Thought from Ancient Times to the End of the Eighteenth Century* (Berkeley: University of California Press, 1967), 310. For accounts of taming animals in early Christian apocryphal literature; see Ingvild Sælid Gilhus, *Animals, Gods, and Humans: Changing Attitudes to Animals in Greek, Roman, and Early Christian Ideas* (London: Routledge, 2006), 257.

109. Salter, *Holy and Noble Beasts*, 147–48.

110. Hobgood-Oster, *Holy Dogs*, 63–80.

111. Hobgood-Oster, *Holy Dogs*, 71.

112. Hobgood-Oster, *Holy Dogs*, 72.

113. Vincent of Beauvais, "De Vita et Actibus Sancti Hieronymi Presbiteri," in *Bibliotheca Mundi. Vincentii Bellovacensis Speculum Quadruplex: Naturale, Doctrinale, Morale, Historiale*, ed., Benedictini Collegii Vedastini, 4 vols., Douai, 1624, vol. 4, Liber XVI. Cap. 18, 623. For the modern scholarship on St. Jerome, see Eugene Rice, *Saint Jerome in the Renaissance* (Baltimore, MD: Johns Hopkins University Press, 1985), 23–48; Herbert Friedmann, *A Bestiary for Saint Jerome: Animal Symbolism in European Religious Art* (Washington DC: Smithsonian Institution Press, 1980), especially first section "The Legend of Saint Jerome in Art," 17–188; Salter, *Holy and Noble Beasts*, 11–24; and Megan Hale Williams, *The Monk and the Book: Jerome and the Making of Christian Scholarship* (Chicago: University of Chicago Press, 2006).

114. A goat, ass, and other animals often came to visit St. Theon's ascetic chamber. St. Gent tamed a wolf and transformed this wolf into his servant. When St. John Chrysostom (c. 345–407) practiced asceticism in the forest, he was benevolent and compassionate toward many beasts around him. St. Giles, a Swedish priest, lived as a hermit in France, with a deer as his friend. St. Zosimas commanded a lion to carry luggage for him. When St. Anthony of Padua (1195–1231) was giving a sermon, it was said that a school of fish came to listen to his teachings. See Lewis G. Regenstein, *Replenish the Earth: A History of Organized Religion's Treatment of Animals and Nature—Including the Bible's Message of Conservation and Kindness toward Animals* (New York: The Crossroad Publishing Company, 1991), 57–61, see chap. 3, "The Early Christian Saints: Compassion and Love for Animals"; Hobgood-Oster, *Holy Dogs*, 67–69; Edward A. Armstrong, *Saint Francis: Nature Mystic; The Derivation and Significance of the Nature Stories in the Franciscan Legend* (Berkeley: University of California Press, 1973); William Edward Hartpole Lecky, *History of European Morals from Augustus to Charlemagne*, 2 vols. (New York: D. Appleton and Company, 1876); Paul Sabatier, *Life of St. Francis of Assisi*, trans. Louise Seymour Houghton (New York: Charles Scribner's Sons, 1902).

115. St. Malchus was a hermit living in the desert for several years. He decided to visit his mother. During his journey back home, he was caught by Ishmaelites and became a slave. He escaped with another Christian, and they were hunted in the desert. When they fled into a cave, they were saved by a lioness. See Roy J. Deferrari, trans., "Life of Malchus,"

in *Early Christian Biographies*, Fathers of the Church Series, vol. 15 (Washington, DC: Catholic University of America Press, 1952), 281-97; Alison Goddard Elliott, *Roads to Paradise: Reading the Lives of the Early Saints* (Hanover, NH: University Press of New England, 1987), 144-67; Salter, *Holy and Noble Beasts*, 18-19.

116.   Reiko Ohnuma, *Unfortunate Destiny*, 148; Ohnuma analyzed this taming ritual as the grand public spectacle in comparison with the Spanish bullfight; see 148-71.

4. DAOISTS TRANSFORMING FEROCIOUS TIGERS

1.   For a summary of the Chinese term *ziran* 自然, which in classical Daoist philosophy "suggests the idealist natural order of civilized societies and the world," see Xiaogan Liu, "Laozi's Philosophy: Textual and Conceptual Analyses," in *Dao Companion to Daoist Philosophy*, ed. Xiaogan Liu (Berlin: Springer, 2006), 81-82.

2.   Citing Buddhist and Confucian sources, Jacques Gernet noted that attitudes towards animals in ancient China could be both compassionate and cruel; see Jacques Gernet, "Pitié pour les animaux," in *De Dunhuang au Japon: Etudes Chinoises et Bouddhiques offertes à Michel Soymié*, ed. Jean-Pierre Drège (Genève: Droz, 1996), 293-300. Scholars suggest that the Daoist religious communities adopted some moral codes for dealing with animals from Confucian and Buddhist teachings. E. N. Anderson and Lisa Raphals, "Daoism and Animals," in *A Communion of Subjects: Animals in Religion, Science, and Ethics*, ed. Paul Waldau and Kimberley Patton (New York: Columbia University Press, 2006), 281; E. N. Anderson compares Daoist and Confucian attitudes toward nature and suggests that early Daoism was neither environmentalism nor social glue, but it was based on an ecological vision; see E. N. Anderson, "Flowering Apricot: Environment, Practice, Folk Religion and Taoism," in *Daoism and Ecology*, ed. N. J. Girardot, James Miller, and Liu Xiaogan (Cambridge, MA: Harvard University Press, 2001), 177.

3.   Anderson and Raphals state that, "Even the tiger, so universally revered in folk cults throughout its range, gets no special treatment in Daoist texts." See E. N. Anderson and Lisa Raphals, "Daoism and Animals," in *A Communion of Subjects*, 281. My study does not support this claim.

4.   The text is titled *The Hereditary Household of the Han Celestial Master* (*Han Tinshi shijia* 漢天師世家, CT 1463), in Zhang Jiyu, ed., *Zhonghua daozang* (Beijing: Huaxia chubanshe, 2004), 46. For a comprehensive study on this text, see Paul Amato, "Rebirth of a Lineage: The Hereditary Household of the Han Celestial Master and Celestial Masters Daoism at Dragon and Tiger Mountain," PhD thesis, Arizona State University, Tempe, 2016. For the discussions on this metaphor about the dragon and tiger, see Wu Hung, "Mapping Early Daoist Art: The Visual Culture of the Wudoumi Dao," in *Daoism and the Arts of China*, ed. Stephen Little and Shawn Eichman (Chicago: The Art Institute of Chicago and Berkeley: University of California Press, 2000), 82. For the discussion on the alchemy and symbolism of tiger and dragon, also see Joseph Needham and Gwei-djen Lu, *Science and Civilisation in China: Volume 5, Chemistry and Chemical Technology*, pt. 5 (Cambridge: Cambridge University Press, 1983), 333.

5.   For the study of this mountain and its significance in the early Daoist tradition, see Zhang Zehong, "Zaoqi Tianshi shixi yu Longhushan Zhang tianshi sijiao," *Shehui kexue yanjiu* 6 (2012): 122-28; later this mountain became the seat of the Zhengyi tradition,

see Miya Noriko, "Ryukosan shi kara mita mongoru meireibun no sekai: shoichikyō kyōdan kenkyū josetsu," *Tōyōshi kenkyū* 63, no. 2 (2004): 94–128.

6.   Shigenobu Ayumi, "Seiōbo: Tenmonde mukaeru kami," *Jinbungaku ronshū* 25 (2007): 159–76; Shigenobu Ayumi, "Seiōbo no genryu: Besuga yoeta zuzōteki eikyō," *Jinbungaku ronshū* 28 (2010): 73–89; Huo Wei, "Hurenyong, Youyi shenshou, Xiwangmu tuxiang de kaocha yu Han Jin shiqi Zhongguo xinan de Zhong Wai wenhua jiaoliu," *Jiuzhou xuelin* 1, no. 2 (2003): 36–92; Li Jinshan, "Xiwangmu ticai huaxiangshi jiqi xiangguan wenti," *Zhongyuan wenwu* 4 (1994): 56–66; Li Jinshan, *Lunan Han huaxiangshi yanjiu* (Beijing: Zhishi chanquan chubanshe, 2008), ch. 9; Nishiwaki Takao, "Seinan Chūgoku niokeru tora no setsuwa," *Hikaku minzoku gakkaihō* 17, no. 1 (1996): 10–19. See Riccardo Fracasso, "Holy Mothers of Ancient China: A New Approach to the Hsi-wang-mu Problem," *T'oung Pao* 74, no. 1/3 (1988): 1–46, where he points out that, "The people of Pa, in fact, traced their origins back to a were-tiger ancestor, that was worshipped both as ancestor of the ruling clan and as mountain-god, and whose cult consisted of human sacrifices and blood-offerings" (17).

7.   Suzanne E. Cahill, *Transcendence and Divine Passion: The Queen Mother of the West in Medieval China* (Stanford, CA: Stanford University Press, 1993), 13.

8.   Suzanne E. Cahill, *Transcendence and Divine Passion*, 26.

9.   See Martha L. Carter, "China and the Mysterious Occident: The Queen Mother of the West and Nanā," *Rivista degli studi orientali*, Nuova Series 79, no. 1/4 (2006): 97–129.

10.   Ching-lang Hou, "The Chinese Belief in Baleful Stars," in *Facets of Taoism: Essays in Chinese Religion*, ed. Holmes Welch and Anna Seidel (New Haven, CT: Yale University Press, 1979), 209–19.

11.   E. N. Anderson and Lisa Raphals, "Daoism and Animals," 286.

12.   Paul R. Goldin, "Why Daoism is not Environmentalism?" *Journal of Chinese Philosophy* 32, no. 1 (2005): 76–77.

13.   John Snarey, "The Natural Environment's Impact on Religious Ethics: A Cross-Cultural Study," *Journal for the Scientific Study of Religion* 35, no. 2 (1996): 85–96.

14.   Yi-fu Tuan, "Discrepancies between Environmental Attitude and Behaviour: Examples from Europe and China," *Canadian Geographer* 12, no. 3 (1968): 175–91. He notes some of the causes of deforestation, such as burning trees in order to deprive dangerous animals of their hiding places.

15.   For the relationship between Daoist hermits and mountains in early medieval China, see Thomas Michael, "Mountains and Early Daoism in the Writings of Ge Hong," *History of Religions* 56, no. 1 (2016): 23–54; and Wei Bin, "Shanzhong de Liuchao shi," *Wenshizhe* 361 (2017): 1–15. Earlier discussion on the religious landscape of the sacred mountain, see James Robson, *Power of Place: The Religious Landscape of the Southern Sacred Peak (Nanyue) in Medieval China*, (Cambridge, MA: Harvard University Press, 2009); Timothy H. Barrett, "Finding a Place for Mountains in Chinese Religion: Bibliographic and Ethnographic Perspectives," *Journal of Chinese Studies* 51 (2010): 357–74.

16.   My discussions on Daoist approaches to snake violence can be found in chapter 5. Even in the seventeenth-century novel the *Complete Story of Han Xiangzi* (*Han Xiangzi quanzhuan*), the tiger and snake were used to test the Daoist transcendent Han Xiang while he cultivated himself in the wildness; see Yang Erzeng, *The Story of Han Xiangzi: The Alchemical*

Adventure of a Daoist Immortal, translated and introduced by Philip Clart (Seattle: University of Washington Press, 2007), 89–93.

17.   Ge Hong, *Baopuzi neipian jiaoshi*, "Dengshe [Ascending Mountains and fording streams],"
chap. 17, ann. Wang Ming (Beijing: Zhonghua shuju, 1985), 299. Le Aiguo briefly notes
the message here in terms of Daoist ecology; see Le Aiguo, *Daojiao shengtaixue* (Beijing:
Shehui kexue wenxian chubanshe, 2005), 250.

18.   Later, in chapter 8, "Shizhi 釋滯 [Resolving obstructions]," Ge Hong states that one who
was willing to become a transcendent should practice guiding the pneuma (*qi*) and taking medicine. Practicing the techniques of guiding the pneuma could prohibit snakes
and tigers, stop the bleeding of wounds, spare the practitioner from suffering hunger
and thirst, and eventually extend the life span; see Ge Hong, *Baopuzi neipian jiaoshi*, 149.
For a short discussion of the Daoist mastery of demons and spirits including the mountain spirit in Ge Hong's writing, see Richard von Glahn, *The Sinister Way: The Divine and
the Demonic in Chinese Religious Culture* (Berkeley: University of California Press, 2004),
88–90; but he does not mention the tiger as the mountain god.

19.   Ge Hong attributes this knowledge to the teaching in the *Secret Record of the Nine Heavens [Jiutian miji 九天秘記]* and the *Hidden Days of the Grand Prime [Taiyi dunjia 太乙遁甲]*.
On the following dates of the longer months, entering the mountain was not a good
idea: the 3rd, 11th, 15th, 18th, 24th, 26th, 30th; and on the following dates of the shorter
months, entering the mountains should also be avoided: the 1st, 5th, 13th, 16th, 26th,
28th. See Ge Hong, *Baopuzi neipian jiaoshi*, 301. Poul Anderson briefly noted this technique of the Numinous Treasury tradition, see Poul Anderson, "Talking to the Gods:
Visionary Divination in Early Daoism (The Sanhuang Tradition)," *Taoist Resources* 5, no. 1
(1994): 10.

20.   Yi-fu Tuan, "Ambiguity in Attitudes toward Environment," *Annals of the Association of
American Geographers* 63, no. 4 (1973): 411–23, esp. 420.

21.   Ge Hong, *Zhouhou beiji fang jiaozhu*, annotated Shen Shunong (Beijing: Renmin weisheng chubanshe, 2016), 248.

22.   Hong Mai 洪邁 notes that this technique comes from the *Arcane Essentials from the Imperial Library [Waitai miyao, juan 40, Xiong hu shangren chuang fang 熊虎傷人瘡方]* compiled in 752 by Wang Tao (670–755). But Hong laughs off the idea that a seven-step spell
could eliminate the tiger's deviant behavior; see Hong Mai, *Rongzhai suibi quanshu leibian
yizhu*, vol. 4, *Rongzhai sibi*, ed. Xu Yimin (Beijing: Shidai wenyi chubanshe, 1993), 818.

23.   In his letter to Xu Mi 許謐, Yang Xi 楊羲 told Ge Xuan's legend. See Tao Hongjing ed.,
Zhengao, vol. 12 (Beijing: Wenwu chubanshe, 1987), 561.

24.   Ge Hong, *Shenxian zhuan*, vol. 4, ann. Hu Shouwei (Beijing: Zhonghua shuju, 2010), 50;
for the English translation of Liu An's biography in this collection, see Robert Ford Campany, *To Live as Long as Heaven and Earth: A Translation and Study of Ge Hong's Traditions of
Divine Transcendents* (Berkeley: University of California Press, 2002), 236. The third-
century Daoist text *Commands and Admonitions for the Families of the Great Dao (Dadao
jialing jie)* also taught that under the Daoist rule a Daoist could travel alone for one thousand *li* because tigers and wolves are tamed; for the English translation of the related
passage, see Stephen R. Bokenkamp, *Early Daoist Scriptures* (Berkeley: University of California Press, 1997), 180.

25. Dunhuang manuscript P. 2452 *Lingbao weiyi jing jue shang* 靈寶威儀經訣上 has noted that Ge Xuan bestowed his teachings to Zheng Siyuan and several Buddhist monks. Zheng received the *Shangqing sanding taizhen daojing* 上清三洞太真道經 from Ge Xuan. A similar story can also be found in the *Dongxuan lingbao yujingshan buxu jing* 洞玄靈寶玉京山步虛經. But Ge Hong's *Baopuzi* states that Zheng Yin 鄭隱 was the one who received the teachings from Ge Xuan. See Wang Chengwen 王承文, *Dunhuang gu Lingbao jing yu Jin Tang Daojiao* (Beijing: Zhonghua shuju, 2002), 86–90, 146; Kamitsuka Yoshiko, "Rikuchō Reihōkyō mieru Kōsenko," in *Sankyō kōshō ronsō*, ed., Mugitani Kunio (Kyoto: Kyōto daigaku jinbun kagaku kenkyūjo, 2005), 1–46; reprinted in Kamitsuka Yoshiko, *Dōkyō kyōten no keisei to bukkyō* (Nagoya: Nagoya Daigaku Shuppankai, 2017), chap. 3. Hsieh Shu-wei, "Chuanshou yu ronghe: *Taiji wuzhenren song yanjiu*," *Zhongyanyuan wenzhesuo jikan* 34 (2009): 262–69; Lü Pengzhi, *Tang qian Daojiao yishi shigang* (Beijing: Zhonghua shuju, 2008), 56–80.

26. Such as *Methods and Writs of Orthodox Unity* (*Zhengyi fawen* 正一法文), *Inner Writs of Three Sovereigns* (*Sanhuang neiwen* 三皇內文), *Charts of the Perfected Forms of Five Marchmounts* (*Wuyue zhenxing tu* 五嶽真形圖), *Scripture of the Divine Elixir Made from Gold Liquid from the Great Clarity* (*Taiqing jinye shendan jing* 太清金液神丹經), and *Five Talismans of the Cavern Mystery* (*Taishang dongxuan lingbao wufu xu* 洞玄靈寶五符序)

27. Zhang Junfang, ed, *Yunji qiqian*, vol. 110, ann. Li Yongcheng (Beijing: Zhonghua shuju, 2003), 2401; Stephen Peter Bumbacher, *The Fragments of the Daoxue Zhuan: Critical Edition, Translation and Analysis of a Medieval Collection of Daoist Biographies* (Bern: Peter Lang, 2000), 338, translated this story. For the introduction to the *Yunji qiqian*, see Wang Chengwen, "The Revelation and Classification of Daoist Scriptures," in *Early Chinese Religion, Part 2: The Period of Division* (220–589 AD), vol. 2, ed. John Lagerwey and Pengzhi Lü (Leiden: Brill, 2010), 776–77.

28. Roel Sterckx, *The Animal and the Daemon in Ancient China* (Albany: State University of New York Press, 2002), 123–163.

29. Ge Hong, *Baopuzi neipian jiaoshi*, 308. Fabrizio Pregadio notes that there is a talisman for avoiding hundreds of snakes and avoiding being harmed by tigers and wolves in this text; see Fabrizio Pregadio, *Great Clarity: Daoism and Alchemy in Early Medieval China* (Stanford, CA: Stanford University Press, 2006), 91–92; he also discussed that Ge Hong applied alchemy techniques for summoning deities in the Jiangnan area (123–39).

30. Zhao Daoyi ed., *Lishi zhenxian tidao tongjian* (CT/DZ 296), vol. 19, the biography of Zhang Zhaocheng, in *Zhonghua daozang*, vol. 47, 346b.

31. See *Xianyuan bianzhu*, juan 2, in *Zhonghua daozang*, vol. 45, 253c–254a.

32. Cf. A. C. Graham, *The Book of Lieh-Tzu, a Classic of Tao* (New York: Columbia University Press, 1990), 42–43. For a modern annotated version of the original text, see Lie Yukou, *Liezi jishi*, ann. Yang Bojun (Beijing: Zhonghua shuju, 1979), 58–59.

33. Liu Xu et al., *Jiu Tang shu*, juan 9, "Xuanzong benji 玄宗本紀" (Beijing: Zhonghua shuju, 1975), 213.

34. Such as *The Precept Scripture of the Highest Lord Lao* (*Taishang laojun jiejing*), see Lai Chi-Tim, "The Demon Statutes of Nüqing and the Problem of the Bureaucratization of the Netherworld in Early Heavenly Master Daoism," *T'oung Pao* 88, no. 4/5 (2002): 251–81; *Master Redpine's Almanac of Petitions* (*Chisongzi zhangli*), see Franciscus Verellen, "The Heavenly Master Liturgical Agenda According to *Chisong zi's Petition Almanac*,"

Cahiers d'extrême-Asie 14 (2004): 291–343; and *The Rules and Precepts of Worshipping the Dao* (Fengdao kejie), see Livia Kohn, *The Daoist Monastic Manual: A Translation of the Fengdao Kejie*, New York: Oxford University Press, 2004.

35. Zhu Xiangxian, ed., *Zhongnanshan shuojingtai lidai zhenxian beiji*, in *Zhonghua daozang*, vol. 48, 603c.

36. Du Guangting, *Xianzhuan shiyi*, vol. 1, in *Du Guangting jizhuan shizhong jijiao*, comp. and ann. Luo Zhengming (Beijing: Zhonghua shuju, 2013), 767.

37. Ge Hong, *Baopuzi jiaoshi*, 310.

38. Ge Hong, *Baopuzi jiaoshi*, 311.

39. Ge Hong, *Baopuzi jiaoshi*, 313; this is called the "prohibition method of three and five (sanwu jinfa 三五禁法)." For the meaning and translation of *qi*, see Stephen R. Bokenkamp, *Early Daoist Scriptures*, 15–20.

40. Wang Ka, *Daojiao jingshi luncong*, see "Dunhuang ben *Taogong chuanshou yi jiaoduji*" (Chengdu: Bashu shushe, 2007), 331–32; Lü Pengzhi, *Tang qianqi Daojiao yishi shigang*, 63.

41. *Zhonghua daozang*, vol. 45, 42. The English translation can be found in Robert Ford Campany, *To Live as Long as Heaven and Earth*, 148.

42. Rolf A. Stein, "Popular Taoism and Popular Religion from the Second to Seventh Centuries," in *Facets of Taoism*, ed. Holmes Welch and Anna Seidel (New Haven, CT: Yale University Press, 1979), 53–81.

43. See Terry F. Kleeman, "Daoism and the Quest for Order," in *Daoism and Ecology*, 68.

44. *Zhonghua daozang*, vol. 8, 643a–b.

45. Wang Chengwen noted that the *Marvelous Essence Scripture* was part of the early medieval Daoist *Three Sovereign Texts* (*Sanhuangwen* 三皇文) from the Numinous Treasury (*Lingbao*) Tradition; see Wang Chengwen, *Dunhuang gu Lingbao jing yu Jin Tang Daojiao*, 220–30. Hsie Shu-wei traces the origins and transmission of the Three Sovereign texts in Daoist tradition; see Hsie Shu-wei "Zhonggu daojiao shi zhong de Sanhuangwen chuantong yanjiu," *Qinghua xuebao* 44, no. 1 (2014): 29–60. More recently, Dominic Steavu offers a comprehensive study on this texts; see Dominic Steavu, *The Writ of the Three Sovereigns: From Local Lore to Institutional Daoism* (Honolulu: University of Hawai'i Press, 2019).

46. *Zhonghua daozang*, vol. 4, 488b–c.

47. Ge Hong, *Baopuzi jiaoshi*, ch. 16, 292.

48. *Zhonghua daozang*, vol. 45, 34, for the reference to the river water see vol. 4. For an English translation of his biography, see Robert Ford Campany, *To Live as Long as Heaven and Earth*, 303. His story also appears in the Daoist text *The Twined Pearls of Transcendent Grove [Xianyuan bianzhou]* compiled by Wang Songnian 王松年, a priest who lived in the Five Dynasties and early Song period. Ge Yue was also said to be able to summon dragons for making rain.

49. *Zhonghua daozang*, vol. 45, 37.

50. This story was cited from *Yeren xianhua* 野人閑話 (compiled by Jing Huan 景煥 in 965), in *Sandong qunxian lu*, ed. Chen Baoguang, vol. 6; and *Zhonghua daozang*, vol. 45, 305b–c.

51. For Fazhong's biography, see Nianchang, *Fozu lidai tongzai*, T. 49, no. 2036, 20, juan 20; For Zhifeng's biography, see Minghe, *Buxu Gaoseng zhuan*, X. 77, no. 1524, juan 7: 419c–420a; Zhuhong, *Yunqi fahui*, J (Jiaxing zang), 33, no. B277, juan 23, 180a.

52. Du Guangting, *Luyi ji*, juan 2, no. 17, in *Du Guangting jizhuan shizhong jijiao*, 31.

53.   Miyazawa Masayori, "Dōkyō reigenki ni tsuite," *Sanko bunka kenkyūjō nenhō* 18 (1986): 1–38; Arao Toshio, "To Kotei Dōkyō reigenki no ohokan ni tsuite," *Tōhō shūkyō* 97 (2001): 20–36; Zhou Xibo offers a study on some manuscripts of the Daoist record of numinous efficacy from Dunhuang, see Zhou Xibo, *Daojiao lingyan ji kaotan: Jingfa yanzheng yu xuanyang* (Taipei: Wenjin chubanshe, 2009).

54.   *Daojiao lingyan ji*, juan 11, Gaoxiang sanhuang neiwen yan; see Du Guangting, *Du Guangting jizhuan shizhong jijiao*, 263. For the study of the fox spirit in early Chinese religions, see Kang Xiaofei, *The Cult of the Fox*, 14–43; she notes the exorcism and the suppression of the fox cult (39–42).

55.   See chapter 1.

56.   Kristopher Schipper, "Daoist Ecology: The Inner Transformation. A Study of the Precepts of the Early Daoist Ecclesia," in *Daoism and Ecology: Ways within a Cosmic Landscape*, ed. N. J. Girardot, James Miller, and Liu Xiaogan (Cambridge, MA: Harvard University Press, 1999), 79.

57.   Du Guangting, *Daojiao lingyan ji*, juan 2, see *Du Guangting jizhuan shizhong jijiao*, 170.

58.   Du Guangting, *Daojiao lingyan ji*, 160.

59.   Du Guangting, *Daojiao lingyan ji*, 340.

60.   Du Guangting, *Daojiao lingyan ji*, 168.

61.   Du Guangting, *Daojiao lingyan ji*, 173.

62.   Many scholars have noted the apologetic strategy in Du Guangting's collection of Daoist stories. See Franciscus Verellen, "Daojiao lingyanji: Zhongguo wan Tang fojiao hufa chuantong de zhuanhuan," *Huaxue* 華學 5 (2001): 38–64; Huang Yong, *Daojiao biji xiaoshuo yanjiu* (Chengdu: Sichuan daxue chubanshe, 2007), 210–48; Zhou Xibo, *Daojiao lingyan ji kaotan*, 25–51; Huang Dongyang, "Du Guangting Daojiao lingyanji de shengsu fansi," *Dongwu zhongwen xuebao* 25 (2013): 51–76; Yusa Noboru, *Tōdai shakai to Dōkyō* (Tōkyō: Tōhō Shoten, 2015), 263–291, compares the story of the Celestial Honored One who Saves from Suffering (jiuku tianzun 救苦天尊) in Du's collection and other sources.

63.   Christine Mollier, *Buddhism and Taoism Face to Face: Scripture, Ritual, and Iconographic Exchange in Medieval China* (Honolulu: University of Hawai'i Press, 2008). Han Jishao 韓吉紹 points out that Buddhist monks and Daoist priests also competed with each other over techniques for longevity in medieval China; see Han Jishao, *Daojiao liandanshu yu Zhongwai wenhua jiaoliu* (Beijing: Zhonghua shuju, 2015), 102–12.

64.   Lynn White Jr., "The Historical Roots of Our Ecologic Crisis," *Science* 155 (1967): 1203–07. For comprehensive criticism of anthropocentrism in Western Philosophy, see Gary Steiner, *Anthropocentrism and its Discontents: The Moral Status of Animals in the History of Western Philosophy* (Pittsburgh, PA: University of Pittsburgh Press, 2005).

65.   Bron Taylor, "The Greening of Religion Hypothesis (Part One): From Lynn White Jr., and Claims That Religions Can Promote Environmentally Destructive Attitudes and Behaviors to Assertions They Are Becoming Environmentally Friendly," *Journal for the Study of Religion, Nature and Culture* 10, no. 3 (2016):" 268–305.

66.   Bron Taylor, Gretel Van Wieren, and Bernard Zaleha, "The Greening of Religion Hypothesis (Part Two): Assessing the Data from Lynn White Jr., to Pope Francis," *Journal for the Study of Religion, Nature and Culture* 10, no. 3 (2016): 306–78; esp. 330–35.

67.   Wang Tao, *Waitai miyao* (Beijing: Renmin weisheng chubanshe, 1955).

68. Chen Hsiu-fen briefly noted there are three recipes shared in both Dunhuang medical manuscripts and *Waitai miyao*, see Chen Hsiu-fen, "Wind Malady as Madness in Medieval China," in, *Medieval Chinese Medicine: The Dunhuang Medical Manuscripts*, ed. Vivienne Lo and Christopher Cullen (London: Routledge, 2005), 356–57.

69. For the Chinese version of the regulation, see *Guofa* 国发, 2018, issue no. 36, "Guowuyuan guanyu yange guanzhi xiniu he hu jiqi zhipin jingying liyong huodong de tongzhi 国务院关于严格管制犀牛和虎及其制品经营利用活动的通知" (index no.: 000014349/2018-00196; http://www.gov.cn/zhengce/content/2018-10/29/content_5335423.htm); for the relevant news in English, see "China to Control Trade in Rhino and Tiger Products," http://english.gov.cn/policies/latest_releases/2018/10/29/content_281476367121088.htm.

70. See Humane Society International, "Humane Society International Expresses Shock as China Lifts 25-Year-Old Ban on Tiger Bone and Rhino Horn Trade," October 29, 2018, http://www.hsi.org/news/press_releases/2018/10/humane-society-international-102918.html.

71. See "China Postpones Regulated Trade of Rhino Horn, Tiger Parts," November 13, 2018, http://www.ecns.cn/news/2018-11-13/detail-ifyzrwsr0795357.shtml, which states: "According to the Environmental Investigation Agency (EIA), there are more than 7,000 captive tigers in China, Thailand, Laos, Vietnam, and South Africa. In China, around 150 companies have permits to sell tiger parts from animals dying in captivity."

72. Emile Durkheim, *The Elementary Forms of the Religious Life*, trans. Joseph Ward Swain (Mineola, NY: Dover Publications, 2008), 40–41.

73. Mircea Eliade, *Patterns in Comparative Religion* (Cleveland, OH: World Publishing Co., 1963), 367–85.

74. Jack Goody, "Religion and Ritual: The Definitional Problem," *The British Journal of Sociology* 12, no. 2 (1961), 142–164, esp. 155.

75. Aaron Gross, *The Question of the Animal and Religion: Theoretical Stakes, Practical Implications* (New York: Columbia University Press, 2015).

5. BUDDHISTS KILLING REPTILES

1. Huijiao, *Gaoseng zhuan*, juan 10, "Baozhi 保志," T. 50, 2059, 394b–c; *Gaoseng zhuan*, juan 11, "Zhu Tanyou 竺曇猷," T. 50, 2059, 395c; Daoxuan, *Xu gaoseng zhuan*, juan 35, "Daomu 道穆," T. 50, 2060, 658b.

2. Chen Tianfu, *Nanyue zongsheng ji*, T. 51, no. 2097, 2: 1079c–1080a; James Robson, *Power of Place: The Religious Landscape of the Southern Sacred Peak (Nanyue) in Medieval China* (Cambridge, MA: Harvard University Asia Center, 2009); Wei Bin, "Shuxie Nanyue: Zhonggu zhongqi Hengshan de wenxian yu jingguan," *Wei Jin Nanbeichao Sui Tang shi ziliao* 31 (2015): 138–62.

3. From the perspective of religious history, the serpent was one of the most important animals in Indo-European culture and religion. It was notorious for tempting Adam and Eve in Abrahamic religions and becoming the symbol of one of the three poisons that result in suffering in Buddhist cosmology. Snakes are also regarded as evil animals in Zoroastrianism; see Mahnaz Moazami, "Evil Animals in the Zoroastrian Religion," *History of Religion* 44, no. 4 (2005): 300–17. For a study on the evolving symbolism of the serpent in the Near Eastern religious tradition, see James H. Charlesworth,

The Good and Evil Serpent: How a Universal Symbol Became Christianized (New Haven, CT: Yale University Press, 2009). For earlier studies on the religious symbolism of the snake, see Balaji Mundkur, *The Cult of the Serpent: An Interdisciplinary Survey of Its Manifestations and Origins* (Albany: State University of New York Press, 1983), and Diane Morgan, *Snakes in Myth, Magic, and History: The Story of a Human Obsession* (Westport, CT: Praeger, 2008).

4. One example can be found on the wall painting of Cave 112. See Dunhuang yanjiuyuan ed., *Dunhuang shiku quanji* [A complete collection of Dunhuang Caves], juan 19: Dongwu hua juan [Volume of animal paintings] (Shanghai: Shanghai renmin chubanshe, 2000), 108.

5. Adapted from Michael J. Puett, *Ambivalence of Creation: Debates Concerning Innovation and Artifice in Early China* (Stanford, CA: Stanford University Press, 2000), 77; original text can be found in Han Fei, *Hanfeizi jijie*, ann. Wang Xianshen (Taipei: Taiwan shangwu yinshuguan, 1969), 685; also see Albert Gavany, "Beyond the Rule of Rulers: The Foundations of Sovereign Power in the *Han Feizi*," in *Dao Companion to the Philosophy of Han Fei*, ed. Paul Goldin (Dordrecht: Springer, 2013), 89.

6. For instance, Christopher Key Chapple, *Nonviolence to Animals, Earth, and Self in Asian Traditions* (Albany: State University of New York Press, 1993); and Chengzhong Pu, *Ethical Treatment of Animals in Early Chinese Buddhism* (Newcastle upon Tyne: Cambridge Scholars Publishing, 2014). But there are always exceptions. For example, as Klaus Vollmer noted, killing animals could be justified in premodern Japanese Buddhism; see Klaus Vollmer, "Buddhism and the Killing of Animals in Premodern Japan," in *Buddhism and Violence*, ed. Michael Zimmermann (Wiesbaden: Reichert Verlag, 2006), 195-211; see also Elizabeth J. Harris, "Violence and Disruption in Society: A Study of the Early Buddhist Texts," Wheel Publication No. 392/393 (Colombo, Sri Lanka: Ecumenical Institute for Study and Dialogue, 1994); Tessa J. Bartholomeusz, *In Defense of Dharma: Just-War Ideology in Buddhist Sri Lanka* (London: Routledge, 2005); Michael Jerryson and Mark Juergensmeyer, eds., *Buddhist Warfare* (New York: Oxford University Press, 2010); Michael K. Jerryson, *Buddhist Fury: Religion and Violence in Southern Thailand* (New York: Oxford University Press, 2011); Vladimir Tikhonov and Torkel Brekke, eds., *Buddhism and Violence: Militarism and Buddhism in Modern Asia* (London: Routledge, 2015).

7. Susan Klein, "Woman as Serpent: The Demonic Feminine in the Noh Play Dōjōji," in *Religious Reflections on the Human Body*, ed. Jane Marie Law (Bloomington: University of Indiana Press, 1995), 100-36; Monica Dix, "Saint or Serpent? Engendering the Female Body in Medieval Japanese Buddhist Narratives," in *The Body in Asia*, ed. Brian S. Turner and Zhang Yangwen (New York: Berghahn, 2009), 43-58; Barbara Ambros, *Women in Japanese Religions* (New York: New York University Press, 2015), 91-92.

8. Terry F. Kleeman noted that in early medieval Sichuan the god who could control the lighting was worshipped as a local cult, and the god appeared as a fearsome serpent; see Terry F. Kleeman, "The Expansion of the Wen-ch'ang Cult," in *Religion and Society in T'ang and Sung China*, ed. Patricia B. Ebrey and Peter N. Gregory (Honolulu: University of Hawai'i Press, 1989), 48-49.

9. Robert F. Campany, "Religious Repertoires and Contestation: A Case Study Based on Buddhist Miracle Tales," *History of Religions* 52, no. 2 (2012): 99-141.

10. Lynne A. Isbell, *The Fruit, the Tree, and the Serpent: Why We See So Well* (Cambridge, MA: Harvard University Press, 2009), 98.

11. Lynne A. Isbell, "Snakes as Agents of Evolutionary Change in Primate Brains," *Journal of Human Evolution* 51, no. 1 (2006): 1–35; Vanessa LoBue, David H. Rakison, and Judy S. DeLoache, "Threat Perception Across the Life Span: Evidence for Multiple Converging Pathways," *Current Directions in Psychological Science* 19, no. 6 (2010): 375–79; Judy S. Deloache and Venessa LoBue, "The Narrow Fellow in the Grass: Human Infants Associate Snakes and Fear," *Developmental Science* 12, no. 1 (2009): 201–07; Vanessa LoBue and Judy S. DeLoache, "Detecting the Snake in the Grass: Attention to Fear-Relevant Stimuli by Adults and Young Children," *Psychological Science* 19, no. 3 (2008): 284–89; Frank C. Keil, "The Roots of Folk Biology," *Proceedings of the National Academy of Sciences of the United States of America* 110, no. 40 (2013): 15857–58; Kevin J. Tierney and Maeve K. Connolly, "A Review of the Evidence for a Biological Basis for Snake Fears in Humans," *The Psychological Record* 63, no. 4 (2013): 919–28; Jonathan W. Stanley, "Snakes: Objects of Religion, Fear, and Myth." *Journal of Integrative Biology* 2, no. 2 (2008): 42–58.

12. Yan Ying, *Yanzi chunqiu yizhu*, ann. Sun Yanlin, Zhou Min, and Miao Ruosu (Jinan: Qilu shushe, 1991), 80; Roel Sterckx used this story to discuss how Yan Ying as a sage master refuted the anomalous character of a species in its natural habitat; see Roel Sterckx, *The Animal and Daemon in Early China* (Albany: State University of New York Press, 2002), 106.

13. Olivia Milburn, *The Spring and Autumn Annals of Master Yan* (Leiden: Brill, 2015), 214.

14. Wang Chong, *Lunheng jiaoshi*, ann. Beijing University (Beijing: Zhonghua shuju, 1979), 1301.

15. Ban Gu, *Han shu* (Beijing: Zhonghua shuju, 1962), 2781; Ouyang Xiu et al., *Xin Tang shu* (Beijing: Zhonghua shuju, 1975), 6345.

16. Ouyang Xun, *Yiwen leiju* (Shanghai: Shanghai guji chubanshe, 1982), 1664–67.

17. Richard E. Strassberg, *A Chinese Bestiary: Strange Creatures from the Guideways through Mountains and Seas* (Berkeley: University of California Press, 2002), 190.

18. Sterckx, *The Animal and Daemon in Early China* 156.

19. Ouyang Xiu et al., *Xin Tang shu*, 1054; another Song scholar, Luo Yuan 羅願 (1136–1184), also noted that though there were numerous snake species, the venomous white-flower snakes were active in the Qichun region. This species of snake was strange because its eyes remained open even after death, whereas other species closed their eyes upon death. He also pointed out that the most venomous snake was the viper with short length, reversing nose, and colorful stripes. Further, in the Lingbiao region (modern Guangdong area), there was a species of two-headed snake. See Luo Yuan, *Erya yi* 爾雅翼, *Sikuquanshu* 32–1a, electronic database and CD-ROM (Hong Kong: Dizhi chuban gongsi, 1999).

20. Du You, *Tongdian* (Beijing: Zhonghua shuju, 1988), vol. 5; Huang Zhengjian, "Shi lun Tangdai qianqi huangdi xiaofei de mouxie cemian: yi Tongdian juanliu suoji changgong wei zhongxin," *Tang yanjiu* 6 (2000): 173–212.

21. Liu Zongyuan, "Bushezhe shuo 捕蛇者說," in *Quan Tang wen*, juan 584, 5897–98. For the English translation, see Liu Zongyuan, "Catching Snakes," trans. Herbert Giles, in *Classical*

Chinese Literature: An Anthology of Translations. Vol. 1: From Antiquity to the Tang Dynasty, ed. John Minford (New York: Columbia University Press, 2000), 1010.

22.   Huijiao, *Gaoseng zhuan*, juan 10, "Baozhi 保志," *T.* 50, no. 2059, 394a.

23.   Gan Bao, *In Search of the Supernatural: The Written Record*, trans. Kenneth J. DeWoskin and James Irving Crump (Stanford, CA: Stanford University Press, 1996), 230–31.

24.   Jivanayakam Cyril Daniel, *The Book of Indian Reptiles and Amphibians* (Mumbai: Oxford University Press, 2002), 74–158. Two of the most common venomous snakes in South Asian Buddhism might be the common krait (*Bungarus caeruleus*) and cobra snake (*Ophiophagus hannah*). For the common krait in India see Ramesh Chandra Sharma ed., *Handbook, Indian Snakes* (Kolkata: Zoological Survey of India, 2003), 188ff. Nevertheless, the sutras often use the snake as a metaphor for expounding their doctrinal discussions.

25.   James P. McDermott, "Animals and Humans in Early Buddhism," *Indo-Iranian Journal* 32, no. 2, (1989): 269–80; Irina Aristarkhova has noted that "the Jain concept of 'Ahimsa' is usually translated as 'nonharm' or 'nonviolence.' In this early translation, 'himsa' was translated as 'injury,' 'sin' and 'killing,' 'damaging' and 'slaying.' As we can see, in early Buddhism, injuring an animal is not allowed either." See Irina Aristarkhova, "Thou Shall Not Harm All Living Beings: Feminism, Jainism, and Animals," *Hypatia* 27, no. 3 (2012): 636–50.

26.   James Stewart, *Vegetarianism and Animal Ethics in Contemporary Buddhism* (London: Routledge, 2015), 41.

27.   Isaline Blew Horner, *Women Under Primitive Buddhism: Laywomen and Almswomen* (London: Routledge, 1930), 287.

28.   Buddhajīva and Zhu Daosheng, *Wufen lü*, juan 21, *T.* 22, no. 1421, 146c3. This minor offense of wrongdoing is called *duṣkṛta*. In contrast, the Mūlasarvāstivāda Vinaya (Carma-vastu) allows monks who have seen a black snake on the street to wear wooden clogs; see Yijing, *Genben shuoyiqieyoubu pinaiye pigeshi*, juan 2, *T.* 23, no. 1447: 1055b15–16.

29.   Buddhajīva and Zhu Daosheng, *Wufen lü*, juan 21, *T.* 22, no. 1421, 184a26.

30.   Isaline Blew Horner, trans., *The Book of the Discipline (Vinaya-Pitaka). Vol. 4: Mahāvagga* (London: Luzac & Co., 1962), 299–300. The Chinese translation of the Sarvāstivāda Vinaya similarly prevented monks from consuming the flesh, fat, blood, and muscle of snakes, but not snake bones; see Puṇyatāra and Kumārajīva, *Shisong lü*, juan 26, *T.* 23, no. 1435, 186c. Many medical texts in medieval China, such as *Gexianweng zhouhou beiji fang* (juan 7), *Zhenglei bencao* 證類本草 (juan 4), claim that snake bones can be used for making medicines to heal diseases.

31.   Yijing, *Genben shuoyiqieyoubu pinaiye zashi*, juan 13, *T.* 24, no. 1451: 263a24–263b5.

32.   Buddhayaśas and Zhu Fonian, *Sifen lü*, juan 42, *T.* 22, no. 1428, 870c13.

33.   Buddhayaśas and Zhu Fonian, *Sifen lü*, juan 42, *T.* 22, no. 1428, 0870c22.

34.   Isaline Blew Horner, trans., *The Book of the Discipline*, 32–35.

35.   Reiko Ohnuma, *Unfortunate Destiny: Animals in the Indian Buddhist Imagination* (New York: Oxford University Press, 2017), 35–40.

36.   Zhiqian, *Zhuanji baiyuan jing*, juan 6, *T.* 4, no. 200, 228a16.

37.   The canonical rules are different from local experience, but contemporary experience in South Asia seems to suggest some exceptions. As Martin Southwold noted, in Polgama, a small village in Sri Lanka, some Buddhists do kill when they have to. He writes: "Most village Buddhists will kill snakes of one particularly dangerous species, the polanga or

Russell's Viper: they know that its bite is normally fatal and that it is also aggressive, attacking unprovoked, and even chasing people." See Martin Southwold, *Buddhism in Life: The Anthropological Study of Religion and the Sinhalese Practice of Buddhism* (Manchester: Manchester University Press, 1983), 67. In studying both canonical literature and medieval Sinhalese literature, Mahinda Deegalle noted that in the Theravada tradition "violence cannot be justified under any circumstance, violence and its manifestations in Buddhist societies can be viewed as a deviation from the teachings of the Buddha." See Mahinda Deegalle, "Is Violence Justified in Theravada Buddhism?" *Social Affairs* 1, no. 1 (2014): 83–94.

38. Kamala Tiyavanich, *Sons of the Buddha: The Early Lives of Three Extraordinary Thai Masters* (Boston: Wisdom, 2007), 208.

39. Melford E. Spiro, *Buddhism and Society: A Great Tradition and Its Burmese Vicissitudes* (Berkeley: University of California Press, 1982), 46.

40. Textually, killing an animal was never an option for the Vinaya master Daoxuan. As I wrote in chapter 1, in his text *Measuring and Handling Light and Heavy Property* (*Liangchu qingzhong yi*), Daoxuan discussed thirteen categories of monastic property in light of the Four-Part Vinaya. For dealing with animals as monastic property, Daoxuan listed three methods: keeping some domestic animals within the monastic community, releasing wild animals to the wilderness, and raising young animals before releasing them.

41. Li Fang, *Taiping guangji huijiao*, ann. Zhang Guofeng 張國風 (Beijing: Beijing yanshan chubanshe, 2011), 8184.

42. Li Fang, *Taiping guangji huijiao*, 8176.

43. Zhipan, *Fozu tongji*, juan 28, *T.* 49, no. 2035, 285c.

44. Zanning, *Song gaoseng zhuan*, juan 20, *T.* 50, no. 2061, 838c.

45. Zanning, *Song gaoseng zhuan*, juan 19, *T.* 50, no. 2061, 829b.

46. William M. Bodiford also noted that in medieval Japan, Rogaku administered the precepts to the reptile spirit so this reptile instantly attained liberation from the realm of reptile; see William M. Bodiford, "The Enlightenment of Kami and Ghosts: Spirit ordinations in Japanese Sōtō Zen," in *Chan Buddhism in Ritual Context*, ed. Bernard Faure (London: RoutledgeCurzon, 2003), 254–55.

47. Buddhabhadra, *Foshuo guan Fo Sanmei hai jing*, juan 5, *T.* 15, no. 643, 668c–669a.

48. Dharmarakṣa, *Daban niepan jing*, juan 23, *T.* 12, no. 374, 499b.

49. Kumārajīva, *Fahua jing*, juan 7, *T.* 9, no. 262, 58a8. For the English translation, see Leon Hurvitz, trans., *Scripture of the Lotus Blossom of the Fine Dharma* (New York: Columbia University Press, 1982), 317.

50. Dunhuang yanjiuyuan, ed., *Dunhuang shiku quanji*, no. 19, "dongwuhua juan" [Volume of animal paintings], ed. Liu Yuquan (Shanghai: Shanghai renmin chubanshe, 2000), 108; a similar wall painting can be found in Mogao Cave 74 (see fig. 3.3), depicting a monk meditating in the center and being surrounded by a lion, a snake, a tiger, a bear, etc.

51. Daoshi, *Fayuan zhulin*, juna 29, *T.* 53, no. 2121, 158a–b. On seeing the snake diminished by the frog's judgment, the fish found the strength to escape the net and kill the snake. The frog judge is identified with the Buddha-to-be, the snake with King Ajātasatru, who, according to Buddhist legend, seized the kingdom from his father (a just king), imprisoned him, and eventually starved him to death. In addition to illustrating the notion of dharma as pragmatic justice, this story indirectly provides some justification for defying an unjust king; see Rupert Gethin, "Keeping the Buddha's Rule: The View from the

Sūtra Piṭaka," in *Buddhism and Law: An Introduction*, ed. Rebecca Redwood French and Mark A. Nathan (Cambridge: Cambridge University Press, 2014), 73.

52.   Religious scholarship has suggested that demons came from the souls of the dead who had been unjustly treated or killed and come back to seek retribution or from the ghosts of the wicked dead; see Joseph Baker, "Who Believes in Religious Evil? An Investigation of Sociological Patterns of Belief in Satan, Hell, and Demons," *Review of Religious Research* 50, no. 2 (2008): 206-20; David Brakke, *Demons and the Making of the Monk: Spiritual Combat in Early Christianity* (Cambridge, MA: Harvard University Press, 2006).

53.   Alan Sponberg, "Attitudes Toward Women and the Feminine in Early Buddhism," in *Buddhism, Sexuality and Gender*, ed. Jose K. Cabezon (Albany: State University of New York Press, 1992), 3-36; Gita Gross, *Buddhism After Patriarchy: A Feminist History, Analysis, and Reconstruction of Buddhism* (Albany: State University of New York Press, 1993); Peter Skilling, "Nuns, Laywomen, Donors, Goddesses: Female Roles in Early Indian Buddhism," *Journal of International Association for Buddhist Studies* 24, no. 2 (2001): 241-74; Kate Crosby, "Gendered Symbols in Theravada Buddhism: Missed Positives in the Representation of the Female," *Xuanzang foxue yanjiu* 9 (2009): 31-47.

54.   P. Steven Sangren, "Female Gender in Chinese Religious Symbols," *Signs* 9 (1983): 4-25; Yü Chün-fang, *Kuan-yin: The Chinese Transformation of Avalokitesvara* (New York: Columbia University Press, 2000).

55.   For a discussion of the fox in the Chinese cosmology of the yin-yang dichotomy, see Kang Xiaofei, *The Cult of the Fox: Power, Gender, and Popular Religion in Late Imperial and Modern China* (New York: Columbia University Press, 2006), 18; in premodern Japan, the fox wife was regarded as the yin imagery, see Michael Bathgate, *The Fox's Craft in Japanese Religion and Culture: Shapeshifters, Transformations, and Duplicities* (London: Routledge, 2004), 40.

56.   The *Shijing* (*The Classic of Poems*), 189, "Sigan 斯干" (86/29); for the English translation, see Arthur Waley, trans., *The Book of Songs* (London: Routledge, 2012, reprint), 283. Roel Sterckx noted that the yin-yang specialist in the Han associated snakes with signs for the involvement of women by citing this poem because snakes were said to be produced by yin; see Roel Sterckx, *The Animal and Daemon in Early China*, 209. This divination was well received in later writings, such as Liu Xiang's 劉向 (79-8 BCE) *New Preface* (*Xinxu* 新序), Wang Fu's 王符 (79-165 CE) *Comments of a Recluse* (*Qianfu lun*), and *The Chapter on Five Phases* (*Wuxing zhi* 五行誌) and *Chapter on Arts and Letters* (*Yiwen zhi*) in the *History of Han Dynasty* (*Hanshu*).

57.   Ouyang Xiu et al., *Xin Tang shu*, 951.

58.   Elizabeth J. Harris, "The Female in Buddhism," in *Buddhist Women across Cultures: Realizations*, ed. Karma Lekshe Tsomo (Albany: State University of New York Press, 1999), 49-65; Karma Lekshe Tsomo, "Is the Bhikṣuṇī Vinaya Sexist?" in *Buddhist Women and Social Justice: Ideals, Challenges, and Achievements*, ed. Karma Lekshe Tsomo (Albany: State University of New York Press, 2012), 66; Bernard Faure, *The Power of Denial: Buddhism, Purity, and Gender* (Princeton, NJ: Princeton University Press, 2003), 319-23.

59.   Bodhiruci, *Da baoji jing*, juan 97, T. 11, no. 310, 545a; Diana Y. Paul, *Women in Buddhism: Images of the Feminine in the Mahāyāna Tradition* (Berkeley: University of California Press, 1985), 41-42.

60. The feminization of the snake and the demonization of the female body can also be found in premodern Japanese folklore; see Barbara Ambros, *Women in Japanese Religions*, 91–92; Ria Koopmans-de Bruijn, "Fabled Liaisons: Serpentine Spouses in Japanese Folktales," in *JAPANimals: History and Culture in Japan's Animal Life*, ed. Gregory M. Pflugfelder and Brett L. Walker (Ann Arbor: University of Michigan Press, 2005), 60–88.

61. *Cibei daochang chanfa*, juan 1, *T.* 45, no. 1909: 922b.

62. Daoxuan claims that women have ten vices and are the same evil as venomous snakes; see *Jingxin jieguan fa*, juan 1, *T.* 45, no. 1893, 1: 824.

63. Li Fang et al., *Taiping guangji huijiao*, 8194.

64. Li Fang et al., *Taiping guangji huijiao*, 8206.

65. Li Fang et al., *Taiping guangji*, juan 107, 727; Chiew Hui Ho, *Diamond Sutra Narratives: Textual Production and Lay Religiosity in Medieval China* (Leiden: Brill, 2019), 187.

66. Meir Shahar, "The Tantric Origins of the Horse King: Haayagrīva and the Chinese Horse Cult," in *Chinese and Tibetan Esoteric Buddhism*, ed. Yael Bentor and Meir Shahar (Leiden: Brill, 2017), 173.

67. Many scholars have discussed the exchanges between Buddhism and Daoism in medieval China. One of the most notable studies can be found in Christine Mollier, *Buddhism and Taoism Face to Face: Scripture, Ritual, and Iconographic Exchange in Medieval China* (Honolulu: University of Hawai'i Press, 2008). My study shows that snakes were objectified during this religious competition.

68. Duan Chengshi, *Youyang zazu jiaojian*, ann. Xu Yimin (Beijing: Zhonghua shuju, 2015), 203; Catherine Despeux and Livia Kohn, *Women in Daoism* (Cambridge, MA: Three Pines Press, 2003), 131–32.

69. E. H. Schafer, "Orpiment and Realgar in Chinese Technology and Tradition," *Journal of American Oriental Society* 75, no. 2 (1955): 73–89; Fabrizio Pregadio, *Great Clarity: Daoism and Alchemy in Medieval China* (Stanford: Stanford University Press, 2006), 138; Paul Copp, *The Body Incantatory: Spells and the Ritual Imagination in Medieval Chinese* (New York: Columbia University Press, 2014), 48.

70. Li Fang, *Taiping guangji huijiao*, 8177–78.

71. In medieval China, the combination of snake and tortoise became the Dark Warrior (Xuanwu 玄武), the guard in the north, one of the four protectors for four directions. The Dark Warrior later transformed into Zhenwu 真武, one of the Daoist deities. For the study of the Zhenwu, see Chao Hsin-yi, *Daoist Ritual, State Religion and Popular Practices: Zhenwu Worship from Song to Ming (960–1644)* (London: Routledge, 2011).

72. Franciscus Verellen, "'Evidential Miracles in Support of Taoism:' The Inversion of a Buddhist Apologetic Tradition in Late Tang China," *T'oung Pao*, 2nd Series 78, no. 4/5 (1992): 217–63.

73. Du Guangting, *Daojiao lingyan ji*, CT 590, 158.

74. Du Guangting, *Daojiao lingyan ji*, 158–59, 160–61, 163–64, 166, 211–12, 238–39.

75. Earlier, the *Treatise on Two Teaching* (Erjiao lun) by Dao'an tells of Zhang Ling's bold claim of being a celestial master and his karmic retribution of being swallowed by a python; see *T.* 52, no. 2103, 8: 140a.

76. Du Guangting, *Daojiao lingyan ji*, 202.

77. In these stories, the appearance of the giant snakes is accompanied by thunder, lightning, and rainstorms. This association of snakes and rainstorms also has a long history in

ancient China; see Qiu Xigui,"On the Burning of Human Victims and the Fashioning of Clay Dragons in Order to Seek Rain in the Shang Dynasty Oracle-Bone Inscriptions," *Early China* 9-10 (1983-1985): 290-306; Takizawa Shunryō, "Ryūja to kiu no shūzoku ni tsuite," *Tōhō shūkyō* 20 (1962): 18-34; Michael Loewe, *Divination, Mythology and Monarchy in Han China* (Cambridge: Cambridge University Press, 1994), 142-59; E. H. Schafer, *The Divine Woman: Dragon Ladies and Rain Maidens in Tang Literature* (Berkeley: University of California Press 1973); Lei Wen, "Qiyu yu Tangdai shehui yanjiu," *Guoxue yanjiu* 8 (2001): 245-89; Kanai Noriyuki, "Sodai no ki u ki hare: Tokuni shu kenka no go o megurite," *Risshō daigaku tōyōshi ronshū* 19 (2015): 1-15; Paul Katz, *Demon Hordes and Burning Boats: The Cult of Marshal Wen in Late Imperial Cheikiang* (Albany: State University of New York Press, 1995), 19-21; Jeffrey Snyder-Reinke, *Dry Spells: State Rainmaking and Local Governance in Late Imperial China.* (Cambridge, MA: Harvard University Press, 2009); Matsumae Takeshi, "Kodaikanzoku no ryu ja suhai to oken," *Chōsen gakuhō* 57 (1970): 1-22; Kawano Akimasa, "Jako to tobyo nichi kan chu no reibutsu shinko ni miru tokutei katei seisui no densho (2)," *Jinbun gakuhō* 374 (2006): 57-130.

78.   Zanning, *Song gaoseng zhuan, T.* 50, no. 2061: 715c; Liu Xu, *Jiu Tang shu*, 1371.

79.   Zhou Yiliang, "Tantrism in China," *Harvard Journal of Asiatic Studies* 8 (1944-1945): 235-332, 269.

80.   In his recent study on Amoghavajra, Geoffrey C. Goble does not touch on this story; see Geoffrey C. Goble, *Chinese Esoteric Buddhism: Amoghavajra, the Ruling Elite, and the Emergence of a Tradition* (New York: Columbia University Press, 2019).

81.   Zhou Yiliang, "Tantrism in China," 304.

82.   According to the Esoteric Buddhist text, the Buddha once taught his disciple Ānanda that the *Kingly Spell of the Great Peacock* (Skt. *Mahāmayuri-vidyārājñī-dhāraṇī*) could be used against snakebite; see the Chinese version, *Fomu da Kongque mingwang jing*, juan 1, *T.* 19, no. 982, 416a; Ronald Davidson, *Indian Esoteric Buddhism: A Social History of the Tantric Movement* (New York: Columbia University Press, 2002), 278.

83.   Fujii Akira, "Mikkyo ni okeru satsu to kōfuku," *Tōyōgaku kenkyū* no. 54 (2017): 376-361 (L); Jens Schlieter, "Compassionate Killing or Conflict Resolution? The Murder of King Langdarma According to Tibetan Buddhist Sources," in *Buddhism and Violence*, ed. Michael Zimmermann (Lumbini, Nepal: International Research Institute, 2006), 131-57.

84.   David B. Gray, "Compassionate Violence?: On the Ethical Implications of Tantric Buddhist Ritual," *Journal of Buddhist Ethics* 14 (2007): 239-71.

85.   Stephen Jenkins, "On the Auspiciousness of Compassionate Violence," *Journal of International Association for Buddhist Studies* 33, no. 1-2 (2011): 299-331.

86.   W. Michale Kelsey, "Salvation of the Snake, The Snake of Salvation: Buddhist-Shinto Conflict and Resolution," *Japanese Journal of Religious Studies* 8, no. 1-2 (1981): 83-113.

87.   Brian Ruppert, "Buddhist Rainmaking in Early Japan: The Dragon King and the Ritual Careers of Esoteric Monks," *History of Religions* 42, no. 2 (2002): 143-74.

88.   Daoxuan, *Xu gaoseng zhuan*, juan 14, *T.* 50, no. 2060, 537b28.

89.   For a detailed study on Meng and his collection, see Chiew Hui Ho, *Diamond Sutra Narratives*, 82-86.

90.   See Meng Xianzhong, Jin'gang *borejingjiyanji, X.* 87, no. 1629; Bernard Faure reads this variant of the snake story as the tension between the universal Buddhist doctrine and

the local spirit. For him, the snake appears as a potentially harmful but eventually benevolent messenger of the invisible world. "The venom of the snake is transmitted into a gift of water, the discovery of a source that allows the construction of a temple." See Bernard Faure, "Space and Place in Chinese Religious Traditions," *History of Religions* 26, no. 4 (1987): 337–56. In light of the Nāga worship tradition in both Hinduism and Buddhism through the ages, some scholars suggest that it was a cultural adaptation, since Nāga worship was always associated with water resources; see Lesley Jo Weaver and Amber R. Campbell Hibbs, "Serpents and Sanitation: A Biological Survey of Snake Worship, Cultural Adaptation, and Parasite Disease in Ancient and Modern India," in *Parasites, Worms, and the Human Body in Religion and* Culture, ed. Brenda Gardenour and Misha Tadd (New York: Peter Lang, 2011), 1–16.

6. BUDDHISTS ENLIGHTENING VIRTUOUS BIRDS

1. For example, James M. Hargett noted that, along with the halcyon kingfisher (*feicui* 翡翠) and the oriole (*ying* 鶯), the parrot (*yingwu* 鸚鵡) is often praised and admired for its beautiful plumage in traditional Chinese literature; see James M. Hargett, "Playing Second Fiddle: The Luan-Bird in Early and Medieval Chinese Literature," *T'oung Pao*, 2nd series, 75, no. 4/5 (1989): 235–36. Schafer examined the importance of the parrot in medieval Chinese social and cultural history; see Edward H. Schafer, "Parrots in Medieval China," in *Studia Serica Bernhard Karlgren Dedicata: Sinological Studies Dedicated to Bernhard Karlgren on His Seventieth Birthday*, ed. Søren Egerod et Else Glahn (Copenhagen: Ejnar Munksgaard, 1959), 271–82.

2. Scientists have conducted research on the learning capacities of mimetic birds in both natural environments and laboratory settings. Experiments have demonstrated that social interaction is important for birds' learning abilities and such a context should be considered. Pepperberg records three observations after two years of training and interaction with humans: (1) "Alex achieved a rudimentary form of communication: contextual/conceptual use of human speech." (2) "He also appeared to possess some limited facility for categorizing objects in a manner not unlike that of humans, and could generalize label use to identify objects that differed somewhat from training items." (3) "The data did not prove that he had advanced capacities for information processing." She concludes: "My research demonstrated that a Grey parrot was capable of far more than simply the ability to mimic human speech." See Irene Maxine Pepperberg, *The Alex Studies: Cognitive and Communicative Abilities of Grey Parrots* (Cambridge, MA: Harvard University Press, 1999), 50–51.

3. Even in medieval Japan, especially from the sixth to twelfth centuries, the parrots appeared as crucial gifts in the foreign relations of Japan; see Minagawa Masaki, "Ōmu no zōtō: nihon kōdai taigai kankeishi kenkyū no hitokoma," in *Chōan toshi bunka to chōsen nihon*, ed. Yano Ken'ichi and Ri Kō (Tokyo: Kyūkoshoin, 2007), 209–31; reprinted in *Nihon kodai ōken to karamono kōeki* (Tokyo: Yoshikawa Kōbunkan, 2014), ch. 8.

4. *Sichuan tongzhi*, juan 15, part 2, in Luo Yuan, *Siku quanshu* (Hong Kong: Dizhi chuban gongsi, 1999).

5. This text first appeared in Yao Xuan, *Tang wen cui*, juan 76, no. 22 (Shanghai: Shanghai guji chubanshe, 1994), under the title *Yingwu sheli ta ji* 鸚鵡舍利塔記; for a detailed study

on various versions of *Tang wen cui*, see Zhang Daya, "Tang wen cui zhijian banben kao," *Donghai daxue tushuguan guanxun* no. 85 (2008): 21–39; later *Wenyuan yinghua* (juan 820), compiled 982–986, included a version from *Tang wen cui* titled *Xichuan yingwu sheli ta ji* 西川鸚鵡舍利塔記; other versions are found in Zongxiao, ed., *Lebang wenlei* [comp. 1200], juan 3, *T.* 47, no. 1969a: 191b-c; and Dong Gao, *Quan Tang wen*, (Beijing: Zhonghua shuju, 1983), juan 453, 4631–4632. For a modern punctuated edition, see Long Xianzhao, ed., *Ba Shu fojiao beiwen jicheng* (Chengdu: Sichuan chubanshe, 2004), 46. I use modern editions of all Wei Gao's essays in Long's collection for my research in this paper.

6. A complete English translation of Wei's parrot text can be found in Daniel B. Stevenson, "Death-Bed Testimonials of the Pure Land Faithful," in *Buddhism in Practice*, ed. Donald S. Lopez Jr. (Princeton, NJ: Princeton University Press, 1995), 599–602; this translation does not include annotations. I cite some passages from his translation but modify them slightly. For a short note on the textual information in this inscription, see John Kieschnick, *A Primer in Chinese Buddhist Writings, Supplement: Epigraphy* (Stanford, CA: Stanford University, 2016), 74–75, accessed July 14, 2022, https://religiousstudies.sites .stanford.edu/sites/g/files/sbiybj5946/f/primer-epigraphy-supplement-part-1.pdf.

7. For a brief explanation of Wei Gao's connection with Buddhism and Wei's commemoration epitaph for the parrot, see Peter N. Gregory, *Tsung-mi and the Sinification of Buddhism* (Honolulu: University of Hawai'i Press, 2002), 45–46; Gregory noted that Wei's text honored the enlightened parrot; also see Bernard Faure, *The Rhetoric of Immediacy: A Cultural Critique of Chan/Zen Buddhism* (Princeton, NJ: Princeton University Press, 1991), 140; John Kieschnick, *The Impact of Buddhism on Chinese Material Culture* (Princeton, NJ: Princeton University Press, 2003), 129, cites *Song Biographies of Eminent Monks*, which states that in his later life Wei Gao became a devout Buddhist.

8. Fan Chengda, *Riding the River Home: A Complete and Annotated Translation of Fan Chengda's (1120–1193) Diary of a Boat Trip to Wu (Wuchuan Lu)*, trans. James M. Hargett (Hong Kong: Chinese University of Hong Kong Press, 2008), 102.

9. For example, Wei Gao was a friend of Chengguan; see Imre Hamar, *A Religious Leader in the Tang: Chengguan's Biography* (Tokyo: International Institute for Buddhist Studies of the International College for Advanced Buddhist Studies, 2002), 74.

10. For instance, the phrase appeared in the inscription of the Dhūta Temple as 蔭法雲於真際，則火宅晨涼；曜慧日於康衢，則重昏夜曉, which Richard B. Mather translated as follows: "They cast the Law-cloud's shadow from the realm of Truth, and thus the Burning House by morn was cool; They shed the Wisdom-sunbeam's light upon the bustling crossroads, and thus the 'heavy gloom' at night grew bright." See Richard B. Mather, "Wang Chin's 'Dhūta Temple Stele Inscription' as an Example of Buddhist Parallel Prose," *Journal of American Oriental Society* 83, no. 3 (1963): 338–59, esp. 346. Forte suggests that the Dhūta Temple inscription serves as a literary model for the stele inscriptions in the Tang dynasty, see Antonino Forte, "A Literary Model for Adam: The Dhuta Monastery Inscription," in Paul Pelliot, *L'inscription nestorienne de Si-ngan-fou*, ed. Antonino Forte (Kyoto: Italian School of East Asian Studies and Paris: Collège de France, 1996), 437–87.

11. In the late Tang dynasty, allusions to this island were very common. For instance, see this poem by Wang Zhenbai, "Xiaobo Hanyang du" [Berthing the Hanyang port in the morning], in *Quan Tang shi*, juan 701, 8062) and the poem by Wang Renyu, "Guo Pingrong

gu diao Hu Hui" [Passing by the Pingrong Valley and offering condolences to Hu Hui], in *Quang Tang shi*, juan 736, 8403–04).

12. For the English translation cited here, see David R. Knechtges, *Wenxuan or Selections of Refined Literature* [by Xiao Tong], vol. 3 (Princeton, NJ: Princeton University Press, 1996), 51. For a comprehensive study of this piece, see William T. Graham Jr., "Mi Heng's 'Rhapsody on a Parrot,'" *Harvard Journal of Asiatic Studies* 39, no. 1 (1979): 39–54; Graham notes various examples in which parrots were a subject of versification. For a recent study on Mi Heng, see Chen Tianyi, "Lishi yu wenxue xushi zhong de Mi Heng," *Furen guowen xuebao* no. 38 (2014): 69–89.

13. Daniel B. Stevenson, "Death-Bed Testimonials of the Pure Land Faithful," 601.

14. As early as the fifth century BCE, the Greek physician and historian Ctesias noted in his book *Indica* that the parrot was from India, see J. M. Bigwood, "Ctesias' Parrot," *The Classical Quarterly* 43, no. 1 (1993): 321–27. Bigwood suggested that Ctesias came to know of this bird during his stay at the Persian court.

15. Fan Ju, *Yunxi youyi*, juan 2, in *Tang Wudai biji xiaoshuo daguan*, ed. Ding Ruming (Shanghai: Shanghai guji chubanshe, 2000), 1277; also Hu Fengdan, *Yingwuzhou xiaozhi* (Wuhan: Hubei jiaoyu chubanshe, 2002), 230.

16. Zhang Du, *Xuanshizhi*, in *Tang Wudai biji xiaoshuo daguan*, juan 9, (Yangzhou: Jiangsu guangling guji keyinshe, 1983), 1061; also see Zanning, "Tang xiyu wangming zhuan 唐西域亡名傳," in *Song gaoseng zhuan*, juan 19, *T.* 50, no. 2061, 830b–c.

17. For an outline of Wei Gao's patronage of Buddhism in Sichuan, see He Xiaorong, "Lun Wei Gao yu fojiao," *Xinan daxue xuebao* 38, no. 5 (2012): 154–59.

18. Zanning, *Song gaoseng zhuan*, juan 19, *T.* 50, no. 2061, 830c.

19. It was collected in the *Quan Tang wen*, juan 453, 4631–32. A modern punctuated edition can be found in Long Xianzhao, ed., *Ba Shu fojiao beiwen jicheng*, 43–44.

20. Wei Gao, "Jiazhou Lingyunsi Da Milefo shixiang ji 嘉州凌雲寺大彌勒石像記," in Long Xianzhao, ed., *Ba Shu fojiao beiwen jicheng*, 45.

21. See Sima Guang et al., *Zizhi tongjian*, juan 193 (Beijing: Zhonghua shuju, 1996); a note by Hu Sanxing (1230–1302) cites Wan Zhen's 萬震 *Record of the Exotic Things in the Southern Territory* [*Nanzhou yiwuzhi* 南州異物志], which states that three kinds of parrots—white, green, and five-colored—lived in the kingdoms south of Jiao prefecture, and that the white and five-color varieties in particular were very intelligent.

22. In the Western Han dynasty, white parrots were regarded as exotic animals. According to the *Miscellaneous Record of the Western Capital City* [*Xijing zaji* 西京雜記] (attributed to Ge Hong), Yuan Guanghan 袁廣漢, a very rich man from Maoling, constructed a private garden in which he raised white parrots, purple mandarin ducks, yaks, green buffalos, and other exotic animals; see Ge Hong, comp., *Xijing zaji* (Taipei: Taiwan guji chubanshe, 1997), 110.

23. Edward H. Schafer, "Parrots in Medieval China," 101.

24. Wang Ting, "Feiniao nengyan: Sui yiqian Zhongguo guanyu yingwu de miaoshu," in *Neilu yazhou shidi qiusuo* (Lanzhou: Lanzhou daxue chubanshe, 2011), 1–15; Li Juan, "Tangdai yingwu gushi de fojiao yinyuan," *Wutaishan yanji* 1 (2009): 25–29; Tan Qianxue, "Yingwuwen tiliang yinguan yu sheng Tang qixiang, *Gugong wenwu yuekan* 20 (2003): 88–91; and Wang Ganghuai, "Tang jing zhong de yingwu," *Shoucangjia* 7 (2004): 31–35; Fan

Shuying, "Cong yiguo xianrui dao shileniao: Tang Xuanzong shiqi dui yingwu xingxiang de yishu yu wenhua suzao," 136–40; Li Xiaorong, "Zhengzhi, zongjiao yu wenxue: Yan Zhaoyin Yingwu mao'er pian fafu," *Fujian shifan daxue xuebao* no. 5 (2013): 65–72.

25.   Dunhuang yanjiuyuan ed., *Dunhuang shiku quanji*, juan 19, "Dongwu hua juan" (Shanghai: Shanghai renmin chubanshe, 2000), 124, no. 106, Yulin Cave 25; 102, no. 83, Mogao Cave 66, north wall; 100, no. 81, Mogao Cave 45.

26.   Edward H. Schafer, "Parrots in Medieval China," 279.

27.   Daniel B. Stevenson, "Death-Bed Testimonials of the Pure Land Faithful," 602.

28.   For the study of Sukhāvatī in early Mahayana Buddhism, see Gregory Schopen, "Sukhāvatī as a Generalized Religious Goal in Sanskrit Mahāyāna Sūtra Literature," *Indo-Iranian Journal* 19 (1977): 177–210.

29.   Reiko Ohnuma, *Unfortunate Destiny: Animals in the Indian Buddhist Imagination* (New York: Oxford University Press, 2017), 31–33.

30.   Kālayaśas, *Guang Wuliangshoufo jing*, T. vol. 12, no. 365: 346a12–22.

31.   Daniel B. Stevenson, "Death-Bed Testimonials of the Pure Land Faithful," 602.

32.   Gregory Schopen, "Sukhāvatī as a Generalized Religious Goal in Sanskrit Mahāyāna Sūtra Literature," 177–210.

33.   For the practice of Pure Land tradition in medieval China, Stevenson notes that there are the mindful recollection of the Buddha and the recitation of the name of Amitabha, see Daniel B. Stevenson, "Pure Land Buddhist Worship and Meditation in China," in *Buddhism in Practice*, ed. Donald S. Lopez Jr. (Princeton, NJ: Princeton University Press, 1995), 359–79 ; and Daniel B. Stevenson, Death-Bed Testimonials of the Pure Land Faithful," 592–602; also Charles B. Jones, "Foundations of Ethics and Practice in Chinese Pure Land Buddhism," *Journal of Buddhist Ethics* 10 (2003): 1–20; Charles B. Jones, "Toward a Typology of Nien-fo: a Study in Methods of Buddha-Invocation in Chinese Pure Land Buddhism," *Pacific World: Journal of the Institute of Buddhist Studies*. 3rd series, 3 (2001): 219–39; for a concise introduction to the pure land practice in medieval China, see Jacqueline I. Stone, *Right Thoughts at the Last Moment: Buddhism and Deathbed Practices in Early Medieval Japan* (Honolulu: University of Hawai'i Press, 2016), 19–21.

34.   Zanning, *Song gaoseng zhuan*, juan 19, T. vol. 50, no. 2061: 830c10–17; He Xiaorong, "Lun Wei Gao yu fojiao," 154–59.

35.   Wendi Adamek, *The Mystique of Transmission: On an Early Chan History and Its Contexts* (New York: Columbia University Press, 2007), 285–86.

36.   Robert Sharf, "On Pure Land Buddhism and Ch'an/Pure Land Syncretism in Medieval China," *T'oung Pao* 88, no. 4–5 (2003): 282–331, esp. 301–09.

37.   See John McRae, *The Northern School and the Formation of Early Ch'an Buddhism* (Honolulu: University of Hawai'i Press, 1986), 223. Bernard Faure also notes that, "Early Chan shows a strong tendency to do away with all mental images, in an attempt to reach the blissful state of non-thinking (Ch., *wuxin* 無心, *wunian* 無念); see Bernard Faure, *Chan Insights and Oversights: An Epistemological Critique of the Chan Tradition* (Princeton, NJ: Princeton University Press, 1993), 184.

38.   Stevenson notes that, "One phenomenon that is a universal sign of sainthood or high spiritual attainment in Chinese Buddhism is the discovery of auspicious relics amid the ashes of the cremated corpse, usually in the form of glassine or jadelike beads." See Daniel B. Stevenson, "Death-Bed Testimonials of the Pure Land Faithful," 594.

39. In the Sui and Tang periods, according to several Buddhist texts, especially the records of Buddhist miraculous responses, during the national-wide movement of distributing relics, many lay Buddhists who received the Bodhisattva precepts reported that they produced relics from their ascetic and meditative practices, but their discoveries of relics usually must be endorsed and therefore authenticated by monastic clergies/monks. See Huaiyu Chen, *The Revival of Buddhist Monasticism in Medieval China* (New York: Peter Lang, 2007), chap. 2.

40. For an influential article discussing the Brazilian Indians who stated that they were parrots and who appeared simultaneously as both human and parrot, blurring the distinction between humans and beasts, see Jonathan Z. Smith, "I Am a Parrot (Red)," *History of Religions* 11, no. 4 (1972): 391–413.

41. Daoxuan, *Guang hongming ji*, juan 1, *T.* 52, No. 2103,1: 98b.

42. The Chinese term *dasheng* 大聖 was shared among several religious traditions in medieval China to refer to saints. The term was used as the title of Guan Zhong 管仲 in the *Book of Guanzi* 管子, later it was used for the Buddha in Buddhist texts, and Buddhism was called the teaching of the Great Sage (*dashengjiao* 大聖教, or commonly abbreviated as *shengjiao* 聖教). In addition, it was used for Jesus Christ in the Chinese text of the "Brilliant Teaching" (Jingjiao 景教, the Syriac church of the East); see Huaiyu Chen, "Suowei Tangdai jingjiao wenxian liangzhong bianwei bushuo," *Tang yanjiu* 3 (1997): 41–52.

43. Daniel B. Stevenson, "Death-bed Testimonials of the Pure Land Faithful," 602. I changed "the secular annals" in Stevenson's translation to "the books of [bamboo] slips."

44. Roel Sterckx, *The Animal and the Daemon in Early China* (Albany: State University of New York Press, 2002), 161, 296–97. Although the parrot was regarded as a pet, for medieval Chinese audiences, it had the ability to speak and understand the feelings of its master. Various ancient Greek thinkers also took an interest in the notion of humans and animals sharing a capacity for speech. For instance, Plato indicated that in the golden age "no creature was wild nor did they eat one another. Men and beasts all spoke the same language." In his *Questions on Genesis*, Philo (of Alexandria) claimed that in the beginning "all animals could probably speak somehow, though human beings spoke more clearly and distinctly." See Robert M. Grant, *Early Christians and Animals* (London: Routledge, 1999), 3.

45. Burton Watson, trans., *Records of the Grand Historian: Qin Dynasty* (New York: Columbia University Press, 1995), 1–2; William H. Nienhauser, ed. and trans., *The Grand Scribe's Records: Volume I, The Basic Annals of Pre-Han China* (Bloomington: Indiana University Press, 2018), 87.

46. Arthur F. Wright, "Fu I and the Rejection of Buddhism," *Journal of the History of Ideas* 12, no. 1 (1951): 33–47. According to Wright, Fu Yi's arguments against Buddhism can be divided into economic, political, nationalistic, sociopsychological, and intellectual categories.

47. Neither the *Qizhi* nor the *Diwang nianli* are extant. Only the titles have survived.

48. Falin, *Poxielun* 破邪論, in Daoxuan, *Guang hongmingji*, juan 11, *T.* 52, no. 2103: 163c12–26. For a comprehensive study on Falin, see Thomas Jülch, *Bodhisattva der Apologetik: die Mission des buddhistischen Tang-Mönchs Falin*, 3 vols. (München: Utz, 2014).

49. In medieval writings, it also appeared as a place name. The so-called Kongsang is located in modern Chenliu, Henan Province. According to *Lüshi chunqiu*, juan 14, a local village

girl found Yiyin as a baby in a hollow mulberry tree. See Lü Buwei, et al., *Lüshi chunqiu jishi* (Shanghai: Shanghai shudian, 1996), 88–89. For the English translation, see John Knoblock and Jeffrey Riegel trans., *The Annals of Lü Buwei* (Stanford, CA: Stanford University Press, 2000), 307.

50.   *The Analects*, 9: 14; see D. C. Lau trans., *Confucius: The Analects* (Hong Kong: The Chinese University Press, 1992), 81.

51.   Falin 法琳 et al., "Shang Qinwang lun qi 上秦王論啟," in Daoxuan, *Guang hongmingji, juan* 11, *T.* 52, no. 2103: 163c12–164a1.

52.   CT 338, *Zhonghua daozang*, vol. 4 (2004), 1; for a brief introduction to this text, see John Lagerwey, "Taishang dongxuan lingbao suming yinyuan mingjing," in *The Taoist Canon: A Historical Companion to the Daozang*, ed. Kristopher Schipper and Franciscus Verellen (Chicago: University of Chicago Press, 2004), 536.

53.   Falin, *Bianzheng lun*, in *Guang hongming ji*, vol. 13; *T.* 52, no. 2103: 528c24–529a4.

54.   "Longjing fengmu 龍精鳳目, longhu fengxing 龍虎鳳行;" See *Xu Fu xiangshu* 許負相書 [Xu Fu's book of physiognomy] in the Dunhuang manuscript CH. 87, section 1; for a modern annotated edition see Zheng Binglin and Wang Jinbo, eds., *Dunhuang xieben xiangshu jiaolu yanjiu* (Beijing: Minzu chubanshe, 2004), 27. The text specifies that people who walk like dragons would achieve the ranks of the three dukes in the central court, and those who walk like tigers would become generals and marshals (31).

55.   See Xu Fu, *Xu Fu xiangshu*, in Zheng Binglin and Wang Jingbo, *Dunhuang xieben xiangshu jiaolu yanjiu* (Beijing: Minzu chubanshe, 2004), 30.

56.   Fan Ye, *Hou Han shu* (Beijing: Zhonghuashuju, 1965), chap. 53, 1741–42.

57.   For a translation of Fan Zhen's "Essay on the Extinction of the Soul," see "The First Chinese Materialist," in Etienne Balazs, *Chinese Civilization and Bureaucracy*, ed. Arthur F. Wright, trans. H. M. Wright (New Haven, CT: Yale University Press, 1964), 255–76.

58.   Thomas Jansen, *Höfische Öffentlichkeit im frühmittelalterlichen China. Debatten im Salon des Prinzen Xiao Ziliang* (Freibourg: Rombach Verlag, 2000); Jacques Gernet, "Sur le corps et l'esprit chez les Chinois," in *Poikilia: études offertes à Jean-Pierre Vernant*, ed. Gilbert Dagron et al, (Paris: Ecole des Hautes études en sciences sociales, 1987), 369–77; Zhang Zhenjun, *Buddhism and Tales of the Supernatural in Early Medieval China: A Study of Liu Yiqing's (403–444) Youming lu*, (Leiden: Brill, 2003), 218–20; Tom de Rauw, "Beyond Buddhist Apology: The Political Use of Buddhism by Emperor Wu of the Liang Dynasty (r. 502–549)," PhD thesis, University of Ghent, 2008.

59.   The translations of these sentences in Fan's essay follow "The First Chinese Materialist," in Etienne Balazs, *Chinese Civilization and Bureaucracy*, 255–76.

60.   Sengyou, *Hongming ji, T.* 52, no. 2102: 56c–57b.

61.   A. C. Graham, trans., *The Book of Lieh-tzŭ: A Classic of the Tao* (New York: Columbia University Press, 1990), 53–55.

62.   Michael Puett, "Humans, Spirits, and Sages in Chinese Late Antiquity: Ge Hong's *Master Who Embraces Simplicity (Baopuzi)*," in *Extrême-Orient, Extrême-Occident*. 29 (2007): 95–119, esp. 96–98.

63.   Nakamura Fumi, "*Mahabarata* dai jusan kan omu to indora no taiwa no kosatsu," *Indo tetsugaku Bukkyōgaku* no. 22 (2007): 288–98; Nakamura Fumi, "Omu to indora no taiwa *mahabarata* dai jusan kan dai go sho no setsuwa wayaku kenkyū," *Otaru Shouka Daigaku Jinbun Kenkyū* no. 115 (2008): 195–209.

64. In contemporary Hinduism and Buddhism in South Asia, the parrot is associated with certain deities, such as Kamadeva, the god of lust, and Madhukara, but not with enlightened beings. See Trilok Chandra Majupuria, *Sacred Animals of Nepal and India* (Lashkar: M. Devi, 2000), 165. It should be noted that there are series of texts in both Sanskrit and Chinese translations about people who bore the name of the parrot in early Buddhist literature, such as the *Karmavibhaṅgadharmagrantha* (Tib. Las-kyi rnam- par ḥgyur-ba shes-bya-baḥi chos-kyi-gshuṅ). Six texts in Chinese translations are about the parrot, including *Yingwujing*, trans. Saṃghadeva, Eastern Jin dynasty, T. 1, no. 26; *Foshuo doudiaojing*, trans. anonymous, Eastern Jin dynasty, T. 1, no. 78; *Foshuo yingwu jing*, trans. Guṇabhadra c. 435–443, T. 1, no. 7; *Fo wei Shoujia zhangzhe shuo yebao chabie jing*, trans. Gautama Dharmajñāna, Sui dynasty, T. 1, no. 80; *Foshuo jingyi youposai suowen jing*, trans. Shihu, Song dynasty, T. 17, no. 755; *Fenbie shan'e baoying jing*, trans. Tianxizai, Song dynasty, T. 1, no. 81. Some Sanskrit fragments of *Karmavibhaṅgadharmagrantha* have been found in Xinjiang and Nepal. For an early study, see A. F. Rudolf Hoernle, *Manuscript Remains of Buddhist Literature Found in Eastern Turkestan* (Oxford: Clarendon Press, 1916), 46–52. For a comprehensive and recent study on Sanskrit fragments from Nepal, see Kudo Noriyuki, *The Karmavibhanga: Transliterations and Annotations of the Original Sanskrit Manuscripts from Nepal* (Tokyo: The International Research Institute for Advanced Buddhology, 2013). For a study of the Tocharian fragment of the *Karmavibhaṅga*, see Tamai Tatsushi, "The Tocharian Karmavibhaṅga*," *Annual Report of The International Research Institute for Advanced Buddhology at Soka University* 18 (2015): 337–81; he notes that this fragment is closer to the Chinese version translated by Gautama Dharmajñāna rather than the Sanskrit fragment; Georges-Jean Pinault, "Concordance des manuscrits tokhariens du fonds Pelliot," in *Instrumenta Tocharica*, ed. Melanie Malzahn (Heidelberg: Winter Verlag, 2007), 169–219, esp. 209–12. A Sogdian fragment of this text has been found in Dunhuang, see A. N. Ragoza, *Sogdiĭskie fragmenty tsentral'no-aziatskogo sobraniya instituta vostokovedeniya* (Moscow: Izd. Nauka, 1980), text 93. This Sogdian fragment may date from the era of Tibetan rule over Dunhuang, see David A. Utz, *A Survey of Buddhist Sogdian Studies* Tokyo: Reiyukai Library, 1978), 8; and Mariko Namba Walter, "Sodgians and Buddhism," *Sino-Platonic Papers* 174 (November 2006): 35. The most visible collection of stories about the parrot in India is the Śukasaptati, which is influenced by early Buddhist literature. For the English translation, see A. N. D. Haksar, *Shuka Saptati: Seventy Tales of the Parrot* (New Delhi: HarperCollins Publishers, 2000). One story about a parrot and a merchant shows that the parrot endowed the virtues of justice and generosity as well as wisdom; see Sakata Teiji, "Ōmu to Shōnin no okamisan: Indo no setsuwa to mukashibanashi o meguru danshō," *Shisō* 623 (1976): 90–104.

65. Dharmanandi, *Ayuwang xihuamu yinyuan jing*, T. 50, no. 2045: 172b.

66. Even in contemporary Indian folklore, talkative women sometimes are connected with parrots; see John R. Perry, "Monty Python and the Mathnavī: The Parrot in Indian, Persian and English Humor," *Iranian Studies* 36, no. 1 (2003): 63–73.

67. An Shigao, *Foshuo mayi jing*, T. 17, no. 732: 532b.

68. Unknown translator, *Foshuo shan'e yinguo jing*, T. 85, no. 2881: 1381a.

69. The manuscript, of 571 lines, was brought to Paris by Paul Pelliot and originally numbered P. 3516. It is now numbered P. Sogd. 5. See D. N. MacKenzie, *The Sūtra of the Causes and Effects of Actions in Sogdian*, London Oriental Series 22, (London: Oxford University

Press, 1970). The Sogdian translation for parrot came from the Chinese word, which indicates that the Sogdian version was based on the Chinese source text.

70.   Huijue, *Xianyujing*, juan 12, *T.* 4, no. 202: 436c07–437a2.

71.   Zhiqian, *Foshuo zhangzhe Yinyue jing*, *T.* 14, no. 531: 809b.

72.   Kivkara and Tanyao, *Za baozang jing*, *T.* 4, no. 203: 485a08–c10. The parrot was endowed with moral and spiritual qualities that allowed it to receive salvation. Robert F. Campany discusses a story that entered China with the translation of the Samyuktaratnapitka Sūtra (*Za baozang jing* 雜寶藏經). This story concerns a compassionate parrot who was rewarded by devas after attempting to save other animals from a forest fire; see Robert F. Campany, *Strange Writing: Anomaly Accounts in Early Medieval China* (Albany: State University of New York Press, 1996), 184–85.

73.   Kang Senghui, *Liudu jijing* [*Ṣaṭ-pāramitā-saṃgraha Sūtra]. *T.* 3, no. 152: 17c1–22.

74.   Kang Senghui, *Liudu jijing*, *T.* 3, no. 152: 34a9–26. For another Jātaka story describing the Buddha's rebirth as a parrot king, see Zhiqian, *Zhuanji baiyuan jing*, *T.* 4, no. 200: 231a17–b27. Chapter 28 of the Buddhist monastic code the Mūlasarvāstivāda Vinaya Kṣudrakavastu 根本說一切有部毘奈耶雜事 includes a story about how a parrot called Juxiang 具相 (Skt. Aṅkita) used his virtue and wisdom to help his lord, a high-ranking official who was the Buddha in a previous life and who helped the King of Viheha achieve his goal of marrying the beautiful daughter of King Pāñcāla 半遮羅. *T.* 24, no. 1451: 342a27–345c8. There are two fragmentary Dunhuang manuscripts with texts titled *Foshuo Dayao shanqiao fangbian jing* 佛說大藥善巧方便經, including P. 3791 and Dunhuang Academy no. 0336. See Yang Sen, "Dunhuang yishu Foshuo Dayao shanqiao fangbian jing juanshang zhaji," *Dunhuang yanjiu* 4 (1989): 108–11.

75.   Chün-fang Yü, *Kuan-yin: the Chinese Transformation of Avalokiteśvara* (New York: Columbia University Press, 2001), 442–47; Wilt L. Idema, "Guanyin's Parrot: A Chinese Buddhist Animal Tale and Its International Context," in *India, Tibet, China: Genesis and Aspects of Traditional Narrative* ed. Alfredo Cadonna (Firenze: Leo S. Olschki, 1999), 103–50.

76.   Li Baiyao, "Shenwu diji," in *Bei Qishu*, juan 2 (Beijing: Zhonghua shuju, 1972).

77.   *Dayunjing shenhuang shouji yishu* 大雲經神皇授記義疏; commonly known as *Dayun jing shu* 大雲經疏. At least two manuscripts of the commentary have been found, S. 2658 and S. 6502 in the Stein collection, the latter of which is longer. For a study of S. 6502, see Lin Shitian, "Wu Zetian chengdi yu tuchen xiangrui: yi S. 6502 Dayunjing shu wei zhongxin," *Dunhuangxue jikan* 2 (2002): 64–72; and Jin Yingkun and Liu Yonghai, "Dunhuang ben Dayunjing shu xinlun: yi Wu Zetian chengdi wei zhongxin," *Wenshi* 4 (2009): 31–46. For a comprehensive translation and study on S. 6502, see Antonino Forte, *Political Propaganda and Ideology in China at the End of the Seventh Century: Inquiry into the Nature, Authors and Function of the Dunhuang Document S. 6502, Followed by an Annotated Translation*, 2nd edition (Kyoto: Scuola Italiana di Studi sull'Asia Orientale, 2005).

78.   The story of Di Renjie's dialogue with Wu Zetian can be found in Sima Qian et al., *Zizhi tongjian*, juan 206 (Beijing: Zhonghua shuju, 1996), 6526.

79.   Lü Zongli, "Chenwei yu Wei Jin Nanbeichao fojiao," *Nanjing daxue xuebao* 4 (2010): 109–22; for a discussion of prophecy tradition in early medieval Chinese political culture,

see Lü Zongli, *Power of the Words: Chen Prophecy in Chinese Politics, AD 265–518* (Bern: Peter Lang, 2003).

80. Minggai 明槩, "Juedui Fu Yi fei fofaseng shi bing biao 決對傅奕廢佛法僧事並表," in Daoxuan, ed., *Guang hongming ji*, juan 12, *T*. 52, no. 2103: 168b-c.

EPILOGUE

1. Lynn White Jr., "The Historical Roots of Our Ecological Crisis," *Science* 155 (1967): 1203–07.
2. Tuan Yi-fu, "Discrepancies Between Environmental Attitude and Behaviour: Examples from Europe and China," *Canadian Geographer* 12, no. 3 (1968): 175–91; Bron Taylor, "The Greening of Religion Hypothesis (Part One): From Lynn White Jr. and Claims that Religions Can Promote Environmentally Destructive Attitudes and Behaviors to Assertions They Are Becoming Environmentally Friendly," *Journal for the Study of Religion, Nature and Culture* 10, no. 3 (2016): 268–305.
3. Aaron Gross, *The Question of the Animal and Religion: Theoretical Stakes, Practical Implications* (New York: Columbia University Press, 2015).
4. Roger Straughan, *Ethics, Morality and Animal Biotechnology* (Swindon: Biotechnology and Biological Sciences Research Council, 1999).
5. Oswald J. Schmitz et al., "Animals and the Zoogeochemistry of the Carbon Cycle." *Science* 362, no. 6419 (2018). DOI: 10.1126/science.aar3213.

Bibliography

CANONICAL TEXTS

Buddhism

ABBREVIATIONS

T = *Taishō shinshū Daizōkyō* 大正新修大藏経, ed. Takakusu Junjirō 高楠順次郎 and
  Watanabe Kaigyoku 渡邊海旭. Tokyo: Taishō Issaikyō Kankōkai, 1924–1929.
X = *Manji shinsan zoku zōkyō* 卍新纂續藏經. Tokyo: Kokusho Kankokai, 1905–1912.

Alphabetized by title.

Ayuwang xihuaimu yinyuan jing 阿育王息壞目因緣經. Dharmanandi (4th century). *T.* 50, no. 2045.
Bianzheng lun 辯正論. Falin (572–640). *T.* 52, no. 2110.
Biqiuni zhuan 比丘尼傳. Baochang (6th century). *T.* 50, no. 2063.
Buxu Gaoseng zhuan 補續高僧傳. Minghe (1588–1640). *X.* 77, no. 1524.
Chu sanzang jiji 出三藏記集. Sengyou (445–518). *T.* 55, no. 2145.
Chuyao jing 出曜經. Zhu Fonian (331?–417?). *T.* 4, no. 212.
Cibei daochang chanfa 慈悲道場懺法. Unknown author. *T.* 45, no. 1909.
Daban niepan jing 大般涅槃經. Dharmarakṣa (385–433). *T.* 12, no. 374.
Da baoji jing 大寶積經. Bodhiruci (572–727). *T.* 11, no. 310.
Da fangbian Fo bao'en jing 大方便佛報恩經. Unknown translator. *T.* 3, no. 156.
Da fangdeng daji jing 大方等大集經. Dharmarakṣa (385–433). *T.* 13, no. 397.
Da loutan jing 大樓炭經. Fali (255?–308?) and Faju (259?–309?). *T.* 1, no. 123.
Dasheng baoyun jing 大乘寶雲經. Mandra (453?–504?) and Saṅghapāla (460–524). *T.* 16, no. 659.
Dasheng yi zhang 大乘義章. Huiyuan (523–592). *T.* 44, no. 1851.
Dichi yiji 地持義記. Huiyuan (523–592). *T.* 85. No. 2803.
Fahua jing 法華經. Kumārajīva (344–413). *T.* 9, no. 262.
Fanwang jing 梵網經. Kumārajīva (344–413). *T.* 24, no. 1484.
Fanyi mingyi ji 翻譯名義集. Fayun (1088–1158). *T.* 54, no. 2131.
Fayuan zhulin 法苑珠林. Daoshi (607?–683). *T.* 53, no. 2122.
Fenbie shan'e baoying jing 分別善惡報應經. Tianxizai (?–1000). *T.* 1, no. 81.

Fo benxing ji jing 佛本行集經. Jñānagupta (523–600). *T.* 3, no. 190.

Fomu da Kongque mingwang zhoujing 佛母大孔雀明王咒經. Amoghavajra (705–774). *T.* 19, no. 982.

Foshuo doudiaojing 佛說兜調經. Unknown translator. *T.* 1, no. 78.

Foshuo guan Fo Sanmei hai jing 佛說觀佛三昧海經. Buddhabhadra (359–429). *T.* 15, no. 643.

Foshuo jingyi youposai suowen jing 佛說淨意優婆塞所問經. Dānapāla (?–1017). *T.* 17, no. 755.

Foshuo lishi apitan lun 佛說立世阿毗曇論. Paramārtha (499–569). *T.* 32, no. 1644.

Foshuo mayi jing 佛說罵意經. An Shigao (113?–171?) *T.* 17, no. 732.

Foshuo shan'e yinguo jing 佛說善惡因果經. Unknown translator. *T.* 85, no. 2881.

Foshuo yingwu jing 佛說鸚鵡經. Guṇabhadra (394–468). *T.* 1, no. 79.

Foshuo zhangzhe Yinyue jing 佛說長者音悅經. Zhiqian (197?–253?). *T.* 14, no. 531.

Fo wei Shoujia zhangzhe shuo yebao chabie jing 佛為首迦長者說業報差別經. Gautama Dharmajñāna (531?–605?). *T.* 1, no. 80.

Fozu lidai tongzai 佛祖历代通载. Nianchang (1282–?). *T.* 49, no. 2036.

Fozu tongji 佛祖統紀. Zhipan (13th century). *T.* 49, no. 2035.

Gaoseng zhuan 高僧傳. Huijiao (497–554). *T.* 50, no. 2059.

Genben shuo yiqieyou bu pinaiye 根本說一切有部毗奈耶. Yijing (635–713). *T.* 23, no. 1442.

Genben shuo yiqieyou bu pinaiye pigeshi 根本說一切有部毗奈耶皮革事. Yijing, trans. *T.* 23, no. 1447.

Genben shuo yiqieyou bu pinaiye zashi 根本說一切有部毗奈耶雜事. Yijing. *T.* 24, no. 1451.

Guang hongming ji 廣弘明集. Daoxuan (596–667). *T.* 52, no. 2103.

Guang Wuliangshoufo jing 觀無量壽佛經. Kālayaśas (383–442). *T.* 12, no. 365.

Guanzhong chuangli jietan tujing 關中創立戒壇圖經. Daoxuan (596–667). *T.* 45, no. 1899.

Hongming ji 弘明集. Sengyou (445–518). *T.* 52, no. 2102.

Hongzan fahua zhuan 弘贊法華傳. Huixiang (7th century). *T.* 51, no. 2067.

Huayanjing zhuanji 華嚴經傳記. Fazang (643–712). *T.* 51, no. 2073.

Jiatai pudenglu 嘉泰普燈錄. Zhengshou (1147–1209). *X.* 79, no. 1559.

Jin'gang borejing jiyanji 金剛般若經集驗記. Meng Xianzhong (8th century). *X.* 87, no. 1629.

Jinglü yixiang 經律異相. Sengmin (467–527) and Baochang (6th century). *T.* 53, no. 2121.

Jingxin jieguan fa 淨心誡觀法. Daoxuan (596–667). *T.* 45, no. 1893.

Lebang wenlei 樂邦文類. Zongxiao (c. 13th century). *T.* 47, no. 1969a.

Liangchu qingzhong yi 量處輕重儀. Daoxuan (596–667). *T.* 45, no. 1895.

Liudu jijing 六度集經. Kang Senghui (181?–280). *T.* 3, no. 152.

Lüjieben shu 律戒本疏. Unknown author. *T.* 85, no. 2788.

Mingfo lun 明佛論. Zongbing (375–443). *T.* 52, no. 2102.

Mohe bore poluomi damingzhou jing 摩訶般若波羅蜜大明呪經. Kumārajīva (344–413). *T.* 8, no. 250.

Mohe sengqi lü 摩訶僧祇律. Buddhabhadra (359–429) and Faxian (338–423). *T.* 22, no. 1425.

Mohe zhiguan 摩訶止觀. Zhiyi (538–597). *T.* 46, no. 1911.

Nanyue zongsheng ji 南嶽總勝集. Chen Tianfu (fl. mid-12th century). *T.* 51, no. 2097.

Neidian xu 內典序. Shen Yue (441–513). *T.* 52, no. 2103.

Poxielun 破邪論. Falin (572–640). *T.* 52, no. 2103.

Pusa dichi jing 菩薩地持經. Dharmarakṣa (385–433). *T.* 30, no. 1581.

Qishi jing 起世經. Jñānagupta (523–600). *T.* 1, no. 24.

Sapoduo pini piposha 薩婆多毗尼毗婆沙. Unknown translator. *T.* 23, no. 1440.

Shanjian lü piposha 善見律毗婆沙. Saṃghabhadra (5th century). *T.* 24, no. 1462.

Shenmie lun 神滅論. Fan Zhen (450–510). *T.* 52, no. 2102.

Shisong lü 十誦律. Puṇyatāra (305?-404) and Kumārajīva (344-413). *T.* 23, no. 1435.

Shizhu piposha lun 十住毗婆沙論. Kumārajīva (344-413). *T.* 26, no. 1521.

Sifen lü 四分律. Buddhayaśas (363?-414?) and Zhu Fonian (331?-417?). *T.* 22, no. 1428.

Song gaoseng zhuan 宋高僧傳. Zanning (919-1001). *T.* 50, no. 2061.

Tuoluoni zaji 陀羅尼雜集. Unknown translator. *T.* 21, no. 1336.

Wufen lü 五分律. Buddhajīva (374?-424?) and Zhu Daosheng (355-434). *T.* 22, no. 1421.

Xianyu jing 賢愚經. Huijue (395?-446?). *T.* 4, no. 202.

Xu gaoseng zhuan 續高僧傳. Daoxuan (596-667). *T.* 50, no. 2060.

Yingwujing 鸚鵡經. Saṃghadeva (316?-385?). *T.* 1, no. 26.

Yiqiejing yinyi 一切經音義. Huilin (737-820). *T.* 54, no. 2128.

Yunqi fahui 雲棲法彙. Zhuhong (1535-1615). *J* (Jiaxing zang 嘉興藏). 33, no. B277.

Za baozang jing 雜寶藏經. Kivkara (422?-473?) and Tanyao (407?-463?). *T.* 4, no. 203.

Zengyi ahan jing 增壹阿含經. Saṃghadeva (316?-385?). *T.* 2, no. 125.

Zheng erjiao lun 正二教論. Ming Sengshao (384?-483). *T.* 52, no. 2102.

Zhengfa nianchu jing 正法念處經. Prajñāruci (476?-544?). *T.* 17, no. 721.

Zhuanji baiyuan jing 撰集百緣經. Zhiqian (197?-253?). *T.* 4, no. 200.

Daoism

Numbers given in the endnotes reference *Zhengtong daozang*: Zhang Jiyu 張繼禹 et al. *Zhonghua daozang* 中華道藏 [Daoist canon of China]. Beijing: Huaxia chubanshe, 2004.

Chisongzi zhangli 赤松子章曆. CT 615.

Dadao jialing jie 大道家令戒. CT 789.

Daojiao lingyan ji 道教靈驗記. Du Guangting (850-933). CT 590.

Dongshen baji miaojing jing 洞神八帝妙精經. CT 640.

Dongxuan lingbao yujingshan buxu jing 洞玄靈寶玉京山步虛經. CT 1439.

Fengdao kejie 奉道科戒. CT 1125.

Han Tinshi shijia 漢天師世家. Zhang Zhengchang (1329-1378). CT 1463.

Lishi zhenxian tidao tongjian 歷世真仙體道通鑑. Zhao Daoyi (fl. 1294-1307). CT 296.

Sandong qunxian lu 三洞群仙錄. Chen Baoguang (13th century). CT 1248.

Sanhuang neiwen 三皇內文. CT 856.

Shenxian zhuan 神仙傳. Ge Hong (283-343). CT 592.

Taipingjing 太平經. CT 1101.

Taiqing jinye shendan jing 太清金液神丹經. CT 880.

Taishang dongxuan lingbao wufu xu 太上洞玄靈寶五符序. CT 388.

Taishang dongxuan lingbao suming yinyuan ming jing 太上洞玄靈寶宿命因緣明經. CT 338.

Taishang dongxuan lingbao yebao yinyuan jing 太上洞玄靈寶業報因緣經. CT 336.

Taishang laojun jiejing 太上老君戒經. CT 784.

Wuyue zhenxing tu 五嶽真形圖. CT 441.

Xianyuan bianzhu 仙苑編珠. Wang Songnian (10th century). CT 596

Yuanshi wulao chishu yupian zhenwen tianshu jing 元始五老赤書玉篇真文天書經. CT 22.

Yunji qiqian 雲笈七籤. Zhang Junfang (11th century). CT 1032.

Zhengao 真誥. CT 1016.

Zhengyi fawen 正一法文. CT 1204.

Zhongnanshan shuojingtai lidai zhenxian beiji 終南山説經臺歷代真仙碑記. Zhu Xiangxian (13th century). CT 956.

Dunhuang Manuscripts

ABBREVIATIONS

BD = The Dunhuang collection at the National Library of China in Beijing
P = The Pelliot Collection at Bibliothèque nationale de France in Paris
S = The Stein Collection at British Library in London

BD 11252: *Taogong chuanshou yi* 陶公傳授儀

Dunhuang Academy no. 0336: *Foshuo Dayao shanqiao fangbian jing* 佛說大藥善巧方便經

P. 2452: *Lingbao weiyi jingjue shang* 靈寶威儀經訣上

P. 2559: *Taogong chuanshou yi* 陶公傳授儀

P. 2940: *Zhaiwan wen* 齋琬文

P. 3791: *Foshuo Dayao shanqiao fangbian jing* 佛說大藥善巧方便經

P. 4513: *Guanyin jing* 觀音經

S. 2658: *Dayunjing shenhuang shouji yishu* 大雲經神皇授記義疏

S. 5637: *Jima wen* 祭馬文

S. 5733: *Taishang dongxuan lingbao wupian zhenwen chishu* 太上洞玄靈寶五篇真文赤書

S. 3750: *Taogong chuanshou yi* 陶公傳授儀

S. 6301: *Taogong chuanshou yi* 陶公傳授儀

S. 6502: *Dayunjing shenhuang shouji yishu* 大雲經神皇授記義疏

COLLECTIONS AND MODERN ANNOTATED EDITIONS OF TRADITIONAL TEXTS AND INSCRIPTIONS

Ban Gu 班固. *Han shu* 漢書. Beijing: Zhonghua shuju, 1962.

Beijing daxue guwenxian yanjiusuo 北京大學古文獻研究所, ed. *Quan Song shi* 全宋詩 [A complete collection of poems from the Song dynasty]. Beijing: Beijing daxue chubanshe, 1998.

Chen Shangjun 陳尚君, ed. *Quan Tang wen bubian* 全唐文補編. Beijing: Zhonghua shuju, 2005.

Ding Ruming 丁如明, ed. *Tang Wudai biji xiaoshuo daguan* 唐五代筆記小說大觀 [The collection of the Biji writings of the Tang and Five Dynasties]. Shanghai: Shanghai guji chubanshe, 2000.

Dong Gao 董誥 et al. *Quan Tang wen* 全唐文. Beijing: Zhonghua shuju, 1983.

Du Guangting 杜光庭. *Du Guangting jizhuan shizhong jijiao* 杜光庭記傳十種輯, ed. and ann. Luo Zhengming. Beijing: Zhonghua shuju, 2013.

Du You 杜佑. *Tongdian* 通典. Beijing: Zhonghua shuju, 1988.

Duan Chengshi 段成式. *Youyang zazu jiaojian* 酉陽雜俎校箋, ann. Xu Yimin 許逸民. Beijing: Zhonghua shuju, 2015.

Dunhuang yanjiuyuan 敦煌研究院 [Dunhuang Academy], ed. *Dunhuang shiku quanji* 敦煌石窟全集 [A complete collection of Dunhuang caves], juan 19, "Dongwu hua juan 動物畫卷 [Volume of animal paintings]. Shanghai: Shanghai renmin chubanshe, 2000.

Fan Ye 范曄. *Hou Han shu* 後漢書. Beijing: Zhonghuashuju, 1965.

Ge Hong 葛洪. *Baopuzi neipian jiaoshi* 抱樸子內篇校釋, annotated Wang Ming. Beijing: Zhong-hua shuju, 1985.

—. *Shenxian zhuan* 神仙傳, ann. Hu Shouwei 胡守為. Beijing: Zhonghua shuju, 2010.

—. *Zhouhou beiji fang jiaozhu* 肘後備急方校注, ann. Shen Shunong 沈澍農, Beijing: Renmin weisheng chubanshe, 2016.

Ge Hong, comp. *Xijing zaji* 西京雜記 [A miscellaneous record of the western capital]. Taipei: Taiwan guji chubanshe, 1997.

Han Fei 韓非. *Hanfeizi jijie* 韓非子集校, ann. Wang Xianshen. Taipei: Taiwan shangwu yinshu-guan, 1969.

Han Yu, "Zhi Dai jian." In *Quan Tang shi*, juan 338, ed. Peng Dingqiu, 3786–87. Beijing: Zhong-hua shuju, 1979.

Hong, Mai 洪邁. *Rongzhai suibi quanshu leibian yizhu* 容齋隨筆全書類編譯註, ed. Xu Yimin 許逸民. Beijing: Shidai wenyi chubanshe, 1993.

Li Baiyao 李百藥. *Bei Qishu* 北齊書 [History of the Northern Qi dynasty]. Beijing: Zhonghua shuju, 1972.

Li Daoping 李道平, ed. *Zhouyi jijie cuanshu* 周易集解纂疏. Beijing: Zhonghua shuju, 2004.

Li Fang 李昉 et al. *Taiping guangji* 太平廣記. Beijing: Zhonghua shuju, 1961.

Li Fang 李昉 et al. *Taiping guangji huijiao* 太平廣記會校, ann. Zhang Guofeng 張國風. Beijing: Bei-jing yanshan chubanshe, 2011.

Li Ximi 李希泌 and Mao Huaxuan 毛華軒, eds. *Tang dazhaoling ji bubian* 唐大詔令集補編. Shang-hai: Shanghai guji chubanshe, 2003.

Li Yanshou 李延壽. *History of Southern Dynasties* (Nan shi 南史). Beijing: Zhonghua shuju, 1975.

Lie Yukou 列禦寇. *Liezi jishi* 列子集釋, ann. Yang Bojun 楊伯峻. Beijing: Zhonghua shuju, 1979.

Liu Xu 劉昫 et al. *Jiu Tang shu* 舊唐書. Beijing: Zhonghua shuju, 1975.

Liu Yiqing 劉義慶. *Shishuo xinyu* 世說新語, trans. Richard Mather. *A New Account of Tales of the World (Shih-Shuo Hsin-Yü),* ann Arbor: Center for Chinese Studies, University of Michigan, Michigan Monographs in Chinese Studies, 2002.

Liu Zhen 劉珍 et al. *Dongguan Han ji*, ann. Wu Shuping 吳樹平. Zhengzhou: Zhongzhou guji chubanshe, 1987.

Long Xianzhao 龍顯昭, ed. *Ba Shu fojiao beiwen jicheng* 巴蜀佛教碑文集成 [A collection of stele inscriptions of Buddhism in Bashu area]. Chengdu: Sichuan chubanshe, 2004.

Lü Buwei 呂不韋 et al. *Lüshi chunqiu jishi* 呂氏春秋集釋 [The collected commentaries on *Master Lü's Spring and Autumn Annals*], ann. Xu Weiyu. Shanghai: Shanghai shudian, 1996.

Luo Yuan 羅願, *Erya yi* 爾雅翼, *Siku quanshu* 四庫全書. Electronic database and CD-ROM. Hong Kong: Dizhi chuban gongsi, 1999.

Ma Xinmin 馬辛民, ed. *Chunqiu Zuozhuan zhengyi* 春秋左傳正義. Beijing: Beijing daxue chuban-she, 1999.

Ma Xinmin 馬辛民 and Li Xueqin 李學勤, eds. *Erya zhushu* 爾雅註疏. Beijing: Beijing daxue chu-banshe, 2000.

Ouyang Xiu 歐陽修 et al. *Xin Tang shu* 新唐書. Beijing: Zhonghua shuju, 1975.

Ouyang Xun 歐陽詢. *Yiwen leiju* 藝文類聚. Shanghai: Shanghai guji chubanshe, 1982.

Pan Anren. "Shezhi fu." In *Wenxuan,* juan 9, ed. Xiao Tong, 415–23 (Shanghai: Shanghai guji chu-banshe, 1986).

Peng Dingqiu 彭定求 et al. *Quan Tang shi* 全唐詩. Beijing: Zhonghua shuju, 1979.

Qiao Dong 喬棟, Li Xianqi 李獻奇, and Shi Jiazhen 史家珍, eds. "Luoyang di'er wenwu gong-zuodui 洛陽市第二文物工作隊." In *Luoyang xinhuo muzhi xubian* 洛陽新獲墓誌續編. Beijing: Kexue chubanshe, 2008.

Sima Guang 司馬光 et al. *Zizhi tongjian* 資治通鑑 [Comprehensive mirror for aid in government]. Beijing: Zhonghua shuju, 1996.

Sima Qian 司馬遷. *Shiji* 史記. Beijing: Zhonghua shuju, 1959.

Tang, Lin 唐臨. *Mingbao ji* 冥報記. Beijing: Zhonghua shuju, 1992.

Tao Hongjing 陶弘景, ed. *Zhengao* 真誥. Beijing: Wenwu chubanshe, 1987.

Wang Chong 王充. *Lunheng jiaoshi* 論衡校釋, ann. Beijing University. Beijing: Zhonghua shuju, 1979.

Wang Meng'ou 王夢鷗 ed. *Liji jinzhu jiyi* 禮記今註今譯. Taipei: Shangwu yinshuguan, 1979.

Wang Renyu 王仁裕. *Kaiyuan Tianbao yishi* 開元天寶遺事. In *Tang Wudai biji xiaoshuo daguan* 唐五代筆記小說大觀, ed. Ding Ruming, 1720. Shanghai: Shanghai guji chubanshe, 2000.

Wang Tao 王燾. *Waitai miyao* 外臺祕要. Beijing: Renmin weisheng chubanshe, 1955.

Wei Shou 魏收. *Wei shu* 魏書. Beijing: Zhonghua shuju, 1974.

Wu Gang 吳鋼 et al. *Quan Tang wen buyi* 全唐文補遺 (*Qian Tang zhi zhai xinji* 千唐誌齋新輯), Xi'an: Sanqin chubanshe, 2006.

Xu Fu 許負. *Xu Fu xiangshu* 許負相書. In Zheng Binglin and Wang Jingbo, *Dunhuang xieben xiangshu jiaolu yanjiu* 敦煌寫本相書校錄研究. Beijing: Minzu chubanshe, 2004.

Yan Juanying 顏娟英, ed. *Beichao fojiao shike tapian baipin* 北朝佛教石刻拓片百品. Taipei: Academica Sinica, 2008.

Yan Ying 晏嬰. *Yanzi chunqiu yizhu* 晏子春秋譯註, ann. Sun Yanlin 孫彥林, Zhou Min 周民, and Miao Ruosu 苗若素. Jinan: Qilu shushe, 1991.

Yao Silian 姚思廉. *Liang shu* 梁書. Beijing: Zhonghua shuju, 1973.

Yao Xuan 姚鉉. *Tang wen cui* 唐文粹 [Selected fine writings from the Tang dynasty]. Shanghai: Shanghai guji chubanshe, 1994.

Zhang Du 張讀, ed. *Xuanshizhi* 宣室志. *Tang Song biji xiaoshuo daguan* 唐宋筆記小說大觀, vol. 1. Yangzhou: Jiangsu guangling guji keyinshe, 1983.

Zhang Junfang 張君房, ed. *Yunji qiqian* 雲笈七籤, ann. Li Yongcheng. Beijing: Zhonghua shuju, 2003.

Zhao Chao 趙超, ed. *Han Wei Liang Jin Nanbeichao muzhi huibian* 漢魏兩晉南北朝墓誌彙編, Tianjin: Tianjin guji chubanshe, 1992.

Zhou Shaoliang 周紹良 and Zhao Chao 趙超, eds. *Tangdai muzhi huibian* 唐代墓誌彙編. Shanghai: Shanghai guji chubanshe, 1992.

SECONDARY SOURCES IN MODERN LANGUAGES

Acharya, Prasanna Kumar. *Architecture of Mānasāra*. New Delhi: Munshiram Manoharlel Publishers Pvt. Ltd., reprinted edition, 1994.

Adamek, Wendi L. *The Mystique of Transmission: On an Early Chan History and Its Contexts*, New York: Columbia University Press, 2007.

Adams, Douglas Q. *A Dictionary of Tocharian B*. Amsterdam: Rodopi, 1999.

Allsen, Thomas T. *The Royal Hunt in Eurasian History*. Philadelphia: University of Pennsylvania Press, 2006.

Amato, Paul. "Rebirth of a Lineage: The Hereditary Household of the Han Celestial Master and Celestial Masters Daoism at Dragon and Tiger Mountain," PhD thesis, Arizona State University, Tempe, 1996.

Ambros, Barbara. *Women in Japanese Religions.* New York: New York University Press, 2015.

Anderson, E. N. "Flowering Apricot: Environment, Practice, Folk Religion and Taoism." In *Daoism and Ecology*, ed. N. J. Girardot, James Miller, and Liu Xiaogan, 157-84. Cambridge, MA: Harvard University Press, 2001.

Anderson, E. N., and Lisa Raphals. "Daoism and Animals." In *A Communion of Subjects: Animals in Religion, Science, and Ethics*, ed. Paul Waldau and Kimberley Patton, 275-90. New York: Columbia University Press, 2006.

Anderson, Poul. "Talking to the Gods: Visionary Divination in Early Daoism (The Sanhuang Tradition)." *Taoist Resources* 5, no. 1 (1994): 1-24.

Arao Toshio 荒尾敏雄. "To Kotei Dōkyō reigenki no ohokan ni tsuite 杜光庭道教靈驗記の應報觀について." *Tōhō shūkyō* 東方宗教 97 (2001): 20-36.

Aristarkhova, Irina. "Thou Shall Not Harm All Living Beings: Feminism, Jainism, and Animals." *Hypatia* 27, no. 3 (2012): 636-50.

Armstrong, Edward A. *Saint Francis: Nature Mystic; The Derivation and Significance of the Nature Stories in the Franciscan Legend.* Berkeley: University of California Press, 1973.

"Art. IV: Notices in Chinese History," *The Chinese Repository* 7, no. 11 (March 1839): 596-97.

Āryaśūra, *Jātakamālā: Or, A Garland of Birth Stories*, trans. Jacob Samuel Speyer. Delhi: Sri Satguru Publications, 1988.

Balazs, Etienne. *Chinese Civilization and Bureaucracy*, ed. Arthur F. Wright, trans, H. M. Wright. New Haven, CT: Yale University Press, 1964.

Barrett, Timothy H. "Finding a Place for Mountains in Chinese Religion: Bibliographic and Ethnographic Perspectives." *Journal of Chinese Studies* 51 (2010): 357-74.

—. "The Monastery Cat in Cross-Cultural Perspective: Cat Poems of the Zen Masters." In *Buddhist Monasticism in East Asia: Places of Practice*, ed. James A. Benn, Lori Meeks, and James Robson, 107-24. London: Routledge, 2009.

—. *The Religious Affiliation of the Chinese Cat: An Essay Towards an Anthropozoological Approach to Comparative Religion.* London: School of Oriental & African Studies, University of London, 1998.

Bartholomeusz, Tessa J. *In Defense of Dharma: Just-War Ideology in Buddhist Sri Lanka.* London: Routledge, 2005.

Bathgate, Michael. *The Fox's Craft in Japanese Religion and Culture: Shapeshifters, Transformations, and Duplicities.* London: Routledge, 2004.

Beggiora, Stefano. "Tigers, Tiger Spirits and Were-tigers in Tribal Orissa." In *Charming Beauties and Frightful Beasts: Non-human Animals in South Asian Myth, Ritual and Folklore*, ed. Fabrizio M. Ferrari and Thomas Dähnhardt, 82-95. Sheffield: Equinox Press, 2013.

Bell, Alexander Peter. *Didactic Narration: Jataka Iconography in Dunhuang with a Catalogue of Jataka Representations in China.* Münster: LIT Verlag, 2000.

Benjamin, Craig. *The Yuezhi: Origin, Migration and the Conquest of Northern Bactria.* Turnhout: Brepols, 2007.

Benn, James, Lori Meeks, and James Robson, eds. *Buddhist Monasticism in East Asia.* London: Routledge,2010.

Berlin, Brent. *Ethnobiological Classification: Principles of Categorization of Plants and Animals in Traditional Societies*, Princeton, NJ: Princeton University Press, 1992.

Bigwood, J. M. "Ctesias' Parrot." *The Classical Quarterly* 43, no. 1 (1993): 321-27.

Blakeley, Donald N. "Listening to the Animals: The Confucian View of Animal Welfare." *Journal of Chinese Philosophy* 30, no. 2 (2003): 137-57.

Bleakley, Alan. *The Animalizing Imagination: Totemism, Textuality and Ecocriticism*. New York: St. Martin's Press, 2000.

Bodiford, William M. "The Enlightenment of Kami and Ghosts: Spirit ordinations in Japanese Sōtō Zen." In *Chan Buddhism in Ritual Context*, ed. Bernard Faure, 250-65. London: RoutledgeCurzon, 2003.

Bokenkamp, Stephen R. *Early Daoist Scriptures*. Berkeley: University of California Press, 1997.

Boomgaard, Peter. *Frontiers of Fear: Tigers and People in the Malay World, 1800–1950*. New Haven, CT: Yale University Press, 2001.

Boucher, Daniel. *Bodhisattvas of the Forest and the Formation of the Mahāyāna: A Study and Translation of the Rāṣṭrapālaparipṛcchā-sūtra*. Honolulu: University of Hawai'i Press, 2008.

Brakke, David. *Demons and the Making of the Monk: Spiritual Combat in Early Christianity*. Cambridge, MA: Harvard University Press, 2006.

Brough, John. "Buddhist Chinese Etymological Notes." *Bulletin of the School of Oriental and African Studies* 38, no. 3 (1975): 581-85.

Brown, Miranda. *The Politics of Mourning in Early China*. Albany: State University of New York Press, 2007.

Cahill, Suzanne E. *Transcendence and Divine Passion: The Queen Mother of the West in Medieval China*. Stanford, CA: Stanford University Press, 1993.

Campany, Robert Ford. "Religious Repertoires and Contestation: A Case Study Based on Buddhist Miracle Tales." *History of Religions* 52, no. 2 (2012): 99-141.

——. *To Live as Long as Heaven and Earth: A Translation and Study of Ge Hong's Traditions of Divine Transcendents*. Berkeley: University of California Press, 2002.

Cao, Deborah. *Animals in China: Law and Society*. Basingstoke: Palgrave Macmillan, 2015.

Carling, Gerd, with Georges-Jean Pinault and Werner Winter, eds. *Dictionary and Thesaurus of Tocharian A, vol. 1: A–J*, Wiesbaden: Otto Harrassowitz Verlag, 2009.

Carroll, Carlos, and Dale G. Miquelle. "Spatial Viability Analysis of Amur Tiger *Panthera tigris altaica* in the Russian Far East: The Role of Protected Areas and Landscape Matrix in Population Persistence." *Journal of Applied Ecology* 43, no. 6 (2006): 1056-68.

Carter, Martha L. "China and the Mysterious Occident: The Queen Mother of the West and Nanā." *Rivista degli studi orientali*, Nuova Series 79, no. 1/4 (2006): 97-129.

Chao Hsin-yi 趙欣怡. *Daoist Ritual, State Religion and Popular Practices: Zhenwu Worship from Song to Ming (960–1644)*. London: Routledge, 2011.

Chapple, Christopher Key. "Animals and Environment in the Buddhist Birth Stories." In *Buddhism and Ecology: The Interconnection of Dharma and Deeds*, ed. Mary Evelyn Tucker and Duncan Ryūken Williams, 131-48. Cambridge, MA: Harvard University Press, 1997.

——. *Karma and Creativity; Nonviolence to Animals, Earth, and Self in Asian Traditions*. Albany: State University of New York Press, 1993.

——. *Nonviolence to Animals, Earth and Self in Asian Traditions*. Albany: State University of New York Press, 1993.

Charlesworth, James H. *The Good and Evil Serpent: How a Universal Symbol Became Christianized*. New Haven, CT: Yale University Press, 2009.

Chen Hsiu-fen. "Wind Malady as Madness in Medieval China: Some Threads From The Dunhuang Medical Manuscript." In *Medieval Chinese Medicine: The Dunhuang Medical Manuscripts*, ed. Vivienne Lo and Christopher Cullen, 345-62. London and New York: Routledge, 2005.

Chen, Huaiyu 陳懷宇. "A Buddhist Classification of Plants and Animals in Early Tang China." *Journal of Asian History* 43, no. 1 (2009): 31–51.

———. *Dongwu yu zhonggu zhengzhi zongjiao zhixu* 動物與中古政治宗教秩序 [Animals in medieval Chinese political and religious order]. Shanghai: Shanghai guji chubanshe, 2012.

———. *The Revival of Buddhist Monasticism in Medieval China*. New York: Peter Lang, 2007.

———. "The Road to Redemption: Killing Snakes in Medieval Chinese Buddhism." *Religions* 10, no. 4 (2019), 247.

———. "Suowei Tangdai jingjiao wenxian liangzhong bianwei bushuo 所謂唐代景教文獻兩種辨偽補說 [Supplementary notes on the authenticity of two so-called Nestorian documents in the Tang dynasty in the Kojima Collection]." *Tang yanjiu* 唐研究3 (1997): 41–52.

———. "Transforming Beasts and Engaging with Local Communities: Tiger Violence in Medieval Chinese Buddhism." *Pakistan Journal of Historical Studies* 3, no. 1 (2018): 31–60.

———. "Yazhou huren chuanshuo zhi wenhuashi bijiao yanjiu 亞洲虎人傳說之文化史比較研究." *Chengda lishi xuebao* 成大歷史學報58 (2020): 21–55.

———. "Yi Liangchu qingzhong yi weili lueshuo Daoxuan lüshi zhi yixue 以量處輕重儀為例略說道宣律師之義學 [Notes on Daoxuan's doctrinal exegesis with special references to *Ritual of Measuring and Handling Light and Heavy Property*]." *Fudan zhexue pinglun* 復旦哲學評論 3 (2006): 78–90.

Chen Tianyi 陳恬儀. "Lishi yu wenxue xushi zhong de Mi Heng 歷史與文學敘事中的禰衡 [Mi Heng in the historical and literary narratives]." *Furen guowen xuebao* 輔仁國文學報 no. 38 (2104): 69–89.

Cheng, Anne. "Filial Piety with a Vengeance: The Tension between Rites and Law in the Han." In *Filial Piety in Chinese Thought and History*, ed. Alan K. L. Chan and Sor-Hoon Tan, 29–43. London: Routledge, 2004.

Chiba Shokan 千葉照観. "Chūgoku ni okeru hōjō shisō no tenkai: seshoku shisō no kannen o chūshin ni 中国における放生思想の展開: 施食思想との関連を中心に." *Tendai gakuhō* 天臺學報 36 (1993): 89–95.

Chou, Yi-Liang (Zhou Yiliang 周一良). "Tantrism in China." *Harvard Journal of Asiatic Studies* 8, no. 3-4 (1945): 235–332.

Ch'u T'ung-tsu 瞿同祖. *Law and Society in Traditional China*. Paris: Mouton, 1961.

———. *Zhongguo falü yu zhongguo shehui*. Beijing: Zhonghua shuju, 1981.

Clough, David. "Putting Animals in Their Place: On the Theological Classification of Animals." In *Animals as Religious Subjects: Transdisciplinary Perspectives*, ed. Celia Deane-Drummond, David L. Clough, and Rebecca Artinian-Kaiser, 209–23. London: Bloomsbury, 2013.

Coggins, Chris. *The Tiger and the Pangolin: Nature, Culture, and Conservation in China*. Honolulu: University of Hawai'i Press, 2003.

Collins, Billie Jean, ed. *A History of the Animal World in the Ancient Near East*, Leiden: Brill, 2002.

Conard, Roswith. "The Domestic Animals in the Cultures of India," *Journal of Indian History* 52 (1974): 76–78.

Copp, Paul. *The Body Incantatory: Spells and the Ritual Imagination in Medieval Chinese*. New York: Columbia University Press, 2014

Crosby, Kate. "Gendered Symbols in Theravada Buddhism: Missed Positives in the Representation of the Female." *Xuanzang foxue yanjiu* 玄奘佛學研究 9 (2009): 31–47.

Daniel, Jivanayakam Cyril. *The Book of Indian Reptiles and Amphibians*. Mumbai: Oxford University Press, 2002.

Davidson, Ronald M. *Indian Esoteric Buddhism: A Social History of the Tantric Movement*. New York: Columbia University Press, 2002.

de Bary, William Theodore et al. *Sources of Chinese Tradition: Volume 1: From Earliest Times to 1600*. New York: Columbia University Press, 2013.

de Groot, Jan Jakob. *The Religious System of China*. Leiden: Brill, 1901.

de Rauw, Tom. "Beyond Buddhist Apology: The Political Use of Buddhism by Emperor Wu of the Liang Dynasty (r. 502-549)," PhD thesis, University of Ghent, 2008.

de Voragine, Jacobus. 1993. *The Golden Legend Readings on the Saints*. Princeton, NJ: Princeton University Press.

Deegalle, Mahinda. "Is Violence Justified in Theravada Buddhism?" *Social Affairs* 1, no. 1 (2014): 83-94.

Deferrari, Roy J., trans. "Life of Malthus." In *Early Christian Biographies*, Fathers of the Church Series, vol. 15, 281-97. Washington, DC: Catholic University of America Press, 1952.

Deloache, Judy S., and Venessa LoBue. "The Narrow Fellow in the Grass: Human Infants Associate Snakes and Fear." *Developmental Science* 12, no. 1 (2009): 201-07.

Despeux, Catherine, and Livia Kohn. *Women in Daoism*. Cambridge, MA: Three Pines Press, 2003.

Dix, Monica. "Saint or Serpent? Engendering the Female Body in Medieval Japanese Buddhist Narratives." In *The Body in Asia*, ed. Brian S. Turner and Zhang Yangwen, 43-58. New York: Berghahn, 2009.

Dudbridge, Glen. *A Portrait of Five Dynasties China: From the Memoirs of Wang Renyu (880–956)*. Oxford: Oxford University Press, 2013.

—. *Religious Experience and Lay Society in T'ang Society: A Reading of Tai Fu's Kuang-I chi*, Cambridge: Cambridge University Press, 2002.

Durkheim, Émile. *The Elementary Forms of Religious Life*, trans. Joseph Ward Swain. Mineola, NY: Dover Publications, 2008.

Dwivedi, O. P. "Satyagraha for Conservation: Awakening the Spirit of Hinduism." In *This Sacred Earth: Religion, Nature, Environment*, ed. Roger S. Gottlieb, 151-63. New York: Routledge, 1996.

Eden, Fanny. *Tigers, Durbars and Kings: Fanny Eden's Indian Journals, 1837–1838*, ed. Janet Durbar. London: John Murray Publishers, 1989.

Edgerton, Franklin. *Buddhist Hybrid Sanskrit Grammar and Dictionary*, 2 vols. New Delhi: Motilal Banarsidass, 1985.

—. *The Pañchatantra Reconstructed*, vol. 2. New Haven, CT: Yale University Press, 1924.

Eichhorn, Werner. "Das Kapitel *Tiger* im T'ai-P'ing Kuang-Chi." *Zeitschrift der Deutschen Morgenländischen Gesellschaft* 104, no. 9, (1954): 140-62.

Eizirik, Eduardo, et al. "Phylogeography, Population History and Conservation Genetics of Jaguars (*Panthera onca*, Mammalia, Felidae)." *Molecular Ecology* 10, no. 1 (2001): 65-79.

Eliade, Mircea. *Patterns in Comparative Religion*. Cleveland, OH: World Publishing Co., 1963.

Ellen, Roy. *The Cultural Relations of Classification: An Analysis of Nuaulu Animal Categories from Central Seram*. Cambridge: Cambridge University Press, 2006.

Elliott, Alison Goddard. *Roads to Paradise: Reading the Lives of the Early Saints*. Hanover, NH: University Press of New England, 1987.

Elvin, Mark. *The Retreat of the Elephants: An Environmental History of China*. New Haven, CT: Yale University Press, 2004.

Emmerick, Ronald E. *Tibetan Texts Concerning Khotan*. London: Oxford University Press, 1967.

Endsjø, Dag Øistein. *Primordial Landscapes, Incorruptible Bodies: Desert Asceticism and the Christian Appropriation of Greek Ideas on Geography, Bodies, and Immortality*. New York: Peter Lang, 2008.

Fan Chengda 范成大. *Riding the River Home: A Complete and Annotated Translation of Fan Chengda's (1120–1193) Diary of a Boat Trip to Wu (Wuchuan Lu)*, trans. James Morris Hargett. Hong Kong: Chinese University of Hong Kong Press, 2008.

Fan Shuying 范淑英. "Cong yiguo xianrui dao shileniao: Tang Xuanzong shiqi dui yingwu xingxiang de yishu yu wenhua suzao 從異國獻瑞到時樂鳥：唐玄宗時期對鸚鵡形象的藝術與文化塑造 [From auspicious offering of foreign countries to the bird of timely joy: The artistic and cultural making of the parrot's images in the Tang emperor Xuanzong's era]." *Xibei meishu* 西北美術 [Fine arts of northwest] 2 (2015): 136–40.

Farmer, Steve, John B. Henderson, and Michael Witzel. "Neurobiology, Layered Texts, and Correlative Cosmologies: A Cross-Cultural Framework for Premodern History." *Bulletin of the Museum of Far Eastern Antiquities* 72 (2000): 48–90.

Faure, Bernard. *The Power of Denial: Buddhism, Purity, and Gender*. Princeton, NJ: Princeton University Press, 2003.

—. "Space and Place in Chinese Religious Traditions." *History of Religions* 26, no. 4 (1987): 337–56.

Fogelin, Lars. *An Archaeological History of Indian Buddhism*. Oxford: Oxford University Press, 2015.

Forte, Antonino. "A Literary Model for Adam: The Dhuta Monastery Inscription." In Paul Pelliot, *L'inscription nestorienne de Si-ngan-fou*, ed. Antonino Forte, 437–87. Kyoto: Italian School of East Asian Studies and Paris: Collège de France, 1996.

—. *Political Propaganda and Ideology in China at the End of the Seventh Century: Inquiry into the Nature, Authors and Function of the Dunhuang Document S. 6502, Followed by an Annotated Translation*. 2nd edition. Kyoto: Scuola Italiana di Studi sull'Asia Orientale, 2005.

Fracasso, Riccardo. "Holy Mothers of Ancient China: A New Approach to the Hsi-wang-mu Problem." *T'oung Pao* 74, no. 1/3 (1988): 1–46.

Franklin, Adrian. *Animals and Modern Cultures: A Sociology of Human–Animal Relations in Modernity*. London: Sage, 1999.

Fraser, Sarah. 2004. *Performing the Visual: The Practice of Buddhist Wall Painting in China and Central Asia, 618–960*. Stanford: Stanford University Press.

Freedman, Maurice. "On the Sociological Study of Chinese Religion." In *Religion and Ritual in Chinese Society*, ed. Arthur P. Wolf, 19–41. Stanford, CA: Stanford University Press, 1974.

Friedmann, Herbert. *A Bestiary for Saint Jerome: Animal Symbolism in European Religious Art*. Washington, DC: Smithsonian Institution Press, 1980.

Fudge, Erica. "A Left-Handed Blow: Writing the History of Animals." In *Representing Animals*, ed. Nigel Rothfels, 3–18. Bloomington: Indiana University Press, 2002.

Fujii Akira 藤井明. "Mikkyo ni okeru satsu to kōfuku 密教における殺と降伏." *Tōyōgaku kenkyū* 東洋学研究 54 (2017): 376–361 (L).

Fujii Kyoko 藤井教公. "Tendai Chigi to bonmōkyō 天台智顗と『梵網経』." *Indogaku bukkyōgaku kenkyū* 印度学仏教学研究 90 (1997): 241–47.

Gan Bao 干寶. *In Search of the Supernatural: The Written Record*, trans. Kenneth J. DeWoskin and James Irving Crump. Stanford, CA: Stanford University Press, 1996.

Gao Yaoting 高曜庭. "Woguo gudai dongwu fenleixue chengjiu de chubu tantao 我國古代動物分類學的初步探討." *Dongwu xuebao* 動物學報 21, no. 4 (1975): 298.

Geertz, Clifford. "Centers, Kings, and Charisma: Reflections on the Symbolics of Power." In *Local Knowledge: Further Essays in Interpretive Anthropology*, 121–46. New York: Basic Books, 2000.

Geissler, Friedmar, and Peter Zieme. "Uigurische *Pañchatantra*-Fragmente." *Turcica* 2 (1970): 32–70.

Gernet, Jacques. *Buddhism in Chinese Society: An Economic History from the Fifth to the Tenth Centuries*, trans. Franciscus Verellen, New York: Columbia University Press, 1995.

——. "Pitié pour les animaux." In *De Dunhuang au Japon: Etudes Chinoises et Bouddhiques offertes à Michel Soymié*, ed. Jean-Pierre Drège, 293–300. Genève: Droz 1996.

——. "Sur le corps et l'esprit chez les Chinois." In *Poikilia: études offertes à Jean-Pierre Vernant*, ed. Gilbert Dagron et al., 369–77. Paris: Ecole des Hautes études en sciences sociales, 1987.

Gethin, Rupert. "Keeping the Buddha's Rule: The View from the Sūtra Piṭaka." In *Buddhism and Law: An Introduction*, ed. Rebecca Redwood French and Mark A. Nathan, 63–77. Cambridge: Cambridge University Press, 2014.

Gilhus, Ingvild Sælid. *Animals, Gods and Humans: Changing Attitudes to Animals in Greek, Roman and Early Christian Ideas*, London: Routledge, 2006.

Glacken, Clarence J. *Traces on the Rhodian Shore: Nature and Culture in Western Thought from Ancient Times to the End of the Eighteenth Century*. Berkeley: University of California Press, 1967.

Goble, Geoffrey C. *Chinese Esoteric Buddhism: Amoghavajra, the Ruling Elite, and the Emergence of a Tradition*. New York: Columbia University Press, 2019.

Goldin, Paul R. "Why Daoism is not Environmentalism?" *Journal of Chinese Philosophy* 32, no. 1 (2005): 76–77.

Goody, Jack. "Religion and Ritual: The Definitional Problem." *The British Journal of Sociology* 12, no. 2 (1961): 142–64.

Goossaert, Vincent. *L'interdit du bœuf en Chine. Agriculture, éthique et sacrifice*. Bibliothèque de l'Institut des hautes études Chinoises, vol. 34. Paris: Collège de France, Institut des hautes études Chinoises, 2005.

Gou Cuihua 苟萃華. "Zhongguo gudai de dongzhiwu fenlei 中國古代的動植物分類." *Kejishi wenji* 科技史文集 4 (1980): 43.

——. *Zhongguo gudai shengwuxue shi* 中國古代生物學史. Beijing: Kexue chubanshe, 1989.

Gou Cuihua et al. "Ye tan Zhongguo gudai de shengwu fenleixue sixiang 也談中國古代的生物分類學思想," *Ziran kexueshi yanjiu* 自然科學史研究 1, no. 4 (1982): 167.

Graham, A. C., trans. *The Book of Lieh-Tzu, a Classic of Tao*. New York: Columbia University Press, 1990.

Graham Jr., William T. "Mi Heng's 'Rhapsody on a Parrot.'" *Harvard Journal of Asiatic Studies* 39, no. 1 (1979): 39–54.

Grant, Robert M. *Early Christians and Animals*. London: Routledge, 1999.

Gray, David B. "Compassionate Violence?: On the Ethical Implications of Tantric Buddhist Ritual." *Journal of Buddhist Ethics* 14 (2007): 239–71.

Green, Susie. *Tiger*. London: Reaktion Books, 2006.

Gregory, Peter N. *Tsung-mi and the Sinification of Buddhism*. Honolulu: University of Hawai'i Press, 2002.

Gross, Aaron. *The Question of the Animal and Religion: Theoretical Stakes, Practical Implications*. New York: Columbia University Press, 2015.

Gross, Gita M. *Buddhism After Patriarchy: A Feminist History, Analysis, and Reconstruction of Buddhism*. Albany: State University of New York Press, 1993.

Grünwedel, Albert. *Alt-Kutscha*. Berlin: D. Reimer, 1920.

Guo, Fu 郭郛, Li Yuese (Joseph Needham), and Cheng Qingtai 成慶泰. *Zhongguo gudai dongwuxue shi* 中國古代動物學史. Beijing: Kexue chubanshe, 1999.

Haksar, A. N. D. *Shuka Saptati: Seventy Tales of the Parrot*. New Delhi: HarperCollins Publishers, 2000.

Hamar, Imre. *A Religious Leader in the Tang: Chengguan's Biography*. Tokyo: International Institute for Buddhist Studies of the International College for Advanced Buddhist Studies, 2002.

Hammond, Charles. "An Excursion in Tiger Lore," *Asia Major* 3rd series 4, no. 1 (1991): 87–100.

—. "The Righteous Tiger and the Grateful Lion." *Monumenta Serica* 43 (1996): 191–211.

Han Jishao 韓吉紹 *Daojiao liandanshu yu Zhongwai wenhua jiaoliu* 道教煉丹術與中外文化交流. Beijing: Zhonghua shuju, 2015.

Hansen, Valerie. *Changing Gods in Medieval China, 1127–1276*. Princeton, NJ: Princeton University Press, 1990.

Hargett, James M. "Playing Second Fiddle: The Luan-Bird in Early and Medieval Chinese Literature," *T'oung Pao* 2nd series 75, no. 4/5 (1989): 235–62.

Harris, Elizabeth J. "The Female in Buddhism." In *Buddhist Women across Cultures: Realizations*, ed. Karma Lekshe Tsomo, 49–65. Albany: State University of New York Press, 1999.

—. "Violence and Disruption in Society: A Study of the Early Buddhist Texts." Wheel Publication No. 392/393. Colombo, Sri Lanka: Ecumenical Institute for Study and Dialogue, 1994.

Harris, Marvin. "The Cultural Ecology of India's Sacred Cattle," *Current Anthropology* 33, no. 1, Supplement: Inquiry and Debate in the Human Sciences: Contributions from Current Anthropology, 1960-1990 (1992): 261–76.

Harrison, Paul M. "Searching for the Origins of the Mahāyāna: What are We Looking for?" *Eastern Buddhist* 28, no. 1 (1995): 48–69.

Hayward, Gregory D., Dale G. Miquelle, Evgeny N. Smirnov, and Chris Nations. "Monitoring Amur Tiger Populations: Characteristics of Track Surveys in Snow." *Wildlife Society Bulletin* 30, no. 4 (2002): 1150–59.

He Xiaorong 何孝榮. "Lun Wei Gao yu fojiao 論韋皋與佛教 [On Wei Gao and Buddhism]." *Xinan daxue xuebao* 西南大學學報 38, no. 5 (2012): 154–59.

Herrington, Sandra. "Subspecies and the Conservation of *Panther tigris*: Preserving Genetic Heterogeneity." In *Tigers of the World: The Biology, Biopolitics, Management and Conservation of an Endangered Species*, ed. Ronald L. Tilson and Ulysses S. Seal, 512–60. Park Ridge, NJ: Notes Publications, 1987.

Ho, Chiew Hui. *Diamond Sutra Narratives: Textual Production and Lay Religiosity in Medieval China*. Leiden: Brill, 2019.

Hobgood-Oster, Laura. *Holy Dogs and Asses: Animals in the Christian Tradition*. Urbana and Chicago: University of Illinois Press, 2008.

Hoernle, A. F. Rudolf. *Manuscript Remains of Buddhist Literature Found in Eastern Turkestan*. Oxford: Clarendon Press, 1916.

Hokazono, Koichi 外薗幸一. "Butten toshite no Śākyasiṃhajātaka nitsuite 仏傳としての Śākyasiṃhajātaka について." *Indogaku bukkyōgaku kenkyū* 印度學仏教學研究 36, no. 1 (1987): 403–401 (L).

Holcombe, Charles. *In the Shadow of the Han: Literati Thought and Society at the Beginning of the Southern Dynasties.* Honolulu: University of Hawai'i Press, 1994.

Horner, Isaline Blew, trans. *The Book of the Discipline* (Vinaya-Pitaka), vol. 4: Mahāvagga. London: Luzac & Co, 1963.

—. *Women Under Primitive Buddhism: Laywomen and Almswomen.* London: Routledge, 1930.

Hou, Ching-lang 侯錦郎. "The Chinese Belief in Baleful Stars." In *Facets of Taoism: Essays in Chinese Religion*, ed. Holmes Welch and Anna Seidel, 193-228. New Haven, CT: Yale University Press, 1979.

Hou Xudong 侯旭東. *Beichao cunmin de shenghuo shijie: Chaoting, Zhouxian yu cunli* 北朝村民的生活世界: 朝廷、州縣與村里. Beijing: Shangwu yinshuguan, 2005.

Hsieh Shu-wei 謝世維. "Zhonggu daojiao shi zhong de Sanhuangwen chuantong yanjiu 中古道教史中的三皇文傳統研究." *Qinghua xuebao* 清華學報 44, no. 1 (2014): 29-60.

—. "Chuanshou yu ronghe: *Taiji wuzhenren song* yanjiu 傳授與融合：太極五真人頌研究," *Zhongyanyuan wenzhesuo jikan* 中研院文哲所集刊 34 (2009): 249-85.

Hu Fengdan 胡鳳丹. *Yingwuzhou xiaozhi* 鸚鵡洲小志 (*A Gazetteer of the Parrot Island*). Wuhan: Hubei jiaoyu chubanshe, 2002.

Huang, I-mei 黃依妹. "Kaisatu Hōjō to Jin no shiso," *Oryō shigaku* 13 (1987): 29-55.

Huang Yong 黃勇 *Daojiao biji xiaoshuo yanjiu* 道教筆記小說研究 (Chengdu: Sichuan daxue chubanshe, 2007.

Huang Zheng 黃徵 and Wu Wei 吳偉, eds. *Dunhuang yuanwen ji* 敦煌願文集. Changsha: Yuelu shushe, 1995.

Huang Zhengjian 黃正建. "Shi lun Tangdai qianqi huangdi xiaofei de mouxie cemian: yi Tongdian juanliu suoji changgong wei zhongxin 試論唐代前期皇帝消費的某些側面：以通典卷六所記常貢為中心." *Tang yanjiu* 唐研究 6 (2000): 173-212.

Hulsewé, A. F. P. *Remnants of Han Law*, Leiden: Brill, 1955.

Huntington, Rania. *Alien Kind: Foxes and Late Imperial Chinese Narrative.* Cambridge, MA: Harvard University Press, 2004.

Huo Wei 霍巍. "Hurenyong, Youyi shenshou, Xiwangmu tuxiang de kaocha yu Han Jin shiqi Zhongguo xinan de Zhong Wai wenhua jiaoliu 胡人俑、有翼神獸、西王母圖像的考察與漢晉時期中國西南的中外文化交流," *Jiuzhou xuelin* 九州學林 1, no. 2 (2003): 36-92.

Hurvitz, Leon, trans. *Scripture of the Lotus Blossom of the Fine Dharma.* New York: Columbia University Press, 1982.

Idema, Wilt L. "Guanyin's Parrot: A Chinese Buddhist Animal Tale and Its International Context." In *India, Tibet, China: Genesis and Aspects of Traditional Narrative*, ed. Alfredo Cadonna 103-50. Firenze: Leo S. Olschki, 1999.

—. *Insects in Chinese Literature: A Study and Anthology.* Amherst, NY: Cambria Press, 2019.

—. *Mouse vs. Cat in Chinese Literature: Tales and Commentary.* Seattle: University of Washington Press, 2019.

Idema, Wilt M., trans. *Personal Salvatio n and Filial Piety: Two Precious Scroll Narratives of Guanyin and Her Acolytes.* Honolulu: University of Hawai'i Press, 2008.

Ikeda On 池田溫. "Chūgoku kodai no mōjū taisaku hōki 中国古代の猛獣対策法規." In *Ritsuryōsei no shomondai: Takikawa Masajirō Hakushi beiju kinen ronshū* 律令制の諸問題：瀧川政次郎博士米寿記念論集, ed. Takikawa Hakushi Beiju Kinenkai, 611-37. Tokyo: Kyūko Shoin, 1984.

Isbell, Lynne A. *The Fruit, the Tree, and the Serpent: Why We See So Well.* Cambridge, MA: Harvard University Press, 2009.

—. "Snakes as Agents of Evolutionary Change in Primate Brains." *Journal of Human Evolution* 51, no. 1 (2006): 1–35.

Jaini, Padmanabh S. "Indian Perspectives on the Spirituality of Animals." In *Buddhist Philosophy and Culture: Essays in Honour of N. A. Jayawickrema*, ed. David J. Kalupahana and W. G. Weeraratne, 169–78. Colombo, Sri Lanka: N. A. Jayawickrema Felicitation Volume Committee, 1987.

Jansen, Thomas. *Höfische Öffentlichkeit im frühmittelalterlichen China. Debatten im Salon des Prinzen Xiao Ziliang*. Freibourg: Rombach Verlag, 2000.

Jenkins, Stephen. "On the Auspiciousness of Compassionate Violence." *Journal of International Association for Buddhist Studies* 33, no. 1–2 (2011): 299–331.

Jennbert, Kristina. "Sheep and Goats in Norse Paganism." In *PECUS. Man and Animal in Antiquity*, ed. Barbro Santillo Frizell, 160–66. Rome: The Swedish Institute in Rome, 2004.

Jerryson, Michael K. *Buddhist Fury: Religion and Violence in Southern Thailand*. New York: Oxford University Press, 2011.

Jerryson, Michael, and Mark Juergensmeyer, eds. *Buddhist Warfare*. New York: Oxford University Press, 2010.

Ji Xianlin 季羨林, with Werner Winter and Georges-Jean Pinault, eds. *Fragments of the Tocharian A Maitreyasamiti-Nāṭaka of the Xinjiang Museum, China*, Berlin: Mouton de Gruyter, 1998.

Jin, Yingkun 金瀅坤 and Liu Yonghai 劉永海. "Dunhuang ben Dayunjing shu xinlun: yi Wu Zetian chengdi wei zhongxin 敦煌本大雲經疏新論：以武則天稱帝為中心 [A new perspective on the Dunhuang manuscript the *Commentary on the Great Cloud Scripture*: With special reference to Wu Zetian's Enthronement]." *Wenshi* 文史 (*Literature and History*) 4 (2009): 31–46.

Jones, Charles. "Foundations of Ethics and Practice in Chinese Pure Land Buddhism." *Journal of Buddhist Ethics* 10 (2003): 1–20.

—. "Toward a Typology of Nien-fo: A Study in Methods of Buddha-Invocation in Chinese Pure Land Buddhism." *Pacific World: Journal of the Institute of Buddhist Studies*. 3rd series, 3 (2001): 219–39.

Jülch, Thomas. *Bodhisattva der Apologetik: die Mission des buddhistischen Tang-Mönchs Falin (Bodhisattva of Apologetics: the Mission of the Tang Buddhist monk Falin)*. 3 vols. München: Utz, 2014.

Kamitsuka Yoshiko 神塚淑子. *Dōkyō kyōten no keisei to bukkyō* 道教経典の形成と仏教. Nagoya: Nagoya Daigaku Shuppankai, 2017.

—. "Rikuchō Reihōkyō mieru Kōsenko 六朝霊宝経に見える葛仙公." In *Sankyō kōshō ronsō* 三教交渉論叢, ed. Mugitani Kunio, 1–46. Kyoto: Kyōto daigaku jinbun kagaku kenkyūjo, 2005.

Kanai Noriyuki 金井徳幸. "Sodai no ki u ki hare: Tokuni shu kenka no go o megurite 宋代の祈雨祈晴: 特に州県下の郷をめぐりて." *Risshō daigaku tōyōshi ronshū* 立正大學東洋史論集 19 (2015): 1–15.

Kang Xiaofei 康笑菲. *The Cult of the Fox: Power, Gender, and Popular Religion in Late Imperial and Modern China*. New York: Columbia University Press, 2006.

Katz, Paul. *Demon Hordes and Burning Boats: The Cult of Marshal Wen in Late Imperial Cheikiang*. Albany: State University of New York Press, 1995.

Kawano Akimasa 川野明正. "Jako to tobyo nichi kan chu no reibutsu shinko ni miru tokutei katei seisui no densho 蛇蟲とトウビョウ:日韓中の霊物信仰にみる特定家庭盛衰の伝承 (2)." *Jinbun gakuhō* 人文學報 374 (2006): 57–130.

Keil, Frank C. "The Roots of Folk Biology." *Proceedings of the National Academy of Sciences of the United States of America* 110, no 40 (2013): 15857-58.

Kelsey, W. Michael. "Salvation of the Snake, The Snake of Salvation: Buddhist-Shinto Conflict and Resolution." *Japanese Journal of Religious Studies* 8, no. 1-2 (1981): 83-113.

Kieschnick, John. *The Eminent Monk: Buddhist Ideals in Medieval Chinese Hagiography.* Honolulu: University of Hawai'i Press, 1997.

——. *A Primer in Chinese Buddhist Writings, Supplement: Epigraphy.* Stanford, CA: Stanford University, 2016. Accessed July 14, 2022. https://religiousstudies.sites.stanford.edu/sites/g/files/sbiybj5946/f/primer-epigraphy-supplement-part-1.pdf.

——. *The Impact of Buddhism on Chinese Material Culture.* Princeton, NJ: Princeton University Press, 2003.

Kleeman, Terry F. "Daoism and the Quest for Order." In *Daoism and Ecology,* ed. N. J. Girardot, James Miller, and Liu Xiaogan, 61-70. Cambridge, MA: Harvard University Press, 2001.

——. "The Expansion of the Wen-ch'ang Cult." In *Religion and Society in T'ang and Sung China,* ed. Patricia B. Ebrey and Peter N. Gregory (Honolulu: University of Hawai'i Press, 1989), 45-73.

Klein, Susan. "Woman as Serpent: The Demonic Feminine in the Noh Play Dōjōji." In *Religious Reflections on the Human Body,* ed. Jane Marie Law, 100-36. Bloomington: University of Indiana Press, 1995.

Knapp, Keith. "The Meaning of Birds on Hunping (Spirit Jars): The Religious Imagination of Second to Fourth century Jiangnan." *Azjiske študije/ Asian Studies* 7, no. 2 (2019): 153-72.

——. "The Use and Understanding of Domestic Animals in Medieval Northern China." *Early Medieval China* 25 (2019): 85-99.

——. "Noble Creatures: Filial and Righteous Animals in Early Medieval Confucian Thought." In *Animals through Chinese History: Earliest Times to 1911,* ed. Roel Sterckx, Martina Siebert, and Dagmar Schäfer, 64-83. Cambridge: Cambridge University Press, 2019.

Knechtges, David R., trans. *Wenxuan or Selections of Refined Literature* [by Xiao Tong]. Princeton, NJ: Princeton University Press, 1996.

Knoblock, John, and Jeffrey Riegel, trans. *The Annals of Lü Buwei.* Stanford, CA: Stanford University Press, 2000.

Kohn, Livia. *The Daoist Monastic Manual: A Translation of the Fengdao Kejie,* New York: Oxford University Press, 2004.

——. "Steel Holy Food and Come Back as a Viper: Conceptions of Karma and Rebirth in Medieval Daoism." *Early Medieval China* 4 (1999): 1-48.

Koopmans-de Bruijn, Ria. "Fabled Liaisons: Serpentine Spouses in Japanese Folktales." In *JAPANimals: History and Culture in Japan's Animal Life,* ed. Gregory M. Pflugfelder and Brett L. Walker, 60-88. Ann Arbor: Center for Japanese Studies, University of Michigan, 2005

Kudo Noriyuki 工藤順之. *The Karmavibhanga: Transliterations and Annotations of the Original Sanskrit Manuscripts from Nepal.* Tokyo: The International Research Institute for Advanced Buddhology, 2013.

Kutcher, Norman. *Mourning in Late Imperial China.* Cambridge: Cambridge University Press, 1999.

Kuwatani, Yuken 桑谷祐顕. "Hōjō shisō ni okeru kyōsei 放生思想における共生." *Nihon bukkyō gakkai nenhō* 日本佛教學會年報64 (1999): 213-27.

La, Na Hee. 2003. "Ideology and Religion in Ancient Korea," *Korea Journal* 43: 4, 10-29.

Lai Chi-tim 黎志添. "The Demon Statutes of Nüqing and the Problem of the Bureaucratization of the Netherworld in Early Heavenly Master Daoism," *T'oung Pao* 88, no. 4/5 (2002):
251–81.

Lai Ruihe, *Tangdai zhongceng wenguan*, chap. 4. Taipei: Lianjing chuban gongsi, 2008.

Lama, Stephanie Tawa. "The Hindu Goddess and Women's Political Representation in South
Asia: Symbolic Resource or Feminine Mystique?" *Revue Internationale de Sociologie* 11, no. 1
(2001): 5–20.

Lamotte, Étienne. *History of Indian Buddhism: From the Origins to the Śaka Era*, trans. Sara Webb-
Boin. Louvain: Université Catholique de Louvain, Institut Orientaliste, 1088.

Lau, D. C. 劉殿爵 trans. *Confucius: The Analects*. Hong Kong: The Chinese University Press, 1992.

Law, Bimal Churn. "Animals in Early Jain and Buddhist Literature." *Indian Culture* 12, no. 1 (1945):
1–13.

Le Aiguo 樂愛國. *Daojiao shengtaixue* 道教生態學. Beijing: Shehui kexue wenxian chubanshe,
2005.

Lecky, William Edward Hartpole. *History of European Morals from Augustus to Charlemagne*, 2 vols.
New York: D. Appleton and Company, 1876.

Le Coq, Albert von. *Chotscho: Facsimile-Wiedergaben der wichtigeren Funde der ersten königlich pre-
ussischen Expedition nach Turfan in Ost-turkistan*, Berlin: D. Reimer, 1913.

——. *Die buddhistische Spätantike in Mittelasien*, vols. 1–5. Berlin: D. Reimer, 1922–1926.

Le Coq, Albert von, and Ernst Waldschmidt, eds., "Neue Bildwerke II." In *Die buddhistische
Spätantike in Mittelasien*, vol. 6. Berlin: D. Reimer, 1928.

Lei Wen 雷聞. "Qiyu yu Tangdai shehui yanjiu 祈雨與唐代社會研究." *Guoxue yanjiu* 國學研究 8
(2001): 245–89.

Lévi, Sylvain, and E. Chavannes. "Les seize arhat protecteurs de la Loi." *Journal Asiatique* 2, no. 8
(1900): 189–304.

Lewis, Gilbert. *Day of Shining Red: An Essay on Understanding Ritual*. Cambridge: Cambridge University, 1980.

Lewis, Michael. "Indian Science for Indian Tigers? Conservation Biology and the Question of
Cultural Values." *Journal of the History of Biology* 38, no. 2 (2005): 185–207.

Li Jinshan 李錦山. *Lunan Han huaxiangshi yanjiu* 魯南漢畫像石研究 (Beijing: Zhishi chanquan
chubanshe, 2008.

——. "Xiwangmu ticai huaxiangshi jiqi xiangguan wenti 西王母題材畫像石及其相關問題,"
Zhongyuan wenwu 中原文物 4 (1994): 56–66.

Li Juan 李娟. "Tangdai yingwu gushi de fojiao yinyuan 唐代鸚鵡故事的佛教因緣 [The Buddhist
affinity of the parrot story in the Tang dynasty]." *Wutaishan yanjiu* 五台山研究 [Studies on
Mount Wutai] 1 (2009): 25–29.

Li Xiaorong 李小榮. "Zhengzhi, zongjiao yu wenxue: Yan Zhaoyin Yingwu mao'er pian fafu 政
治、宗教與文學: 閻朝隱《鸚鵡貓兒篇》發覆 [Politics, religion, and literature: A reading of Yan
Zhaoyin's writing on parrot and cat]." *Fujian shifan daxue xuebao* 福建師範大學學報 no. 5
(2013): 65–72.

Lin Fu-shih 林富士. "The Images and Status of Shamans in Ancient China. In *Early Chinese Religion*, Part 1, ed. John Lagerwey and Marc Kalinowski, 397–458. Leiden: Brill, 2009.

Lin Shitian 林世田. "Wuzetian chengdi yu tuchen xiangrui: yi S. 6502 Dayunjing shu wei
zhongxin 武則天稱帝與圖讖祥瑞: 以 S. 6502 大雲經疏為中心 (The Enthronement of Wu
Zetian and the Auspicious Signs of the Illustrated Prognostics: With Special Reference to

the S. 6502 the *Commentary on the Great Cloud Scripture*)" *Dunhuangxue jikan* 敦煌學輯刊 (*Dunhuang Studies Quarterly*) 2 (2002): 64–72.

Lippiello, Tiziana. *Auspicious Omens and Miracles in Ancient China: Han, Three Kingdoms and Six Dynasties*. Sankt Augustin: Monumenta Serica Institute, 2001.

Liu Houbin 劉後濱. "Tangdai xianling de xuanshou 唐代縣令的選授." *Zhongguo lishi bowuguan guankan* 中國歷史博物館館刊 3 (2007): 51–58.

Liu Xiaogan 劉笑敢. "Laozi's Philosophy: Textual and Conceptual Analyses." In *Dao Companion to Daoist Philosophy*, ed. Liu Xiaogan, 71–100. Berlin: Springer.

Liu Yukou 列禦寇. 1990. *The Book of Lieh-tzŭ: A Classic of the Tao*, trans. A. C. Graham. New York: Columbia University Press.

Liu Zongyuan 柳宗元. "Bushezhe shuo 捕蛇者說" and "Zhashuo 褶說." In *Quang Tan wen*, juan 584, 5898–99. Beijing: Zhonghua shuju, 1983.

——. "Catching Snakes," trans. Herbert Giles. In *Classical Chinese Literature: An Anthology of Translations. Vol. 1: From Antiquity to the Tang Dynasty*, ed. John Minford, 1010. New York: Columbia University Press, 2000.

Lloyd, Geoffrey E. R. *Ancient Worlds, Modern Reflections: Philosophical Perspectives on Greek and China*. Oxford: Oxford University Press, 2006.

LoBue, Vanessa, David H. Rakison, and Judy S. DeLoache. "Threat Perception Across the Life Span: Evidence for Multiple Converging Pathways." *Current Directions in Psychological Science* 19, no. 6 (2010): 375–79.

LoBue, Vanessa, and Judy S. DeLoache. "Detecting the Snake in the Grass: Attention to Fear-Relevant Stimuli by Adults and Young Children." *Psychological Science* 19, no. 3 (2008): 284–89.

Loewe, Michael. *Divination, Mythology and Monarchy in Han China*. Cambridge: Cambridge University Press, 1994.

Lü Pengzhi 呂鵬志. *Tang qianqi Daojiao yishi shigang* 唐前期道教儀式史綱. Beijing: Zhonghua shuju, 2008.

Lü Zongli 呂宗力. *Power of the Words: Chen Prophecy in Chinese Politics, AD 265–518*. Bern: Peter Lang, 2003.

Luo Manling 羅曼玲. "Remembering Kaiyuan and Tianbao: The Construction of Mosaic Memory in Medieval Historical Miscellanies." *T'oung Pao* 97, no. 4/5 (2011): 263–300.

MacKenzie, D. N. "Buddhist Terminology in Sogdian: A Glossary." *Asia Major* 18, no. 1 (1971): 28–89.

——. *The Sūtra of the Causes and Effects of Actions in Sogdian*. London Oriental Series 22. London: Oxford University Press, 1970.

Magnin, Paul. "Donateurs et joueurs en l'honneur de Buddha." In *De Dunhuang au Japon, Études chinoises et bouddhiques offertes à Michel Soymié*, ed. Jean-Pierre Drège, 103–38. Genève: Librairie Droz, 1996.

Mainka, Susan A., and Judy A. Mills. "Wildlife and Traditional Chinese Medicine: Supply and Demand for Wildlife Species." *Journal of Zoo and Wildlife Medicine* 26, no. 2 (1995): 193–200.

Majupuria, Trilok Chandra. *Sacred Animals of Nepal and India*. Lashkar: M. Devi, 2000.

——. *Sacred and Symbolic Animals of Nepal: Animals in the Art, Culture, Myths and Legends of the Hindus and Buddhists*. Kathmandu: Sahayogi Prakashan Tripureswar, 1977.

Mangum, Teresa. "Dog Years, Human Fears." In *Representing Animals*, ed. Nigel Rothfels 35–37. Bloomington: Indiana University Press, 2002.

Marks, Robert B. *Tigers, Rice, Silk, and Silt: Environment and Economy in Late Imperial South China.* Cambridge: Cambridge University Press, 1998.

Marshak, Boris I. *Legends, Tales, and Fables in the Art of Sogdiana.* New York: Bibliotheca Persica Press, 2002.

—. "The Tiger, Raised from the Dead: Two Murals from Panjikent," *Bulletin of the Asia Institute,* New Series 10 (1996): 207-17.

Marshak, Boris I., and Franz Grenet. "L'arte sogdiana (IV-IX secolo)." In *Le arti in Asia Centrale,* ed. Pierre Chuvin, 114-63. Milano: Garzanti, 2002.

Mason, David A. *The Spirit of the Mountain: Korea's San-Shin and Traditions of Mountain Worship.* Seoul: Hollym, 1999.

Masubuchi Tatsuo 増淵龍夫. *Chūgoku kodai no shakai to kokka* 中国古代の社会と国家 (*Society and State in Ancient China*). Tokyo: Iwanami Shoten, 1996.

Mather, Richard B. "Wang Chin's 'Dhūta Temple Stele Inscription' as an Example of Buddhist Parallel Prose." *Journal of American Oriental Society* 83, no 3 (1963): 338-59.

Matsumae Takeshi 松前健. "Kodaikanzoku no ryu ja suhai to oken 古代韓族の竜蛇崇拝と王権." *Chōsen gakuhō* 朝鮮學報 57 (1970): 1-22.

Mayo, Lewis. "The Order of Birds in Guiyi jun Dunhuang." *East Asian History* 20 (2000): 1-59.

McDermott, James P. "Animals and Humans in Early Buddhism," *Indo-Iranian Journal* 32, no. 2, (1989): 269-80.

McMullen, David. "Bureaucrats and Cosmology: The Ritual Code of T'ang China." *Ritual of Royalty: Power and Ceremonial in Traditional Societies,* ed. David Cannadine and Simon Price, 181-236. Cambridge: Cambridge University Press, 1987.

McRae, John. *The Northern School and the Formation of Early Ch'an Buddhism.* Honolulu: University of Hawai'i Press, 1986.

Metzger, Thomas A. "Was Neo-Confucianism 'Tangential' to the Elite Culture of Late Imperial China?" *The American Asian Review* 4, no. 1 (1986): 1-33.

Michael, Thomas. "Mountains and Early Daoism in the Writings of Ge Hong." *History of Religions* 56, no. 1 (2016): 23-54.

Milburn, Olivia. *The Spring and Autumn Annals of Master Yan.* Leiden: Brill, 2015.

Minagawa Masaki 皆川雅樹. "Ōmu no zōtō: nihon kōdai taigai kankeishi kenkyū no hitokoma 鸚鵡の贈答−日本古代対外関係史研究の一齣 [The parrot as the gift: One observation on studying the history of foreign relations in ancient Japan]." In *Nihon kodai ōken to karamono kōeki* 日本古代王権と唐物交易 [The kingship of ancient Japan and the material exchanges with Tang China], ed. Yano Ken'ichi and Ri Kō. Tokyo: Yoshikawa Kōbunkan, 2007.

Miya Noriko 宮紀子. "Ryukosan shi kara mita mongoru meireibun no sekai: shoichikyō kyōdan kenkyū josetsu 龍虎山志からみたモンゴル命令文の世界:正一教教團研究序説." *Tōyōshi kenkyū* 東洋史研究 63, no. 2 (2004): 94-128.

Miyazawa Masayori 宮沢正順. "Dōkyō reigenki ni tsuite 道教霊験記について." *Sanko bunka kenkyūjō nenhō* 三康文化研究所年報 通号 18 (1986): 1-38.

Moazami, Mahnaz. "Evil Animals in the Zoroastrian Religion." *History of Religion* 44, no. 4 (2005): 300-17.

Mollier, Christine. *Buddhism and Taoism Face to Face: Scripture, Ritual, and Iconographic Exchange in Medieval China.* Honolulu: University of Hawai'i Press, 2008.

Monier-Williams, Monier. *A Sanskrit-English Dictionary.* New Delhi: Asian Educational Services, 2009.

Morgan, Diane. *Snakes in Myth, Magic, and History: The Story of a Human Obsession.* Westport, CT: Praeger, 2008.

Mundkur, Balaji. *The Cult of the Serpent: An Interdisciplinary Survey of Its Manifestations and Origins.* Albany: State University of New York Press, 1983.

Nakamura Fumi 中村史. "*Mahabarata* dai jusan kan omu to indora no taiwa no kosatsu マハーバーラタ第13巻 '鸚鵡とインドラ' の対話の考察 [*Mahābhārata*, vol. 13: A study on the conversation between parrot and Indra]." *Indo tetsugaku Bukkyōgaku* 印度哲學佛教學 (*Studies on Indian Philosophy and Buddhism*) no. 22 (2007): 288–98.

—. "Omu to indora no taiwa *mahabarata* dai jusan kan dai go sho no setsuwa wayaku kenkyū 鸚鵡とインドラの対話–『マハーバーラタ』第13巻第5章の説話-和訳研究 [The conversation between parrot and Indra: Japanese translation and study on the story in *Mahābhārata*, vol. 13, ch. 5]." *Otaru Shouka Daigaku Jinbun Kenkyū* 小樽商科大学人文研究 [*Humanities Research of Otaru Business University*] no. 115 (2008): 195–209.

Namura Takatsuna 苗村高綱. "Chigi daishi no hōjōchi ni tsuite 智者大師の放生池について." *Shūgakuin ronjū* 宗学院論輯 22 (1976): 72–85.

Nattier, Jan. *A Guide to the Earliest Chinese Buddhist Translations: Texts from the Eastern Han and Three Kingdoms Periods.* Tokyo: The International Research Institute for Advanced Buddhology, Soka University, 2008.

Needham, Joseph, and Gwei-djen Lu 魯桂珍. *Science and Civilisation in China: Volume 5, Chemistry and Chemical Technology,* pt. 5. Cambridge: Cambridge University Press.

Nelson, Janet. *Politics and Ritual in Early Medieval Europe.* London: Hambledon Press, 1986.

Nienhauser William H., ed. and trans. *The Grand Scribe's Records: Volume I, The Basic Annals of Pre-Han China.* Bloomington: Indiana University Press, 2018.

Norman, K. R. "Middle Indo-Aryan." In *Indo-European Numerals,* ed. Jadranka Gvozdanovich, 199–241. Berlin: Mouton de Gruyter, 1992.

—. "Solitary as Rhinoceros Horn." *Buddhist Studies Review* 13 (1996): 133–42.

Nyland, Michael. "Confucian Piety and Individualism in Han China." *Journal of American Oriental Society* 116 (1996): 1–27.

Ogata Isamu 尾形勇. *Chūgoku kodai no ie, to kokka: Kōtei shihaika no chitsujo kōzō* 中國古代の「家」と國家: 皇帝支配下の秩序構造. Tokyo: Iwanami Shoten, 1979.

Ohnuma, Reiko. "The Gift of the Body and the Gift of Dharma." *History of Religions* 37, no. 4 (1998): 323–59.

—. *Head, Eyes, Flesh, and Blood: Giving Away the Body in Indian Buddhist Literature.* New York: Columbia University Press, 2007.

—. *Unfortunate Destiny: Animals in the Indian Buddhist Imagination.* New York: Oxford University Press, 2017.

Oldenberg, Hermann. *Die Religion des Veda.* Berlin: Verlag von Wilhelm Hertz, 1894; second edition, 1916. [English version] *The Religion of the Veda,* trans. Shridhar B. Shrotri. Delhi: Motilal Banarsidass, 1988.

Olsen, Sandra L., Susan Grant, Alice M Choyke, and Laszlo Bartosiewicz. *Horses and Humans: The Evolution of the Human-Equine Relationship.* British Archaeological Report, International Series 1560, Oxford, 2006.

Ölmez, M. "Ein weiteres alttürkischen Pañchatantra-Fragment." *Ural-Altaische Jahrbücher* N. F. 12 (1993): 179–91.

Page, Tony. *What Does Buddhism Say About Animals.* London: UVAKIS Publications, 1998.

Paul, Diana Y. *Women in Buddhism: Images of the Feminine in the Mahāyāna Tradition.* Berkeley: University of California Press, 1985.

Pepperberg, Irene Maxine. *The Alex Studies: Cognitive and Communicative Abilities of Grey Parrots.* Cambridge, MA: Harvard University Press, 1999.

Peterson, Anna. "Review: Religious Studies and the Animal Turn." *History of Religions* 56, no. 2 (2016): 232–45.

Phelps, Norm. *The Great Compassion: Buddhism and Animal Rights.* New York: Lantern Books., 2004.

Phineas, Charles. "Household Pets and Urban Alienation," *Journal of Social History* 7 (1974): 3, 338–43.

Pinault, Georges-Jean. "Concordance des manuscrits tokhariens du fonds Pelliot [Concordance of the Tocharian Manuscripts of the Pelliot Collection]." In *Instrumenta Tocharica*, ed. Melanie Malzahn, 163–219. Heidelberg: Winter Verlag, 2007.

Posey, Darrell and William Leslie Overal, eds. *Ethnobiology: Implications and Applications. Proceedings of the First International Congress of Ethnobiology.* Belém: Museu Paraense Emílio Goeldi, 1990.

Pregadio, Fabrizio. *Great Clarity: Daoism and Alchemy in Early Medieval China.* Stanford, CA: Stanford University Press, 2006.

Pu Chengzhong 蒲成中. *Ethical Treatment of Animals in Early Chinese Buddhism: Beliefs and Practices.* Newcastle upon Tyne: Cambridge Scholars Publishing, 2014.

Puett, Michael J. *Ambivalence of Creation: Debates Concerning Innovation and Artifice in Early China.* Stanford, CA: Stanford University Press, 2000.

——. "Humans, Spirits, and Sages in Chinese Late Antiquity: Ge Hong's *Master Who Embraces Simplicity (Baopuzi).*" *Extrême-Orient, Extrême-Occident.* 29 (2007): 95–119.

Pulleyblank, Edwin G. "Why Tocharians?" *Journal of Indo-European Studies* 23 (1995): 427–48.

Qiu Luming 仇鹿鳴. "Quanli yu guanzhong: Dezhengbei suojian Tangdai de zhongyang yu difang 權力與觀眾：德政碑所見唐代的中央與地方." In *Chang'an yu Hebei zhijian: Zhongwan Tang de zhengzhi yu wenhua* 長安與河北之間：中晚唐的政治與文化, 124–73. Beijing: Beijing shifan daxue chubanshe, 2018.

Qiu Xigui 裘錫圭. "On the Burning of Human Victims and the Fashioning of Clay Dragons in Order to Seek Rain in the Shang Dynasty Oracle-Bone Inscriptions." *Early China* 9–10 (1983–1985): 290–306.

Queen, Sarah A. *From Chronicle to Canon: The Hermeneutics of the Spring and Autumn, According to Tung Chung-shu,* Cambridge: Cambridge University Press, 1996.

Ragoza, A. N. *Sogdiĭskie fragmenty tsentral'no-aziatskogo sobraniya instituta vostokovedeniya.* Moscow: Izd. Nauka, 1980.

Raschmann, Simone-Christine, and Ablet Semet. "Neues zur alttürkischen 'Geschichte von der hungrigen Tigerin.'" In *Aspects of Research into Central Asian Buddhism: In Memoriam Kōgi Kudara,* ed. Peter Zieme, 237–75. Turnhout, Belgium: Brepols, 2008.

Regenstein, Lewis G. *Replenish the Earth: A History of Organized Religion's Treatment of Animals and Nature—Including the Bible's Message of Conservation and Kindness toward Animals.* New York: The Crossroad Publishing, 1991.

Reinders, Eric. "Animals, Attitude toward: Buddhist Perspective." In *Encyclopedia of Monasticism,* ed. William M. Johnston, 30–31. Chicago: Fitzroy Dearborn, 2000.

Ren Shuang 任爽 *Tangdai lizhi yanjiu* 唐代禮制研究. Shenyang: Dongbei shifan daxue chubanshe, 1999.

Rice, Eugene. *Saint Jerome in the Renaissance.* Baltimore, MD: Johns Hopkins University Press, 1985.

Robson, James. *Power of Place: The Religious Landscape of the Southern Sacred Peak (Nanyue) in Medieval China.* Cambridge, MA: Harvard University Asia Center, 2009.

Sabatier, Paul. *Life of St. Francis of Assisi,* trans. Louise Seymour Houghton. New York: Charles Scribner's Sons, 1902.

Sakata Teiji 坂田貞二. "Ōmu to Shōnin no okamisan—Indo no setsuwa to mukashibanashi o meguru danshō 鸚鵡と商人のおかみさん—インドの説話と昔話をめぐる断章 [Parrot and merchant's wife: Miscellaneous notes on India's narrative and legendary stories]." *Shisō* 思想 [*Thought*] 623 (1976): 90-104.

Salisbury, Joyce E. *The Beast Within: Animals in the Middle Ages.* London: Routledge, 1994.

Salisbury, Joyce E., ed. *The Medieval World of Nature: A Book of Essays.* New York and London: Garland Publishing, 1993.

Salomon, Richard. *A Gandhārī Version of the Rhinoceros Sūtra.* Seattle: University of Washington Press, 2000.

Salter, David. *Holy and Noble Beasts: Encounters with Animals in Medieval Literature.* Cambridge: D. S. Brewer, 2001.

Sangren, P. Steven. "Female Gender in Chinese Religious Symbols." *Signs* 9 (1983): 4-25.

—. *History and Magical Power in a Chinese Community.* Stanford, CA: Stanford University Press, 1987.

Sarton, George. *Introduction to the History of Science.* Baltimore, MD: Williams & Wilkins Co., 1927.

Schafer, Edward H. "Cultural History of the Elaphure," *Sinologica* 4 (1956): 251-74.

—. *The Divine Woman: Dragon Ladies and Rain Maidens in Tang Literature.* Berkeley: University of California Press, 1973.

—. *The Golden Peaches of Samarkand: A Study in T'ang Exotics,* Berkeley: University of California Press, 1963.

—."Hunting Parks and Animal Enclosures in Ancient China," *Journal of the Economic and Social History of the Orient* 11, pp. (1968): 318-43.

—. "Orpiment and Realgar in Chinese Technology and Tradition." *Journal of American Oriental Society* 75, no. 2 (1955): 73-89.

—. "Parrots in Medieval China." In *Studia Serica Bernhard Karlgren Dedicata: Sinological Studies Dedicated to Bernhard Karlgren on His Seventieth Birthday,* ed. Søren Egerod et Else Glahn, 271-82. Copenhagen: Ejnar Munksgaard, 1959.

—. *The Vermilion Bird: T'ang Images of the South.* Berkeley: University of California Press, 1967.

Schaller, George B. *The Deer and the Tiger: A Study of Wildlife in India.* Chicago: University of Chicago Press, 1967.

Scheidel, Walter. "Comparing Comparisons: Ancient East and West." In *Ancient Greece and China Compared,* ed. G. E. R. Lloyd and Jingyi Jenny Zhao (Cambridge: Cambridge University Press, 2018), 40-58.

Schipper, Kristopher. "Daoist Ecology: The Inner Transformation. A Study of the Precepts of the Early Daoist Ecclesia," in *Daoism and Ecology: Ways Within a Cosmic Landscape,* ed. N. J. Girardot, James Miller, and Liu Xiaogan, 79-94. Cambridge, MA: Harvard University Press, 1999.

Schipper, Kristopher, and Franciscus Verellen, eds. *The Taoist Canon: A Historical Companion to the Daozang*. Chicago: University of Chicago Press, 2004.

Schlieter, Jens. "Compassionate Killing or Conflict Resolution? The Murder of King Langdarma according to Tibetan Buddhist Sources." In *Buddhism and Violence*, ed. Michael Zimmermann, 131-57. Lumbini, Nepal: International Research Institute, 2006.

Schmithausen, Lambert. *Buddhism and Nature: The Lecture Delivered on the Occasion of the EXPO 1990. An Enlarged Version with Notes*. Tokyo: International Institute for Buddhist Studies, 1991.

—. "The Early Buddhist Tradition and Ecological Ethics." *Journal of Buddhist Ethics* 4 (1997): 1-74.

—. *Martrī and Magic: Aspects of the Buddhist Attitude Toward the Dangerous in Nature*. Wien: Verlag der Österreichischen Akademie der Wissenschaften, 1997.

—. *Plants as Sentient Beings in Earliest Buddhism*. Faculty of Asian Studies, Australian National University, Canberra, 1991.

Schmitz, Oswald J., et al. 2018. "Animals and the Zoogeochemistry of the Carbon Cycle." *Science* 362, no. 6419 (2018). DOI: 10.1126/science.aar3213.

Schopen, Gregory. "Sukhāvatī as a Generalized Religious Goal in Sanskrit Mahāyāna Sūtra Literature." *Indo-Iranian Journal* 19 (1977): 177-210; reprinted with the update in Gregory Schopen, *Figments and Fragments of Mahāyāna Buddhism in India: More Collected Papers* (Honolulu: University of Hawai'i Press, 2005), 154-89.

Seidensticker, John, Sarah Christie, and Peter Jackson, eds. *Riding the Tiger: Tiger Conservation in Human-Dominated Landscapes*, Cambridge: Cambridge University Press, 1999.

Shahar, Meir. "The Chinese Cult of the Horse King: Divine Protector of Equines." In *Animals and Human Society in Asia: Historical and Ethical Perspectives*, ed. Rotem Rosen, Michal Biran, Meir Shahar, and Gideon Shelach, 355-90. Basingstoke: Palgrave Macmillan, 2019.

—. "The Tantric Origins of the Horse King: Haayagrīva and the Chinese Horse Cult." In *Chinese and Tibetan Esoteric Buddhism*, ed. Yael Bentor and Meir Shahar, 147-90. Leiden: Brill, 2017.

Sharf, Robert H. "On Pure Land Buddhism and Ch'an/Pure Land Syncretism in Medieval China." *T'oung Pao* 88, no. 4-5 (2003): 282-331.

Sharma, Ramesh Chandra, ed. *Handbook, Indian Snakes*. Kolkata: Zoological Survey of India, 2003.

Shigenobu Ayumi 重信あゆみ. "Seiōbo no genryu: Besuga yoeta zuzōteki eikyō 西王母の源流: ベスが与えた図像的影響." *Jinbungaku ronshū* 人文学論集 28 (2010): 73-89.

—. "Seiōbo: Tenmonde mukaeru kami 西王母: 天門で迎える神," *Jinbungaku ronshū* 人文学論集 25 (2007): 159-76;

Shinohara, Koichi 筱原亨一. "Animals in Medieval Chinese Biographies of Buddhist Monks." *Religions* 10, no. 6 (2019): 348.

Sillitoe, Paul. "Ethnobiology and Applied Anthropology: Rapprochement of the Academic with the Practical." *Journal of the Royal Anthropological Institute* 12 (2006): S119-S142.

Sima Qian 司馬遷. *The Grand Scribe's Records: Volume I, The Basic Annals of Pre-Han China*, trans. and ed. William H. Nienhauser. Bloomington: Indiana University Press, 1994.

—. *Records of the Grand Historian: Qin Dynasty*. 3rd edition, trans. Burton Watson. New York: Columbia University Press, 1995.

Simpson, George G. *Principles of Animal Taxonomy.* New York: Columbia University Press, 1962.

Sims-Williams, Nicholas. "Indian Elements in Parthian and Sogdian." In *Sprachen des Buddhismus in Zentralasien,* ed. K. Röhborn and W. Veenker, 132–41. Wiesbaden: Otto Harrassowitz, 1983.

Skilling, Peter. "Nuns, Laywomen, Donors, Goddesses: Female Roles in Early Indian Buddhism." *Journal of International Association for Buddhist Studies* 24, no. 2 (2001): 241–74.

Smith, Joanna F. Handlin. "Liberating Animals in Ming-Qing China: Buddhist Inspiration and Elite Imagination." *Journal of Asian Studies* 58, no. 1 (1999): 51–84.

Smith, Jonathan Z. "I Am a Parrot (Red)." *History of Religions* 11, no. 4, 391–413.

Snarey, John. "The Natural Environment's Impact on Religious Ethics: A Cross-Cultural Study." *Journal for the Scientific Study of Religion* 35, no. 2 (1996): 85–96.

Snyder-Reinke, Jeffrey. *Dry Spells: State Rainmaking and Local Governance in Late Imperial China.* Cambridge, MA: Harvard University Press, 2009.

Southwold, Martin. *Buddhism in Life: The Anthropological Study of Religion and the Sinhalese Practice of Buddhism.* Manchester: Manchester University Press, 1983.

Spiro, Melford E. *Buddhism and Society: A Great Tradition and Its Burmese Vicissitudes.* Berkeley: University of California Press, 1982.

Sponberg, Alan. "Attitudes Toward Women and the Feminine in Early Buddhism." In *Buddhism, Sexualilty and Gender,* ed. Jose K. Cabezon, 3–36. Albany: State University of New York Press, 1992.

Spring, Madeline K. *Animal Allegories in T'ang China,* New Haven, CT: American Oriental Society, 1993.

Srivastav, Asheem, and Suvira Srivastav. *Asiatic Lion on the Brink.* Dehra Dun: Beshen Singh Mahendra Pal Pal Singh, 1999.

Stanley, Jonathan W. "Snakes: Objects of Religion, Fear, and Myth." *Journal of Integrative Biology* 2, no. 2 (2008): 42–58.

Steavu, Dominic. *The Writ of the Three Sovereigns: From Local Lore to Institutional Daoism.* Honolulu: University of Hawai'i Press, 2019.

Stein, Rolf A. "Religious Daoism and Popular Religion from the Second to Seventh Centuries." In *Facets of Taoism,* ed. Holmes Welch and Anna Seidel, 53–81. New Haven, CT: Yale University Press, 1979.

Steiner, Gary. *Anthropocentrism and Its Discontents: The Moral Status of Animals in the History of western Philosophy.* Pittsburgh, PA: University of Pittsburgh Press, 2005.

Sterckx, Roel. *The Animal and the Daemon in Ancient China.* Albany: State University of New York Press, 2002.

——. "Animal Classification in Ancient China." *East Asian Science, Technology and Medicine* 23 (2005): 96–123.

——. "Transforming the Beasts: Animals and Music in Early China." *T'oung Pao,* 2nd series 86, no. 1/3 (2000): 1–46.

Sterckx, Roel, Martina Siebert, and Dagmar Schäfer, eds. *Animals Through Chinese History. Earliest Times to 1911.* Cambridge: Cambridge University Press, 2019.

Stevenson, Daniel B. "Death-Bed Testimonials of the Pure Land Faithful." In *Buddhism in Practice,* ed. Donald S. Lopez Jr., 592–602. Princeton, NJ: Princeton University Press, 1995.

——. "Pure Land Buddhist Worship and Meditation in China." In *Buddhism in Practice,* ed. Donald S. Lopez Jr., 359–79, Princeton, NJ: Princeton University Press, 1995.

Stewart, James. *Vegetarianism and Animal Ethics in Contemporary Buddhism*. London: Routledge, 2015.

Strassberg, Richard E. *A Chinese Bestiary: Strange Creatures from the Guideways through Mountains and Seas*. Berkeley: University of California Press, 2002.

Straughan, Roger. *Ethics, Morality and Animal Biotechnology*. Swindon: Biotechnology and Biological Sciences Research Council, 1999.

Strong, John. "The Legend of the Lion-Roarer: A Study of the Buddhist Arhat Piṇḍola Bhāradvāja." *Numen* 26, no. 1 (1979): 50–88.

Sullivan, Herbert P. "A Re-examination of the Religion of the Indus Civilization." *History of Religions* 4, no 1 (1964): 115–25.

Sun Zhengjun 孫正軍. "Zhonggu liangli shuxie de liangzhong moshi 中古良吏書寫的兩種模式." *Lishi yanjiu* 歷史研究3 (2014): 4–21.

Sung Hou-mei 宋后楣. *Decoded Messages: The Symbolic Language of Chinese Animal Painting*. New Haven, CT: Yale University Press, 2009.

Tamai Tatsushi 玉井达士. "The Tocharian Karmavibhaṅga*." *Annual Report of The International Research Institute for Advanced Buddhology at Soka University* 18 (2015): 337–81.

Tambiah, Stanley J. "Animals Are Good to Think and Good to Prohibit." In *Culture, Thought, and Social Action: An Anthropological Perspective*, 192–211. Cambridge, MA: Harvard University Press, 1985.

Tan Qianxue 譚前學. "Yingwuwen tiliang yinguan yu sheng Tang qixiang 鸚鵡紋提梁銀罐與盛唐氣象 [The parrot-patterned silver pot with hanging holder and the atmosphere of the high Tang]." *Gugong wenwu yuekan* 故宮文物月刊20 (2003): 88–91.

Taylor, Bron. "The Greening of Religion Hypothesis (Part One): From Lynn White Jr. and Claims that Religions Can Promote Environmentally Destructive Attitudes and Behaviors to Assertions They Are Becoming Environmentally Friendly," *Journal for the Study of Religion, Nature and Culture* 10, no. 3 (2016): 268–305.

Taylor, Bron, Gretel Van Wieren, and Bernard Zaleha, "The Greening of Religion Hypothesis (Part Two): Assessing the Data from Lynn White Jr. to Pope Francis," *Journal for the Study of Religion, Nature and Culture* 10, no. 3 (2016): 306–78.

Taylor, Rodney. "Of Animals and Humans: The Confucian Perspective." In *A Communion of Subjects: Animals in Religion, Science, and Ethics*, ed. Paul Waldau and Kimberley Patton, 293–307. New York: Columbia University Press, 2006.

Takizawa Shunryō 滝沢俊亮. "Ryūja to kiu no shūzoku ni tsuite 龍蛇と祈雨の習俗について," *Tōhō shūkyō* 東方宗教 20 (1962): 18–34.

Teiser, Stephen F. *Ghost Festival in Medieval China*. Princeton, NJ: Princeton University Press, 1988.

——. *Reinventing the Wheel: Paintings of Rebirth in Medieval Buddhist Temples*. Seattle: University of Washington Press, 2006.

——. *The Scripture on the Ten Kings and the Making of Purgatory in Medieval Chinese Buddhism*, Honolulu: University of Hawai'i Press, 1994.

Thomas, Richard. "Perceptions versus Reality: Changing Attitudes Towards Pets in Medieval and Post-medieval England." In *Just Skin and Bones? New Perspectives on Human-Animal Relations in the Historical Past*, ed. Aleksander Pluskowski, 95–104. Oxford: Archaeopress, 2005.

Tierney, Kevin J., and Maeve K. Connolly. "A Review of the Evidence for a Biological Basis for Snake Fears in Humans." *The Psychological Record* 63, no. 4 (2013): 919–28.

Tikhonov, Vladimir, and Torkel Brekke, eds. *Buddhism and Violence: Militarism and Buddhism in Modern Asia*. London: Routledge, 2015.

Tiyavanich, Kamala. *Sons of the Buddha: The Early Lives of Three Extraordinary Thai Masters*. Boston: Wisdom, 2007.

Tokyo National Museum, ed. 1975. Chinese *Paintings of the Yuan Dynasty on Buddhist and Taoist Figure Subjects*. Tokyo: Tokyo National Museum, 1975.

Tourunen, Auli. "A Zooarchaeological Study of the Medieval and Post-Medieval Town of Turku." PhD thesis, Humanistic Faculty of the University of Turku, Turku, 2008.

Tremblay, Xavier. *Pour une histoire de la Sérinde: Le Manicheisme parmi les peuples et religions d'Asie Centrale a'apres les sources primaires*. Wien: Verlag der Österreichischen Akademie der Wissenschaften, 2001.

Trizin, Sakya. *A Buddhist View on Befriending and Defending Animals*. Portland, OR: Orgyan Chogye Chonzo Ling, 1989.

Tsomo, Karma Lekshe. "Is the Bhikṣuṇī Vinaya Sexist?" In *Buddhist Women and Social Justice: Ideals, Challenges, and Achievements*, ed. Karma Lekshe Tsomo, 45-72. Albany: State University of New York Press, 2012.

Tuan, Yi-fu 段義孚. "Ambiguity in Attitudes toward Environment." *Annals of the Association of American Geographers* 63, no. 4 (1973): 411-423.

—. "Discrepancies Between Environmental Attitude and Behaviour: Examples from Europe and China." *Canadian Geographer* 12, no. 3 (1968): 175-91.

Tucker, Mary Evelyn, and Duncan Ryūken Williams, eds. *Buddhism and Ecology: The Interconnection of Dharma and Deeds*. Cambridge, MA: Harvard University Center for the Study of World Religions, 1998.

Twitchett, Denis. *Financial Administration Under the T'ang*. 2nd edition. Cambridge: Cambridge University Press, 1970.

Upadhyaya, Manorama. *Royal Authority in Ancient India*. Jodhpur: Books Treasure, 2007.

Utz, David A. *A Survey of Buddhist Sogdian Studies*. Tokyo: Reiyukai Library, 1978.

Vandermeersch, Léon. "Ritualisme et juridisme." In *Essais sur le rituel, Colloque du centenaire de la Section des Sciences religieuses de l'Ecole Practique des Hautes Etudes*, vol. 2, ed. A. Blondeau and K. Schipper. Louvain and Paris: Peeters, 1990; reprinted in *Etudes sinologiques*, 209-20. Paris: Presses Universitaires de France, 1994.

Verellen, Franciscus. "The Heavenly Master Liturgical Agenda According to *Chisong zi's Petition Almanac*," *Cahiers d'extréme-Asie* 14 (2004): 291-343.

—. "Daojiao lingyanji: Zhongguo wan Tang fojiao hufa chuantong de zhuanhuan, 道教靈驗記: 中國晚唐佛教護法傳統的轉換," *Huaxue* 華學 5 (2001): 38-64.

Vollmer, Klaus. "Buddhism and the Killing of Animals in Premodern Japan." In *Buddhism and Violence*, ed. Michael Zimmermann, 195-211. Wiesbaden: Reichert Verlag, 2006.

von Glahn, Richard. *The Sinister Way: The Divine and the Demonic in Chinese Religious Culture*. Berkeley: University of California Press, 2004.

Wagoner, Phillip B. 1996. "'Sultan among Hindu Kings:' Dress, Titles, and the Islamicization of Hindu Culture at Vijayanagara." *Journal of Asian Studies* 55: 4, 851-880.

Waldau, Paul, and Kimberley Patton, eds. "Buddhism and Animals Rights." In *Contemporary Buddhist Ethics*, ed. Damien Keown, 81-112. Richmond, Surrey, England: Curzon Press, 2000.

—. *A Communion of Subjects: Animals in Religion, Science and Ethics.* New York: Oxford University Press, 2004.

—. *The Specter of Speciesism: Buddhist and Christian Views of Animals.* New York: Oxford University Press, 2001.

Waley, Arthur, trans. *The Book of Songs.* London: Routledge, 2002, reprint.

Walter, Mariko Namba. "Sodgians and Buddhism." *Sino-Platonic Papers* 174 (November 2006): 35.

Wang Chengwen 王承文. "The Revelation and Classification of Daoist Scriptures," in *Early Chinese Religion, Part Two: The Period of Division (220–589 AD)*, ed. John Lagerwey and Pengzhi Lü, vol. 2, 785–898. Leiden: Brill, 2010.

—. *Dunhuang gu Lingbao jing yu Jin Tang Daojiao* 敦煌古靈寶經與晉唐道教. Beijing: Zhonghua shuju, 2002.

Wang, Ting 王頲. "Feiniao nengyan: Sui yiqian Zhongguo guanyu yingwu de miaoshu 飛鳥能言隋以前中國關於鸚鵡的描述 [Flying birds an speak: The descriptions on the parrots in pre-Sui China]." In *Neilu yazhou shidi qiusuo* 內陸亞洲史地求索 [Studies on inner Asian history and geography], 1–15. Lanzhou: Lanzhou daxue chubanshe, 2001.

Watson, Burton, trans. *Records of the Grand Historian: Qin Dynasty* [by Sima Qian]. New York: Columbia University Press, 1993.

Watson, James L. "The Structure of Chinese Funerary Rites: Elementary Forms, Ritual Sequence, and the Primacy of Performance." In *Death Ritual in Late Imperial and Modern China*, ed. James L. Watson and Evelyn S. Rawski, 3–19. Berkeley: University of California Press, 1988.

Weaver, Lesley Jo, and Amber R. Campbell Hibbs. "Serpents and Sanitation: A Biological Survey of Snake Worship, Cultural Adaptation, and Parasite Disease in Ancient and Modern India." In *Parasites, Worms, and the Human Body in Religion and Culture*, ed. Brenda Gardenour and Misha Tadd, 1–16. New York: Peter Lang, 2011.

Wechsler, Howard J. *Mirror to the Son of Heaven: Wei Cheng at the Court of T'ang T'ai-tsung.* New Haven: Yale University Press, 1974.

—. *Offerings of Jade and Silk: Ritual and Symbol in the Legitimation of the T'ang Dynasty.* New Haven, CT: Yale University Press, 1985.

Wei Bin 魏斌. "Shanzhong de Liuchao shi 山中的六朝史," *Wenshizhe* 文史哲 361 (2017): 1–15.

—. "Shuxie Nanyue: Zhonggu zhongqi Hengshan de wenxian yu jingguan 書寫南嶽: 中古早期衡山的文獻與景觀 (Writing Southern Marchmount: The Literature and Landscape in Mount Heng in Early Medieval China)," *Wei Jin Nanbeichao Sui Tang shi ziliao* 魏晋南北朝隋唐史资料 31 (2015): 138–62.

Weng Junxiong 翁俊雄. "Tangdai hu xiang de xingzong: Jianlun Tangdai hu xiang jizai zengduo de yuanyin 唐代虎、象的行蹤—兼論唐代虎、象記載增多的原因." *Tang Yanjiu* 唐研究 3 (1997): 381–94.

Wessing, Robert. "Symbolic Animals in the Land between the Waters: Markers of Place and Transition." *Asian Folklore Studies* 65, no. 2 (2006): 205–39.

Whatley, E. Gordon, Anne B. Thompson, and Robert K. Upchurch, eds. *Saints' Lives in Middle English Collections.* Kalamazoo, MI: Medieval Institute Publications, 2004.

White Jr., Lynn. "The Historical Roots of Our Ecological Crisis." *Science* 155 (1967): 1203–07.

Williams, C. A. S. *Chinese Symbolism and Art Motifs: A Comprehensive Handbook on Symbolism in Chinese Art through the Ages*, 4th edition. Tokyo: Tuttle Publishing, 1974.

Williams, Duncan. "Animal Liberation, Death, and the State: Rites to Release Animals in Medieval Japan." In *Buddhism and Ecology: The Interconnection of Dharma and Deed*, ed. Mary Evelyn Tucker and Duncan Williams, 149–64. Cambridge, MA: Harvard University Press, 1997.

Williams, Megan Hale. *The Monk and the Book: Jerome and the Making of Christian Scholarship*. Chicago: University of Chicago Press, 2006.

Wilson, Don E., and DeeAnn M. Reeder, eds. *Mammal Species of the World: A Taxonomic and Geographic Reference*. 3rd edition. Baltimore, MD: John Hopkins University Press, 2005.

Wright, Arthur F. "Fu I and the Rejection of Buddhism." *Journal of the History of Ideas* 12, no. 1 (1951): 33–47.

Wu Hung 巫鴻. "Mapping Early Daoist Art: The Visual Culture of the Wudoumi Dao," in *Daoism and the Arts of China*, ed. Stephen Little and Shawn Eichman, 77–93. Chicago: The Art Institute of Chicago and Berkeley: University of California Press, 2000.

Xu Tingyun 徐庭雲. "Sui Tang Wudai shiqi de shengtai huangjin 隋唐五代時期的生態環境." *Guoxue yanjiu* 國學研究 8 (2001): 209–44.

Yang, C. K. 楊慶堃. "The Functional Relationship between Confucian Thought and Chinese Religion." In *Chinese Thought and Institutions*, ed. John K. Fairbank, 269–290. Chicago: University of Chicago Press, 1957.

——. *Religion in Chinese Society: A Study of Contemporary Social Functions of Religion and Some of Their Historical Factors*. Berkeley: University of California Press, 1961.

Yang Erzeng 楊爾曾. *The Story of Han Xiangzi: The Alchemical Adventure of a Daoist Immortal*, trans. Philip Clart. Seattle: University of Washington Press, 2007.

Ye Wei 葉煒. *Nanbeichao Sui Tang guanli fentu yanjiu* 南北朝隋唐官吏分途研究. Beijing: Beijing daxue chubanshe, 2009.

Yu, Chün-fang 于君方. *Kuan-yin: The Chinese Transformation of Avalokitesvara*. New York: Columbia University Press, 2000.

——. *Renewal of Buddhism in China: Chu-Hung and the Late Ming Synthesis*. New York: Columbia University Press, 1981.

Yusa Noboru 遊佐昇. *Tōdai shakai to Dōkyō* 唐代社会と道教. Tōkyō: Tōhō Shoten, 2015.

Zhang Daya 張達雅. "Tang wencui zhijian banben kao 唐文萃知見版本考 (Studies on Known Editions of the *Selected Fine Writings of the Tang Dynasty*)." *Donghai daxue tushuguan guanxun* 東海大學圖書館館訊 (*Tunghai University Library Newsletter*) no. 85 (2008): 21–39.

Zhang Mengwen 張孟聞. "Zhongguo shengwu fenleixue shi shulun 中國生物分類學史述論 [A preliminary discussion on the history of biological taxonomy in China]." *Zhongguo keji shiliao* 中國科技史料 [Historical sources on Chinese science and technology] no. 6 (1987): 3–27.

Zhang Zehong 張澤洪. "Zaoqi Tianshi shixi yu Longhushan Zhang tianshi sijiao 早期天师世系与龙虎山张天师嗣教." *Shehui kexue yanjiu* 會科學研究 6 (2012): 122–28.

Zhang Zhenjun 張振軍. *Buddhism and Tales of the Supernatural in Early Medieval China: A Study of Liu Yiqing's (403–444) Youming lu*. Leiden: Brill, 2003.

Zheng, Binglin 鄭炳林 and Wang Jinbo 王晶波. *Dunhuang xieben xiangshu jiaolu yanjiu* 敦煌寫本相書校錄研究 [Annotations and studies on the book of physiognomy in Dunhuang manuscripts]. Beijing: Minzu chubanshe, 2004.

Zhou Xibo 周西波. *Daojiao lingyan ji kaotan: Jingfa yanzheng yu xuanyang* 道教靈驗記考探：經法驗證與宣揚. Taipei: Wenjin chubanshe, 2009.

Zhou Yiliang 周一良. "Tantrism in China." *Harvard Journal of Asiatic Studies* 8 (1944-1945): 235-332.

——. *Wei Jin Nanbeichao shi zhazhi* 魏晉南北朝史札記. Beijing: Zhonghua shuju, 1985.

Zimmer, Heinrich. *Myths and Symbols in Indian Art and Civilization.* Bollingen Series XI. Princeton, NJ: Princeton University Press, 1972.

Zimmermann, Francis. *The Jungle and the Aroma of Meats: An Ecological Theme in Hindu Medicine.* Delhi: Motilal Banaesidaa Publishers, 1999.

Zou Shuwen 鄒樹文. "Zhongguo gudai de dongwu fenleixue 中國古代的動物分類學." In *Zhongguo kejishi tantao* 中國科技史探討, ed. Li Guohao 李國豪, Zhang Mengwen 張孟聞, and Cao Tianqin 曹天欽, 511-24. Hongkong: Zhonghua shuju xianggang fenju, 1986.

Index

Locators in italic refer to figures.